Managing Diversity, Equity, and Inclusion in Public Service Organizations

Managing Diversity, Equity, and Inclusion in Public Service Organizations: A Liberatory Justice Approach is a textbook designed to facilitate critical and courageous conversations that recognize our differences, including our privileged and marginalized social identities, and engage readers in the principles and practice of solidarity to transform systems of oppression. Examining dimensions of race, gender, sexual orientation, disabilities, and their intersectionality in the context of diverse, multigenerational organizations, this leading-edge new textbook redefines and reimagines the role of public service in fostering meaningful, authentic, sustainable, and transformative change.

While diversity is now a standard topic in books on public personnel and human resource management, authors Rashmi Chordiya and Meghna Sabharwal offer a deeper, nuanced, and reflective understanding of many of the systematic and often covert ways in which marginalized and minoritized groups can face barriers to full and equal participation in decision-making, access to resources, and opportunities for advancement and growth. Taking a holistic, liberatory public service approach, the book explores what it would mean if public service systems were reimagined, and goals aligned and transformed, to serve an "all means all" public.

Other unique features of this book include developing a nuanced understanding of trauma of oppression from neurobiological, sociological, and historical perspectives. This book supports the reader in exploring ways of cultivating individual and organizational competencies and capacities for envisioning and implementing trauma-informed, repair and healing-centered approaches to public service that compassionately center the margins. To encourage learner engagement and to connect theory to practice, this book offers several case studies. Each chapter contains a description of big ideas, big questions, and key concepts and teachings offered in that chapter, as well as chapter summaries and deep dive resources. Throughout the book, the authors offer boxed invitations to pause and use reflective prompts to engage readers with the core concepts and key teachings of the book. *Managing Diversity, Equity, and Inclusion in Public Service Organizations* is required reading for all current and future public administrators and nonprofit leaders.

Rashmi Chordiya (She | Her) is an associate professor of public administration at Seattle University's Department of Public Affairs and Nonprofit Leadership, USA. Her research focuses on bridging critical academic scholarship and social justice movement visions and theories to advance the theory and praxis of liberatory justice in public service. She approaches diversity and social justice work from an embodied lens that is trauma-informed, repair and healing-centered, and compassionately centering the margins. Her peer-reviewed journal articles are published in prestigious public administration journals.

Meghna Sabharwal is a National Academy of Public Administration (NAPA) Fellow and a professor in the public and nonprofit management program, as well as the Associate Provost of Faculty Success at the University of Texas at Dallas, USA. Her extensive research portfolio centers around public human resources management with a particular focus on workforce diversity, equity and inclusion, high skilled immigration, and comparative public human resources. She is the editor-in-chief of the *Review of Public Personnel Administration*. She is the recipient of several national and international awards.

"This book looks anew at old problems. For the optimist, the book shows the way forward. For the realist, it acknowledges hurdles to be jumped. For the pessimist, it explains liberatory precepts and makes them accessible for discussion."

Mary E. Guy, *University of Colorado Distinguished Professor, USA*

"Deep and accessible. Gentle and courageous. This book inspires a renewed commitment to the human-centered public service our communities need and deserve. With loving clarity and great care, Chordiya and Sabharwal illuminate a path for each of us – and the institutions we steward – to see our need for connection, transformation, trust, wholeness, and healing as the building blocks of the future of public service. This uplifting and exciting contribution is a gift!"

Adana Protonentis, *MPA, Co-Owner and Director of Liberatory Learning, Kindred Consulting*

"Rarely does a book come along that has the power to change everything you know about the public sector. But Chordiya and Sabharwal have done just that. With their thoughtful, thorough, and meaningful words, they offer us the liberatory public service as a way to transform our organizations and ourselves. This is a must read for public servants, students, and faculty in public administration, political science, and criminal justice."

Stephanie Dolamore, *Maryland Developmental Disabilities Council, Maryland, USA*

"While we've made a lot of progress in studying diversity, this amazing work by Chordiya and Sabharwal is exactly what public administration needs right now to move our field down the path to embracing justice in our teaching and research. It will be transformative, and I cannot wait to adopt it in class."

Jessica E. Sowa, *Joseph R. Biden, Jr. School of Public Policy & Administration, University of Delaware, USA*

"Chordiya and Sabharwal have written a necessary text at a time of great need for those of us who care about good and just governance. Their book envisions the kind of change our students crave. The pages are brave, well-researched, and reasonable, and will infuse life into the most important debates facing public administration today."

Nuri Heckler, *Co-Editor-in-Chief*, Administrative Theory & Praxis

Managing Diversity, Equity, and Inclusion in Public Service Organizations

A Liberatory Justice Approach

Rashmi Chordiya and Meghna Sabharwal

NEW YORK AND LONDON

Designed cover image: © Getty Images

First published 2024
by Routledge
605 Third Avenue, New York, NY 10158

and by Routledge
4 Park Square, Milton Park, Abingdon, Oxon, OX14 4RN

Routledge is an imprint of the Taylor & Francis Group, an informa business

Library of Congress Cataloging-in-Publication Data
Names: Chordiya, Rashmi, author. | Sabharwal, Meghna, author.
Title: Managing diversity, equity, and inclusion in public service organizations : a liberatory justice approach / Rashmi Chordiya and Meghna Sabharwal.
Description: New York : Routledge, 2024. | Includes bibliographical references and index.
Identifiers: LCCN 2024001248 (print) | LCCN 2024001249 (ebook) | ISBN 9781032670652 (hbk) | ISBN 9781032670645 (pbk) | ISBN 9781032670669 (ebk)
Subjects: LCSH: Public administration--Social aspects. | Diversity in the workplace. | Social integration. | Intersectionality (Sociology)--Political aspects.
Classification: LCC JF1351 .C4615 2024 (print) | LCC JF1351 (ebook) | DDC 352.608--dc23/eng/20240412
LC record available at https://lccn.loc.gov/2024001248
LC ebook record available at https://lccn.loc.gov/2024001249

ISBN: 978-1-032-67065-2 (hbk)
ISBN: 978-1-032-67064-5 (pbk)
ISBN: 978-1-032-67066-9 (ebk)

DOI: 10.4324/9781032670669

Typeset in Sabon LT Pro
by KnowledgeWorks Global Ltd.

To all people who are most impacted by the inequities in our systems. Your voices, perspectives, lived experiences, and leadership must be at the core of all social justice and public service work. We dedicate this book to you.

Rashmi Chordiya and Meghna Sabharwal

Contents

Acknowledgments

Rashmi Chordiya

I am deeply grateful for my life on our beautiful planet Earth – the land, the water, the air, that supports me and sustains my life and all life. I want to do better as a sibling and a relative to you. I am grateful for the Coast Salish and Duwamish land that I am on, where I have written most of this book. I am grateful for all the First peoples of this land – all Coast Salish peoples, all the Duwamish peoples, the past, the present, and the future generations.

I acknowledge all the social justice transformative leaders, my ancestors in India, the freedom fighters, all Black, Indigenous, and People of Color teachers, visionaries, and movement builders. As I write this book, I honor you and remember that liberatory work is rooted in collective and intergenerational efforts – the present and the future generations that have and will continue to carry forward the torch of liberatory justice. I hold you all, in my heart, my spirit, and I pray for wisdom and courage as I journey my path of social justice and collective liberation.

I want to express my deepest gratitude to you, Dr. Meghna Sabharwal, for your beautiful big generous heart and brilliance. Thank you for choosing me as your co-author. Thank you for being an extraordinary mentor, a thoughtful collaborator, and a loving kind friend that you are. Writing this book with you has been a profoundly joyful and nourishing experience for me. You inspire me, motivate me, and are one of my strong anchors. Thank you for believing in me. I am blessed to have you in my life.

I am grateful for all my friends and colleagues who helped review many chapters of this book with deep thought and care. Adana Protonentis – I am thankful for your friendship and thought partnership in my life. Dr. Stephanie Dolamore, thank you for your positive and affirming support, my friend. Dr. Mary Guy, Dr. Jessica Sowa, Dr. Nuri Heckler, Dr. Zach Woods, Prof. Paul Carlson, thank you for your validations and thoughtful reviews of our chapters. All your comments, suggestions, clarifying questions, and feedback helped Meghna and me to make this book stronger, clearer, and more accessible for our diverse audience.

Sahil, without your partnership, I cannot imagine how I could have started or completed this book project. Thank you for being the source of my strength, joy, and nourishment. You always help me find the confidence and the clarity I need. I am deeply blessed for our daughter, Saphira. Saphira, my "Chaku-pie," you are the most amazing "big kiddo." Your laughter, hugs, kisses and three-year-old wisdom and genius, inspires me and gives mummy all the medicine and the strength she needs to keep on going on. I am grateful for Saphira's preschool – all teachers and staff. Thank you for providing Saphira with the care and safe environment she needs to learn, grow, and belong. You all are a key part of my support system.

Mummy, Pappa – I am blessed to be your daughter. Senu Mummy and Daddy, I am lucky to be a family with you. I do not take this blessing and privilege for granted. You all have always modeled for me what justice and love look like and feel like in practice. You are my teachers and my spirit protectors. I am deeply grateful for all my elders, my grandmother, my beloved late grandfather, all my relatives, and my community members.

Last, but not the least, I want to acknowledge and thank you my Seattle University community – my department, my colleagues, friends, and students. I appreciate all the care, concern, and gentleness you offer – it has helped me to meaningfully begin and bring this project to a place of completion.

Meghna Sabharwal

I want to extend my deepest gratitude to the numerous mentors who have been instrumental in turning this book from a mere vision into a reality. While it's challenging to mention everyone due to the extensive list, I particularly wish to express my appreciation to Norma Riccucci for her unwavering support. I am also immensely grateful to Mary Guy, Jessica Sowa, and Sean McCandless for accompanying me on this equity-focused journey. The completion of our manuscript wouldn't have been possible without the tireless efforts of my dedicated graduate students, including Abdollah (Abdi) Zeraatpisheh, Savannah Sipos, Aurora M. Becerra, and Chanyoung Han.

I could not do this book without my co-author Dr. Rashmi Chordiya. Her vision and expertise have been instrumental in shaping the Liberatory Public Service (LPS) framework. Together, we've navigated through the intricacies of conceptualization of the LPS framework. Her unwavering commitment, enthusiasm, and expertise have not only influenced the depth of our discussions but have also introduced me to many new learnings along the way. Working alongside Rashmi has been an inspiring and enlightening experience. I am thrilled about the doors this work will open and the conversations it will spark. Thank you, Rashmi, for being not just a co-author but the visionary architect behind this profound work.

I would like to thank my UTD colleagues. I acknowledge and express gratitude for the ancestral land of the Caddo, Wichita, and Comanche people that we stand on. I recognize the legacy of colonization and the harm caused by the forced removal of Indigenous people from these lands. As a member of the UT Dallas community, I continue to benefit from the contributions of Indigenous students and colleagues on our campus, and I am committed to building solidarity and advance the ongoing work of centering of the Native culture that is essential to our community. As an educator, I remain dedicated to dismantling barriers for all my students, particularly those who are multiply marginalized and deeply affected by the numerous inequities prevalent in our higher education systems and beyond.

Finally, I want to recognize my family – my parents and sister, my husband, Nikhil Gupta, and my son, Aakash Sabharwal Gupta – for their incredible patience while I dedicated myself to this project. It was a difficult choice, and I've missed a few of my nine-year-old son's soccer games on weekends to focus on this book. Their unwavering support, love, and encouragement have been pivotal in making this book possible.

Preface

As we write this book, we acknowledge the co-existence of multiple forces, including those that are challenging democratic systems, and those that are affirming and calling for a deeper, authentic, and mature democracy. In these contexts, the theory and praxis of public service takes on a profound significance. It requires public servants to build capacity to hold and navigate intense contradictions. Public service is not merely about creating public policies, carrying out bureaucratic duties or administrative tasks; rather, it embodies the very essence of societal well-being, justice, equity, and inclusion.

In this book, we argue that public service has a growing potential for engaging in praxis of solidarity to transform systems of oppression and create liberatory, life affirming and life enriching systems that serve all public. As we embark on the journey into the heart of "Liberatory Public Service," this book seeks to redefine and reimagine the role of public service in fostering meaningful, authentic, sustainable, and transformative change.

In recent times, the call for liberatory justice in public service has grown louder, challenging traditional paradigms, and urging us to confront systemic inequities that persist within our organizations/institutions and our communities. We hope this book serves as a compass for those who wish to navigate this challenging terrain, offering analysis, conceptual and theoretical insights, and actionable approaches to advance public service toward a diverse, equitable, inclusive, and liberatory future.

In this book, we build on the existing foundations of diversity, equity, and inclusion work and aspire for application and integration of an emerging framework of liberatory public service (LPS). We offer the framework of LPS as a vision, a process, and a practice of creating the conditions for liberation to emerge through alignments across policy work, administrative work, structure and culture change work, and an embodied social justice leadership that serves – "*all means all*" public. LPS involves the systematic removal of oppressive policies, administrative, and cultural barriers, one step at a time, until we collectively eliminate all forms of oppressive policies, administrative, and cultural barriers. LPS means our public safety, peace keeping, immigration, welfare, education, healthcare, housing, environmental, public utilities, public transit, and all other public service systems, are reimagined, our (settler) colonial lineages are acknowledged, and our goals, visions and values are transformed to serve "all means all" public.

We emphasize, LPS is not about simply dismantling structures or removing burdens to create a void. It is about replacing burdensome systems and procedures that are exclusionary, marginalizing, causing hurt and harm, with nourishing systems, inclusive cultures, procedures, and infrastructures that are rooted in collective work, accountability, transparency, demonstrate care. LPS is about integrating inner and systemic transformation to foster public service that is, are trauma-informed, repair and healing-oriented, and compassionately centering the margins.

This book takes a scaffolded approach, and each chapter builds on concepts, ideas, frameworks, and reflections offered in the previous chapters. In Parts I and II, we explore the core concepts, frameworks, and theoretical approaches that serve as building blocks of LPS framework. We seek to connect the dots and weave together a tapestry of social justice and liberatory frameworks that have been developed within both critical academic scholarship as well as within social justice movement spaces. In Part III, we reflect on applications and integrations of LPS in public service using specific contexts of racial justice, gender and LGBTQIA+ justice, and disability justice.

Throughout this book, we focus on the organizational, institutional, and societal context of the United States as it is the current focus of our teaching, service, and scholarship. However, we believe the ideas, theories, and practices explored in this book will be relevant to advance just, equitable and inclusive public policies and public administration across cultural and societal contexts. Throughout this book, we share our discernments and seek to lift-up and center the lessons from social justice frameworks aimed at fostering *a trauma-informed, repair and healing-oriented public service, which compassionately centers the margins*. These core ideas form the basis of an emergent LPS framework that we explore throughout this book. We believe these concepts can be innovated and adapted to advance the theory and praxis of LPS in diverse societal, cultural, and organizational contexts.

In many ways this book serves as a starting point for us. As we grow this work, we are committed to expanding and deepening the scholarship of LPS in cross-national and diverse cultural contexts, particularly in the Global South, as there are immense opportunities for cross-learning and development for public service organizations serving across national, geographical, and cultural contexts. Similarly, while it is beyond the scope of this or any single book to cover all key topics and contexts of diversity, equity, inclusion, and liberatory justice (DEILJ) work, we hope that the theoretical frameworks and reflections on intersectional praxis of DEILJ explored through the chapters of this book serve to advance courageous conversations and embodied social justice leadership praxis across societal contexts and public service domains.

In the following pages, we invite you to engage with the ideas offered in this book critically and reflect on your own roles and spheres of influence. Whether you are an aspiring public servant, an advocate for social justice focused change, or a concerned citizen, this book aims to empower you with the knowledge, inspiration, and a discipline of hope[1] needed to contribute to a more equitable and just society through the vehicle of public service. We hope our book, serves as a meaningful resource for you and leads you to many other books, especially those authored by disabled, queer, trans, non-binary, Two-Spirit, Black, Indigenous, and People of Color authors, teachers, visionaries, and movement builders (many of which we highlight throughout this book and in our deep dive resources sections).

A Note for Our Diverse Audience: This Book Is For You

While we sincerely hope this book serves a diverse audience, our primary audience includes interested learners, advocates, allies, champions, and change agents across leadership levels, who are invested in advancing the work of diversity, equity, inclusion, and liberatory justice (DEILJ) for all people. This book is for public service scholars, practitioners, students, and educators who seek to cultivate a nuanced, imaginative, and intersectional approach to foster DEILJ in their work and within their spheres of influence. This book is for lifelong students and learners of public service who care deeply about an education that will support their liberatory social justice journeys. It is for scholars and practitioners of public service who are looking for theoretical frameworks, perspectives, tools, and ideas emerging from both critical academic scholarship and social justice movement spaces, to support transformative DEILJ work. It is for end users of public services who desire tools and strategies to support their relationships with public service professionals and public service organizations.

We believe an equitable, inclusive, and liberatory praxis of public service benefits all people. We write this book with the hope of furthering our collective work toward imagination and co-creation of an equitable, inclusive, and liberatory society. With that hope and intention in mind, we invite all members of public service community and our broader society – Black, Indigenous, and People of Color (BIPOC) across generations, white people, queer people, cis and trans people, people with disabilities, people of the Global South and of the Global North, allies, advocates, accomplices, those who see themselves in equity work, and those who have felt left out by equity work – to engage with, experience, and explore this book. We write this book with care for you as our audience and our global public service community in our hearts and minds.

An Embodied Invitation

In approaching our perspectives and analysis, we strive to center and follow the leadership of those most impacted. We recognize that movement toward social justice necessitates the work of developing a liberatory consciousness rooted in the values of interdependence, allyship, belonging, accountability, and decolonizing solidarity. We understand that social justice at its core is the work of healing justice – it is about doing the work of repair and supporting the work of healing from trauma of oppression. We emphasize that liberatory work is both the work of interrupting and ending systems of oppression, and it is the work of imagination, creation, innovation, and collaboration that necessitates collective visioning, actions, shared leadership, and solidarity for a sustainable DEILJ-focused change.

As we write this book, we also acknowledge the heavy weight of social justice topics we cover in this book, particularly, for multiply marginalized disabled, queer, trans, Black, Indigenous, and negatively racialized People of Color (QTBIPOC) across generations. We also acknowledge that all people, and especially multiply marginalized people, are not consistently invited to take space for processing all the ways in which these topics impact their bodyminds, such as emotionally, psychologically, intellectually, and physically. We seek to interrupt separating our cognitive experience of oppression from that of our bodies and foster an embodied approach to learning and development that invites you to process content holistically with your bodymind.

Throughout this book, as we share our perspectives, analysis, and reflections, our approach is invitational. We avoid explicit or graphic description of violence against anybody, especially marginalized bodies of color. We offer heavy-content and trigger warnings, invitations and prompts to pause, and embodied practices to connect with your bodymind.[2]

If you are able and willing, as you engage with this book, please keep a notebook/paper and pen/pencil close to you, to practice journaling. We invite you to take the time and space you need to breathe with ease, to move bodies in ways that feel accessible, whether it is by rocking, stretching, tapping your feet, or any other forms of movements that offer you comfort and a sense of intentional and mindful connection with your body. We invite you to honor your capacity by engaging with this book at a pace that feels accessible and meaningful to you; to step away if necessary and return when your bodyminds feel ready enough to continue. We rely on these practices to avoid disembodiment or disconnection with our bodyminds and to support a practice of embodied intentionality as we engage with DEILJ work.

We also recognize that the content, descriptions, interpretations, analysis, and perspectives shared in this book are both strengthened and subject to limitations in terms of our own intersectional (advantaged and disadvantaged) social identities and perspectives. We both (Rashmi and Meghna) identify as cisgender, straight, currently non-disabled, middle-aged, women of color born and raised in India, who currently have access to higher education and career opportunities, and as non-Dalit and non-Adivasi (non-Indigenous) women of color, we recognize our privileges in a prevailing casteist system. Our social justice work is deeply shaped by both our oppressed and oppressor identities. It is also informed and shaped by our own developing work of building liberatory consciousness. This acknowledgment is not a statement that diminishes our work, knowledge, and writing, rather it helps us humbly contextualize and clarify for our audience that we undertake this work within a larger context and an ecosystem of complex, inter-generational liberatory social justice work. This acknowledgement of our social identities also helps us remain humbly anchored, to find our roles, and to find our way to practice and build solidarity for collective liberation.

Notes

1 We humbly acknowledge and thank Mariame Kaba for her framing of "Hope Is a Discipline (Kaba 2021).
2 With deep humility and gratitude, we wish to acknowledge that these practices are our adaptations inspired from our discernments and learnings with teachers Resmaa Menakem in the Foundations of Somatic Abolitionism program; Rev angel Kyodo williams, Staci Haines, Deborah Dana, and Dr. Sara King of the Embodied Social Justice Leadership Program; and many teachers of the Integrative Somatic Trauma Therapy Program with the Embody Lab.

References

Kaba, Mariame. 2021. Hope Is a Discipline: Mariame Kaba on Dismantling the Carceral State Interview by Jeremy Scahill. https://theintercept.com/2021/03/17/intercepted-mariame-kaba-abolitionist-organizing/.

Part I

Introduction

Core Concepts

Intentions and Objectives

In Part I, we begin this book with a foundational understanding of core concepts related to diversity, equity, inclusion, and liberatory justice (DEILJ) praxis. We explore definitions and nuanced meanings of terms diversity, equity, inclusion, and liberatory justice and other related ideas.

Throughout this book, we develop an understanding of the building blocks and the key tenets that make up the framework of liberatory public service (LPS). LPS seeks to transform the systems of oppression and move us toward collective liberation. Therefore, it is important to understand what the meaning of oppression is. We dedicate these initial chapters to developing a nuanced understanding of the systems of oppression. In Chapter 2, we explore the key characteristics of oppression, and how does it work at individual and collective levels and how can we interrupt it.

DOI: 10.4324/9781032670669-1

1 Diversity, Equity, Inclusion, and Liberatory Justice (DEILJ)

Abstract

In the wake of the widespread and resonating demands for social and racial justice voiced during the 2020 Black Lives Matter movement, there is a growing mass awareness of white supremacy and anti-Black racism. There continues to be an emerging and pressing need within public service organizations to place a greater emphasis on allocating resources toward initiatives aimed at fostering diversity, equity, inclusion, and liberatory justice (DEILJ) to counter various forms of oppression. There is also a widespread recognition of the historical and systemic injustices and disparities, including an analysis of how social inequities manifest in public policies, administrative decision-making, and management practices. The aim of this book is to advance existing literature on DEILJ and introduce a framework of Liberatory Public Service (LPS). The building blocks and the key tenets of the LPS framework will be explored throughout this book. In this chapter, we intend to start at the beginning and offer a comprehensive grounding into definitions and nuanced meanings of the core concepts of DEILJ.

Introduction

In the wake of the widespread and resonating demands voiced during the 2020 Black Lives Matter movement and the increased awareness of anti-Black racism on both national and global scales, there is an emerging and pressing need within public service organizations to place a greater emphasis on allocating resources toward initiatives aimed at fostering diversity, equity, inclusion, and liberatory justice (DEILJ). There is now a more widespread recognition of the historical and systemic injustices and disparities, including how they have manifested in public policies, administrative decision-making, and management practices.

These glaring injustices and inequities were heightened during the COVID-19 pandemic, which had a disproportionately devastating impact

DOI: 10.4324/9781032670669-2

on multiply marginalized[1] communities of color. Our recent shared experiences have underscored the necessity of giving higher priority to investing-in and institutionalizing DEILJ work in public service contexts. Integrating DEILJ work as an organizational and institutional priority is recognized as a means to interrupt and ultimately put an end to cycles of systemic harm and oppression.

Despite the significance of DEILJ efforts to improve our daily lives and our vision for a just and humane democratic society, there continues to be a growing resistance against DEILJ in various parts of the United States. Without fully listening to the needs expressed by multiply marginalized Black, Indigenous, and People of Color (BIPOC) communities, systems of oppression (such as racism and white supremacy) fueled by fear and scarcity mindset persist through a severe movement backlash. These include legislative initiatives to hinder movement toward greater diversity, equity, inclusion, and liberatory justice (DEILJ).

In this book, our dedication is to build on existing literature and offer a framework of liberatory public service (LPS) that could shape the work of DEILJ in public service contexts. LPS is a vision, a process, and a practice of creating the conditions for liberation to emerge through alignments across policy work, administrative work, structure and culture change work, and leadership praxis that serves – *"all means all"* public. It involves the systematic removal of oppressive policies, administrative, and cultural barriers, one step at a time, until we collectively eliminate all forms of oppressive policies, administrative, and cultural barriers.

LPS is not about simply dismantling structures or removing burdens to create a void. LPS is about replacing burdensome systems and procedures that are exclusionary, marginalizing, causing hurt and harm, with, nourishing systems, inclusive and life-affirming cultures that are rooted in collective work, shared accountability, transparency, and demonstrate care. LPS is about integrating inner and systemic transformation to foster public service that is trauma-informed, repair and healing-oriented, and compassionately centering the margins.

The building blocks and the key tenets of the LPS framework will be explored through chapters offered in Part II and Part III of this book. In this chapter, we intend to first offer a comprehensive grounding into definitions and nuanced meanings of the terms, diversity, equity, inclusion, and liberatory justice.

The Meaning of "Diversity"?

Diversity is a fact. We are different in appearances and experiences of our bodies and minds. We are different based on the color of our skin, age, our body parts, our sexuality, our gender identities, the functioning of our minds, our emotional states and behaviors, our neurobiology, and psychology. We are also different because of our social groupings based on the contexts of our geographical locations, as well as cultural, ethnic, and religious contexts.

However, in the emergent field of "diversity, equity and inclusion +," (DEI+) when we refer to the term diversity, we often focus not only on the range of human diversity based on differences in our bodies and minds, cultural, geographical, ethnic, and religious contexts; rather, we also examine how individual and social differences have been weaponized to place values of superiority and inferiority on human beings based on socially constructed categorizations.

Systems of oppression continue to exploit our differences, historically and into present times through fear and scarcity-based divisive strategies. As we explore in this book, forming of hierarchies and divisions, along with other strategies of oppression such as domination, exploitation, elimination, erasure, and marginalization are operationalized through institutionalized structures, cultures, and entire systems. These systems perpetuate oppression through divisive strategies that advantage, empower, and co-opt the favored dominant groups and disadvantage, disempower, and exclude the marginalized and minoritized groups.

The meaning of diversity has been shaped by our long historical context of oppression, domination, wars and other forms of human tragedies and its meaning continues to evolve. As the work of diversity, equity, and inclusion diffuses through public service organizations and institutions, public service community often refers to diversity to mean the groups that have been marginalized. However, we argue that such a reference is inaccurate and incomplete. Because diversity, in fact, includes both: Social groups that have been included, advantaged, and favored by systems and structures of power as well as those that have been disadvantaged, excluded, and marginalized.

The work of advancing diversity thus entails fostering proportional, meaningful, and empowered representation of diverse social groups, including those with dominant social locations and, particularly, those with marginalized social locations. Because our organizations and institutions have historically favored people from dominant social groups (such as white people, cisgender men, non-disabled people, middle-aged people, heteronormative people, Christian people); dominant groups are overrepresented within our organizations as compared to the populations we serve. As a result, the efforts to promote diversity often center around rectifying the historical and ongoing underrepresentation of social groups who have been marginalized and excluded, ensuring they have a meaningful voice and influence.

Diversity and Representative Bureaucracy

The idea or concept of diversity is not new to the public service community. In fact, by some accounts, public administration (PA) is one of the earliest fields to step up and embrace the ideas of representation and social equity (Frederickson 2010). Many members of the public administration (PA) community may be familiar with the concept of representative bureaucracy. The concept of representative bureaucracy suggests that when government agencies reflect the demographic makeup of the general population, they are more likely to act in ways that serve the interests of that population (Mosher 1968).

This idea can take on two forms: Passive representation and active representation. Passive representation occurs where government organizations hire and promote individuals in similar proportions to the demographics of society. These include women, LGBTQIA+ people, people with disabilities, and BIPOC people. Passive representation becomes active representation when public service professionals and administrators who share demographic characteristics with the public they serve, lead to the development and implementation of programs and policies that specifically benefit the represented population. This theoretical framework recognizes the potential connection between representation and the decisions made within bureaucracies, particularly in how they impact interests of minoritized and marginalized populations (Bishu and Kennedy 2020; Mosher 1968).

Even though the greater goal of diversity work is to go beyond passive representation and promote empowered active representation of underrepresented populations; it is important to recognize many advantages of passive representation in terms of fostering symbolic representation. This form of representation can be meaningful for individuals, particularly those from historically marginalized groups, by fostering positive attitudes, beliefs, and organizational climate. For example, the presence of a teacher of a similar background as the students can better student performance. Similar trends appear in the contexts of law enforcement, employment complaints, child support, rural home loans, undocumented immigrants, and parental school involvement (Hawes 2021; Meier and Nicholson-Crotty 2006; Riccucci, Van Ryzin, and Lavena 2014; Theobald and Haider-Markel 2009).

Therefore, in the context of public service organizations, we can understand diversity to mean passive, active, and symbolic representation of a wide range of social identities, lived experiences, voices, and perspectives present throughout our communities, organizations, and *across all levels of leadership and organizational operations*.

"The Diversity Edge"

There is abundant research demonstrating "the diversity edge" for organizations that proactively cultivate diversity rather than through performative tactics that "tokenize" members of minoritized and marginalized groups (Ely and Thomas 2020; Kanter 1977). When diversity is proactively nurtured within public service organizations and teams, across its levels of leadership and operations, the diversity edge manifests through improved social equity outcomes (Bradbury and Kellough 2011; Meier 2023), better performance outcomes (e.g., Andrews, Ashworth, and Meier 2014), and improved employee outcomes such as greater organizational commitment and reduced turnover intentions (e.g., Ashikali and Groeneveld 2015; Chordiya 2019, 2022a, 2022b).

Diverse organizations are more competent in meeting the needs of their clients and communities and they experience improved perceptions of performance and trustworthiness among communities (Riccucci et al. 2014; Riccucci and Van Ryzin 2017). Diverse organizations are also found to be more innovative in their problem-solving approaches (Lorenzo 2017; Østergaard, Timmermans, and Kristinsson 2011; Rock and Grant 2016). There is abundant empirical evidence of the positive influence of social identity representation (race, gender, sexuality, disability, etc.) on policy outcomes for marginalized communities in areas including education, law enforcement, politics, healthcare, welfare, federal employment, and fire service (Andrews et al. 2014; Bishu and Kennedy 2020; Bradbury and Kellough 2011; Dolan 2000; Meier 2023).

Thus, ensuring greater workforce diversity has become an essential value upheld by political actors and institutions alike. Recognizing the importance of representation in PA, policymakers and organizations strive to create inclusive and diverse bureaucracies. This commitment to representative bureaucracy stems from the understanding that a diverse workforce contributes to better decision-making, fosters trust among citizens, and supports the principles of social equity and democratic governance.

To achieve the diversity edge, organizations must proactively invest in diversity, such as, by ensuring there is a critical mass (not just one or few people) representing marginalized groups and interests across organizational leadership, from street levels to the top; through effective management of diverse groups and teams (including management of disagreements and conflicts); and by creating organizational conditions for felt experience of inclusion and belonging, where voices and perspectives of diverse members are invited and valued, particularly members identifying with marginalized and underrepresented groups (e.g., Bishu and Kennedy 2020; Choi and Rainey 2010; Chordiya 2019, 2022a, 2022b;

Hays-Thomas 2016; Mor Barak 2016; Sabharwal 2014). In the next section, we explore the concepts of inclusion and belonging.

Inclusion and Belonging

When organizations are striving for diversity, particularly, in contexts where majority of the leadership identifies with dominant social groups, there is often an implicit or explicit acknowledgment that the organization seeks to diversify from a given dominant group (e.g., white, cisgender men, straight, non-disabled, middle-aged people). However, increasing diversity is not just about recruitment and hiring of candidates identifying with minoritized and marginalized communities. For example, many of us are familiar with organizations who use misleading images and information on websites and share stories of a few members from marginalized groups to improve their numbers for recruitment of students, staff, clients, customers, and to increase profits.

We argue that increasing diversity requires us to work backward and focus on creating conditions of inclusion and belonging that can improve retention. For example, through equitable and inclusive policies, structures, procedures, and culture that invests in retention of students, staff, clients, and volunteers, particularly those with marginalized and minoritized identities.

The work of improving organizational diversity necessitates effort to bring shifts in culture and power structures in service of equity, inclusion, and belonging of those individuals and groups it seeks to recruit. For example, it is disempowering, tokenizing, and harmful to recruit one or few minoritized individuals and expect them to do all the DEI work for the organization without channelizing adequate support systems and resources in their direction.

The work of advancing diversity of marginalized groups through inclusion and belonging when envisioned and practiced from good faith and integrity seeks to shifts power toward embodied and empowered representation of marginalized groups. It seeks to tackle hidden biases in organizational operations and in policies, procedures, protocol, structures, cultures. It creates a welcoming environment where every organizational member feels they belong. In inclusive organizations, people are valued and respected; the inherent humanity and dignity of people are always honored.

A culture of inclusion and belonging is important for people to feel a sense of connection, purpose, and fulfillment as they contribute toward organizational goals, values, vision, and mission. Inclusion and belonging are key elements for nurturing pro-diversity and multicultural organizations. Inclusion means actively embracing diversity, while belonging is the result of these inclusive actions.

Inclusion is a day-to-day practice of facilitating an active engagement and participation of diverse individuals who identify with dominant and marginalized groups. Inclusion means providing a platform for individuals to express their perspectives, ideas, and concerns, and actively involving them in decision-making processes that are of consequence to them (Sabharwal 2014).

A culture of inclusion is related to many positive outcomes for organizations, employees, and the communities they serve. For example, research indicates that inclusion boosts employee engagement, productivity, and the perception of fairness in the organization (Hoang, Suh, and Sabharwal 2022). An inclusive organizational culture is linked to reduced turnover intentions among its employees, particularly those identifying with marginalized groups (Chordiya 2019, 2022a, 2022b). When people feel valued and motivated to contribute, it also sparks creativity. Inclusive cultures attract and retain top talent, as job seekers look for organizations that emphasize diversity, equity, and inclusion. Additionally, it helps build a positive reputation within the larger community, showing a commitment to social responsibility and equality.

Belonging can be described as an embodied experience (i.e., connected to bodymind and spirit) when people feel they can truly belong to themselves and each other. It is about an embodied sense of being connected, welcome, accepted, and valued in given physical or virtual space that they are a part of. While it is vitally important need for humans to belong to groups and communities that they are a part of; belonging is different from "fitting in" or assimilation. Brené Brown (2019) notes, "*true belonging doesn't require that we change who we are; it requires that we be who we are.*"

Similarly, in describing their spiritual journey to belonging, rev angel Kyodo williams notes (2021b),

> I realized that I had to have a fundamental belonging that was not predicated on something external, because if that were the case, I would always be in tension with what is going on outside that I actually can't control. So that if I'm going to have any sense of self-agency, of being able to be in alignment with myself and understand my own truth– not pulled by the external forces, by the waves of outside, by what people say, by the fashion, by the time, by the era, by gender, by the prescriptions of society, the prescriptions of my family, the prescriptions of my church, my culture, faith, all of those things–I had to get to someplace that was going to be essentially my own. And so, I have this concept of one's own belonging, of belonging to oneself first and foremost, and cultivating that as the reference point for discernment about all of the other ways in which we belong.
>
> (p. 2)

Thus, a culture that seeks to foster belonging recognizes that belonging means to, first and foremost, belong to oneself (Brown 2019; williams 2021a, 2021b). However, in organizational contexts, it is also important to recognize a contradiction – that a practice of self-belonging or to be authentic could mean taking disproportionate risks for minoritized and marginalized individuals. It is therefore important for organizations that truly care about diversity, inclusion, and belonging to foster a psychologically safe-enough culture for people to take risks and to belong. A culture where people, particularly multiply marginalized BIPOC people, can belong to themselves and should not have to worry about retaliations for being their authentic selves and for expressing their authentic views and perspectives (Brown and Burke 2021; Burey 2020).

As beautifully and powerfully noted by john a. powell of the Othering and Belonging Institute at the University of California Berkeley, the organizational practice of cultivating belonging means, "more than just being seen. Belonging entails having a meaningful voice and the opportunity to participate in the design of social and cultural structures. Belonging means having the right to contribute to, and make demands on, society and political institutions" (powell, cited in Grant-Thomas 2016, p. 2). In the next section, we explore the concept of psychological safety and its significance to foster diversity, inclusion, and belonging.

Psychological Safety: A Key to Diversity, Inclusion, and Belonging

Psychological safety is an important element in fostering diversity, inclusion, and belonging. Psychological safety means providing a safe-enough environment for taking interpersonal risks. It allows members to freely share their opinions, ideas, and perspectives without worrying about retaliation, backlash, or punishment. In such a setting, individuals feel at ease admitting mistakes, asking questions, and seeking help without being judged. This authenticity enhances collaboration, problem-solving, and decision-making. Leaders can encourage psychological safety by prioritizing open communication, transparency, and inclusivity to create a supportive culture (Edmondson 2014, 2018).

However, the meaning of psychologically safe environment is also often misunderstood. Psychological safety is about creating an environment where people feel secure in expressing themselves, taking risks, and learning, while maintaining respect for boundaries, standards, and accountability. It is not a lack of responsibility or a license for harmful behavior. Rather, it is a foundation for healthy communication, growth, and collaboration (Edmondson 2014, 2018). In Table 1.1, we describe what psychological safety means in workplace/learning contexts and what it does not mean.

Table 1.1 What Psychological Safety Is and Is Not

Psychological Safety Means	*Psychological Safety Does Not Mean*
Encouraging and supporting candor.	Being "nice" or "polite" to avoid discomfort.
Freedom to express thoughts and perspectives.	Saying anything you want.
Constructively expressing needs, feelings, and legitimate concerns.	Letting go emotions as you please.
Allocating tasks and coaching when needed.	Leadership taking a laissez-faire approach.
A space where people feel a sense of ease and support.	A space free of any inner discomfort.
Taking measured risks after considering possible scenarios.	Taking risks and hoping for the best.
Everything is considered.	Everything is tolerated.

Sources: Author's adaptation of a resource offered by Bakjac Consulting 2022; Based on Amy Edmondson's framework of psychological safety (2014, 2018).

A Reflection Invitation: Inclusion, Belonging, and Psychological Safety

Below we offer some prompts for individual and collective (or group) reflection. Some of these prompts could trigger unexpected emotions and feelings. We invite gentleness, care, and compassion for self and the collective as you engage in this reflection.

We encourage practice of consent, confidentiality, and respect for boundaries if this reflection opportunity is used in a collective. We invite you to honor your context, embodied wholeness, capacity as you engage in this reflection: stop if you need to, move, breathe, hydrate, and offer and receive "No" as a compassionate response, especially if you are engaging in a collective reflection.

We offer several prompts for reflection and invite you to start and continue to reflect on prompts that resonate the most with you.

Suggested Reflection Prompts

1 *Based on the above discussion of diversity, inclusion, belonging, and psychological safety, what is resonating for you? What is causing dissonance? What else would you add to the above discussion to make it feel more complete for you? (For example, "I would add <write your statement>").*
2 *Reflect on a time when you felt both included and a strong sense of belonging in a group or a community. What made you feel this*

sense of belonging, and how did it impact your experience? How did this environment contribute to your overall feelings of psychological safety and well-being?

3 *Can you recall a time when you felt excluded or like you didn't belong? What were the circumstances, and how did it make you feel? How did that experience impact your feelings of psychological safety? What could have been done differently to make you feel more included and safer?*
4 *Think about the role of communication in creating psychological safety. How has effective and open communication positively impacted your sense of psychological safety, inclusion, and belonging in different contexts?*
5 *In your workplace or other group settings, have you experienced leaders who actively promote psychological safety to foster inclusion and belonging as a part of their leadership practice? How has this influenced the overall culture of inclusion and belonging? Are there any leadership behaviors and practices that stood out/resonated with you?*
6 *What actions or interventions can be taken at leadership and collective levels to interrupt unsafety in workplace/learning/service contexts. What organizational conditions will be necessary to move toward an inclusive and psychologically safe environment where people can feel a sense of belonging?*
7 *What are the challenges, risks, and rewards involved in moving organizational cultures toward inclusion, belonging, and psychological safety. We invite you to respond to this prompt based on your own experienced perspectives as well as based on suitable research.*
8 *In Table 1.2, we outline some practices and approaches for creating inclusive organizations. What else would you add to this list of ideas? What actions and behaviors can you/do you practice to foster psychological safety, inclusion, and belonging within your spheres of influence?*

In the next section, we dive into the concepts of equality, equity, and liberatory justice. We begin by offering a brief context of how social equity has become a foundational pillar of PA.

Invitation to Pause: *However, before diving in, we want to acknowledge we have already covered several key concepts. We invite a pause here, even if for a minute, to breathe, move, take care of your bodyminds. We invite you to take a longer pause here, if you need, and return to the next sections, when you are ready.*

Table 1.2 Approaches and Practices to Create Inclusive Organizations

- Develop self-awareness to recognize and address biases at individual and systemic levels.
- Actively seek out and incorporate diverse voices, especially those that are marginalized in decision-making processes.
- Establish compassionate boundaries and psychologically safe spaces for employees/team members to engage in critical conversations and critical actions.
- Provide education, learning, and development opportunities that go beyond mandatory training. Coaching and mentoring opportunities are included.
- Listen attentively to employees and cultivate curiosity.
- Use inclusive language in communication.
- Provide opportunities for employees to engage in cross-cultural interactions and build relationships.
- Implement inclusive policies and practices that support equal opportunities and accessibility.
- Regularly assess and address any barriers or biases that may impede inclusion.
- Promote equity by addressing disparities and ensuring fair treatment and advancement opportunities for all.
- Regularly solicit feedback from employees and actively respond to their concerns or suggestions regarding exclusion.
- Hold individuals in positions of power accountable and consider who may be excluded.

Source: Created by the authors.

Social Equity: A Foundational Pillar of Public Administration

Public administration is an applied field. PA professionals are tasked with the implementation of laws. Implementing laws is a complex task. Laws are not always straightforward, making uniform application challenging. In the early days of the field, the idea of bureaucratic neutrality, that seeks to implement laws and policies neutrally was idealized. However, neutrality is not practically achievable, as PA involves interpreting the law and exercising discretion. In the field of PA, there is wider and concrete recognition that everyday operational tasks and decision-making of public servants from street level bureaucrats to top executives necessitates the ethic of social equity (Frederickson 2010).

The early generations of the field of PA essentially operated under the assumption that efficient and effective government administration inherently benefited all citizens equally. However, during the 1960s with the growing civil rights movement, there was a stronger acknowledgment and greater realization of the stark reality that the outcomes of government policies and the actions of public administrators in implementing those policies favored certain citizens while leaving others at a disadvantage. Issues related to racial and class inequality and injustice became glaringly evident and ignited widespread anger, indignation, outrage, and passion. Widespread protests, particularly in response to racial injustice and an unpopular Vietnam War, brought these issues to the forefront (Frederickson 2010).

It was within this intense atmosphere, a group of PA practitioners and scholars gathered at the inaugural Minnowbrook conference at Syracuse University in 1968. Through this conference, the term "social equity" found its place in literature and, subsequently, in the practices of PA, accompanied by a collection of associated concepts and shared values (Frederickson 2010).

Through the 1960s and 1970s, there was a growing recognition of social equity as a core value of PA. PA began to acknowledge that certain public programs were executed with significantly greater efficiency and effectiveness for some citizens compared to others. Public administrators could not reasonably distance themselves from practices that clearly resulted in unfairness and injustice. Consequently, the argument for social equity as an additional ethical pillar within PA gained prominence. Ultimately, social equity assumed its place alongside efficiency and economy as the third core principle in the field of PA (Blessett et al. 2019; Frederickson 1990, 2010; Gooden and Portillo 2011; Guy and McCandless 2012, 2020).

In his compelling presentation of arguments advocating for social equity as a core value of PA, George Frederickson's (1990) asks us, especially, the skeptics among us to consider:

> To say that a service may be well managed and that a service may be efficient and economical, still begs these questions: Well managed for whom? Efficient for whom? Economical for whom? We have generally assumed in public administration a convenient oneness with the public. We have not focused our attention or concern on the issue of variations in social and economic conditions. It is of great convenience, both theoretically and practically, to assume that citizen A is the same as citizen B and that they both receive public services in equal measure. This assumption may be convenient, but it is obviously both illogical and empirically inaccurate.
>
> (Frederickson 1990, p. 228)

Invitation to Pause: *We invite a pause here to breathe into this quote and reflect even if for a few moments. Allow these words to land in your bodymind.*

As a result of persistent ongoing efforts from scholars and practitioners, there is a growing call and recognition within PA community that social equity is not just a distinct pillar but a foundational cornerstone of PA (Blessett et al. 2019). In the next section, we explore the nuances between social equity and justice approaches based on the logics of equality, equity, and liberatory justice.

Equality vs. Equity vs. Liberatory Justice

Figure 1.1 is often used in the DEI learning contexts and may be familiar to you. The Center for Story-Based Strategy and Interaction Institute for Social Change co-developed this image through a collaborative effort. This image uses a baseball game metaphor and depicts three people with different heights watching the game from across the fence/obstacle that blocks the viewing of the game. The image has three panels, panel one depicts the equality metaphor, panel two depicts the equity metaphor, and panel three depicts the liberation metaphor, respectively (Center for Story-based Strategy n.d.).

In the first panel depicting the equality metaphor, all three people have one box each to give them an elevation above the ground to watch the game. As a result, the tallest person, with a height advantage in this scenario, is elevated in height quite above the fence. The relatively shorter person is elevated just above the fence is now able to watch the game. For the shortest person, who is most disadvantaged in height in this scenario, despite the box, has their view totally blocked by the fence and are not able to watch the game. One box does not offer them the elevation they need above the ground to be able to watch the game.[2]

Equality

As one may notice in this image, we often understand and operationalize equality through sameness, for example, allocation of same or equal resources. Equality can be appealing as a concept and an approach to public policy/administrative decision-making. However, it also has a major flaw.

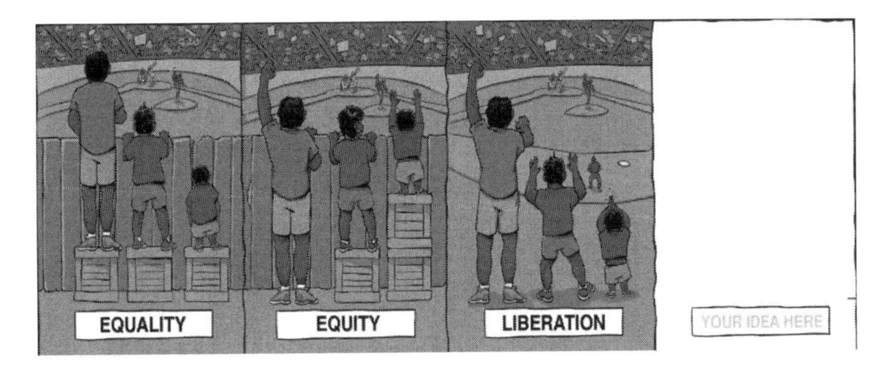

Figure 1.1 Equality vs. Equity vs. Liberation

Image Credit: Equality/Equity/Liberation image is a collaboration between Center for Story-Based Strategy & Interaction Institute for Social Change. The "#4th Box" was created by Andrew Weizeman. CC BY-NC 4.0 DEED.

Equality-based approaches use the one-size-fits-all logic and do not fully account for the historical, inter-generational, socio-cultural, and individual contexts and needs of all people we intend to serve, especially those who are the most disadvantaged (powell, Menendian, and Ake 2019).

Solutions based on one-size-fits-all approaches are not always necessary and do not always work for everybody. As depicted in the image, the one-box solution worked for the person in the middle, but it was not needed by the tallest person, and it did not work for the shortest person depicted in the image. To offer another example from a public policy area, Medicare for All is likely to work for people who experience inequities due to lack of access to health care insurance or are underinsured, however, it offers an incomplete solution for people and communities who not only lack insurance but are also disadvantaged by lack of access to hospitals or health care providers (powell et al. 2019). Furthermore, the solutions designed using the one-size-fits-all logic are often biased to favor those who are in the middle and ignore the needs of those at the margins.

Equity

Equity-based approaches serve as effective alternatives to address this flaw in equality-based approaches. The logic of equity in public policy making and administrative decision-making invites us to follow the leadership of those most impacted by inequities and to take evidence-based, targeted, approaches to solving problems of inequities. The focus is to identify inequities posed by systemic biases and problem-solving to address those inequities. Equity-based approaches are rooted in values of sharing and redistributing resources to address systemic inequities.

For example, as depicted in Figure 1.1, the design of the fence is biased and inequitable, because it is designed based on the height assumptions of a tall person and ignores the reality of differences in heights, particularly, among relatively shorter people. The equity approach involved redistributing the resources, in this case, the elevated platform from the tall person who did not need it, because the fence is designed to meet their height and body needs, to the shortest people who needed it the most. Thus, equity-based approaches involve creative and collaborative problem-solving to address systemic biases by providing greater access to those that are not considered/are neglected by dominant designs, structures, and cultures.

Equity-based approaches recognize that our dominant systems, by design, have historical and institutional biases embedded in them. These biases often work in favor of people with dominant identities as their needs and contexts were represented and properly considered in decision-making process, while disadvantaging those with marginalized identities whose needs were excluded or neglected in decision-making process. However, the challenge and limitation of equity-based approaches is that, in practice, they often seek to provide greater access to minoritized and marginalized people without necessarily transforming inequities embedded within the system. Equity-based approaches can be limited when they work to reform, not transform, existing systems. A liberatory justice approach seeks to address this limitation.

Liberatory Justice

A liberatory justice approach focuses on identifying and transforming the conditions that allow social inequities and injustices to persist. For example, as depicted in the imagery, equity-based approaches may focus on providing boxes (i.e., resources) based on the needs of the individual/group, without addressing the barrier that created unequal access in the first place. On the other hand, liberatory justice goes deeper and invites us to interrogate the existence and persistence of systemic barriers.

Liberatory justice seeks transformation. It goes beyond simply reforming existing systems to make them more equitable and accessible. It is focused on transformative work that seeks to change conditions that allow inequities to be reproduced, it seeks to remove all forms of barriers (i.e., inequities) that can have an adverse, marginalizing, and disempowering impact on any group. It necessitates collective efforts and shared leadership approaches that are community and survivor-led and seeks to replace inequitable systems with, structures, cultures, policies, protocols, and practices that meaningfully prioritize the needs of those who are multiply marginalized by inequities (Kaba 2021; Page and Woodland 2023; Sins Invalid 2019).

Liberatory justice work is rooted in the visionary and creative politics of both resistance and creation. It seeks to both remove systemic biases against marginalized populations and advance proactive politics of inclusion, belonging and freedom from oppression. For example, liberatory justice is the work of both anti-racism and creating pro-Black, pro-Indigenous, pro-disabled, pro-LGBTQIA+, feminist cultures, and infrastructures (Acker 1990; Chordiya and Protonentis 2024; Sins Invalid 2019; Suarez et al. 2023).

Liberatory justice is a goal and a process. As a process, liberatory justice work could involve creating microcosms of diversity, inclusion, belonging and safety within our own spheres of influence – the ones that reflect the world we envision and desire. Liberatory justice practice is action-oriented, imaginative, and explorative. It is not free of failures. However, when engaging in liberatory justice practice, we learn to fail forward. We become intentional and proactive to avoid missteps, hurt and harm; learn from mistakes when they inevitably happen as is in case of any human creative work, own responsibility for our actions, do the necessary work of repair while being in generative relationships and avoid repeating the same mistakes (brown 2020).

We cannot achieve liberatory justice without engaging in a liberatory politics of cultivating inclusion, generative relationships, and belonging that shifts power and follows the leadership of those most impacted by inequities. Liberatory justice work does not happen in isolation. It happens in a collective. It necessitates integration of both inner transformation and collective transformation. In other words, it requires us to engage in the disciplined practice of transforming ourselves as we work to transform the worlds we envision and deeply desire (williams n.d.).

Summary and Key Teachings

In this chapter, we explored the nuanced concepts of diversity, equality, equity, inclusion, psychological safety, belonging and liberatory justice. We also explored the context of social equity work in PA. The key teachings of this chapter focus on understanding that diversity is a nuanced concept that is evolving and should be understood within the broader historical context of oppression and liberatory resistance work. Diversity in the context of PA includes passive or demographic representation, however, it is incomplete without active representation of public service workers who are responsive to the needs of diverse people and communities we intend to serve.

We explored the distinctions between equality, equity, and liberatory justice. We also discussed the limitations of equality-based approaches that often use one-size-fits-all solutions to solve problems posed by inequities. Equity-based approaches help to address some of the limitations of equality or one-size-fits-all approaches by developing needs and context-based solutions to solve problems posed by existing inequities. Finally, we reflected on the meaning of liberatory justice. Liberatory justice is a political work and process of removing inequities and transforming the conditions (including policies, administrative procedures, structures, designs, and cultures) that created inequities and contributed towards harm into systems and cultures that are oriented towards repair, healing and are life-affirming.

Deep Dive Resources [Full Citations in References]

1 brown, adrienne maree. 2020. We Will Not Cancel Us: And Other Dreams of Transformative Justice.

2 Frederickson, H. George. 1990. "Public Administration and Social Equity."
3 McDowell, Ceasar. 2015. "Democracy from the Margins."
4 powell, john a. 2019. Podcast: Targeted Universalism, with john a. powell | Othering & Belonging Institute Interview by Marc Abizeid.
5 Racial Equity Tools. n.d. "Act, Strategies, Caucus and Affinity Groups."

Notes

1 Throughout this book we use "multiply" (muhl-ti-plee) as an adverb and it means, in several different ways or respects. Collins (2008) offered a language of "multiply marginalized" to describe different and intersectional ways in which oppression is experienced by people with more than one socially disadvantaged identities.
2 The creators of this story-based strategy to imagine social change acknowledge that the metaphor is not complete and has its own limitations. One of the critiques of the metaphor is that the story told through this image may be too simple and linear. About the sequencing of the panels, does the liberation panel come first, before the fence was built, or does it come last after the fence was removed? The creators of this image recently added a fourth box (#the 4th box) created by Andrew Weizeman. The creators added the fourth box to serve users in imagining what could come after liberation. In other words, what could happen, if we removed all the obstacles?

References

Acker, Joan. 1990. "Hierarchies, Jobs, Bodies: A Theory of Gendered Organizations." *Gender & Society* 4 (2): 139–58. https://doi.org/10.1177/089124390004002002

Andrews, Rhys, Rachel Ashworth, and Kenneth J. Meier. 2014. "Representative Bureaucracy and Fire Service Performance." *International Public Management Journal* 17 (1): 1–24. https://doi.org/10.1080/10967494.2014.874253

Ashikali, Tanachia, and Sandra Groeneveld. 2015. "Diversity Management in Public Organizations and Its Effect on Employees' Affective Commitment: The Role of Transformational Leadership and the Inclusiveness of the Organizational Culture." *Review of Public Personnel Administration* 35 (2): 146–68. https://doi.org/10.1177/0734371X13511088

Bakjac Consulting. 2022. "What Does Psychological Safety at Work Actually Look Like?" Bakjac Consulting. February 27, 2022. http://www.bakjacconsulting.com/michelles-blog/2022/2/27/what-does-psychological-safety-at-work-actually-look-like

Bishu, Sebawit G., and Alexis R. Kennedy. 2020. "Trends and Gaps: A Meta-Review of Representative Bureaucracy." *Review of Public Personnel Administration* 40 (4): 559–88. https://doi.org/10.1177/0734371X19830154

Blessett, Brandi, Jennifer Dodge, Beverly Edmond, Holly T Goerdel, Susan T Gooden, Andrea M Headley, Norma M Riccucci, and Brian N Williams. 2019.

"Social Equity in Public Administration: A Call to Action." *Perspectives on Public Management and Governance* 2 (4): 283–99. https://doi.org/10.1093/ppmgov/gvz016

Bradbury, Mark, and J. Edward Kellough. 2011. "Representative Bureaucracy: Assessing the Evidence on Active Representation." *The American Review of Public Administration* 41 (2): 157–67. https://doi.org/10.1177/0275074010367823

brown, adrienne maree. 2020. *We Will Not Cancel Us: And Other Dreams of Transformative Justice.*

Brown, Brené. 2019. *Braving the Wilderness: The Quest for True Belonging and the Courage to Stand Alone.* Reprint ed. New York: Random House Trade Paperbacks.

Brown, Brené, and Tarana Burke. 2021. "Introduction to You Are Your Best Thing: A Conversation." Dare to Lead Hub. *Brené Brown* (blog). January 25, 2021. https://brenebrown.com/blog/2021/01/25/introduction-to-you-are-your-best-thing-a-conversation/

Burey, Jodi-Ann. 2020. "The Future of Work: Jodi-Ann Burey." Presented at the UW Communication Leadership Graduate Program, Washington, USA, March 13. https://www.youtube.com/watch?v=NZSuSnHr4Y8

Center for Story-based Strategy. n.d. "#the4thBox." Center for Story-Based Strategy. n.d. https://www.storybasedstrategy.org/the4thbox

Chordiya, Rashmi. 2019. "Are Federal Child Care Programs Sufficient for Employee Retention? Critical Examination From a Gendered Perspective." *The American Review of Public Administration* 49 (3): 338–52. https://doi.org/10.1177/0275074018804662

________. 2022a. "Organizational Inclusion and Turnover Intentions of Federal Employees With Disabilities." *Review of Public Personnel Administration* 42 (1): 60–87. https://doi.org/10.1177/0734371X20942305

________. 2022b. "A Study of Interracial Differences in Turnover Intentions: The Mitigating Role of Pro-Diversity and Justice-Oriented Management." *Public Personnel Management* 51 (2): 235–60. https://doi.org/10.1177/00910260211061824

Chordiya, Rashmi, and Adana Protonentis. 2024. "Healing from White Supremacy Culture and Ableism: Disability Justice as an Antidote." *Journal of Social Equity and Public Administration.* 2 (1): 127–52. *https://doi.org/10.24926/jsepa.v2i1.4856.*

Choi, Sungjoo, and Hal G. Rainey. 2010. "Managing Diversity in U.S. Federal Agencies: Effects of Diversity and Diversity Management on Employee Perceptions of Organizational Performance." *Public Administration Review* 70 (1): 109–21. https://doi.org/10.1111/j.1540-6210.2009.02115.x

Collins, Patricia Hill. 2008. *Black Feminist Thought: Knowledge, Consciousness, and the Politics of Empowerment.* New York: Routledge.

Dolan, Julie. 2000. "The Senior Executive Service: Gender, Attitudes, and Representative Bureaucracy." *Journal of Public Administration Research and Theory* 10 (3): 513–30. https://doi.org/10.1093/oxfordjournals.jpart.a024279

Edmondson, Amy C. 2014. *"Building a Psychologically Safe Workplace." Presented at the TEDxHGSE, May 4.* https://www.youtube.com/watch?v=LhoLuui9gX8

_______. 2018. *The Fearless Organization: Creating Psychological Safety in the Workplace for Learning, Innovation, and Growth*. 1st ed. Hoboken, New Jersey: Wiley.

Ely, Robin J., and David A. Thomas. 2020. "Getting Serious About Diversity: Enough Already with the Business Case." *Harvard Business Review*, November 1, 2020. https://hbr.org/2020/11/getting-serious-about-diversity-enough-already-with-the-business-case

Frederickson, H. George. 1990. "Public Administration and Social Equity." *Public Administration Review* 50 (2): 228–37. https://doi.org/10.2307/976870

_______. 2010. "The State of Social Equity in American Public Administration." In *Social Equity and Public Administration: Origins, Developments, and Applications: Origins, Developments, and Applications*, 95–105. Armonk: Taylor & Francis Group. http://ebookcentral.proquest.com/lib/seattleu/detail.action?docID=501521

Grant-Thomas, Andrew. 2016. "Editors' Introduction, Issue One." *Othering and Belonging* (blog). June 29, 2016. https://www.otheringandbelonging.org/editors-introduction/

Gooden, Susan, and Shannon Portillo. 2011. "Advancing Social Equity in the Minnowbrook Tradition." *Journal of Public Administration Research and Theory* 21 (suppl_1): i61–76. https://doi.org/10.1093/jopart/muq067

Guy, Mary E., and Sean A. McCandless. 2012. "Social Equity: Its Legacy, Its Promise." *Public Administration Review* 72: S5–13.

_______. 2020. *Achieving Social Equity: From Problems to Solutions*: Melvin & Leigh, Publishers.

Hawes, Daniel, P. 2021. "Symbolic Representation, Cooperation, and Undocumented Immigrants: The Role of Representation in Improving Assessments of Cooperative Behaviors in Education." The American Review of Public Administration 51 (8): 605–18. https://doi.org/10.1177/0275074021103192

Hays-Thomas, Rosemary. 2016. *Managing Workplace Diversity and Inclusion: A Psychological Perspective*. 1st ed. New York: Routledge.

Hoang, Trang, Jiwon Suh, and Meghna Sabharwal. 2022. "Beyond a Numbers Game? Impact of Diversity and Inclusion on the Perception of Organizational Justice." *Public Administration Review 82 (3): 537–55. https://doi.org/10.1111/puar.13463.*

Kaba, Mariame. 2021. *We Do This 'Til We Free Us: Abolitionist Organizing and Transforming Justice*. Edited by Tamara K. Nopper. Chicago: Haymarket Books.

Kanter, Rosabeth Moss. 1977. "Some Effects of Proportions on Group Life: Skewed Sex Ratios and Responses to Token Women." *American Journal of Sociology* 82 (5): 965–90. https://doi.org/10.1086/226425

Lorenzo, Rocío. 2017. "How Diversity Makes Teams More Innovative | Rocío Lorenzo | TED." Presented at the TED, November 15. https://www.youtube.com/watch?v=lPtPG2lAmm4

McDowell, Ceasar. 2015. "Democracy from the Margins | Ceasar McDowell | TEDxIndianaUniversity." TEDx Talks. https://www.youtube.com/watch?v=irkqd0q9a9k&ab_channel=TEDxTalks

Meier, Kenneth. 2023. "Representative Bureaucracy and Social Equity: Bias, Perceived Fairness and Efficacy." *Journal of Social Equity and Public Administration* 1 (1): 23–38. https://doi.org/10.24926/jsepa.v1i1.4814

Meier, Kenneth J., and Jill Nicholson-Crotty. 2006. "Gender, Representative Bureaucracy, and Law Enforcement: The Case of Sexual Assault." Public Administration Review 66(6): 850–60. https://doi.org/10.1111/j.1540-6210.2006.00653.x

Mor Barak, Michalle E. 2016. *Managing Diversity: Toward a Globally Inclusive Workplace.* 4th ed. Los Angeles: SAGE Publications, Inc.

Mosher, Frederick C. 1968. *Democracy and the Public Service.* New York: Oxford University Press.

Østergaard, Christian R., Bram Timmermans, and Kari Kristinsson. 2011. "Does a Different View Create Something New? The Effect of Employee Diversity on Innovation." *Research Policy* 40 (3): 500–509. https://doi.org/10.1016/j.respol.2010.11.004

Page, Cara, and Erica Woodland. 2023. *Healing Justice Lineages: Dreaming at the Crossroads of Liberation, Collective Care, and Safety.* Berkeley, California: North Atlantic Books.

powell, john a. 2019. Podcast: Targeted Universalism, with john a. powell | Othering & Belonging Institute Interview by Marc Abizeid. https://belonging.berkeley.edu/podcast-targeted-universalism-john-powell

powell, john a., Stephen Menendian, and Wendy Ake. 2019. "Targeted Universalism: Policy & Practice." Berkeley, CA: Haas Institute for a Fair and Inclusive Society at UC Berkeley. file:///C:/Users/chordiyarash/Downloads/targeted_universalism_primer.pdf

Racial Equity Tools. n.d. "Act, Strategies, Caucus and Affinity Groups." Racial Equity Tools. n.d. https://www.racialequitytools.org/resources/act/strategies/caucus-and-affinity-groups

Riccucci, Norma M., and Gregg G. Van Ryzin. 2017. "Representative Bureaucracy: A Lever to Enhance Social Equity, Coproduction, and Democracy." *Public Administration Review* 77 (1): 21–30. https://doi.org/10.1111/puar.12649

Riccucci, Norma M., Gregg G. Van Ryzin, and Cecilia F. Lavena. 2014. "Representative Bureaucracy in Policing: Does It Increase Perceived Legitimacy?" *Journal of Public Administration Research and Theory* 24 (3): 537–51. https://doi.org/10.1093/jopart/muu006

Rock, David, and Heidi Grant. 2016. "Why Diverse Teams Are Smarter." *Harvard Business Review*, November 4, 2016. https://hbr.org/2016/11/why-diverse-teams-are-smarter

Sabharwal, Meghna. 2014. "Is Diversity Management Sufficient? Organizational Inclusion to Further Performance." *Public Personnel Management* 43 (2): 197–217. https://doi.org/10.1177/0091026014522202

Sins Invalid. 2019. "Skin, Tooth, and Bone: The Basis of Movement Is Our People, A Disability Justice Primer." https://www.sinsinvalid.org/skin-tooth-and-bone

Suarez, Cyndi, and Staff at Non Profit Quarterly. 2023. *Building A Pro-Black World: Moving Beyond DE&I Work and Creating Spaces for Black People to Thrive. 1st edition. Wiley.*

Theobald, Nick A., and Donald P. Haider-Markel. 2009. "Race, Bureaucracy, and Symbolic Representation: Interactions between Citizens and Police." *Journal of Public Administration Research and Theory* 19(2): 409–26. https://doi.org/10.1093/jopart/mun006

williams, Rev. angel Kyodo. n.d. "Angel Kyodo Williams 'Love and Justice Are Not Two. without Inner Change, There Can Be No Outer Change; without Collective Change, No Change Matters.'" n.d. https://angelkyodowilliams.com/

williams, Rev angel Kyodo. 2021a. The Core of Belonging Interview by Tami Simon. Transcript. https://www.resources.soundstrue.com/podcast/the-core-of-belonging/

________. 2021b. *Belonging: From Fear to Freedom on the Path to True Community*. Unabridged ed. Sounds True.

2 Understanding Oppression

What It Is, How It Works, and How to Interrupt It?

Abstract

One of the first steps toward cultivating a liberatory public service (LPS) is developing a critical awareness and analysis of systems of oppression. In this chapter, we focus on theoretical frameworks that help us explore the following questions: What is oppression? How does it work? How can we interrupt it and move toward liberatory justice? The key teachings of this chapter include learning to recognize the key characteristics of oppression. Drawing from existing sociology literature, we highlight that oppression is hierarchical and divisive, dehumanizing, pervasive and cumulative, has multiple and intersectional manifestations, is persistent, mutating, and durable, and has consequences for all. We also explore how systems of oppression work at multiple levels such as micro (i.e., individual level), meso (i.e., institutional, and organizational level), and macro (i.e., social, structural, and cultural level). Another key teaching explored in this chapter is acknowledging that we are all socialized into systems of oppression and learn to internalize domination and oppression. We, especially as public servants, also have the choice and power to interrupt the cycle of socialization into oppressive systems and enter the path of developing a liberatory consciousness to foster collective joy, love, and freedom. We acknowledge the work of building liberatory consciousness is not easy, but it is necessary. Developing a liberatory consciousness involves unlearning our socialization into oppressive behaviors and learning behaviors and practices rooted in mutuality, solidarity, and reciprocity. It necessitates repair and healing, including collective healing. And it is important to be discerning of our embodied needs, limits, and capacities while moving at a pace that feels liberatory, compassionate, and meaningful.

What Is Oppression?

One of the first steps toward cultivating a liberatory public service (LPS) is developing a critical awareness and analysis of systems of oppression. The meaning of the term oppression has evolved over time. Traditionally

DOI: 10.4324/9781032670669-3

the term oppression has referred to the use of brute force and exercise of tyranny by a ruling group. It carries a strong connotation of conquest and colonial domination and something evil (Young 1990).

However, in addition to describing the tyranny of a ruling group over those who are ruled, social justice movements of 1960s and 1970s nuanced the concept of oppression to include everyday experiences of structural and systemic oppression. This expanded understanding of oppression sheds light on every day structural patterns of conscious and unconscious biases, unexamined norms, habits, rules, and taken-for-granted assumptions reproduced through our major economic, political, and cultural institutions. These structured patterns and biases have privileging and marginalizing consequences for dominant and non-dominant groups, respectively (Young 1990).

The patterns of structural oppression are reproduced and persist through unexamined and inequitable policies, procedures, structural and cultural factors. They are biased to advantage the favored dominant groups in our society (such as white people, non-disabled people) and disadvantage those who are not in the dominant groups (such as people of color, disabled people, women, and nonbinary and trans people). A nuanced and structural understanding of oppression helps us recognize harms caused by policy and administrative decisions.

For example, decision to dump public waste in low-income neighborhoods whose majority residents are people of color, or disproportionate lack of access to public benefits and resources (such as educational, health, and recreational infrastructure) in low-income neighborhoods, or a lower safety net for essential workers who are often low-income and people of color. Dismantling systemic oppression will take more than getting rid of the tyrannical ruler or rules and making new laws; it will necessitate a wider social, economic, political, and cultural transformation (Young 1990).

Key Characteristics of Systems of Oppression

To eliminate oppression from our systems, structures, and cultures, we must be vigilant of its key characteristics and how they are reproduced. Scholars Hardiman, Jackson, and Griffin (2007) as well as Lee Anne Bell (2022) contributed to the development of conceptual frameworks that help us understand systems of oppression as an overarching social phenomenon. They identify and describe the key characteristics of oppression that reveal how systems of oppression are constructed and maintained in structured, cultural, and institutional ways in overt and covert manners.

Such an analysis of oppression can help diversity, equity, inclusion, and liberatory justice (DEILJ) workers in public and nonprofit sector contexts to identify oppressive systems and work to interrupt and transform them in their personal and professional lives. Below we synthesize the six key features of oppression identified by Bell (2022). Bell (2022) notes, oppression is (1) hierarchical and divisive, (2) dehumanizing, (3) pervasive and cumulative, (4) with multiple and intersectional manifestations, (5) persistent, mutating, and durable, and (6) with consequences for all.

Hierarchical and Divisive

A key tool of oppression is the use of divisive strategies. Systems of oppression use superiority-based, fear-based, scarcity-based, and urgency-based mindsets, to create division of humanity and regulate access to resources, participation, belonging, social respect, and self-actualization.

Systems of oppression rupture bonds of solidarity and kinship. We are sorted and ranked by socially constructed categories leading to emergence of social groups based on race, gender, sexuality, age, religion, caste, class, disability, and other such context and culture-specific social markers. Categorization and hierarchy are normalized, and oppressive outcomes are made to seem logical and inevitable. We enter unequal, hierarchical relationships to one another at systemic, structural, and institutional levels that by design favor and advantage some groups over others (Bell 2022).

Dehumanizing

Systems of oppression use dehumanization as a strategy to divide people into "in groups" and "outgroups." Strategies for "othering" include dehumanizing language (including dehumanizing body language), images, narratives, stereotypes, and prejudices. Groups that are defined as "others" are denied wholeness and humanity. Symbolic and physical violence, exclusion, mistreatment, devaluation of their bodies and minds through harm, exploitation, and abuse are legitimatized.

[Content Warning: Emotionally Heavy Materials] For example, in 1851, American physician Samuel A. Cartwright's fabricated theories of "Drapetomania" and "Dysaesthesia Aethiopica" to assert that enslaved laborers suffered from bodily and mental ailments, purportedly making them lazy and prone to escaping from their enslavers. These fabricated theories were meant to dehumanize enslaved African Americans using ableist logics and in support of the oppressive and racialized system of slavery (Chin 2021).

In our current times, techniques and logics of dehumanization are used to "other" and rationalize anti-LGBTQIA+ agendas, to minimize and invalidate sufferings of low-income groups and people living in poverty, to disenfranchise, exclude and discriminate against people with disabilities, to devalue bodyminds and take-for-granted contributions of Black, Indigenous, and negatively racialized People of Color in our organizations and in our society without any meaningful support, resourcing, recognition, and sharing of power.

For example, when it comes to the issue of persisting housing crisis, one of the key logics of dehumanization is to attribute blame on individuals while ignoring systemic biases and realities. These include systemic inequities related to rising home prices, unemployment, lack of health care and communal care, lack of safety nets, large scale socio-economic impacts of emergencies and crises such as COVID-19. Even though these systemic inequities contribute toward the existence and persistence of housing crisis in the first place, oppression persists and is normalized when we make attribution errors and blame individuals for their circumstances rather than challenge and resist inequitable systems that made/allowed those conditions to be a possibility in the first place.

Pervasive and Cumulative

Systems of oppression exist by design. They are pervasive and cumulative across time and institutions. However, without a critical lens of awareness, they remain hidden. They are deeply embedded into our systems through intentional or unintentional biases. They are normalized, naturalized, and woven into our social fabric, dominant historical narratives, legal systems, economic policies, and educational systems. The stacking and layering of biased policies, procedures, and cultural norms over time function to normalize, rationalize, and institutionalize injustices and inequities (Bell 2022).

At individual and interpersonal levels, the systems of socialization contribute toward internalization of our dominant and marginalized roles within oppressive systems. We are told what our place is and learn to maintain the status quo by conforming with the rules, norms, and behavioral expectations within oppressive systems. Individuals who question prevailing norms and resist conformity face the potential of encountering backlash and reprisals. This pervasive and cumulative nature of oppression makes it hard to identify, analyze, and challenge it (Hardiman et al. 2007). As Carter G. Woodson (1999) noted in his writings,

> When you control a man's thinking you do not have to worry about his actions. You do not have to tell him not to stand here or go yonder. He will find his "proper place" and will stay in it. You do not need to send him to the back door. He will go without being told. In fact, if there is no back door, he will cut one for his special benefit. His education makes it necessary.

Multiple and Intersectional Manifestations

Systems of oppression have multiple manifestations such as ableism, racism, ageism and youth oppression, classism, casteism, religious oppression, sexism, heterosexism, and trans oppression. These manifestations of oppression affect us all through biased systems and structures. Their impact can either be advantageous or marginalizing, depending on our proximity to or distance from power structures. All manifestations of social oppression interlock with one another and therefore addressing one manifestation is inadequate and ineffective to achieve the goals of social justice (Hardiman et al. 2007).

Intersectionality is a term used to refer to the interlocking or overlapping systems of oppression and how different manifestations of oppression or "isms" are mutually dependent and reinforcing (Crenshaw 2016, 2020). Furthermore, intersectionality also makes us aware that the privilege and marginalization experienced by our identities is dynamic and context specific. This means that for many of us, we hold (systemically) oppressed and oppressor identities at different points in time and in various spaces we live, work, learn, and play (Hancock 2011).

Intersectionality also invites us to remain vigilant of vertical and horizontal forms of oppression. Vertical oppression involves conscious and unconscious dehumanization and marginalization by dominant group members of minoritized group members (e.g., white person refusing to be examined by a doctor of color; a straight person refusing to serve a gay person, or a male supervisor harassing a female employee).

Here, it is important to note the distinction between individual prejudice and system of oppression. For example, while individuals with marginalized identities may harbor prejudice against dominant group members, this prejudice does not have structural, institutional, and cultural support that characterizes vertical oppression exercised by members of dominant groups against marginalized group members. Therefore, the terms reverse racism and reverse sexism are inaccurate descriptions of the individual prejudice exercised by marginalized group members toward dominant group members. These acts of prejudice are individualized and lack structural and systemic support (Hardiman et al. 2007).

Horizontal oppression is an outcome of "hierarchical and divisive" characteristic of oppression that may stem from fear and scarcity mindset, misinformation, ignorance, and insecurity. Members of oppressed groups may exhibit rage, prejudice, discrimination, and exclusion against other members of oppressed groups.

For example, cisgender and straight people of color may exclude members of their groups who identify as gay, or non-binary, or transgender and do not conform with existing gender norms. People of color with access to income/wealth opportunities may invalidate or dehumanize low-income, poor, or people of color experiencing homelessness. Horizontal oppression may also function within advantaged groups when members of advantaged or dominant groups challenge systems of oppression. For example, when white people who challenge racism are called racial slurs or experience explicit or implicit threats and exclusion (Hardiman et al. 2007).

It is important to notice and understand these common patterns in forms of horizontal and vertical, multiple, and intersectional manifestations of oppression. At the same time we need to be vigilant and mindfully aware that the intensities of harm, hurt, and wounding vary based on our contexts and lived experiences within systems of oppression. Equating or comparing experiences of oppression and harm, naming them as common/same experiences across diverse social identities, without any nuance and an understanding of our differences can get in the way of resisting oppression and building solidarity.

For example, white women, BIPOC women, white and BIPOC LGBQ+ women, white and BIPOC trans women are located differently. And in building solidarity, it is important to understand how systems embedded in patriarchy, racism, heterosexism, and trans oppression impact women differently based on their multiply marginalized social locations. Intersectionality also teaches us that it is important to interrupt oppression olympics (e.g., who has it worse). We need to cultivate a compassionate expansiveness and depth to hold space for solidarity, it is important that we are centering the needs, contexts, and lived experiences of those among us who are at the margins of margins (Glenn 2015; Hancock, 2011).

Persistent, Durable, and Mutating

Systems of oppression are persistent, durable, and mutating. They persist within our institutions and organizations as well as broader societal culture, across historical timelines and span across generations. Systems of oppression are durable and mutating, which means they shift and adapt to changing circumstances. They are deeply embedded within all systems and resistant to change (Bell 2022).

Movement backlash is a common pattern through which systems of oppression resist change toward social justice and liberation. For example, with global awareness of diversity in terms of gender identity and sexual orientation, increased visibility, and movement for equity and inclusion of LGBTQIA+ people, there has been increasing movement backlash. Within United States, 574 bills that seek to harm and marginalize trans communities were introduced as of October 2023 across 49 states – 83 were passed, 366 are actively being considered, and 125 failed, and these numbers are ever increasing. These bills range from book bans, to challenging gender fluidity and shifts in culture to promote use of pronouns as a trans affirming strategy, gender affirming care, athletics and even clothing (Trans Legislation Tracker 2023).

To offer another example, in retaliation to the 2020 Black Lives Matter movement, there has been movement backlash in form of banning books that explore the topic of racism in the United States' contexts, targeting of diversity, equity, inclusion, and justice focused offices and work in institutions of higher education and government organizations, and spread of misinformation in media sources about Critical Race Theory (CRT) being divisive. (A side note: We explore the meaning and the importance of CRT in chapter 8).

Oppression tactics of movement backlash are not new. For example, there was backlash against the gains of the Civil Rights Movement of the 1960s and 1970s. After segregation and discrimination against Black people was legally prohibited, there was an emergence of "color-blind racism" which allowed schools to remain segregated in reality by means of property taxes, red lining, and school "choice" programs. These forms of color-blind racism persist in our present-day times. At organizational and interpersonal levels, dominant group members who have access to power and privileges can exhibit backlash politics through retaliation against members of the team/organization who challenge dominant norms of organizational behaviors.

Consequences for All

Systems of oppression have consequences for *everybody*. While the direct intensity of oppression in terms of existential and survival crisis may be most felt by those who are disadvantaged, disenfranchised, and othered within the systems of oppression, as long as these systems persist, those who remain advantaged and privileged pay a social, moral, and ethical price. The reality of justice and democracy remains elusive until all people are free from interconnected systems of oppression.

We want to acknowledge that this piece may feel particularly challenging for those who may hold multiply advantaged positionalities. Based on experiences of being privileged by many systems, one may think, feel, and argue that "the current systems are working just fine (for me)."

The meritocracy-based arguments are often along this same line of thought. The meritocracy argument centers on the idea that success and opportunities should be on merit-based criteria that focus on individual abilities, skills, and effort rather than on factors like social class, family background, racial and other social identities, or other non-merit-based criteria. These arguments do not fully consider the historical, intergenerational, and persistent institutional burdens of systems of oppression.

If you identify as someone who is curious and needs more clarification or perspectives on how systems of oppression have consequences for all, including those with advantaged social positionalities, we invite you to sit with the following questions and notice what emerges for you? We want to acknowledge, you may not find all answers in this moment and this reflection invitation may take a long time; you might need new observations, deeply listening to non-dominant perspectives, especially of those people and groups who have lived experiences of being at the margin, and critical experiences to fully process and reach a place of discernment and understanding. However, if you are able and willing, we invite deep curiosity and openness on your part to consider and reflect:

i *"How is my liberation and freedom connected to liberation and freedom of others?" Think of any "ism" – racism, (hetero) sexism, trans oppression, ageism, youth oppression, ableism, classism.*
ii *"Can harm and suffering and freedom coexist in our organizations and our societies? Can one be free without all being free?"*
iii *"When one human life is devalued and dehumanized, in what ways does it devalue and dehumanize all human lives (including mine)?"*
iv *"If I am not experiencing the effects of oppression directly, if I cannot see, feel, and experience it directly myself, because, my privilege makes it so, does it mean oppression does not exist? What happens if I lose my privilege?"*
v *We invite you to ask yourself the hard question – are you counting on your privilege to avoid experiences of trauma and hardship, or can you count on our current systems (policies, structures, cultural norms) to provide you with the safety net and support systems you need to survive and thrive despite hardships. For example, if you have not currently experienced harm, trauma, and violence from climate change – cyclones, fires, floods, does it mean our systems can protect you and people you love, including your future generations, forever? Doesn't climate change have consequences for all? Doesn't social injustice and systems of oppression have consequences for all?*

We invite you to reflect on Rev. Martin Luther King Jr.'s quote from his Letter from Birmingham Jail (1963, p. 1), "*Injustice anywhere is a threat to justice everywhere. We are caught in an inescapable network of mutuality, tied in a single garment of destiny. Whatever affects one directly affects all indirectly.*" What does this quote mean to you?

Invitation to Pause and Reflect

We invite you to pause here. If it feels accessible, take one or more deep breaths, hydrate your body, move your body, soothe your body in ways that feel kind and compassionate.

If/when you feel ready, take a few moments to notice. Notice what is emerging for you based on the discussions offered so far. What sensations and feelings are your feeling?

Is there a sense of resonance or dissonance, overwhelm or calm or mixed sensations, confusion or clarity, validation, or challenge? Just notice. Do not analyze. Take your time with this pause and reflection. We invite you to return to the next section when you feel ready and resourced in your body mind.

How Do the Systems of Oppression Work?

Sociologists have conceptualized a multi-level and multi-dimensional functioning of the systems of oppression. In general, oppression could be understood to operate in at least three broad levels of social organization – a micro level (i.e., individual, and interpersonal levels), a meso level (i.e., institutional, and organizational levels), and a macro level (i.e., systemic – legal, structural, and cultural levels).

Hardiman et al. (2007) conceptualized a three-dimensional matrix of oppression. They describe that oppression is constructed, maintained, and reproduced at three broad levels of a social organization – individual, institutional, and societal/cultural. At these three levels oppression manifests at both conscious/explicit and unconscious/implicit levels.

Oppression is manifested at individual levels through attitudes and behaviors; at institutional levels through policies, procedures, practices, and norms; and at societal/cultural levels through values, beliefs, and customs. Like individuals, institutions can also have biases that manifest at conscious (e.g., official) and unconscious (e.g., unofficial) levels. Like individuals, institutions may demonstrate attitudinal manifestations of oppression (e.g., through organizational policies) and behavioral manifestations (e.g., through organizational behaviors and practices) (Hardiman et al. 2007).

All three – societal/cultural, institutional, and individual levels – are interconnected and interlock with one another. Institutions and organizations function to maintain the socialization of individuals to internalize and perpetuate oppressive systems. This function is carried out through biased policies, infrastructures, cultural norms and values, and practices developed and maintained to serve the dominant groups. Individuals act as vehicles (or carriers) that enable and/or enact discriminatory policies and practices of the institutions through their internalized attitudes and behaviors. At a societal level, a network of institutions and organizations that make up the society carry out oppressive cultural norms, beliefs, and values (Hardiman et al. 2007).

Oppression at Individual Level

Oppression manifests at individual levels through conscious or unconscious attitudes and interpersonal behaviors that contribute toward discrimination, negative biases, micro-aggressive and gaslighting behaviors, stigma, shaming, and exclusion. For example, in workplace contexts, research studies have revealed that interpersonal behaviors manifesting negative biases, stigma and prejudice against people with disabilities are some of the biggest barriers to employment and career growth opportunities for people with disabilities (Chordiya 2022a).

Cycle of Socialization and Internalized Oppression

Another aspect of individual manifestation of oppression is internalized subordination and internalized domination. Internalization is one of the most covert and therefore powerful features of oppression. Socialization is a key mechanism through which we as individuals, who are born into existing systems of domination and subordination learn to play unequal roles prescribed by an inequitable social system of oppression.

Bobbie Harro (2018b) conceptualized a model called "cycle of socialization" to describe the process of socialization into systems of oppression. Harro (2018b) notes that the process of socialization is "pervasive (coming from all sides and sources), consistent (patterned and predictable), circular (self-supporting), self-perpetuating (intradependent) and often invisible (unconscious and unnamed)." (p. 27)

THE BEGINNING

The socialization process begins even before our birth. Our social identities (race, gender, sex, caste, class, religion) are ascribed to us at birth with no choice on our part, and thus outside of our control. It is therefore meaningless to blame each other for the identities we have. We are born innocent and into an already well-established system of oppression.

Individuals born into dominant groups receive unearned privileges and advantages solely due to their association with these groups. This occurs because our social and institutional systems are inherently structured to support/favor certain groups while marginalizing and disenfranchising others. Socialization into dominant identities can contribute toward a false sense of superiority or "being better than" which can perpetuate internalized domination.

When born in subordinated groups we may experience devaluation, shaming, stigma, marginalization, and exclusion. Being born into socially marginalized groups can contribute toward a false sense of inferiority or "being less than"- however, being born into a systemically marginalized social group (e.g., being born in poverty or a marginalized gender or racial group) does not mean we are "lesser human beings" or "flawed" - it is important to remember that *we are not flawed*, rather we are born into a flawed system that persists through oppressive tools of shaming, marginalization, and domination. Furthermore, because we all have multiple social identities, many of us may experience both dominant or oppressor and marginalized or oppressed identities. For example, someone may experience privilege due to their national origin, citizenship status, class status, sexuality, or education and may also be disadvantaged due to their racial or disability identity – thus holding oppressed (disadvantaged) and oppressor (advantaged) identities (Harro 2018b).

FIRST SOCIALIZATION

Immediately upon our births, our first socialization happens through the people we love and trust the most, our families, caregivers, adults who are raising us. They shape our concept of self and self-perceptions (how we think about ourselves) and our interpersonal perceptions (how we relate to others). They also shape our worldviews, the societal norms, and rules we must follow, and teach us the roles we play (e.g., gender norms; class norms). They also shape our expectations of the future, and our dreams (Harro 2018b).

INSTITUTIONAL AND CULTURAL SOCIALIZATION

As we grow, we begin to attend schools, places of worship, medical facilities, visit public places, and seek several services. Our contact with external institutions and organizations continues to grow and our sources of socialization are multiplied. The institutions we interact with teach us how to be, how to conduct ourselves, whom to look up to, whom to look down on, what rules to follow and what roles to play.

The assumptions we develop and messages we learn from our socialization at home may be reinforced or contradicted by these institutions. We are inundated with unexamined and stereotypical messages through media, internet, popular culture, video games, cultural and religious holidays, language patterns and more. We learn about in-groups and outgroups. Through well-established structured systems and unquestioned cultural ways, we receive biased and prejudiced messages that shape how we think and how we relate to one another (Harro 2018b).

ENFORCEMENTS

The system of socialization is a well-designed process that includes tools and techniques to maintain itself through rewards for conforming and punishments for non-conformity. Enforcements make it challenging to ignore, challenge, or contradict the messages received through the dominant process of socialization. We are taught not to practice courage, not to rock the boat (Harro 2018b).

RESULTS

The results of the systematic learning through socialization in oppressive systems and maintaining them are harmful for all involved. For those in dominant groups, unexamined privilege can inhibit growth and human development as well as lead to the internalization of oppressive behaviors and beliefs (Harro 2018b).

Internalized domination refers to ways in which members of dominant social groups, through socialization process, learn attitudes and behaviors that reflect entitlement and privilege. A key characteristic of internalized domination and privilege is that because group's culture is dominant and normalized, members of this group view resources and opportunities as earned and as part of the natural order of things rather than a result of social system that advantages them (Hardiman et al. 2007).

When our internalized domination remains unexamined, we might explicitly or implicitly become implicated with systems of oppression to perpetuate its cycle by participating (instead of interrupting) in our roles as oppressors or dominant group members. We might rationalize our privilege by blaming others for their living conditions without any kind of systems analysis. We might dehumanize our fellow human beings. We might live with fear, hatred, scarcity, ignorance, obliviousness, and insecurity. We might experience toxicity within us and in the world around us (Hardiman et al. 2007).

For those in marginalized groups, unexamined oppression can also inhibit growth and maturing as human beings. The process of socialization may have the result of internalized oppression or internalized subordination (Harro 2018b). Internalized subordination refers to ways in which members of marginalized groups, through socialization processes, internalize shame, stigma, negative biases, and devaluation of their own group (Hardiman et al. 2007).

It is important to view these tensions and dilemmas around internalized subordination with curiosity, without shame and judgment, and even with self-compassion as we find our way toward a practice of developing liberatory consciousness. We must acknowledge that a number of these behaviors may be learned from the need to survive and cope within the systems of oppression. Another dimension in the result of socialization process is experience of dissonance, anger, and guilt that may emerge from one's unexamined participation with the process of socialization. These negative or uncomfortable emotions are a common experience and if we remain open and curious, practice (self) empathy and (self) compassion, these emotions could even move us toward liberatory action and transformation (Harro 2018b).

ACTION

When we reach the results of the socialization process, we face the decision of what to do next? The easiest thing may seem to be "do nothing." By failing to interrupt the cycle of socialization we participate in its continuation. Harro 2018b, 32) note:

> This cycle (of socialization) has a life of its own. It doesn't need our active support because it has its own centrifugal force. It goes on, and unless we choose to interrupt it, it will continue to go on. Our silence is consent. Until our discomfort becomes larger than our comfort, we will probably stay in this cycle.

When we might begin to examine our decision to "do nothing" and ask ourselves the question "What has kept me in this cycle for so long?," we might discover that at the core of this cycle are patterns of fear, ignorance, confusion, insecurity, and destructive power or feeling of powerlessness (Harro 2018b).

An Invitation to Pause and Reflect: Cycle of Socialization

We have covered several key concepts related to understanding oppression. We invite you to pause here. If it feels accessible, take one or more deep breaths, hydrate your body, move your body, soothe your body in ways that feel kind and compassionate.

If/when you feel ready, take a few moments to notice. Notice what is emerging for you based on the discussions offered so far. What sensations and feelings are your feeling? Notice.

If you are able and willing, we invite you to further reflect using the following suggested prompts:

a *Begin with identifying an "ism" for reflection (e.g., racism, ableism, sexism, trans oppression).*
b *Using Bobbie* Harro's (2018b) *"Cycle of Socialization" framework (or other similar framework), reflect on your experience of internalized socialization in relation to the "ism" you've identified. Focus on the selected "ism." We encourage you to reflect on*

each of the stages within the cycle of socialization and in relation to your own experience with socialization of internalized domination and internalized oppression.

Authors' note: We intend this reflection to be for personal practice. If you choose to share your reflections with others, we invite deep care and intentionality. If you choose to share, we suggest you share this reflection with your diversity and inclusion leadership coach/mentor/trainer/professor or with trusted peers in a community of learning and practice. In any case, we invite practice of consent and confidentiality in contexts of collective reflections as foundations to build trust and relationality (We discuss more about the practice of consent and confidentiality in chapter 4).

Oppression at Institutional Level

The institutional level refers to both the broad fields such as public service, public administration, healthcare, criminal legal system, education, media, and specific organizational units it encompasses such as an agency, a university, a team, a department, college, or a school. At institutional levels, conscious and unconscious (e.g., official, and unofficial) attitudes (e.g., policies) and behaviors (e.g., practices) help to produce, reproduce, and maintain the systems of oppression and its multiple manifestations (Hardiman et al. 2007). An example of official policies includes dress codes and unofficial attitudes include norms about dressing, hairstyles, appearance, and presentation that privilege the groups that are used as a standard for developing these norms and marginalize and dehumanize groups who do not/cannot conform to these norms (D'Agostino et al. 2022).

Changes in laws, official policies, structures are indispensable, yet, unfortunately, inadequate measures to interrupt and end institutional and organizational oppression. Organizational and institutional transformation necessitates supporting legal and policy change with necessary shifts in culture, infrastructure, power structures, procedures, and practices to favor social equity and justice (Chordiya 2019, 2022a, 2022b; Chordiya and Protonentis, 2024).

For example, in heteronormative organizations, heterosexuality is the dominant norm. Heterosexual people do not have to "come out." Heterosexual individuals and couples may experience themselves as "normal" or "standard," and institutional policies, procedures, infrastructures, and culture are designed to meet their "standard" needs (e.g., health care policies, medical benefits, leave benefits, support through pregnancy and/or adoption, support during medical or other emergencies). On the other hand, heteronormative and cisnormative organizations may remind LGBTQIA+ people through official and unofficial policies and practices that they do not fit the norm, starting with the process of "coming out" to receive support and to meet their everyday needs as individuals, parents, families, and/or couples.

Oppression at Societal/Cultural Level

The systems of oppression and its multiple manifestations are instrumental at societal and cultural levels through dominant policies, structures, norms, and practices (Hardiman et al. 2007). In an oppressive society, patterns of oppression (i.e., dominant structures, policies, procedures, and practices) go unexamined and reproduce the cycles of domination and marginalization (Portillo, Humphrey, and Bearfield 2022; Riccucci 2022). Through processes of socialization, institutions, and individuals interact with broader society and culture to construct and maintain the patterns of oppression exhibited at the larger social, structural, and cultural level (Adams, Varghese, and Zúñiga 2022). Case Study 2.1 provides an example of systemic racism in sports in the United States.

Case Study 2.1: Combating Hair Discrimination, Addressing Systemic Racism, and Promoting Inclusivity in Sports and Education

[Content Warning: Emotionally Heavy Materials]

On April 1, 2022, a troubling incident unfolded just moments before a young Black female athlete was set to compete. Officials at a meet in Jackson, Mississippi, informed her that she must remove beads from her braided hair or face disqualification, citing a rule from the Mississippi High School Activities Association (MHSAA) Powerlifting handbook. After being informed of the conditions, the athlete's mostly white teammates and coaches huddled around her to help her remove the braids at an ultrafast speed to prevent disqualification.

Many athletes and legal experts claim that in the case of powerlifting, a non-contact individual sport, the prohibition of hair adornments, such as beads, appears unnecessary and discriminatory. Persons wearing hair beads frequently participate in various physical activities without posing any risk to themselves or others. Moreover, the MHSAA's powerlifting rule concerning hair allows certain hard hair items like rubber bands and bobby pins but bans others like beads, disproportionately impacting Black students with culturally significant hairstyles.

Unfortunately, this incident is not an isolated case but part of a larger pattern of discriminatory practices faced by Black students in the United States regarding their culturally significant hairstyles. In March 2021, a Black high school student athlete in Oregon was instructed to remove her hair beads to participate in a volleyball match, leading her to cut her hair and express a sense of loss of identity. In April 2021, a Black female student in North Carolina was told to remove her hair beads during a high school softball game. In September 2021, a Black six-year-old child was prohibited from playing in a recreational soccer game due to her hair clips and bows, leaving her emotionally distressed.

These discriminatory actions result in lost educational and extracurricular opportunities and, in some cases, breach state and federal laws. For example, targeting students with culturally significant hairstyles breaches Title VI of the Civil Rights Act of 1964 which prohibits discrimination based on stereotypes and characteristics associated with race, color, and national origin.

Recognizing the systemic nature of hair discrimination, the National Federation of State High School Associations (NFHS) has taken measurable steps to remove discriminatory language about use of hard hair items and implement rules that permits hair adornments, provided that the hair does not pose a safety threat. MHSAA's noted that it plans to revise the rule banning hair beads. Such a response by the MSHAA is a step forward, but there is a larger, more systemic need to confront this kind of oppression.

There are large-scale efforts to make the CROWN Act a federal law as well as a state law across all 50 states. The CROWN Act, which stands for "Creating a Respectful and Open World for Natural Hair," prohibits race-based hair discrimination, such as denial of employment and educational opportunities because of hair texture or protective hairstyles including braids, hair bead/hair adornments, locs, twists or bantu knots. As of October 2023, the CROWN Act is a law in 23 states.

This case study seeks to highlight that hair discrimination is deeply rooted in systemic racism and serves to uphold white spaces. Policies that forbid natural hairstyles, including afros, braids, bantu knots, and locs, have been used to justify the exclusion of Black individuals from classrooms and workplaces. The absence of nationwide legal protections against hair discrimination places the burden on Black people to either risk consequences at school or work for embracing their natural hair or conform to Eurocentric standards of professionalism and beauty.

Suggested Discussion Questions

1 What are the key issues presented in this case study, and how do they relate to systemic oppression through racism and discrimination?
2 What is the significance of the term "white spaces" in the context of this case study? How do policies that target natural Black hairstyles contribute to preserving white spaces?
3 As described previously in this chapter, one of the features of oppression is that it is persistent, mutating, and durable. How is this feature operational in this case study?
4 Discuss the importance of the CROWN Act and its potential impact on ending hair discrimination. In addition to policy changes, what other structural and cultural changes will be necessary to end hair discrimination in organizations such as schools, sports, and workplaces?

(*Sources*: Legal Defense Fund, 2022; Saunders 2022)

Oppression and Implicit Biases

As we have noted so far, to build a critical awareness of systems of oppression we must understand how bias against marginalized people/groups is pervasive not only at individual levels but also at institutional and societal levels. Bias against marginalized people/groups is a powerful tool of oppression. It creeps into various aspects of our daily lives, often operating subtly and without our conscious awareness. It manifests through prejudices, stereotypes, and discriminatory behaviors and practices, shaping the distribution of power and privilege.

Within institutions, implicit negative biases can influence decision-making processes, leading to unequal treatment and opportunities for different groups of individuals. Hiring practices, promotions, and resource allocation can be affected, perpetuating disparities, and hindering equal representation and progress. Since people are a part of the systems and institutions, individual biases are reflected in the policies and systems that we operate within. These form the basis of systemic barriers that impact marginalized groups, disproportionately. Often the biases operate at an unconscious level, shaping the decision and behaviors of individuals without our explicit awareness.

All humans have biases, as it's a natural part of who we are. Our mental shortcuts help us make quick decisions and survive as a species. If we have a brain, we have bias. That same brain gives us the power to examine and counteract our biases. When unexamined, biases at individual and institutional levels can have harmful and marginalizing consequences for individuals and groups who are subject to these negative biases. Part of maturing as human beings and especially in the context of anti-oppression and liberatory work necessitates findings structured ways to test/examine/check our individual, collective, and structural assumptions and biases that may have harmful or hurtful consequences. Only when we explicitly check/question our assumptions can we notice our implicit biases and interrupt them.

Biases may manifest at conscious and/or unconscious levels. Conscious or overt bias happens when people/institutions are aware of their biases and act on them intentionally (e.g., racial segregation). On the other hand, implicit bias operates at a subconscious level, making it hard to recognize or admit. Implicit bias may be confusing as they may sometimes be based on good intentions and yet have harmful impacts. For example, a manager might ignore promotion opportunities for an employee who is pregnant, without consulting them, based on benevolent sexist assumptions about pregnant peoples' needs, hopes, and wishes. Operating from benevolent (yet sexist) assumptions and stereotypes can cause the manager to ignore their pregnant employees' career needs and goals, and thus contribute to harmful impact on their career.

Common Biases

Some common types of implicit biases include affinity bias, conformity bias, self-serving bias, attribution error, the halo effect, the horns effect, and proximity bias.

1 Affinity bias is when we naturally prefer people who are like us in terms of background, interests, experiences, and values.
2 Conformity bias, on the other hand, is when we adopt the opinions of a group, setting aside our own thoughts. This often happens in social groups to fit in or follow those in power.
3 Self-serving bias is another type of bias where we tend to attribute our successes to our own qualities and skills, while we blame external factors or others for our failures. This bias can be more common in people with privileged or dominant identities, as it reinforces a sense of entitlement and overlooks the contributions and experiences of marginalized groups.
4 Attribution error, also known as the fundamental attribution error (FAE), involves the tendency to attribute the negative behavior/mistakes of others to internal or dispositional factors while attributing one's own negative behavior/mistakes to external or situational factors. For example, if someone else runs a red light or a stop sign, we may attribute their behavior as reckless driving; whereas if we ourselves ran a red light or a stop sign, we may attribute our behavior to a situational

factor such as "being in a rush to get somewhere," "being preoccupied with my sick child in the backseat."

5 The Halo Effect and the Horns Effect are two biases that influence how people perceive and judge others. They are based on the idea that a single positive or negative trait or quality can heavily influence overall perceptions, leading to biased judgments. If someone is perceived as having one positive trait (e.g., physical attractiveness, intelligence, charisma), it can "cast a halo" over their entire personality, causing people to assume that other aspects of the person are also positive. On the other hand, if someone is perceived as having one negative trait (e.g., a heavy accent, dressing style, lacking charisma), it can create a negative bias or a Horns effect that extends to other aspects of the person's personality or abilities.

6 Proximity bias is a term describing the tendency of individuals in positions of authority to favor employees who are physically present in the office while potentially overlooking those who engage remotely. This bias is rooted in the outdated assumption that in-office workers are more productive. Proximity bias has the potential to profoundly impact the remote workforce, leading to feelings of isolation and reduced engagement. It is especially crucial to address this bias in the era of remote and hybrid work arrangements.

These biases are not exhaustive, and individuals and institutions may exhibit a combination of them in various situations. Recognizing these biases is the first step in mitigating their influence and making more rational, objective, inclusive, and equitable decisions. It requires self-reflection, building self-awareness, continuous education to learn and unlearn, and a willingness to challenge our own preconceptions.

Interrupting Oppression and Developing a Liberatory Consciousness

As we have explored, systems of oppression are instrumental at all three levels (individual, institutional/organizational, and societal/cultural) and manifest in multiple forms (such as racism, sexism, heterosexism, trans oppression, ableism, and ageism) that interlock with each other. Therefore, our path toward DEILJ must include theory and praxis that address the nuance and multi-dimensional nature of anti-oppression and liberatory work. As DEILJ change workers we must remain sharp and consistent in our dual focus of transforming the world around us as well as transforming ourselves.

Harro's (2018b) "cycle of socialization" (described previously) details the process of socialization which prepares individuals to perform roles of dominant or subordinated groups within a system of oppression. The next two theoretical frameworks can guide us in thinking about our individual transformation journeys, to recognize and unlearn internalized oppression and learn new ways of being that are aligned with values of self-belonging, inclusion, and liberatory justice. These two frameworks are Barbara Love's Liberatory Consciousness framework (2018) and Bobbie Harro's (2018a) Cycle of Liberation framework.

Barbara Love's Liberatory Consciousness Framework

Love (2018) notes that a system of oppression exists by design and no single human can be charged with creation of oppressive systems as they function today. At the same time, all humans now living, learn to internalize the attitudes, understandings, patterns of thoughts and behaviors that allow them to function in and collaborate with systems of oppression, whether they are favored and advantaged, or othered and disadvantaged by the system. The force of the socialization process is covert and powerful, and it begins at birth. Humans are a product of socialization, and we learn to "be" and "live life" by following habits of mind and thoughts that are instilled in us.

Within a socialization system rooted in the logic of domination and oppression, DEILJ change agents shoulder the responsibility of continually cultivating their liberatory consciousness. This involves disrupting the prevailing patterns of the socialization process, which tends to perpetuate domination, oppression, and "othering." Instead, the aim is to harness available resources and energy toward the pursuit of liberation (Love 2018).

There are four key elements in Love's framing of liberatory consciousness work. The first element of developing a liberatory consciousness is building and deepening critical awareness of oppression. It means "noticing what happens in the world around you" (Love 2018, 600). The second element of the liberatory consciousness work is the practice of critical analysis. Critical analysis is the process of examining "the why" of a phenomenon/situation and what needs to be done about it.

The third element of the liberatory consciousness work involves building/deepening one's capacities and consistently engaging in the practice of critical action to make liberatory change happen. The fourth and the final element of the liberatory consciousness works is practice of allyship rooted in accountability (Love 2018). This practice involves an understanding of accountability in a proactive sense; as something that we do and not something that is done to us. This liberatory approach to accountability stems from a desire to be in the right relationship with others and is motivated by respect, mutuality and interdependence (brown 2017; Couchois Duncan and Smith 2022).

Bobbie Harro's Cycle of Liberation Framework

Bobbie Harro's (2018) cycle of liberation framework is an offering based on their research, discovery, and discernment of some paths that were successful at creating long-lasting liberatory change that addressed the causes of oppression at its core and people's roles in it. While describing the purpose of the cycle of liberation framework, Harro (2018a) notes, the

> Purpose (of the cycle of liberation) is to organize and name a process that may otherwise be elusive, with the goal of helping people to find their pathway to liberation. It could be characterized as a map of changing terrain where not everyone goes in the same direction or to the same destination or at the same speed, so it should not be taken as a "how to," but rather as a description of what has worked for some.
> (p. 619)

Like the cycle of socialization (discussed above), the path toward liberatory change has cycle-like patterns and is called "the cycle of liberation." However, these two cycles are distinct in their phases as well as their core values. Whereas the core of cycle of socialization is steeped in fear, ignorance, confusion, insecurity, and powerlessness (Harro 2018b), the fuel that drives cycle of liberation is filled with hope, balance, joy, self-esteem, support, security, a spiritual base, and authentic practice of love for self and others (Harro 2018a).

While the cycle of socialization teaches us to learn and perform our given roles within a system of oppression, the cycle of liberation guides us in carving our own path of liberatory consciousness. Below we describe the key milestones or patterns of events that Harro (2018a) discovered to be common to successful liberatory efforts. It is important to note that in this cyclical process, there is no specific beginning or end point. When humans seek to interrupt their cycle of socialization and choose to enter the cycle of liberation, they may start at any point and will likely repeat or recycle many times in the process (Harro 2018a).

Like Love (2018), Harro's (2018a) framing of a liberatory journey begins when we begin to experience ourselves differently in the world than we have in our past. Harro (2018a) calls this phase "waking up," wherein we begin to experience inner change at our core, embodied level, wherein we experience a cognitive dissonance, where something that made sense (or an assumption we took for granted) does not make sense anymore. This may be a result of a critical incident or a slow evolutionary process that shifts our worldview.

Once we begin our journey of awakening and become critically aware of the realities of oppression whether it is in the context of racism, or sexism or heterosexism or trans oppression, or ageism or ableism and more, at some point in our liberatory consciousness journey we are likely to reach the "getting ready" phase (Harro 2018a; Love 2018). Like Love's (2018) framing of critical awareness and critical analysis, the "getting ready" phase involves consciously engaging in the liberatory work of reflection, education, and consciousness raising to learn (and/or create) and unlearn (and/or dismantle) behavioral aspects of ourselves, our narratives, and our worldviews based on our new perspectives.

"Getting ready" at an intrapersonal or an inner change level remains incomplete without transitioning into "reaching out" at interpersonal or collective level. This transition marks the beginning of "reaching out" phase where we seek to integrate inner change with collective change (i.e., connecting intrapersonal to interpersonal change). In this phase, we begin to expose ourselves to a wider range of differences and experiences than we had before. This involves stretching (not stressing) our comfort zones and playing with and gently leaning into discomfort.

For example, we may begin to practice our liberatory skills and tools with others (e.g., non-violent communication, empathy for self and others, curiosity, and patience), experiment with expressing our new ideas and perspectives, and learning to find our voice and speak up as best as we can with authenticity and integrity in situations when we disagree. In this phase, we also receive feedback from others about our changing selves – sometimes we may receive discouraging feedback (such as pressure to not "rock the boat") or even retaliatory behaviors. Other times, the feedback may be encouraging (such as making new friends and relationships because of speaking up) (Harro 2018a).

The next phase in the cycle of liberation involves "building community" and involves at least two types of meaningful relationship building and dialoguing on a regular basis- both are critical. The first is dialoguing with people who share our social identities and are similarly situated as ourselves, in terms of being advantaged or disadvantaged or both, to build a support base in resisting oppression. An example might be building meaningful relationships and dialogue in employee affinity groups or employee resource groups or a community of practice to cultivate support system in resisting oppression.

The second is dialoguing with people who do not share our social identities and are situated differently from ourselves, in terms of being advantaged or disadvantaged or both. The intention is to gain nuanced and layered understanding of oppression and build coalitions and solidarity (Harro 2018a). An example might be building relationships and solidarity across differences through communities of practice for LPS. It is important to remember that our communities may comprise of even two or three people for a long time, and that is enough. Starting with critical dialogues or conversations and returning to critical dialogues or conversations is the key to coalition building, to collectively dream, envision, co-create and diffuse DEILJ innovations.

The next three phases in cycle of liberation focus on "coalescing" to "co-create" and "maintain" liberatory change (Harro 2018a). These are aligned with Love's (2018) framing of critical action and allyship rooted in accountability. As we coalesce, we begin to discover the power of coalitions, of solidarity, of allyship rooted in accountability to make a difference and interrupt the vicious cycles of oppression. In this process, we metabolize our energies away from frustration, anger, shame, and mistrust and move toward hope, repair, healing, shared power, relationships, and trust building.

We coalesce to build collectives and communities that work to co-create and diffuse liberatory ideas (innovations) and cultures within our individual and collective spheres of influence and expanding and deepening those spheres of influence. For example, coalitions influence organizational policies, structures, procedures, cultures, and leadership to transform and foster liberatory values. Finally, one of the hardest parts of transformative change work is maintaining the change by adapting, strengthening, deepening, and integrating change in the daily habits and rituals of individuals and collectives (Harro 2018a).

A Reflection Invitation: Cultivating a Liberatory Consciousness[1]

Using either Barbara Love's (2018) liberatory consciousness framework or Bobbie Harro's (2018a) cycle of liberation framework, we invite you to reflect on the following suggested prompts.

a *In what ways can the selected theoretical framework support your inner transformation journey toward cultivating a liberatory consciousness and decolonizing solidarity for social justice within your personal and professional work.*
b *Considering your social identity and positionality, identify and describe a leadership metaphor (find ideas below) that best aligns with your vision of becoming a diversity and social justice centered leader. Identify and describe the core values and skilled behaviors that you are cultivating toward the practice of living into this vision of becoming a diversity and social justice centered leader.*

Be sure to reflect on your journey of integrating inner transformation and social transformation. Here are some metaphors for how you might envision yourself in relation to people you intend to serve. Feel free to add your/other metaphors to this list.

A banyan tree providing shade to travelers (any tree metaphor is welcome); caregiver to the vulnerable; healer to the hurt; advocate to the jury; salesperson to potential buyers; preacher to the sinful; sheepdog to sheep; website to surfers; guru to followers; gardener to plants; tour guide to travelers in a bus; nectar to bees; fertilizer to crops; pesticide to crops; trainer to gym-goer; judge to the condemned; guide to rock-climber; team-player to fellow team-members.

Case Study 2.2: Navigating Power and Privilege in Advocacy: A Manager's Dilemma

In a recent diversity and inclusion training session conducted by one of the authors at a municipal government, an intriguing perspective emerged from a white female manager named Janet Walls (pseudo name is used to protect the identity of the manager). During a group discussion on advocating for BIPOC colleagues within the organization, Janet shared her thoughts and concerns about her role as a white person in a position of power and privilege.

Janet expressed her desire to be an advocate for perspectives of BIPOC colleagues and to use her influence to bring about positive change. However, she acknowledged the complexities inherent in her positionality. She was acutely aware that, as a white woman, she holds a lot of privilege and she couldn't fully understand the lived experiences of Black, Indigenous, and People of Color (BIPOC) colleagues. Janet recognized that it was not her place to tell their stories or speak on their behalf. She wanted to avoid unintentionally overshadowing their voices or perpetuating further marginalization.

Janet expressed the need for more clarity on how to be an effective advocate and leader. On one hand, she wanted to leverage her position and power within the organization to address systemic racialized inequalities and champion equity and inclusion. On the other hand, she recognized the importance of centering BIPOC individuals' experiences and perspectives, ensuring they had the autonomy and agency to advocate for themselves.

As Janet grappled with these dilemmas, she sought guidance on how to navigate her role effectively. She understood that her self-awareness of privilege alone was not enough. She wanted to find a way to support and elevate marginalized voices without unintentionally perpetuating harmful dynamics or diminishing their agency. Now faced with this ethical challenge, Janet sought to strike the right balance in her advocacy efforts and contribute to creating a more equitable and inclusive organizational culture.

Suggested Discussion Questions

- What are the potential challenges and dilemmas faced by individuals in positions of power and privilege who aim to advocate for minoritized groups?
- How might Janet's self-awareness of her privilege influence her ability to be an effective and accountable ally/advocate for minoritized perspectives?
- What strategies, approaches, and practices can Janet employ to support and elevate marginalized perspectives while practicing accountability, and honoring agency and autonomy of her BIPOC colleagues?
- How important is it for a manager to first build relationships with her BIPOC colleagues that are anchored in trust, reciprocity, and mutuality? What are some of the norms and practices managers can use to cultivate collegial relationships anchored in values of solidarity in workplace contexts?
- How can organizations create an ethical environment that encourages individuals in positions of power and privilege to advocate for minoritized groups in a responsible, transparent, accountable, and effective manner?

Building Capacity to Hold Contradictions: Starting With and Returning to "the Why" and "the Who"

Developing a liberatory consciousness is not an easy quest as forces of oppression are strong. Furthermore, in the work of building liberatory consciousness, public servants and public administrators must constantly wrestle with recognition and reckoning of many hard truths and contradictions. Contradictions may surface as ethical dilemmas during administrative decision-making that is focused on advancing equity and liberation, while operating within the larger context of oppressive capitalism. Contradictions and tensions also emerge from operating in the context of historical legacies and uninterrupted, unexamined cycles of historical, intergenerational, persistent institutional and personal trauma (Menakem 2017) perpetuated directly or indirectly through public policies and administrative decisions.

The liberatory journey is not linear nor can we expect a destination – the work is circular (a cycle we enter) and expansive, it is life's work and a way of being. This journey is also not without pain; transformation is often painful. The invitation is to expect and engage with discomfort and unsettling experiences as we slowly and steadily keep stretching ourselves to create greater embodied capacity for purposefully holding contradictions and tensions. The invitation is to lean into interdependence and find and cultivate relationships within a collective (e.g., a community of practice) that can serve as a support system, a source of strength, joy, inspiration, and motivation – one that can keep us accountable to our liberatory values.

DEILJ change workers need to start and keep returning to "the why" and "the who" that drives and motivates us. We need to constantly reflect, articulate, and return to our why, our purpose. And remember who are the people (e.g., our planet, our kin, our community, our ancestors, our future generations) that nourish us, motivate us, and inspire us to sustain through the challenges of social justice and liberatory work.

For many of us our why may reside in our care and commitment to public service and social justice. Many of us seek an alternative way of being that does not have to depend on domination, dehumanization, and subordination of fellow living beings, our kin, and our planet for survival and growth. Rather, we seek a way of "Be-ing" that is harmony, interdependence and mutuality with one another and our planet Earth that makes life possible in the first place. We might discover that our purpose why, and the people who, drive our DEILJ change work are rooted in a place of embodied love and compassion to end suffering and to birth and sustain freedom.

Reflect on the "Why" and the "Who" that drive and sustain your commitment to public service and liberatory DEILJ change work?

An Invitation to Reflect

We invite you to pause, take a deep breath if that is accessible, move your body, hydrate yourself. Using the reflection box, journal the purpose 'why' and the people 'who' drive and sustain your commitment to public service and DEILJ change work? (Notice, sometimes, "the who" could be your "why").

Summary and Key Teachings

In this chapter, we focused on developing an understanding of oppression. We discussed the key characteristics of oppression. We learned that oppression is: (1) hierarchical and divisive, (2) dehumanizing, (3) pervasive and cumulative, (4) with multiple and intersectional manifestations, (5) persistent, mutating, and durable, and (6) with consequences for all. Systems of oppression work at multiple levels such as micro (i.e., individual level), meso (i.e., institutional, and organizational level), and macro (i.e., social, structural, and cultural level). We are all socialized into systems of oppression and learn to internalize domination and oppression. However, we can interrupt the cycle of socialization into oppressive systems and enter the path of developing a liberatory consciousness to foster collective joy, love, and freedom. Developing a liberatory consciousness involves unlearning our socialization into oppressive behaviors and learning behaviors and practices rooted in mutuality, solidarity, and reciprocity.

We also reflected on the contradictions and tensions involved in cultivating a liberatory praxis for public service and public administration professionals operating within systems of oppression (e.g., racialized capitalism). Love's (2018) and Harro's (2018a) frameworks of liberation help us focus on starting with liberatory work within the public administration community at various levels – local, state, national, and global. The idea is to start small and continue to nurture and amplify the impact of liberatory praxis within our growing spheres of influence.

We need to be and can be the transformation we need to see in the world. We can approach liberatory work one goal at a time, one task at a time, one project at a time, one practice at a time. We can create liberatory microcosms within our spheres of influence (friends, families, neighbors, team members, organizations, communities we serve, and other collectives). We can deepen and expand that liberatory reach through consistent practice as we grow our spheres of influence in coalition with other DEILJ change workers. As Rev. angel Kyodo williams (n.d.) powerfully notes, we must remember that "love and justice are not two. without inner change, there can be no outer change; without collective change, no change matters."

Deep Dive Resources [Full Citations in References]

1 Hardiman, Rita, and Bailey Jackson. 2007. "Conceptual Foundations for Social Justice Education."
2 Harro, Bobbie. 2018a. "Cycle of Liberation."
3 Harro, Bobbie. 2018b. "Cycle of Socialization."
4 Love, Barbara J. 2018. "Developing a Liberatory Consciousness."

Note

1 Adapted from Alan Mortiboys (2011) and David Green (2021).

References

Adams, Maurianne, Rani Varghese, and Ximena Zúñiga. 2022. "Core Concepts for Teaching Social Justice Education." In *Teaching for Diversity and Social Justice*, edited by Maurianne Adams, Lee Anne Bell, Diane J. Goodman, Davey Shlasko, Rachel R. Briggs, and Romina Pacheco, 4th ed. New York, NY: Routledge.

brown, adrienne maree. 2017. *Emergent Strategy: Shaping Change, Changing Worlds*. Reprint ed. Chico, CA: AK Press.

Bell, Lee Anne. 2022. "Theoretical Foundations for Social Justice Education." In *Teaching for Diversity and Social Justice*, edited by Maurianne Adams, Lee Anne Bell, Diane J. Goodman, Davey Shlasko, Rachel R. Briggs, and Romina Pacheco, 4th ed. New York, NY: Routledge.

Chin, Natalie M. 2021. "Centering Disability Justice ADA Symposium." *Syracuse Law Review* 71 (3): 683–750.

Chordiya, Rashmi. 2019. "Are Federal Child Care Programs Sufficient for Employee Retention? Critical Examination From a Gendered Perspective." *The American Review of Public Administration* 49 (3): 338–52. https://doi.org/10.1177/0275074018804662

———. 2022a. "Organizational Inclusion and Turnover Intentions of Federal Employees With Disabilities." *Review of Public Personnel Administration* 42 (1): 60–87. https://doi.org/10.1177/0734371X20942305

———. 2022b. "A Study of Interracial Differences in Turnover Intentions: The Mitigating Role of Pro-Diversity and Justice-Oriented Management." *Public Personnel Management* 51 (2): 235–60. https://doi.org/10.1177/00910260211061824

Chordiya, Rashmi, and Adana Protonentis. 2024. "Healing from Intersectional White Supremacy Culture and Ableism: Disability Justice as an Antidote." *Journal of Social Equity and Public Administration* 2 (1): 127–52. https://doi.org/10.24926/jsepa.v2i1.4856

Couchois Duncan, Aja, and Kad Smith. 2022. "The Liberatory World We Want to Create: Loving Accountability and the Limitations of Cancel Culture." *Non Profit News | Nonprofit Quarterly*, May 19, 2022. https://nonprofitquarterly.org/the-liberatory-world-we-want-to-create-loving-accountability-and-the-limitations-of-cancel-culture/

Crenshaw, Kimberlé. 2016. "Transcript of 'The Urgency of Intersectionality.'" TED Ideas Worth Spreading. October 2016. https://www.ted.com/talks/kimberle_crenshaw_the_urgency_of_intersectionality/transcript

———. 2020. She Coined the Term 'Intersectionality' Over 30 Years Ago. Here's What It Means to Her Today Interview by Katy Steinmetz. TIME. https://time.com/5786710/kimberle-crenshaw-intersectionality/

D'Agostino, Maria, Helisse Levine, Meghna Sabharwal, and Al C Johnson-Manning. 2022. "Organizational Practices and Second-Generation Gender Bias: A Qualitative Inquiry into the Career Progression of U.S. State-Level Managers." *The American Review of Public Administration* 52 (5): 335–50. https://doi.org/10.1177/02750740221086605

David, Green. (2021). "Investigating Your Practice Through Metaphor" Ignatian Pedagogy Series| Reflective Practice. Seattle: Seattle University.

Glenn, Evelyn Nakano. 2015. "Settler Colonialism as Structure: A Framework for Comparative Studies of U.S. Race and Gender Formation." *Sociology of Race and Ethnicity* 1 (1): 52–72. https://doi.org/10.1177/2332649214560440.

Hancock, Ange-Marie. 2011. *Solidarity Politics for Millennials: A Guide to Ending the Oppression Olympics*. New York: Springer.

Hardiman, Rita, Bailey Jackson, and Pat Griffin. 2007. "Conceptual Foundations for Social Justice Education." In *Teaching for Diversity and Social Justice*, 2nd ed., edited by Maurianne Adams, Lee Anne Bell, and Pat Griffin, 35–66. New York, NY: Routledge/Taylor & Francis Group.

Harro, Bobbie. 2018a. "Cycle of Liberation." In *Readings for Diversity and Social Justice*, edited by Maurianne Adams, Warren J. Blumenfeld, D. Chase J. Catalano, Keri Dejong, Heather W. Hackman, Larissa E. Hopkins, Barbara Love, Madeline L. Peters, Davey Shlasko, and Ximena Zuniga, 4th ed., 627–34. New York, NY: Routledge.

———. 2018b. "Cycle of Socialization." In *Readings for Diversity and Social Justice*, edited by Maurianne Adams, Warren J. Blumenfeld, D. Chase J. Catalano, Keri Dejong, Heather W. Hackman, Larissa E. Hopkins, Barbara Love, Madeline L. Peters, Davey Shlasko, and Ximena Zuniga, 4th ed., 27–33. New York, NY: Routledge.

King, Martin Luther Jr. 1963. "Letter from Birmingham Jail," August 1963. chrome-extension://efaidnbmnnnibpcajpcglclefindmkaj/https://www.csuchico.edu/iege/_assets/documents/susi-letter-from-birmingham-jail.pdf

Legal Defense Fund. 2022. "LDF Sends Letter Regarding Student Forced to Remove Her Hair Beads to Participate in a Powerlifting Sporting Event to Mississippi High School Activities Association." *Legal Defense Fund* (blog). April 25, 2022. https://www.naacpldf.org/news/ldf-sends-letter-regarding-student-forced-to-remove-her-hair-beads-to-participate-in-a-powerlifting-sporting-event-to-mississippi-high-school-activities-association/

Love, Barbara J. 2018. "Developing a Liberatory Consciousness." In *Readings for Diversity and Social Justice*, edited by Maurianne Adams, Warren J. Blumenfeld, D. Chase J. Catalano, Keri Dejong, Heather W. Hackman, Larissa E. Hopkins, Barbara Love, Madeline L. Peters, Davey Shlasko, and Ximena Zuniga, 4th ed., 610–15. New York, NY: Routledge.

Mortiboys, Alan. 2011. *Teaching With Emotional Intelligence: A Step-by-Step Guide for Higher and Further Education Professionals*. 2nd ed. London: Routledge.

Portillo, Shannon K., Nicole Humphrey, and Domonic A. Bearfield. 2022. *The Myth of Bureaucratic Neutrality*. 1st ed. New York, NY: Routledge.

Riccucci, Norma M. 2022. *Critical Race Theory: Exploring Its Application to Public Administration. Elements in Public and Nonprofit Administration*. Cambridge: Cambridge University Press. https://doi.org/10.1017/9781009122986

Saunders, Angel. 2022. "Black Student-Athlete Forced to Remove Hair Beads to Remain in Competition." *REVOLT* (blog). April 8, 2022. https://www.revolt.tv/article/2022-04-08/161840/black-student-athlete-forced-to-remove-hair-beads-to-remain-in-competition/

Trans Legislation Tracker. 2023. "2023 Anti-Trans Bills: Trans Legislation Tracker." 2023. https://translegislation.com.

williams, Rev angel Kyodo. n.d. "Rev. Angel Kyodo Williams 'Love and Justice Are Not Two. without Inner Change, There Can Be No Outer Change; without Collective Change, No Change Matters.'" n.d. https://revangel.com/

Woodson, Carter Godwin. 1999. *The Mis-Education of the Negro*. Edited by Tony Darnell. 12th Media Services.

Young, Iris Marion. 1990. "Five Faces of Oppression." In *Justice and the Politics of Difference*, 39–65. Princeton, NJ: Princeton University Press.

Part II

Building Blocks of a Liberatory Public Service Framework

Intentions and Objectives

In Part II, we examine multiple theoretical frameworks rooted in critical academic scholarship, as well as literature co-created by organizers and visionary leaders within our social justice movements. These frameworks are the building blocks that inspire, inform, and shape our vision for a liberatory public service (LPS). Our intention is not to offer an exhaustive list of theories and frameworks focused on anti-oppression and liberatory justice work; rather the goal is to demonstrate and reflect on the importance of social justice movement theories and critical academic scholarship as guiding stars for our individual and collective exploration and imagination of LPS.

The big ideas that we explore in Part II include:

a The significance of cultivating a trauma-informed and healing-centered (TIHC) practice in public service work. What are the immediate, intermediate, and long-term actions for cultivating a TIHC public service? (Chapters 3 and 4)
b The critical need to compassionately center the margins and follow the leadership of those most impacted in our equity and LPS approaches (Chapters 5 and 6)
c How can we develop and sustain individual and organizational competence and capacity for diversity, equity, inclusion, and liberatory justice (DEILJ)? (Chapters 5 and 6)

Invitation to Pause and Reflect

As you read these theoretical frameworks, we invite you to remember to pause as often as you need, to take deep breaths, move your body, hydrate yourself, and care for your body and mind as is accessible to you. We

DOI: 10.4324/9781032670669-4

invite you to use these breaks as opportunities to notice/sit with/journal/reflect on the content using following prompts.

- What is resonating with you?
- What is causing dissonance?
- What else would you add or how would you adapt these frameworks to make them your own and meaningful for your own individual and collective practice?

3 Trauma-Informed and Healing-Centered Public Service

Abstract

In this chapter, we uplift the need to recognize emotional labor and neurobiologically challenging nature of public service and diversity, equity, inclusion, and liberatory justice (DEILJ) work. We affirm consistent calls to cultivate an ethics of care, relationality, and interdependence in public service contexts to serve both the public and the public servants. Building on existing interdisciplinary literature we extend a call for trauma-informed and healing centered (TIHC) public service organizations. This chapter seeks to offer an expansive and nuanced understanding of trauma. We offer an understanding of trauma from both neurobiological perspectives as well as socio-psychological perspectives. Collectively, these perspectives inform us about historical, inter-generational, persistent institutional, and personal trauma of oppression, and hence, the need to center repair and healing as a core approach for LPS. We discuss the need to foster TIHC approaches in public service to avoid harm and re-traumatization for populations we serve and to engage in the challenging and necessary work of repair to address historical and systemic oppression. We envision TIHC public service to acknowledge and address historical, inter-generational, and persistent institutional trauma from oppression. TIHC public service framework seeks to examine the ways trauma from oppression is reproduced in public service contexts. It seeks to cultivate supportive and life-affirming organizational systems and cultures where individuals and collectives can engage in the process of repairing and healing from trauma of oppression.

What Is Trauma and Why Should We Care About It in Public Service?

Trauma is the body's protective response (such as fight, flight, freeze, appease, and disconnect) to an event – or a series of events – that it understands as potentially dangerous (Haines 2019; Menakem 2017,

DOI: 10.4324/9781032670669-5

2019). It is the body's highly adaptive mechanism to find safety and to protect itself (Haines 2019; Menakem 2017, 2019). Because our trauma responses (such as fight, flight, freeze, appease, and disconnect) originate in our bodies, the healing of our trauma must also include approaches that seek to heal our bodyminds and spirit (Dana 2021a; Haines 2019; Menakem 2017, 2019).

Resmaa Menakem, a trauma-specialist dedicated to racial and social justice work, highlights that *trauma remains stuck in our bodies* until it is processed and metabolized. Therefore, we need embodied or somatic practices to heal from experiences of trauma. He offers us a simple, yet profound definition of trauma – *"Trauma is anything that happens too much, too fast, too soon coupled with something that should have happened and that didn't"* (Menakem 2019, at 5:20 minutes).

Notice in the Menakem's (2019) definition of trauma, it is "anything that happens too much, too fast, too soon and *is coupled with something that should have happened and didn't" (emphasized by authors)*. This emphasized aspect is an important key to understanding trauma. To understand the quote *"something that should have happened and did not,"* more concretely, we invite you to reflect on following broad examples:

"Somebody should have helped and did not."
"Something should have been said and that did not happen."

Invitation to Pause: *We invite a pause here to breathe into this quote and reflect. Allow these words to land in your bodymind. Notice what is emerging for you.*

It is important to note that trauma is not a weakness. Trauma is also not an event. Trauma is the body's protective response to an event that it understands as potentially harmful or dangerous. Traumatic events refer to experiences of personal as well as collective harm and loss.

(**Content Warning: Heavy and Potentially Triggering Content**) Personal trauma is when harm and loss is experienced at an individual level (e.g., trauma from domestic violence, trauma from a car accident, trauma from harmful experiences in childhood such as child sexual abuse). Collective trauma is when a whole group of people with a shared identity experience harm and loss in similar ways. Events or series of events contributing to collective trauma include historical, inter-generational, persistent institutional, and personal harm and trauma from systemic oppression (e.g., trauma of racism and white supremacy, trauma of colonization, trauma of genocide and wars, trauma of displacement, trauma of living in poverty) (Brave Heart n.d.; DeGruy 2005; Krawec 2022; Menakem 2017).

In this chapter, we call for trauma-informed and healing-centered (TIHC) public service organizations that can:

a Hold space for meaningful and courageous conversations about trauma, including historical, inter-generational, and persistent institutional trauma from systemic oppression.
b Critically examine how trauma from oppression is reproduced and maintained through our institutionalized policies, structures, procedures, protocols, and cultural norms and practices.
c Cultivate critical action to avoid harm and re-traumatization; recognize individual and collective grief; as well as build supportive and life-affirming cultures and conditions where individuals and collectives can engage in the process of healing trauma.

Throughout this chapter and this book, we expand on these ideas and reaffirm a call for TIHC public service. In the next sub-section, we explore the need for TIHC public approaches from an emotional labor perspective. We argue that TIHC approaches can help to prevent burnout as well as to resource, nourish, and support well-being of public servants as they engage in tasks that demand emotional labor of varying intensities.

Subsequently, we explore an understanding of embodied trauma and its neurobiological connections from the perspective of polyvagal theory. We also discuss theoretical frameworks that have expanded our comprehension of personal and collective trauma from oppression (such as racialized oppression) that persists through history, across generations, and reproduced through institutions.

Furthermore, we explore the concepts of "attempted spirit murder" and spiritual trauma, which highlights the spiritual wounding and harm caused by systemic violence, prejudice and discrimination experienced by kids, youth, and adults with marginalized (such as BIPOC, LGBTQIA+ and disability) identities. We also explore the importance of spirit restorers and spirit protectors for healing spiritual trauma. Finally, we discuss the core principles of trauma-informed approaches that can serve as a starting point for developing TIHC public service praxis. As this outline suggests, we are exploring several key concepts in this chapter. So, we offer a gentle reminder to engage with the content at a pace that feels manageable, accessible, and meaningful for your bodymind.

Need for Trauma-Informed Healing-Centered Public Service: An Emotional Labor Perspective

Trauma theories and trauma-informed approaches have traditionally been developed and applied in fields like neurobiology, psychology, and social work. These professions involve direct and close interactions with people experiencing/navigating the effects of trauma and respond by incorporating trauma-informed approaches. However, the principles of trauma-informed practice have found resonance across various disciplines, including public health, education, and even within social justice advocacy spaces. We assert that the significance of trauma-informed public service extends beyond social work, psychology, and neurobiology to encompass all forms of public service and administrative job roles that necessitate a commitment to ethics of care in job performance and thus demand emotional labor (Burnier 2009; Dolamore 2021; Guy, Newman, and Mastracci 2014).

Emotional labor is a job demand that requires emotional effort, management, and regulation of one's emotions as part of job performance (Hochschild 1983). Engaging in emotional labor is pivotal in the interactions between public servants and the public they serve. It is essential for effective and equitable performance of public service jobs and to demonstrate care (Guy, Newman, and Mastracci 2014).

Emotional labor involves three main elements: Surface acting, deep acting, and emotional dissonance or false face acting. Surface acting is when an individual displays emotion that is not genuinely felt (Hochschild 1983). For example, in citizen interactions, public servants need to remain calm and empathetic when dealing with upset or distressed citizens, provide information with a friendly demeanor, or navigate difficult conversations with diplomacy.

In contrast to surface acting, deep acting involves trying to genuinely feel the emotions that are expected (Hochschild 1983). In healthcare, social services, and emergency services, public servants must show empathy, compassion, and patience when dealing with individuals facing issues of unsafety, health, financial, or social challenges (Guy et al. 2014).

Emotional dissonance or false face acting occurs when there is a disconnect between the emotions a person feels and the emotions they are expected to display. False face acting refers to emotional labor when an individual suppresses their emotion and displays a different emotion (Guy et al. 2014; Hochschild 1983). For example, during crises, such as natural disasters, pandemics, or social unrest, public servants are often on the front lines. They must manage their own emotions, while providing guidance, support, and reassurance to affected individuals and communities.

Thus, emotional labor is vital for performance of public service jobs and can place heavy demands on a public servant's body and mind (henceforth referred as, bodymind). Public servants must interact with communities and people in both favorable as well as challenging situations that can trigger stress and trauma responses. Public service professionals need to cultivate skills to be responsive to the varying contexts of each person served, including their stress and trauma responses. At the same time, public servants must practice self-awareness of their own trauma histories and trauma responses and be vigilant to avoid harm and re-traumatization while operating from a position of power.

In public administration, emotional labor extends beyond individual interactions. Leaders and administrators must also foster a caring and supportive organizational culture. This involves recognizing and acknowledging the emotional toll that the work may take on employees and providing the necessary resources and support systems to promote well-being and resilience (Guy et al. 2014).

Overall, emotional labor research reveals that public administrators' care work and emotional labor are crucial in building trust and legitimacy for the government and public institutions. When communities perceive that public servants genuinely care about their well-being and are committed to serving their needs, it can enhance public trust in government and foster a positive relationship between the public and the state.

TIHC approaches are essential elements to cultivate an ethics of care, equity, relationality, and resilience in service of both – the public and the public servants (Burnier 2003, 2009; Dolamore and Whitebread 2022; Headley et al. 2023; Meyer, Johnson III, and McCandless 2022). From an emotional labor perspective, TIHC approaches help us acknowledge the whole personhood of public service professionals. It helps to recognize that public servants must often engage in work that can exact heavy emotional lifting and neurobiological stresses when responding to traumatic events. Furthermore, it acknowledges the need for trauma-informed practices to avoid harm and re-traumatization when operating from positions of power. These job demands, if they are not well resourced, can have long-lasting impacts of distress on public servants bodyminds.

For example, consider that in their everyday job, public transit operators (e.g., a bus driver), must practice care to serve passengers needing assistance (such as wheelchair users, or elderly passengers, or passengers with infants and kids). They also frequently encounter irate passengers, disputes, or disruptive behaviors among passengers. Such situations demand conflict resolution skills and require emotional labor. Teachers need to practice patience and care for students with varying backgrounds and needs. They need to cultivate positively supportive classroom climate and attitudes to support students with learning difficulties, struggling with traumatic childhood experiences, emotional struggles, or behavioral challenges.

Public policy makers and administrative officials need to interact, serve, negotiate, and balance the interests and demands of various constituents, advocacy groups, and political parties. Healthcare workers, emergency dispatchers (911 call responders), crisis responders (e.g., firefighters, paramedics, disaster response teams), social workers, often interact with individuals and families during critical moments of life struggles and including survival situations. They often interact with people coping with grief, loss, and uncertainty.

Police officers need to respond to various emergencies, including situations involving violence, harm, and tragedy and may involve victims/survivors, witnesses, or suspects in distress. These situation demands various types of emotional labor, often at the same time, as police officers must display empathy, compassion, emotional restraint, calm under pressure, and regulate their own emotions to make sound decisions to ensure safety for themselves and others.

Invitation to Pause: *These are intense situations. We invite a pause to practice self-care, take one or move deep breaths, hydrate, move your body, and let these sentences land in your bodyminds.*

Across the board, we can observe that emotional labor is a core component of public service jobs. Public servants including public policy makers and administrators, police officers, welfare officers, social workers, emergency dispatchers, crisis responders, health care workers, teachers, and bus drivers serve public in favorable, and unfavorable conditions that may potentially trigger trauma responses and requiring varying intensities of emotional labor. The performance of these jobs involves various levels of emotional, physical, psychological, and neurobiological stresses. They demand a deep practice of self-compassion and compassion for others to support the public's needs for care, safety, healing, and resilience.

Therefore, consistent with emotional labor and trauma-informed care focused literature, we call for TIHC public service approaches that proactively cultivate policies, structures and cultures anchored in values of care, nurture, and nourishment. TIHC means supporting and building individual and organizational resilience that can help public servants to cope with emotional and neurobiological stresses of their jobs. When public servants are well nourished and have trauma-informed organizational support systems to practice embodied healing and self-compassion, they can approach public service work, including emotionally and neurobiologically taxing job functions from a place of nourishment, rather than depletion, burnout, and compassion fatigue (e.g., refer Guy et al. 2014; Headley et al. 2023; Mastracci, Guy, and Newman 2015; Substance Abuse and Mental Health Services Administration 2014).

In the next section, we offer a neurobiological understanding of trauma from the perspective of polyvagal theory. We explore polyvagal-informed practices that can help to find neurobiological anchors and emotional regulation in moments of distress and challenging public service, including in the context of diversity, equity, inclusion, and liberatory justice (DEILJ) focused work.

Understanding Trauma: A Polyvagal Perspective

Polyvagal theory is a neurobiological framework developed by Dr. Stephen Porges to understand the role of the autonomic (involuntary) nervous system in regulating social engagement, emotional experiences, stress, and trauma responses (Porges 1995, 2009). The "vagal" in polyvagal theory refers to the vagus nerve. The vagus nerve, also fondly known as the "wandering nerve" is the tenth cranial nerve (CN X). It is in fact the longest network of nerve fibers extending from the brainstem (i.e., base of the brain region) to the abdomen (i.e., our belly area).

As depicted in Figure 3.1, the vagus nerve originates in our brainstem and runs down both sides of the neck and travels down through the throat, the lungs, and heart before diving down into the abdomen and digestive system (i.e., the belly region) (Dana 2021a; Menakem 2017; Seladi-Schulman 2022).

A Note About Limitations of Polyvagal Theory

Before we dive deeper into the core principles of polyvagal theory and their implications for TIHC public service, including DEILJ work, we wish

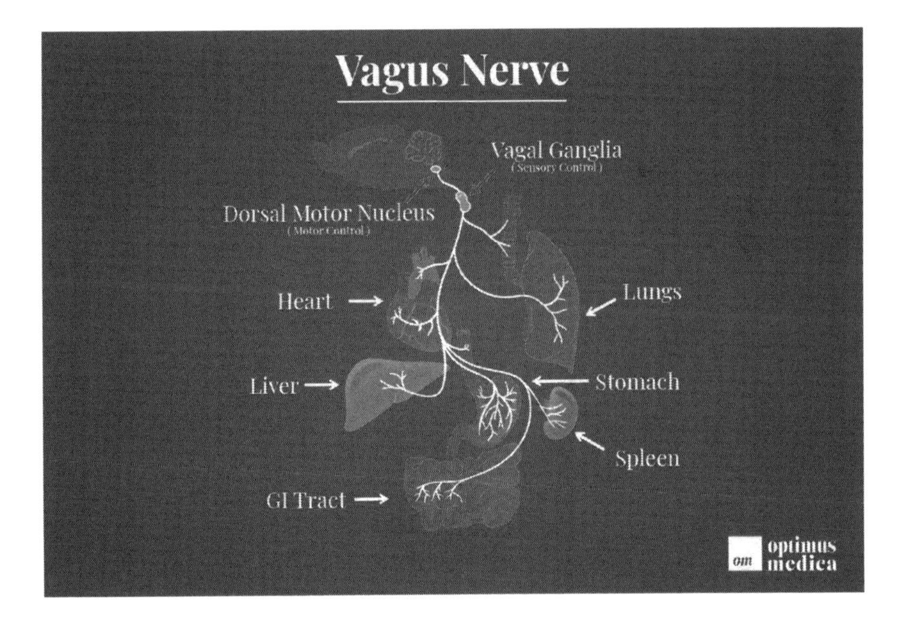

Figure 3.1 The vagus nerve is the longest nerve of the nerve fibers in our central nervous system. It is fondly called the "Wanderer Nerve" as it travels throughout the body and interacts with many major organ systems

Sources: West 2021, Optimus Medica; Original Sources of Image: Chang Rui B. 2019, Chang et al. 2015. Used with permission.

to acknowledge two of the key limitations of this scientific theory and our intentions. First, a commonly noted limitation of this theory, as is common with scientific theories, is that it requires more extensive work to be applied effectively and clearly to support well-being of all range of human differences and lived experiences. This is particularly pertinent in the context of the full range of neurobiological diversity, psychological diversity, and individual differences.

Second, polyvagal theory can often be misinterpreted and misunderstood, especially in practice, to overemphasize the need for emotional regulation without fully acknowledging the importance of the conditioned survival tendencies in the form of embodied activation or disconnection and shutdown. In the following paragraphs, we further clarify the need for polyvagal-informed practice in public service as well as the caveats, cautions, and contradictions related to this practice.

We also wish to acknowledge that we do not identify as professional therapists and our discussion here is not intended to be prescriptive in any way, especially in psychological ways. Our intent is to introduce trauma frameworks that can help us expand our comprehension of individual and collective trauma, it's connection to body, and the need to foster a TIHC public service. We strongly recommend that you review our suggested references to develop a deeper and nuanced understanding of trauma and polyvagal theory. With that acknowledgment, let's dive into the core principles of the polyvagal theory.

The Core Principles of the Polyvagal Theory

The three key principles of polyvagal theory are: (a) Autonomic Hierarchy. (b) Neuroception. (c) Coregulation (Dana 2021a, 2021b).

a. Autonomic Hierarchy

The principle of autonomic hierarchy describes how, through the process of evolution, our nervous system came to be organized around three building blocks. In neurobiological terms, these three building blocks are called: (a) ventral vagal system, related to states of safety, calm, and connection (evolved around 200 million years ago), (b) sympathetic system, related to states of fight, flight mobilization (evolved around 400 million years ago), and (c) dorsal vagal system, related to states of disconnect and disappear (evolved around 500 million years ago) (Dana 2021a).

These elements along with other components of our autonomic nervous system play a fundamental role in regulating autonomic or involuntary bodily functions such as heart rate, respiration, blood pressure, rest, and digest, and more. They work to maintain the body's internal balance or homeostasis. However, when recruited in survival mode, these three building blocks also help our body to appropriately respond to threats through fight, flight, freeze, appease, dissociate, and shutdown responses (Dana 2021a).

The principle of autonomic hierarchy of the polyvagal theory refers to the predictable order in which our nervous system works (Porges n.d., 2009; Dana 2021a). Deborah Dana (2021a) uses the metaphor of a ladder to explain this autonomic hierarchy and the preset pathways of our nervous system. This principle suggests that as we move through our everyday life, our autonomic nervous system moves through various embodied states associated with the three building blocks, however, this movement always occurs in a preset hierarchical order.

At the top of the ladder or the hierarchy of the three states of our nervous system is the state of embodied safety, calm and connection that originates in the ventral vagal system. When our ventral vagal system (related to safety, calm, and connection) is overwhelmed with distress, we move through sympathetic nervous state (i.e., energize and mobilize) which triggers fight, flight, mobilize stress, and trauma responses. If the sources of our distress continue to remain unresolved, we move to our dorsal vagal state (i.e., disconnect and disappear) which is related to embodied responses of disconnection/dissociation and shutdown.

The ventral vagal system is linked to the socially engaged parts of our autonomic nervous system. When we are in our ventral vagal state (i.e., safety, calm, and connection), we feel safe and settled in our bodies, we feel connected to ourselves and other living beings. Within the realm of our ventral vagal system, we are anchored in safety and connection, our heart rate is steady, and our breath is natural and full. We can self-regulate and co-regulate (Dana 2021a, 2021b).

Next on the autonomic hierarchy is our sympathetic nervous system (i.e., our energize and mobilize system). It provides us with the vital energy to move around the world. It works in cooperation with our ventral vagal (i.e., safety, calm, and connection) system to energize us, regulate our heart rate, blood pressure, and breathing patterns. However, when we feel distressed or too challenged, our ventral vagal system is overwhelmed, and we move out of the state of safety, calm, and connection. When we lack capacity or resources to cope with the challenge of the moment in time, our ventral vagal system goes into background (or offline, if you will). Consequently, we lose our capacity to feel settled, calm, and regulated.

In these moments, our sympathetic nervous system being next in the autonomic hierarchy gets recruited and mobilizes our fight and flight responses. Some of the flavors of this state include feelings of overwhelm and anxiety, irritation, the world seems unfriendly and chaotic to our nervous system (Dana 2021a, 2021b; Porges 1995, 2009, n.d.). Examples from everyday life include a long list of tasks to complete and feeling irritated, feeling frustrated, being in traffic and losing temper. In the context of DEILJ conversations, we may feel like arguing or putting down somebody in moments of disagreement.

Last in this hierarchy is the oldest part of our autonomic nervous system, namely our dorsal vagal system (i.e., disconnect and disappear responses). The day-to-day, non-reactive responsibility of our dorsal vagal branch is to regulate healthy digestion (i.e., rest and digest functions). When we feel distressed, and our actions within the zone of sympathetic activation do not resolve the issue of the moment, and our nervous system continues to feel overwhelmed, we drop into the dorsal vagal state of disconnect and disappear. Examples of this state include feeling buried under a heavy load of work and cannot get out, a state of exhaustion, burnout, a state of despair, disconnection, and powerlessness (Dana 2021a). These are all common states of our nervous systems, and their understanding is relevant to professional contexts of public service work, including the DEILJ work.

An understanding of the principle of autonomic hierarchy and our embodied trauma responses (such as fight, flight, freeze, appease, and disconnect) can help us build self-awareness and cultivate individual and collective resilience to effectively engage in trauma-informed public service and DEILJ work. Susan Gooden (2014) wrote about race and social equity being a nervous area of government. In the field of public administration, we have an ongoing conversation about the need to create brave spaces in our classrooms and our organizations to engage in courageous conversations about DEILJ (e.g., refer to Love, Gaynor, and Blesset 2016; Starke, Heckler, and Mackey 2018).

An understanding of our nervous system is significant to cultivating brave spaces as it helps us understand our embodied responses and a range of feelings and emotions experienced during courageous DEILJ conversations. These include a range of emotions from nervousness, anxiousness, frustration, rage, and despair to hope, love, connection, and belonging.

It helps us acknowledge and normalize our embodied experiences such as shakiness in our voice, the elevated heart rate, and our gut reactions that are sometimes hard to explain, at least in the moment when we experience uncertainty, emotional exposure, and risks (i.e., feel vulnerable; Brown 2010) during courageous conversations. In context of DEILJ conversations, an embodied practice of engaging with vulnerability, including speaking with shaky voice, trembling, elevated heart rate, can be considered as positive signs of courage, embracing the discomfort, and stretching our capacity to learn, grow, and mature as DEILJ and public service practitioners. From a polyvagal perspective, these embodied experiences are far from embarrassing or signs of weakness or low self-confidence; rather these are signs that we care, are willing to be outside of our comfort zones, and opening ourselves to being vulnerable and brave.

It is important to note that the communication carried along the vagal pathway (i.e., through the vagus nerve) is bidirectional, *with eighty percent of information originating in the body and moving to the brain and twenty percent information flowing from the brain to our body*. From a DEILJ perspective, this means that during difficult and vulnerable conversations, the story we tell ourselves really originates from our bodies and depends on the state of our autonomic nervous system.

Depending on the state of our bodies (i.e., autonomic nervous system) in any given moment and context, we may tell ourselves at least three different stories. A story of safety and connection (a story originated in the ventral vagal system) or a story of win-lose, power-over, judgment, and criticism or blame (for self and others) (a story originated in the sympathetic system), or a story of hopelessness, resignation, powerlessness, disconnection, and disembodiment (a story originated in the dorsal vagal system).

The invitation of polyvagal theory is that – when we feel resourced and nourished enough in our bodymind and spirit, we can practice curiosity about these stories and ask – "what is the story I am telling myself? For this situation, what is my ventral vagal story (i.e., of calm and connection)? What is my sympathetic system's story (i.e., of fight, flight, mobilize)? What is my dorsal vagal story (i.e., of disconnect and disappear)?" This curiosity might lead to finding at least three different narratives or stories to experience a situation (Brown 2018; Dana 2021a, 2021b).

From a practice perspective, in the context of everyday life and particularly in the context of DEILJ conversations, one may also be curious: How do we stay anchored in our ventral vagal or bring emotional states of regulation it back online? If we are feeling unsettled, how can we return to feelings of connection, safety, and regulation?

In response to these questions, Dana (2021a, 2021b) offers that – first, it is important to practice self-compassion and remember that the goal of polyvagal-informed practice is not to always be in the state of ventral vagal calm, connection, and regulation; that would be impractical (some might call such an approach toxic positivity). Due to the daily stress of our lives, and particularly in the contexts of public service work and DEILJ praxis, we are bound to move into states of sympathetic activation and dorsal vagal disconnection and that's okay. The goal of polyvagal-informed practice is to build capacity to move through the different states of our autonomic hierarchy (i.e., ventral vagal system, sympathetic system, and dorsal vagal system) with fluidity and flexibility, *as best as we can* in our given context.

Second, Dana (2021a, 2021b) notes, we must recognize this practice cannot be forced, and the experience of coming back online or of being offline varies based on our neurobiological diversity, our trauma histories, psychological and individual differences. Therefore, it is most important to not shame our sympathetic (i.e., fight-flight) and dorsal vagal (i.e., disconnect and disappear) survival responses. Rather the polyvagal invitation is to be curious about them and honor the wisdom offered by our embodied survival responses.

Finally, it is important to recognize that this is a very important and difficult practice. It takes time, it takes resources and a support system that can offer coregulation. It takes a disciplined effort, and patience to cultivate skills and practices that can help us flexibly navigate different states of our autonomic nervous system (Dana 2021a, 2021b). For example, when practicing running a marathon, or becoming a yogi, or a weightlifter, or a singer, any artist, a persuasive communicator, a data analyst, a mathematician, to develop a mastery at any skill or capacity in life, we must train and condition our bodymind, work every day with discipline and develop a practice that will help us attain our goals. The same logic applies to developing a flexible and fluid practice of finding our way back to regulated mindful presence. It requires consistent working with our bodymind as best as we can with the support and resources we have. Below we offer some examples of beginning practices that can help us develop embodied anchors to experience flavors of calm and connection.

When an embodied connection (such as to our breath, our body) becomes accessible to our nervous system, one of the first steps is to develop a practice of noticing. Notice the patterns in our embodied reactions to feelings of unsettledness (i.e., sympathetic activation), as well as disconnection, and disembodiment (i.e., dorsal vagal activation). The other practices focused on building deeper connection with the ventral vagal anchors are shared below. We invite you to explore practices that feel most accessible to your bodymind.

- Taking deep breaths throughout the day: Exhales and sighs which helps to reset our nervous systems.
- Moving your body (e.g., shaking it off, literally or going for a run or doing a physically engaging body movement practice after an emotionally challenging task or conversation to discharge the sympathetic energy).
- Centering your body, such as focusing on the places where your body is feeling supported (e.g., feet, back) or places where you can feel the movement of your breath (e.g., chest, belly).
- Rocking your body.
- Humming (to music, a song, or a prayer you like).
- Placing hands on the heart or face in ways that feel soothing (based on Dana 2021a; Menakem 2017).

We want to acknowledge that these are some of the beginning practices that can help us find an embodied anchor or connection. These practices can be deepened based on your strengths and interests and especially with the help of a trauma-informed, somatic or embodied training and/or coaching.

A Reflection Invitation: Connecting with Ventral Vagal Anchors

In what ways do you/can you create time and space to connect with the things that help you feel comfortable and safe (i.e., your ventral vagal anchors). Ventral vagal anchors could be people, places, times of the day, objects, and actions that help you feel at ease, and safe (E.g., walks, food, meeting friends, therapy, breathing practices, swimming, running, dance, mindfulness, yoga/exercise).

- *What are your ventral vagal anchors?*
- *In what ways do they nourish your bodymind?*
- *How can you cultivate a consistent (daily) practice of intentionally connecting with your ventral vagal anchors?*

In the context of DEILJ conversations, from a polyvagal perspective, the key practice is to develop an awareness and relationship with our nervous systems. The invitation is to cultivate a level of fluidity and flexibility to move through these three states of our nervous system and find our way back to ventral vagal anchors. Another piece is to notice when we move away from our ventral vagal state and to step back or step away to offer ourselves self-empathy and self-compassion needed to feel a sense of safety and connection.

Similarly, during DEILJ conversations, in moments of tension and rupture (e.g., with a colleague, student, manager, or professor) the polyvagal invitation is to engage with the work of repair (e.g., through offering and receiving meaningful apology) from a place of curiosity about each other needs, and embodied empathy for self and others. Of course, all of this is easier said than done and context and power dynamics play a big role in the practice. However, developing an embodied leadership practice for DEILJ at individual and collective levels is key to sustaining critical conversations and critical actions. It involves a recognition that not just our brains, but rather our nervous system, our hearts (literally), and our bodies are involved in DEILJ work and therefore we need to care for our individual and collective nervous systems while doing this work in trauma-informed ways. Next, we discuss the principles of neuroception and coregulation.

b. Neuroception

The second principle of polyvagal theory is called Neuroception. It refers to the internal surveillance system of our autonomic nervous system. The term "neuro" refers to nervous system and "ception" means awareness. This principle suggests that our nervous system has a built-in surveillance system that looks for signs of safety and signs of danger. It means that our perceptions, the way we make sense of the world around us, the stories we tell about our experiences, our behavioral actions, and reactions, all begin with neuroception (i.e., the embodied sense of safety and danger, in other words, whether our body is feeling safe or threatened in a given moment) (Dana 2021a; Menakem 2017).

As noted in the previous section, the communication carried along the vagal pathway (i.e., through the vagus nerve) is bidirectional, with eighty percent of information originating in the body and moving to the brain and twenty percent information flowing from the brain to our body. Our trauma responses are activated when our body sends a signal (i.e., neuroception) to our brain that something in our environment is physically or psychologically threatening. From a survival perspective, our neuroception is attuned more strongly to the signs of danger, rather than cues of safety. Therefore, our trauma responses can be activated at signs of real and/or perceived danger or threat. Examples of perceived threat in everyday contexts could be when we receive criticism about our work and this experience can trigger our defensiveness. Our trauma responses manifest in the body as a form of our adaptive survival response which becomes a conditioned tendency (or a behavioral habit) we use to react in moments of overwhelm or stress (Haines 2019; Menakem 2017).

It is often hard to make sense of our trauma response, at least cognitively, because we lose its context over time. Menakem (2017, 2019, 2020) notes, because trauma is decontextualized overtime, our trauma responses may seem like over-the-top reactions to small problems, however, they are in fact rekindling old pain or discomfort and our body is addressing it with reflexive energy that is unresolved or not metabolized and stuck in our nervous system. To return the example of receiving criticism about our work, over-the-top defensiveness could signal that experiencing criticism about our work is rekindling an old pain, for example, related to shame or perfectionism. Our work then is to notice our trauma response as gently as we can, be curious about the old (embodied) pain it is evoking and offer this pain the care and attention it needs. From this place, we will likely find our way toward metabolizing this pain and healing it.

However, it is important to be attentive against misuse or overuse of the language of trauma to describe discomfort, difficult experiences, and political or ideological struggles. Misattributing trauma in this way minimizes and decenters survivors' experiences, making it difficult to develop real strategies to process and heal from trauma (Menakem 2017; Page and Woodland 2023).

In the context of TIHC public service and DEILJ work, this principle of neuroception teaches us to cultivate a self-awareness about our trauma responses in gentle, self-compassionate ways, and work toward our own healing journey. As the saying goes, "hurt people, hurt people." In public service context, this principle invites us to practice self-empathy, self-compassion, and healing for justice. It teaches us to approach public service and DEILJ work from a place of kindness, gentleness, and nourishment for self and others. It teaches us the importance of creating a culture and a container that supports individual and collective practice of connecting with the signs of safety.

To offer a simple, yet important practice example, this may mean that we develop enough pauses for self and our collectives, during our meetings and gatherings to include centering practices (at regular intervals) that can help us find anchors in our breath or movement or an object, to slow down as needed, to hydrate and nourish ourselves. These practices do not have to be strict, extensive, or fancy, they can be brief and adaptive, and must always be based on consent and context. Sometimes, cultivating these practices may mean simply giving ourselves and our group members permission to connect with our bodyminds as needed and in ways that feel accessible.

The principle of neuroception also teaches us that our nervous system, for a very good survival reason, is attuned more strongly to signs of danger rather than cues of safety. As we mature in our embodied practice, the invitation is to focus on nurturing and recognizing cues that send a message to our bodies that we are safe in this moment, that we can turn off our defensive systems, that we are okay. As noted by Stephen Porges, "*good therapy and good social relations, good parenting, good teaching, (good leadership), it's all about the same thing—how do you turn off defensiveness? When you turn defense systems off, you have accessibility to different cortical areas for more profound understanding, learning, and skill development*" (Porges n.d., *p. 2; parentheses added by authors*).

c. Coregulation

The third and the final principle of polyvagal theory is that as human beings, we need to find safe connections with others in the experience of coregulation. Coregulation or the experience of feeling regulated and settled with others is a deeply fundamental human need, stemming from the very beginning of life and necessary for our survival. This universal human need goes beyond the first years of our life. Dana (2021a) notes, "While the world seems increasingly focused on self-regulation and independence, coregulation is the foundation for safely navigating daily living" (p. 10).

In the context of TIHC public service and DEILJ work, this principle teaches us the importance of cultivating interdependence and collectives such as peer, affinity, and mutual support groups. DEILJ work needs to happen in collectives with interdependence, mutuality, and reciprocity as key values guiding our work. From a polyvagal perspective, a key task for embodied public service and social justice leadership practitioners is to cultivate communal spaces and identity-based affinity (e.g., race-based, gender-based affinity groups) where people can regularly gather to offer coregulation, to share individual and collective knowledge and wisdom, and cultivate sites of healing from grief and trauma of oppression.

Polyvagal Theory: Concluding Thoughts on Implications for Practice

An understanding of our nervous system and the polyvagal theory has significant implications for DEILJ work and to foster a TIHC public service. It offers profound insights into how our nervous system reacts to trauma and stress. It can help us recognize and process our trauma and stress responses, particularly when engaging in challenging DEILJ conversations, while handling emotionally demanding public service tasks or responding to traumatic events and crisis situations. Our trauma and stress responses have a significant impact on our individual and collective well-being.

Polyvagal theory can help us at individual levels as well as in the contexts of public service work to cultivate an awareness of our trauma and stress responses in moments of overwhelm. These include our fight, flight, freeze, appease, and disconnect responses that originate in our nervous system.

Polyvagal theory emphasizes the need to develop a connection with our nervous system, or in other words, to befriend our nervous system (Dana 2021a, 2021b). By befriending our nervous system, we can recognize patterns of activation (e.g., feeling triggered into fight or flight responses at workplace), as well as immobilization, disconnection, and shutdown (e.g., feeling indifferent or going through the motions of living without really feeling anything) that occurs when our nervous system feels overwhelmed in day-to-day life (Dana 2021a, 2021b).

In public service and DEILJ work contexts that demand high-level emotional self-awareness, emotional labor, and emotional regulation, polyvagal-informed practices can help us connect with our nervous system and find embodied resources and support systems before, during, and after moments of intense emotional labor, stress, and overwhelm. Polyvagal-informed leadership praxis is an invitation to connect with embodied anchors in our bodyminds, cultivate practices to develop deeper self-awareness, and become a regulating presence for self and others in moments of tension and conflicts (Dana 2021a, 2021b).

In the next section, we continue to build on polyvagal theory and explore the framework of "somatic abolitionism" that highlights the connections between trauma and body as well as between systems of oppression and experiences of collective trauma.

Collective Trauma, Oppression, and Body

In his 2017 book titled, "My Grandmother's Hands: Racialized Trauma and the Pathway to Mending Our Hearts and Bodies," Black Healer and Trauma Specialist Resmaa Menakem introduces the concept of "somatic abolitionism." Somatic abolitionism calls upon us to understand and address racialized trauma not only at an intellectual or emotional level, but also at a somatic level. "Soma" refers to the wholeness of mind, body, and spirit (Haines 2019). Menakem (2017) translates the understanding of our autonomic (or involuntary) nervous system and particularly the vital role of our vagus nerve in responding to traumatic events and applies and integrates it to develop an embodied understanding of racialized trauma and white body supremacy.

His conceptualization of somatic abolitionism challenges the notion that healing from trauma of oppression (such as racism and ableism) can be accomplished solely through intellectual awareness and discussions about the "ism," or strategic planning, or policy and structural changes. This means we cannot solve the complex problems of historical, intergenerational, and persistent institutional oppression and trauma by simply thinking about them, critically examining them, and formulating strategic plans, with just our thinking brain. Trauma including trauma from oppression remains stuck in our bodies unless we proactively seek to process it and heal it. Therefore, our anti-oppression and liberatory justice work necessitates building a connection with our nervous system and healing our bodyminds (Haines 2019; Menakem 2019, 2020).

While policy and structural changes are fundamentally necessary ingredients of systemic change toward social justice and liberation, this work is incomplete and inadequate unless we are committed to and engage with DEILJ work with our bodyminds and spirit. Cultivating TIHC public service and DEILJ necessitates building capacity to transform the oppression embedded within us and our dominant cultures at an embodied level.

Somatic abolitionism framework highlights that work of healing from racialized trauma (and trauma of oppression) necessitates both somatic or embodied inner transformation as well as a broader cultural shift that acknowledges public health crisis of trauma and need to heal our bodyminds and spirit individually and in collectives (Menakem 2017, 2019; Substance Abuse and Mental Health Services Administration 2014).

Somatic abolitionism recognizes that harms and trauma experienced due to systems of oppression have occurred at collective/community levels (e.g., to Indigenous people, to Black people, to Jewish people, to Muslim people) and we need to heal as a people in communities and collectives (i.e., collective healing). Somatic abolitionism calls for transformation of our culture from a culture of oppression and disembodiment that allows perpetuation of trauma and cycles of oppression, to a culture where collective healing at an embodied level becomes a norm (Menakem 2017).

Healing from trauma, including collective trauma (e.g., of racialized oppression), will require us to engage in not only policy and structural transformation but also cultural transformation that favors and facilitates embodied practices of coregulation (remember the third principle of polyvagal theory). It is through coregulation, that is, by being in community and collectives *where we feel a sense of autonomy, belonging, inclusion, trust, and safety*, that we can metabolize and begin our journey toward healing trauma. In the context of DEILJ work, cultivating a practice of coregulation through relationality, trust, inclusion, belonging, and safety in communal spaces is aligned with and necessary to build solidarity and sustainable coalitions for systemic transformation toward liberation (e.g., refer to Harro's (2018) cycle of liberation discussed in Chapter 2).

In the next section, we explore frameworks that offer a deeper and nuanced understanding of historical, inter-generational, and persistent institutional trauma. As a reminder, we intend the following discussion to serve introductory purposes and invite you to dive deeper into additional references and resources offered at the end of this chapter to develop a more thorough understanding of these frameworks.

The Historical, Inter-Generational, and Institutional Trauma

Long before the field of epigenetics[1] had advanced scientific findings about inter-generational nature of trauma, spiritual and cultural work by Black, Indigenous, and People of Color (BIPOC) scholars, practitioners, and liberation workers have recognized the need to heal from unresolved grief and trauma that can be passed down by generations. BIPOC scholars have advanced and nuanced our understanding of trauma, resilience and, have for long advocated the need for healing as a collective. Below we include insights offered by such scholars and practitioners.

Indigenous scholar, Dr. Maria Yellow Horse Brave Heart conceptualized "historical trauma" and "unresolved grief" in 1980s while exploring the generational impact of genocide on Indigenous people. Dr. Braveheart defines historical trauma as a "cumulative emotional and psychological wounding over the lifespan and across generations, emanating from massive group trauma" (Brave Heart n.d., slide 4). She also notes that "historical unresolved grief accompanies that trauma" (Brave Heart n.d., slide 4).

She notes, "children of massacre survivors, children of boarding school survivors, pass on the trauma to their descendants. For healing to begin, it is critical that we concentrate on healing the next seven generations. It's important that we incorporate our ceremonies in the healing process as well as develop Native research on historical trauma and its interventions. Our historical trauma, including individual current lifespan trauma, must be acknowledged, and validated" (Dr. Brave Heart quoted in Chavez n.d., p. 1).

In 2005, Dr. Joy DeGruy, published a book titled "Post Traumatic Slave Syndrome: America's Legacy of Enduring Injury and Healing." Focusing on the experiences of African Americans in the United States, Dr. DeGruy, discusses the need for societal acknowledgment of historical and intergenerational trauma. They highlight, acknowledging and addressing historical and inter-generational trauma can contribute to more equitable and just social systems.

Dr. DeGruy's (2005) work addresses the long-lasting effects of historical trauma, such as slavery and systemic racism, and how these experiences continue to influence individuals, families, and communities today. Dr. DeGruy's introduced the concept of "post traumatic slave syndrome" (P.T.S.S.) to describe the emotional and psychological consequences that have been passed down through generations due to the trauma of slavery and its aftermath. Their work examines how these historical traumas and resilience have shaped African American culture, behavior, and identity, and how they continue to impact contemporary society. Dr. DeGruy emphasizes the importance of investing in cultural strengths (including in the areas of spirituality, music, art, and literature), family support, and community networks to foster healing and resilience.

Through his book "My Grandmothers Hand's" Resmaa Menakem (2017) offered a framing of trauma as "historical, intergenerational, persistent institutional and personal trauma." This framing of trauma builds on pioneering, and powerful contributions of Indigenous and Black, Women Scholars and Healers of Color such as Dr. Brave Heart, Dr. DeGruy and helps us recognize that trauma is passed at a cellular level, from person to person, and generation to generation. It passes through abuse and unsafety created by our systems, structures, institutions, and cultural norms and through our genes through modifying our gene expression (Menakem 2017; Howie, Chuda, and Kerry 2019).

As public service workers, an understanding of historical, inter-generational, institutional trauma of oppression can offer us much needed contexts for solving complex and layered problems of social inequities and injustices and better meet the needs of the public that have been systematically excluded, oppressed, and marginalized. It can help us overcome individual blame bias and build greater awareness of systemic biases that we may often overlook in our public policy making, administrative decisions, and implementation work. It can help us create nurturing systems that interrupt trauma from oppression and foster resilience.

An understanding of historical, inter-generational, and persistent institutional trauma can help us notice that systems we work in often make it so that the whole picture or context (i.e., the historical, generational, and institutional context) of oppression is not allowed to be easily discernable. What we often experience as challenging behaviors, habitual patterns, and actions could be a trauma response that is decontextualized over time (which is one of the ways in which oppression works). Lack of awareness around decontextualizing can contribute toward attribution errors or biases of blaming individuals instead of accurately locating system blames. This in turn, perpetuates the cycle of trauma, oppression, and inequities.

Interrupting the cycle of trauma would involve understanding the layered and complex nature of trauma. It would necessitate building individual public servants and institutional capacity and competence for approaching traumatic experiences from a place of being resourced and nourished, with patience, care, curiosity, openness, solidarity, and humility. It would necessitate cultivating a culture that supports the work of healing and building resilience.

Reflection Box for Journaling: Interrupting Cycles of Trauma and Oppression and Fostering Healing

A Reflection Invitation: Interrupting Cycles of Trauma and Oppression and Fostering Healing

This chapter so far has explored the meaning of trauma that trauma resides in our bodies and hence the healing work must begin in our bodies. We also explored the need for trauma-informed and healing centered public service as trauma from oppression manifests through historical, intergenerational, persistent institutional, and personal trauma. We acknowledge that this is a lot of information, maybe new information to process. We invite you to pause here and notice what you need. Take one or more deep breaths if they are accessible, connect with your body, move, hydrate, and take care of your needs. We invite you to return to this reflection and the rest of the chapter when you feel able and ready.

When you return, if you are able and willing, we invite you to notice and journal your reflections using the following suggested prompts. As you respond/return to these prompts, prioritize and focus on prompts that resonate with you in this moment and move at a pace that feels kind and nourishing.

1 *What is resonating; what is causing dissonance; what questions, concerns, and contradictions are emerging for you? What needs to be acknowledged? What should be let go?*
2 *What does the understanding of historical, inter-generational, persistent institutional, and personal trauma from oppression mean for your practice as a public service professional and/or for your DEILJ praxis?*

   - *We invite you to sit in small groups of trusted peers and/or identity-based affinity groups. Working together, imagine and dream about the first and next steps we can take as public servants to become a healing presence (we do not have to be a healer to be a healing presence) within our spheres of influence and in our communities? What support systems and resources will we need to cultivate to sustain such a practice at mind, body, and spiritual levels?*
   - *We invite you to dream and envision the immediate, intermediate, and long-term actions to bring systemic, structural, and cultural transformation at institutional/organizational levels, to interrupt cycles of trauma and oppression and, potentially become spaces that support and contribute toward individual and collective healing?*

Spiritual Wounding, Spiritual Trauma, and Healing: The Power of Spirit Protectors and Restorers

In her seminal work, "The Alchemy of Race and Rights: Diary of a Law Professor" (1992), Professor Patricia Williams, a distinguished legal scholar, introduced the concept of "spirit murder." She illuminated how racism, prejudice, and discrimination leave deep and lasting emotional and spiritual wounds on the individual and collective psyche of marginalized communities, especially focusing on BIPOC communities in the United States.

Williams (1992) emphasized that while one's physical body might endure, spiritual and emotional injuries have profound, long-term consequences for the individual and the collective. The emotional and spiritual wounds inflicted by structural inequality, prejudice, discrimination, and domination are often swift and potent. But these injuries are seldom acknowledged, as marginalized individuals strive to survive within institutions marked by Eurocentrism, patriarchy, capitalism, hetero/cisnormativity, citizenship-based norms, and ableism, furthering the harm and trauma. As individuals enter survival mode, they may become unaware of the depths of the wounds they bear. This is a shared experience for many, including people of color, cisgender women, LGBTQIA+ people, people with disabilities, and other marginalized/minoritized groups (Revilla 2021).

Scholars such as Hines and Wilmost (2018) and Love (2016) have drawn attention to how the U.S. education system perpetuates acts of spirit murder against young Black bodies daily. For example, refer to case study 2.1 on "Combating Hair Discrimination, Addressing Systemic Racism, and Promoting Inclusivity in Sports and Education" discussed in Chapter 2. Rather than creating nurturing, equitable, and engaging learning environments for Black students, attempted spirit murder occurs through acts such as physical, psychological, and emotional violence by school police officers and other officials, disproportionate school discipline, the erasure of Black history in the curriculum, the silencing of Black voices, cultural discrimination, and the demonization of cultural wealth brought by Black families. These experiences can leave Black children feeling humiliated, demotivated, and unappreciated over and over again.

Within organizational and workplace contexts, attempted spirit murder may occur when individuals experience trauma from repeated discrimination, marginalization, exclusion and not belonging, within oppressive systems such as racism, classism, sexism, heterosexism, trans oppression, anti-immigrant attitudes, ableism, and ageism. Within organizational settings, attempted spirit murder can have the power to spiritually and emotionally "murder and destroy not only people's dreams but also their very essence and desire to exist" (Revilla 2021, 37).

Professor Anita Tijerina Revilla, in their article titled "Attempted Spirit Murder: Who Are Your Spirit Protectors and Your Spirit Restorers?" (2021), expands upon Williams' (1992) concept of spirit murder and introduces the concepts of spirit protectors and spirit restorers. Revilla (2021) argues that individuals targeted by attempted spirit murder can either internalize the practice or resist it. Resistors survive by having access to or being able to form spirit restorative teams, including peers, mentors, family, and community members who transform into spirit protectors and restorers.

Revilla (2021) defines "spirit protectors and spirit restorers" as individuals, places, organizations, beliefs, and practices, including art, poetry, books, music, and dance. These elements provide the strength needed to resist and survive attempted spirit murder and restore wounded spirits, even in the face of repeated attacks and woundings. Revilla calls for an expanded vision of social justice praxis that encompasses holistic spirit restoration and protection.

A Reflection Invitation: Attempted Spirit Murder and The Need for Spirit Protectors and Spirit Restorers (Adapted from *Revilla 2021, p. 41 and p. 43*)

This invitation is to reflect and intentionally respond/return to these questions when you have the headspace. The invitation is to proactively construct spirit restorative and protective networks within our families, friends, among our colleagues, affinity groups and communities (including community of practice).

1 *Who serves as your spirit protectors? Remember these can be, but are not limited to, individuals, places, organizations, beliefs, and practices, including art, poetry, books, music, and dance.*
2 *Do you have a support system or a spirit restorative team to intervene if/when you face attempted spirit murder?*
3 *In what ways are you actively involved in the process of restoring and healing your spirit and bodymind?*
4 *How do you ensure that you haven't internalized the role of a spirit murderer?*
5 *Are you fulfilling the role of a spirit protector yourself? What role will you take on in safeguarding your own spirit and the spirits of those around you?*
6 *How will you embark on the healing process, especially in the face of emotional and institutional violence that you may have encountered?*

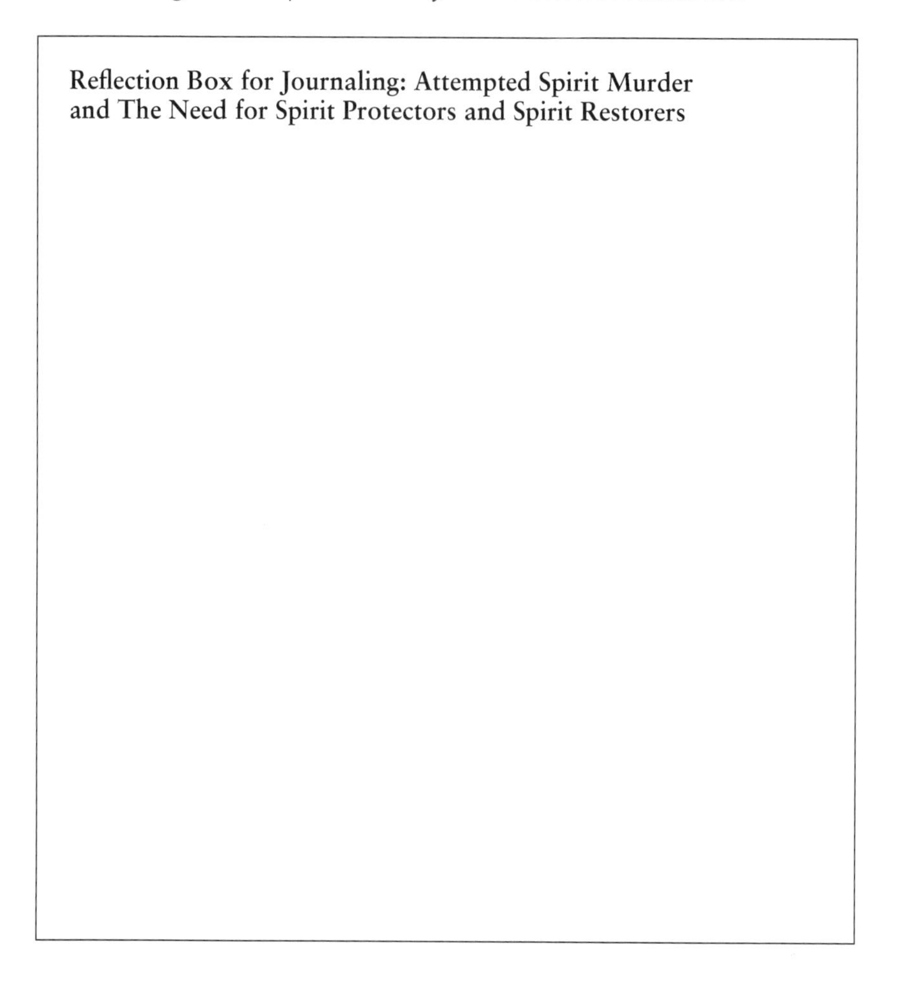
Reflection Box for Journaling: Attempted Spirit Murder and The Need for Spirit Protectors and Spirit Restorers

In the next section, we introduce core principles of trauma-informed approaches. These principles can aid the journey of cultivating TIHC public service and DEILJ work by offering ideas, tools, and inspiration for beginning and deepening practices.

Trauma-Informed Approaches

Trauma-informed approaches acknowledge the widespread impact of historical, inter-generational, institutional, personal, trauma (including impact of spirit murder and spiritual trauma) on individuals and communities. Trauma-informed approaches aim to create an organizational/educational/workplace environment that promotes safety, empowerment, and supports healing.

There have been increasing calls for applications of trauma-informed approaches across various public service settings, including healthcare, education, social services, and mental health. Through this chapter, we extend this call and argue that the principles of trauma-informed approaches are essential ingredients to foster DEILJ and a TIHC public service.

There are several key principles of trauma-informed practice. These principles can guide public service professionals in interrupting oppression and promoting healing, resilience, and recovery within diverse public service contexts. Below we describe the six main principles of trauma-informed approaches as articulated and advocated by the Substance Abuse and Mental Health Services Administration (2014) of the U.S. Department of Health and Human Services.

1 **Safety**: Throughout the organization, staff, and the people they serve, whether children, youth, or adults, experience a profound sense of physical and psychological safety. The physical environment is designed to maximize safety, while interpersonal interactions actively foster a sense of safety. Importantly, the organization places a strong emphasis on *interpreting safety in accordance with the perspectives and definitions of those receiving its services.*
2 **Trustworthiness and Transparency**: Organizational procedures, decisions, and protocols are carried out transparently, aiming to foster and uphold trust with clients, family members, community, among staff and all others connected to the organization.
3 **Peer Support and Collaboration**: Peer support and mutual aid are key vehicles for establishing safety and hope, building trust, enhancing collaboration, and affirming stories and lived experience to promote recovery and healing from trauma. The term "peers" refers to individuals with lived experiences of trauma, family members of children who have experienced traumatic events and are key caregivers in their recovery. Peers have also been referred to as "trauma survivors."
4 **Collaboration and Mutuality**: Significant emphasis is placed on fostering partnerships and equalizing power dynamics, not only between staff and clients but also among the organizational staff, ranging from clerical and housekeeping personnel to professional staff and administrators. This underscores the understanding that healing takes place within relationships and through the meaningful distribution/sharing of power and decision-making. The organization acknowledges that everyone has a part to play in adopting a trauma-informed approach. It's a recognition that one doesn't need to be a therapist to contribute therapeutically or to be healing presence.
5 **Empowerment, Voice, and Choice**: Across the organization, there is a concerted effort to acknowledge and leverage the strengths and experiences

of individuals, including the people served by the organization. Autonomy and agency are not only recognized but deeply respected.

The organization holds a firm belief in the fundamental importance of those it serves, emphasizing strengths, resilience and the innate capacity of individuals, organizations, and communities to heal and advance along the path of recovery from trauma. Procedures are in place to ensure that individuals have a voice in decisions that impact their lives, facilitating the restoration of their sense of control.

In every facet of its operations, workforce development, and service delivery, the organization is dedicated to promoting empowerment, both for its staff and the clients and communities they serve. The organization prioritizes the safety and well-being of both its staff and service recipients. There is a keen awareness of power dynamics and a commitment to addressing historical and persisting imbalances where clients'/communities voices and choices were marginalized, and coercive measures were employed. Clients/communities are actively supported in developing self-advocacy skills.

6 **Cultural, Historical, and Gender Sensitivity**: The organization takes proactive steps to challenge cultural stereotypes and prejudices, regardless of factors such as race, ethnicity, sexual orientation, age, religion, gender identity, disability identity, income, or geography. It ensures access to gender-responsive services. The organization harnesses the healing potential of traditional cultural connections. It integrates policies, protocols, and procedures that are sensitive to the racial, ethnic, and cultural needs and contexts of those it serves. There is an intentional effort to acknowledge and addresses historical, inter-generational, persistent institutional, and personal trauma.

In the next section, we conclude by offering a summary of key teachings and big ideas covered in this chapter.

Summary and Key Teachings

In this chapter, we uplift the need to recognize emotional labor and neurobiologically challenging nature of public service and DEILJ work (Guy et al. 2014; Mastracci et al. 2015). We affirm consistent calls to cultivate an ethics of care, relationality, and interdependence in public service contexts (Burnier 2003; Guy et al. 2014, 2009; Dolamore and Whitebread 2022; Meyer, Johnson, and McCandless 2022; Stensöta 2011).

Furthermore, we build on existing interdisciplinary literature and extend a call for TIHC public service. We envision TIHC public service to acknowledge historical, inter-generational, and persistent institutional trauma from oppression, to examine the ways trauma from oppression is reproduced in public service contexts, and to cultivate supportive and affirming organizational systems and cultures where individuals and collectives can engage in the process of repair and healing from trauma of oppression.

This chapter seeks to offer an expansive and nuanced understanding of trauma. We developed an understanding of trauma from both neurobiological perspectives as well as socio-psychological perspectives that inform us about historical, inter-generational, persistent institutional, and personal trauma. One of the key teachings offered in this chapter is that trauma is the body's protective response to an event or series of events that are potentially dangerous. Our trauma responses originate in our bodies and, when unresolved, trauma can remain stuck in our bodies. Our healing work, including healing from trauma of oppression, therefore, must also be engaged at an embodied level.

Another key teaching offered in this chapter is related to collective trauma from oppression. Because the trauma of systemic oppression (such as racialized trauma) happens to a collective or a community (i.e., to a group) with shared identity, culture, or context, it is important for DEILJ praxis to cultivate spaces and collectives that can foster communal healing. Overall, we advocate for TIHC approaches in public service settings and for DEILJ praxis. In the next chapter, we go deeper into the idea of nurturing collectives for courageous DEILJ conversations and critical actions.

Deep Dive Resources (Full Citations in References]

BOOKS

1 Dana, Deborah. 2021a. *Anchored: How to Befriend Your Nervous System Using Polyvagal Theory.*
2 Menakem, Resmaa. 2017. *My Grandmother's Hands: Racialized Trauma and the Pathway to Mending Our Hearts and Bodies.*
3 Joy DeGruy. 2005. Post Traumatic Slave Syndrome: America's Legacy of Enduring Injury and Healing.

Interviews and Articles

4 Brave Heart, Maria Yellow Horse, Josephine Chase, Jennifer Elkins, and Deborah B. Altschul. 2011. "Historical Trauma Among Indigenous Peoples of the Americas: Concepts, Research, and Clinical Considerations." *Journal of Psychoactive Drugs* 43 (4): 282–90. https://doi.org/10.1080/02791072.2011.628913
5 Menakem, Resmaa. 2019. Francesca Maximé – ReRooted – Ep. 13 – Resmaa Menakem – Be Here Now Network 2022 Interview by Francesca Maximé. https://beherenownetwork.com/francesca-maxime-rerooted-ep-13-resmaa-menakem/.

6 Dana, Deborah. 2021b. Becoming an Active Operator of Your Nervous System (With Deborah Dana) Interview by Tami Simon. https://resources.soundstrue.com/podcast/becoming-an-active-operator-of-your-nervous-system/.

Note

1 Epigenetics is the study of how your behaviors and environment can cause changes that affect the way your genes work. Unlike genetic changes, epigenetic changes are reversible and do not change your DNA sequence, but they can change how your body reads a DNA sequence (Centers for Disease Control and Prevention 2022, p. 1).

References

Brave Heart, Maria Yellow Horse. n.d. "The Return to the Sacred Path: Reflections on the Development of Historical Trauma Healing." https://www.ihs.gov/sites/telebehavioral/themes/responsive2017/display_objects/documents/slides/historicaltrauma/htreturnsacredpath0513.pdf

Brave Heart, Maria Yellow Horse, Josephine Chase, Jennifer Elkins, and Deborah B. Altschul. 2011. "Historical Trauma Among Indigenous Peoples of the Americas: Concepts, Research, and Clinical Considerations." *Journal of Psychoactive Drugs* 43 (4): 282–90. https://doi.org/10.1080/02791072.2011.628913.

Brown, Brené. 2010. "Brené Brown: The Power of Vulnerability | TED Talk." 2010. https://www.ted.com/talks/brene_brown_the_power_of_vulnerability

———. 2018. *Dare to Lead: Brave Work. Tough Conversations. Whole Hearts.* First ed. Edition. New York, NY: Random House.

Burnier, DeLysa. 2003. "Other Voices/Other Rooms: Towards a Care-Centered Public Administration." *Administrative Theory & Praxis* 25 (4): 529–44.

———. 2009. "Markets No More: Toward a Care-Centered Public Administration." *Administrative Theory & Praxis* 31 (3): 396–402.

Centers for Disease Control and Prevention. 2022. "What Is Epigenetics? | CDC." Centers for Disease Control and Prevention. August 15, 2022. https://www.cdc.gov/genomics/disease/epigenetics.htm

Chang, Rui B. 2019. "Body Thermal Responses and the Vagus Nerve." *Neuroscience Letters* 698: 209–16.

Chang, Rui B., David E. Strochlic, Erika K. Williams, Benjamin D. Umans, and Stephen D. Liberles. 2015. "Vagal Sensory Neuron Subtypes That Differentially Control Breathing." *Cell* 161 (3): 622–33.

Chavez, Nora. n.d. "Shouldering Grief: Validating Native American Historical Trauma." *NM CARES Health Disparities Center*, n.d. https://hsc.unm.edu/programs/nmcareshd/docs/story_heart.pdf

Dana, Deborah. 2021a. *Anchored: How to Befriend Your Nervous System Using Polyvagal Theory*. Boulder, CO: Sounds True.

———. 2021b. Becoming an Active Operator of Your Nervous System (With Deborah Dana) Interview by Tami Simon. https://resources.soundstrue.com/podcast/becoming-an-active-operator-of-your-nervous-system/

DeGruy, Joy. 2005. *Post Traumatic Slave Syndrome: America's Legacy of Enduring Injury and Healing.* 1st ed. Milwaukie, OR: Uptone Press.

Dolamore, Stephanie. 2021. "Detecting Empathy in Public Organizations: Creating a More Relational Public Administration." *Administrative Theory & Praxis (Taylor & Francis Ltd)* 43 (1): 58–81. https://doi.org/10.1080/10841806.2019.1700458

Dolamore, Stephanie, and Geoffrey Whitebread. 2022. "Recalibrating Public Service: Valuing Engagement, Empathy, Social Equity, and Ethics in Public Administration." *Public Integrity* 24 (4–5): 375–86. https://doi.org/10.1080/10999922.2021.2014223

Gooden, Susan T. 2014. *Race and Social Equity: A Nervous Area of Government.* Armonk, NY: Routledge.

Guy, Mary E., Meredith A. Newman, and Sharon H. Mastracci. 2014. *Emotional Labor: Putting the Service in Public Service.* Armonk, NY: Routledge.

Haines, Staci. 2019. *The Politics of Trauma: Somatics, Healing, and Social Justice.* Illustrated ed. Berkeley, CA: North Atlantic Books.

Harro, Bobbie. 2018. "Cycle of Liberation." In *Readings for Diversity and Social Justice*, edited by Maurianne Adams, Warren J. Blumenfeld, D. Chase J. Catalano, Keri Dejong, Heather W. Hackman, Larissa E. Hopkins, Barbara Love, Madeline L. Peters, Davey Shlasko, and Ximena Zuniga, 4th ed., 627–34. New York, NY: Routledge.

Headley, Andrea M., Kaila Witkowski, Christa Remington, N. Emel Ganapati, and Santina Contreras. 2023. "Trauma-Informed Organizational Climate and Its Impact on Burnout in First Response Agencies During COVID-19." *Public Administration Review* n/a (n/a). https://doi.org/10.1111/puar.13764

Hines, Dorothy E., and Jennifer M. Wilmot. 2018. "From Spirit-Murdering to Spirit-Healing: Addressing Anti-Black Aggressions and the Inhumane Discipline of Black Children." *Multicultural Perspectives* 20 (2): 62–69. https://doi.org/10.1080/15210960.2018.1447064

Hochschild, Arlie Russell. 1983. "The Managed Heart: Commercialization of Human Feeling. Highlighted, Underlined and Noted edition." *California, US: University of California.*

Howie, Hunter, Chuda M. Rijal, and Kerry J. Ressler. 2019. "A Review of Epigenetic Contributions to Post-Traumatic Stress Disorder." *Dialogues in Clinical Neuroscience* 21 (4): 417–28. https://doi.org/10.31887/DCNS.2019.21.4/kressler

Krawec, Patty. 2022. *Becoming Kin: An Indigenous Call to Unforgetting the Past and Reimagining Our Future.* Minneapolis, MN: Broadleaf Books.

Love, Bettina L. 2016. "Anti-Black State Violence, Classroom Edition: The Spirit Murdering of Black Children." *Journal of Curriculum and Pedagogy* 13 (1): 22–25.

Love, Jeannine M., Tia Sherèe Gaynor, and Brandi Blessett. 2016. "Facilitating Difficult Dialogues in the Classroom: A Pedagogical Imperative." *Administrative Theory & Praxis* 38 (4): 227–33. https://doi.org/10.1080/10841806.2016.1237839

Mastracci, Sharon H., Mary E. Guy, and Meredith A. Newman. 2015. *Emotional Labor and Crisis Response: Working on the Razor's Edge.* New York, NY: Routledge. https://doi.org/10.4324/9781315704869

Menakem, Resmaa. 2017. *My Grandmother's Hands: Racialized Trauma and the Pathway to Mending Our Hearts and Bodies*. Illustrated ed. Las Vegas, NV: Central Recovery Press.

———. 2019. Francesca Maximé – ReRooted – Ep. 13 – Resmaa Menakem – Be Here Now Network 2022 Interview by Francesca Maximé. https://beherenownetwork.com/francesca-maxime-rerooted-ep-13-resmaa-menakem/

———. 2020. Resmaa Menakem — 'Notice the Rage; Notice the Silence' Interview by Krista Tippett. Transcript. https://onbeing.org/programs/resmaa-menakem-notice-the-rage-notice-the-silence/

Meyer, Seth J., Richard Greggory Johnson, and Sean McCandless. 2022. "Meet the New Es: Empathy, Engagement, Equity, and Ethics in Public Administration." *Public Integrity* 24 (4–5): 353–63. https://doi.org/10.1080/10999922.2022.2074764

Page, Cara, and Erica Woodland. 2023. *Healing Justice Lineages: Dreaming at the Crossroads of Liberation, Collective Care, and Safety*. Berkeley, CA: North Atlantic Books.

Porges, Stephen W. 1995. "Orienting in a Defensive World: Mammalian Modifications of Our Evolutionary Heritage. A Polyvagal Theory." *Psychophysiology* 32 (4): 301–18. https://doi.org/10.1111/j.1469-8986.1995.tb01213.x

Porges, Stephen W. 2009. "The Polyvagal Theory: New Insights into Adaptive Reactions of the Autonomic Nervous System." *Cleveland Clinic Journal of Medicine* 76 (Suppl 2): S86–90. https://doi.org/10.3949/ccjm.76.s2.17

Porges, Stephen W. n.d. Wearing Your Heart on Your Face: The Polyvagal Circuit in the Consulting Room Interview by Ryan Howes. PESI: A Nonprofit Organization.https://www.pesi.com/blog/details/967/wearing-your-heart-on-your-face-the-polyvagal-circuit

Revilla, Anita Tijerina. 2021. "Attempted Spirit Murder Who Are Your Spirit Protectors and Your Spirit Restorers?" *The Journal of Educational Foundations* 34 (1): 31–46.

Seladi-Schulman, Jill. 2022. "Vagus Nerve: Function, Stimulation, and More." Healthline. July 22, 2022. https://www.healthline.com/human-body-maps/vagus-nerve

Starke, Anthony M., Nuri Heckler, and Janiece Mackey. 2018. "Administrative Racism: Public Administration Education and Race." *Journal of Public Affairs Education* 24 (4): 469–89. https://doi.org/10.1080/15236803.2018.1426428

Stensöta, Helena. 2011. "A Public Ethics of Care for Administration and Implementation." In 1–14. *Western Political Science Association Annual Meeting Paper*. https://ssrn.com/abstract=1766979.

Substance Abuse and Mental Health Services Administration. 2014. "SAMHSA's Concept of Trauma and Guidance for a Trauma-Informed Approach." HHS Publication No. (SMA) 14–4884. Rockville, MD: Substance Abuse and Mental Health Services Administration, U.S. Department of Health and Human Services.

West, Zack. 2021. "Vagus Nerve: The Most Important Part of Your Body." *Optimus Medica* (blog). May 30, 2021. https://www.optimusmedica.com/vagus-nerve/

Williams, Patricia J. 1992. *The Alchemy of Race and Rights*. Cambridge, MA: Harvard University Press.

4 Nurturing Collectives

Building Capacity for Courageous DEILJ Conversations

Abstract

Social equity is a core value in public administration and public service professions. There is a growing call from social justice movements to practice solidarity to resist manifestations of oppression in public service contexts. To advance social equity and justice work, it is critical that we continue to focus on transforming oppressive public policies, administrative procedures, protocols, and practices. However, the work of transformation and liberation happens through collective efforts. Public service professionals and organizations will need to nurture collectives that share a vision for liberatory social justice and seek to follow the leadership of those most impacted by systemic inequities and injustices. In this chapter, we explore the need for building individual and organizational capacity to hold space for courageous DEILJ conversations. Courageous DEILJ conversations are embodied, interpersonal, and emotional in nature. Courageous DEILJ conversations can lead to critical and meaningful actions and relationships. However, the emotional labor, disciplined practice, and intentionality involved in facilitating and engaging in courageous conversations is often underestimated. In this chapter, we offer nine principles as a starting point to build necessary norms and practices that can support and sustain courageous DEILJ conversations for meaningful and transformative action.

An Introduction: What are Courageous DEILJ Conversations and Why We Need Them?

Across the United States and globally, there is widespread movement for advancing equity, social justice, and collective liberation. However, there has also been intense movement backlash. We witness divisive, dehumanizing, blaming, and shaming conversations that reflect superiority complex, fear, and insecurity. Book bans, anti-LGBTQIA+ bills, anti-immigration sentiments, and religious prejudices are tactics of oppression that are often embedded in fear, insecurity, and a scarcity mindset.

DOI: 10.4324/9781032670669-6

In this context, there is a growing need to nurture individual and collective capacities to hold space for critical and courageous conversations about diversity, equity, inclusion, and liberatory justice (DEILJ) in service of collective liberation. Building capacities to initiate and sustain courageous DEILJ conversations is critical to fostering meaningful relationships and solidarity that can help us envision and realize collective liberation.

Within organizational contexts, courageous DEILJ conversations are distinct from many other types of team or group conversations, primarily, because of their embodied nature. Critical and courageous DEILJ conversations require both thinking and feeling work. They bring our bodies and our minds into a conversation. At their core, courageous DEILJ conversations are relational in nature. They necessitate building relationships, including first with ourselves.

As students, educators, leaders, professionals, and administrators engaged in public service, we enter DEILJ work within our own contexts of oppression and lived experiences within systems of oppression. Many of us enter this work with oppressed and oppressor identities, that is, we may be both advantaged and disadvantaged by our dominant systems, structures, and cultures. When we are talking about differences in lived experiences and inequities as it relates to racial, or gender, or disability identities, courageous DEILJ conversations invite us to recognize our differences, go beyond our comfort zones and embrace the vulnerability (i.e., the risk, uncertainty, and emotional exposure) that is intrinsic to these conversations (Brown 2010, 2018).

As we have explored in chapter 3, DEILJ conversations can activate our nervous systems and therefore necessitate a consistent practice of building self-awareness, self-care (and collective care), and of befriending our nervous systems (Dana 2021). DEILJ work demands more than our intellectual and cognitive labor, it is relational, embodied, and often is emotionally and psychologically taxing. Based on our own contexts and trauma histories, we may find ourselves navigating a landmine of triggering information, heavy content, triggering actions and behaviors. This remains a reality of courageous DEILJ conversations even when we try to come to this work with the best of our intentions, commitment to solidarity and accountability, and with deep care and intentionality.

Courageous DEILJ conversations require us to build necessary support systems for practice of accountability, to be willing to do the work of repair when rupture happens, and to build individual and collective resilience to stay in this work sustainably. Building capacity for critical and courageous DEILJ conversations requires deepening our practice of mindful embodied presence. We must learn to discern and hold space for both tenderness and fierceness, be compassionate to self and others, challenge and affirm each other with grace, respect individual and collective strengths, support each other's growing edges, develop self and collective efficacy to practice courage to speak our truth and live into our values, be confident in our perspectives, and practice curiosity about others' needs and viewpoints.

We are living in times of rapidly changing climate and deepening call from current generations of movement builders and leaders for co-creating a just and humane world for all beings[1]. As an inter-generational community of students, educators, scholars, professionals, administrators, and leaders of public administration, we face the ethical choices to engage with transformative and radical changes to our lives and our organizations. If we are to make transformative change, we need to build collaborative partnerships and solidarity across differences, like never before. So how do we nurture collectives for liberatory praxis? How do we move forward together? How do we move forward sustainably?

In context of the United States, due to inter-generational social justice movements led by multiply marginalized Black, Indigenous, and People of Color (BIPOC) leaders and communities and with solidarity from white allies, there exists a strong foundation of the Civil Rights Act and anti-discrimination laws. These transformative and landmark laws and policies have been pivotal wins to advance equity and justice for all; however, we must also remember that systems of oppression are persistent, mutating, and durable (as discussed in Chapter 2). Oppression continues to persist in forms of overt and covert discrimination and prejudice and hence the work of resistance and our striving for collective liberation goes on.

In this inter-generational relay of liberatory social justice work, one of the key tasks for our present generation of public service professionals and administrators is to build a liberatory culture. A liberatory culture that will help us sustain resistance to oppression as well as to generate a greater momentum of co-creative, innovative, and transformative change work that follows the leadership of those most impacted by inequities and injustices. For this we need to nurture collectives anchored in mutuality, reciprocity, and guided by shared visions for liberatory social justice.

Part of that nurturing and culture building work is to create a sustained and strong container to hold space for courageous DEILJ conversations. Spaces where our differences are valued, where disagreements are used as opportunities to gain insights into each other's perspectives, and our conversations and conflicts are generative and transformative. However, we must also not underestimate the energetic charge of DEILJ conversations and create necessary guardrails and boundaries to center minoritized and marginalized perspectives, to acknowledge and avoid power dynamics, hurt, harm, and re-traumatization that can occur intentionally or unintentionally while engaging in these conversations.

The Energetic Charge of Courageous DEILJ Conversations

Courageous DEILJ conversations will require us to be present with our minds and bodies, and sense the vibrations, feelings, and energy in our collective spaces. We must learn to discern when to step up and when to step back. They challenge us to act from a place of compassion for self and others in moments of tension and major disagreements. If we choose to engage with these vibrations, feelings, and energy meaningfully and mindfully, DEILJ conversations have the potential to create strong energetic connection across bodyminds present in a space.

From a polyvagal perspective (discussed in Chapter 3), sometimes, in moments of uncertainty and emotional vulnerability in DEILJ conversations, we may sense the energetic charge as a feeling of nervousness in our bodyminds. In moments of tension, conflict, or disagreements, we may feel a sense of aggression or hostility toward others, signaling activation of our nervous system's fight responses (e.g., to put down a person with whom we disagree). Other times, the energy may be felt as a rush to move on to the next topic on the meeting agenda or to leave the meeting space or to simply tune out when we wish to avoid or resist receiving a difference of perspective, signaling activation of our nervous system's flight response. Sometimes, we may feel a sense of disengagement or a sense of despair or hopelessness and depletion signaling a disconnect and disappear response of our nervous system (based on authors' interpretation of Dana 2021).

It is important that we pay attention to our embodied reactions and energy. When we ignore, deny, or blame others for triggering/activating these uncomfortable/challenging embodied experiences, without any curiosity of the old pain that these activations may be signaling that need our attention and care, we stifle opportunities for growth, maturity, and transformation within ourselves and our organizations (Gooden 2014; Menakem 2017; williams 2021b). However, when we choose to sit with difficult emotions and feel our feelings, when we give ourselves permission to acknowledge our (unmet) needs and practice compassion for self and others (as best as we can), and practice curiosity about others' needs and intentions (as best as we can), we might create a breathing room for a slow yet unstoppable growth, maturity and even transformation to happen (Menakem 2017; Rosenberg 2015; williams 2021b).

As public service professionals, when we commit our time, energy, and a disciplined practice to building our capacity to embrace (rather than avoid, deny, or blame others for) these embodied experiences, we create a breathing room for a sense of wholeness, connection, and belonging to come alive. We can hold differences in perspectives and lived experiences. We can disagree without dehumanizing oneself or others. We can shift away from exclusionary and disempowering politics to inclusionary and empowering politics of centering the marginalized and minoritized voices and perspectives. Embodied DEILJ conversations, when practiced with self-awareness, care, and intentionality to live into our values, could act as a fuel, as a source of motivation, pleasure, and nourishment to co-create micro-moments and micro-movements of liberatory present and to build liberatory futures.

Courageous DEILJ conversations are happening/waiting to happen in our meeting rooms, in our classrooms, in our workshops and trainings, in our townhalls, in our council meetings, in our committees, in our employee resource groups, in our affinity groups, in our organizational executive and boardrooms. Facilitating or holding space for courageous DEILJ conversations that intend to go deeper than superficial acknowledgments of oppression and the one that seeks to build support for collective belonging, action, and transformation is not a task or responsibility that we can take for granted or lightly. It necessitates sustained work before, during, and after the conversation is held.

Integrating Inner Transformation and Collective Transformation[2]

Nurturing collectives and holding space for courageous DEILJ conversation necessitates a dual focus toward both inner and collective transformation. When done with integrity, courageous DEILJ conversations necessitate an embodied, wholehearted acknowledgment of hurt and harm caused by systemic inequities and oppression. They necessitate critical analyses of systems and structures of power and oppression that a collective could work to transform. While raising collective consciousness is crucial, the focus on inner transformation is also necessary.

Building critical consciousness involves asking ourselves difficult questions about how deeply we are entangled and invested in systems of oppression that we are advocating to change, and why? As public service professionals, we must examine why and how systems of oppression are produced and reproduced within our governments and bureaucracies. Who has power and who does not? Why is it so? How and why are we complicit in maintaining dominant systems and power structures? How can we interrupt it within our spheres of influence? How can we expand our spheres of influence? What is our vision of collective liberation? What are the challenges, risks, and rewards? What collective resources and support systems will we need to nurture to realize shared visions for social justice and collective liberation?

Audre Lorde reminds us,

> The true focus of revolutionary change is never merely the oppressive situations which we seek to escape, but that piece of the oppressor which is planted deep within each of us, and which knows only the oppressors' tactics, the oppressors' relationships.
>
> (Lorde 1984, p. 123)

An Invitation to Pause: We invite you to pause and allow this quote to land in your bodymind, breathe into this quote and reflect on what it means for you.

Doing the work of inner transformation requires deepening our capacity and building a consistent practice of courage, rigor, and discipline to:

- Avoid reproducing capitalistic cultural norms steeped in "power over" approaches and replacing them with "power with" and solidarity-based approaches.
- Avoid binary "either/or" thinking and replacing it with broad and inclusive "both/and" approaches that can hold contradictions.
- Avoid short-term thinking and instant gratification and lean into the wisdom of patience and long-term sustainability (Mitchell 2018).

In context of public service work, there are many ways in which these dominant cultural norms show up in our decision-making, protocols, processes, and practices. For example, we put disproportionate emphasis on "either/or" capitalistic conceptualization of efficiency even when it could become exploitative (of land, labor, and people), reproduce domination, and work against the principles of effectiveness and equity (Gooden 2014, 2017). We are socialized to internalize the dominant norms of "short-term thinking" and pressure to "getting things done" without building adequate flow of support systems and resources to also ensure that we are also "getting it right" (Alkadry, Blessett, and Patterson 2015).

Similarly, we are socialized to internalize the pressure to "do more with less" under the garb of capitalist values of efficiency even when it becomes exploitative and leads to employee burnout and turnover. We are socialized to overlook trust building and core public administration values of equity and ethics of care (Mastracci 2021). We measure efficiency of our work narrowly in terms of "how much, and how many," and overlook or assign less weighting to the performance measures that help us assess effectiveness of our work in terms of "how well" and equity in terms of "for whom" (Chordiya and Protonentis 2024; Frederickson 2005) and "by whom" (Portillo, Bearfield, and Humphrey 2020).

Other challenges and odds that continue to get in the way of liberatory DEILJ work include deeply entrenched taken-for-granted assumptions and beliefs of bureaucratic neutrality even when evidence suggests many conscious and unconscious systemic biases that are built into our existing systems continue to minoritize and marginalize Black, Indigenous, and negatively racialized People of Color with multiple marginalized identities (Portillo et al. 2020, 2022).

For example, Portillo et al. (2020) examine the testing and written exams-based hiring and promotion processes in our local governments. They demonstrate how institutionalized inequities are perpetuated through rationalized myth of bureaucratic neutrality, disregarding ample evidence that testing methods result in institutionalized racial inequities in hiring and promotion and are unrelated to job performance outcomes.

To offer some other explanatory organizational examples, our systemic biases and dominant cultural norms (such as either/or thinking, short-term thinking, scarcity and urgency mindset, and power-over approaches) manifest through our:

- **Organizational designs and structures:** For example, when we continue to use buildings without a ramp access or sensory rooms, or all gender bathroom options. When we use communication tools that are not accessible to people who are d/Deaf and hard of hearing, and/or Blind, low-vision, or sight-limited people. When we require in-person attendance, even when remote or hybrid (i.e., in person + remote) participation is a feasible option or reasonable accommodation to meet one's access needs. When we lack organizational designs and infrastructures to support attendees to join and facilitators to facilitate conversations/gatherings in meaningful ways that allow for hybrid options (for example, when commute is challenging due to weather conditions or other reasons, or as they care for themselves or a loved one). When we continue to use job evaluation methods and pay structures that undervalue or omit job demands and skills that are related to female-dominated jobs (Chordiya et al. 2023; Chordiya and Hubbell 2022).
- **Organizational processes:** For example, when we use written tests in hiring and promotions that lack evidence of validity and result in marginalizing women, people of color, older people, and people with disabilities. When we continue to use processes that place undue administrative burdens on students and employees with disabilities when they seek educational and workplace accommodations. When we do not proactively change/revise/develop our processes to include feedback and address needs from diverse users of our processes.
- **Organizational programs:** For example, when our cultural programs are extractive or tokenize communities of color or ignore them altogether.

These are just a few explanatory examples of attitudes, beliefs, and taken-for-granted assumptions that are part of wider cultural norms in public service organization's contexts that create systems of advantage and disadvantage based on one's social identity. We need courageous DEILJ conversations in public service contexts to nurture collectives that can help us identify and interrupt systemic biases, and to challenge, affirm, support, and hold each other accountable in doing transformative social equity and justice work.

Clean Pain and Dirty Pain in Public Service Contexts

Public service professionals working to serve diverse communities and operating within the contexts of systemic oppression often confront hard and painful ethical choices. Resmaa Menakem refers to these choices as "dirty pain and clean pain" (Menakem 2017, 166).

Dirty pain flows through avoidance, blame, and denial. For example, when we choose "out of sight, out of mind" attitudes and behaviors, or when we fail to take responsibility for our own learning and growth. It is a pain we may feel when we try to rationalize oppression and our roles within systems of oppression, when we feel dissonance from acting out of alignment with our values and justifying those actions. It is a pain we seek to numb; and, because it is based on avoidance, blame, and denial, it cannot become a source of any transformative change. Dirty pain can show up in our decision-making and DEILJ conversations when we act from a place of hurt and wounding. It reproduces the cycle of revenge, hurt and harm within us and for those around us (Menakem 2017, 2021).

Clean pain is a pain that we must experience and process for growth and transformation to happen. It is the pain we feel when we choose integrity over fear, patience over aggression (Menakem 2017; Mitchell 2018). It is the pain we feel when we must make difficult choices, when we choose what is right over what is easy[3], when we choose to be in alignment with our values, and when we choose to embrace patience in moments of uncertainty. It is the pain we feel when we reckon with our mistakes, hurt, and the harm we may have caused, gather courage to apologize and take the responsibility to make amends. It is the pain we feel when, instead of numbing, we allow our bodyminds to surrender to the experience (Brown 2018; Menakem 2017; Mingus 2019).

The concept of "clean pain" is not new to public administration. For example, one of the key theses of Susan T. Gooden's (2014) book titled "Race and Social Equity: A Nervous Area of Government" is that – changes in laws, and rules, and policies are incomplete and remain merely aspirational about promoting racial justice when they are not matched

A Reflection Box: Courageous Conversations

by pro-BIPOC, racially equitable, protocols, processes, and practices to implement those rules and policies. Racially just and equitable implementation approaches will require public service professionals and administrators to become embodied social justice leaders who can experience and metabolize clean pain with compassion for self and others.

A Reflection Invitation: Courageous Conversations

We invite you to pause here. If it feels accessible, take one or more deep breaths, hydrate your body, move your body, soothe your body in ways that feel kind and compassionate.

If/when you feel ready, take a few moments to notice. Notice what is emerging for you based on the discussions offered so far. Is there a sense of resonance or dissonance, overwhelm or calm or mixed sensations, confusion or clarity, validation, or challenge? Just notice. Take your time with this pause and reflection.

If you are able and willing, we invite you to recall an experience of having conversations about race and social justice in a diverse, racially mixed group. Because this is intended to be an introductory practice, we invite you to reflect on an experience that is not too intense in terms of conflict or disagreements, perhaps, one or two on the scale of one to ten, one being low intensity and ten being very intense.

We invite you to remember the embodied charge of that conversation. Try to remember and notice whether there was clean pain or dirty pain showing up in that conversation. Try to remember what type of pain was showing up within you- clean pain or dirty pain?

Pause. Breathe. Move. Reflect. Do it again if you need.

Journal your observation and reflections, using the reflection box. If the experience is feeling too intense, STOP. Notice. Be Gentle. Breathe. Move. Do not force your bodymind to engage in the reflection practice if you are feeling depleted and/or activated. Be gentle to yourself. Return to the reflection when you feel you have the embodied capacity to process it.

We bet all of us have experienced some flavor of a DEILJ conversation escalating too fast, getting out of control, alienating, depleting, and creating tension among people involved and leaving much room for work of repair and accountability to happen which does not happen because we choose dirty pain over clean pain, and the cycle of unproductive DEILJ conversations continues.

Dirty pain shows up in public administration and public service when we act from a place of hurt and wounding, from a place of shame, or when we hide behind technical rationality to avoid hard conversations and actions around social equity (Brown 2012, 2018; Starke, Heckler, and Mackey 2018). When we opt for the "color-blind" paradigm to evade conversations about the importance of racial equity, rather than taking race-conscious actions to ensure equitable outcomes for all (Gooden 2014).

When we use a "race-blind" or "gender-blind" or "color-blind" approach, we make flawed assumptions that everyone has had the exact same experiences. Dirty pain shows up when we choose to ignore individual struggles, pain, and hurt. When we use efficiency and the politics of "doing more with less" to garb exploitation. Dirty pain shows up when we engage in equity and public service work from a place of savior complex and paternalism or when we center or attract attention and energy to ourselves in a spaces and conversations that are meant to center those most impacted by inequities (Chordiya and Protonentis 2024; Alkadry et al. 2015; Alkadry and Blessett 2010).

Menakem (2017, 166) notes, "*clean pain is about letting go of what is familiar but harmful, finding the best parts of yourself, and making a leap-with no guarantee of safety or praise.*" He also notes that it is "*by walking into that (clean) pain, experiencing it fully, and moving through it, you metabolize it and put an end to it*" (Menakem 2017, 166).

This process of engaging in clean pain allows us to grow and mature as human beings, to build our capacity for further growth, and create room in our nervous system for other things. In DEILJ focused work, we need to create strong and sustainable containers that can hold and meaningfully channelize the energetic charge and pain that shows up in courageous conversations.

So, how can we create these strong and sustainable containers and condition our body minds, our nervous systems (that triggers, our fight, flight, freeze, appease, and disconnect responses in situations of discomfort) and build capacity to process and metabolize clean pain? How can we create a nourishing soil to plant seeds for expansive and deep radical imagination, creativity, playful problem solving, and generative and reciprocal relationships with one another? To develop an embodied social justice leadership would necessitate a commitment to training, practice, patience, conditioning, stretching, and most importantly, discipline. As the visionary leader of the civil rights' movement, the late Vincent Harding (2019) observed,

> That whole idea of discipline is one that clearly, we have cast aside except when we're talking about technological development or military development. And it seems to me that we need, again, to recognize that to develop the best humanity, the best spirit, the best community, there needs to be discipline, practices of exploring. How do you do that? How do we work together? How — to go back to our conversation — how do we talk together in ways that will open up our best capacities and our best gifts?
>
> My own feeling that I try to share again and again, is that when it comes to creating a multiracial, multiethnic, multireligious, democratic

> society, we are still a developing nation. We've only been really thinking about this for about half a century. But my own deep, deep conviction is that knowledge, like all knowledge, is available to us if we seek it.
>
> I think that that determination to find a truly democratic society and to create the truly beloved community, those are things that can be available to us if we're willing to work with each other and work with the universe on developing them. They don't come free and easy. They are tough, tough tasks for us to take on (p. 3).

Cultivating Courageous Conversations: The Importance of Culture

Culture plays a foundational role in building life affirming institutions and liberatory systems. In her book, Sacred Instructions: Indigenous Wisdom for Living Spirit Based Change, Sherri Mitchell (2018) describes the importance of core cultural values that could serve as our guiding stars in this co-creative journey. Mitchell writes, "Our core cultural values help us to identify who we've been, who we are, and who we will become as a people... (These values) guide our relationships and the work that we do in the world. They are transmitted behavior patterns that influence all aspects of life, from art, beliefs, and thought processes to structures of government" (pp. 146–148).

In her book, "We Will Not Cancel Us: And Other Dreams of Transformative Justice," adrienne maree brown (2020) observes that the vision of social justice and transformative justice movement work touches everything. Her writings amplify the perspectives and principles guiding our social justice movements. She writes that each one of us and each of our institutions and organizations have a "fractal responsibility" in advancing a world that is equitable, inclusive, and just. To build liberatory futures where we share abundant capacity to generate belonging for all, we need to build life-affirming institutions and liberatory systems in the present. She writes that every action we take, even our smallest choices today will become our future norms (brown 2020, pp. 2–3).

These calls from movement visionaries, leaders, and educators for dreaming and co-creating futures anchored in life-affirming and liberatory cultural norms and values are consistent with the calls within the community of public service scholars and practitioners that invite us to:

a Interrupt and dismantle color-blind racism and replace it with systems and cultures informed by race and social equity consciousness (e.g., Gooden 2014).

b To push back and challenge decision-making that uses technical rationality and the myth of bureaucratic neutrality to rationalize, deny or overlook cultural and historical contexts of social inequities that shapes the work of government (e.g., Alexander and Stivers 2020; Portillo et al. 2022; Starke et al. 2018).
c To center the public ethics of care, which acknowledges that we humans are interdependent beings and hence our approaches to government work, must put relations and responsibilities at the heart of any ethical analysis. In words of Helena Stensöta (2011), "*We are, and need to be, related to each other as humans, but we also have relations and responsibilities to other entities such as our surrounding context and nature*" (p. 7).

Principled Norms and Practices for Courageous DEILJ Conversations

In this section, we share our learnings and discernments related to the cultural values, norms, and practices that could serve as anchors to nurture collectives and foster courageous conversations we need to advance the liberatory praxis of DEILJ. We outline them in Table 4.1. We also include a description of the meaning of the terms, language, and practices we offer.

Table 4.1 Principled Norms and Practices for Courageous Conversations

1 Consent and Confidentiality.
2 Embodiment and Honoring Wholeness.
   a Embodied approaches.
   b Embodied empathy (for self and others).
   c Prioritize self-compassion and healing for justice.
3 Acknowledging Power Dynamics and Centering the Margins.
4 Compassionate and Decolonizing Accountability.
5 Building Shame Resilience and Psychological Safety.
6 Rupture, Repair, and Reciprocity.
   a Building generative relationships anchored in resilience and reciprocity.
   b Use dialogues and even moments of conflict generatively as opportunities to learn about each other's differences, to build connections and transformation.
   c Holding generous assumptions and practicing curiosity about each other's intentions.
   d Taking responsibility for impact of our words and actions and, doing the necessary work of repair when mistakes and rupture happens.

(*Continued*)

Table 4.1 (Continued)

7 Constructive Critiques and Humanizing Call-Outs (or Call-Ins).

   a Avoid using the tactics of domination and revenge such as – public humiliation and shaming, punishing, cancelling, dehumanizing verbally or nonverbally (e.g., through body language).
   b Affirm and challenge each other with grace, consent, and dignity.
   c Use "Oops" and "Ouch."
   d Circle Back.

8 Take Responsibility for Our Own Learning and Feelings.

   a Listen to and honor our embodied limits and boundaries.
   b Do not expect ourselves or others to communicate on behalf of our/their gender, racial groups, ethnic groups, religious groups, abilities, and class (or the groups we perceive them to be a part of).
   c Do not expect ourselves or others to perform emotional labor to educate.
   d Honor reflective silence as a powerful tool to process ideas, thoughts, and feelings.
   e Distinguish between intent and impact.
   f We speak our truth. Use "I" statements.

9 Practice Inclusive Communications.

   a Practice inclusive language.
   b Observe the "one mic, one voice" rule.
   c Gently nudge if someone (i.e., peers and/or facilitator) is dominating the conversation.

Courageous Conversations | Reflective Practice for Cultivating Self-Empathy and Collective Empathy

We invite groups and collectives to use/adapt these prompts as needed for intention setting, and practice of empathy for self and others to prepare for courageous conversations. As educators, we have found it helpful in our contexts to invite participants to use post-it notes to write their reflections. We then invite all participants to create a collage of anonymously shared reflections using these post-it notes for everyone to witness.

We invite you to follow-up this practice with a shared embodied acknowledgement (e.g., by looking around the room, at each other, with a collective smile, a collective breathing or gentle movement practice) to recognize our shared humanity. We invite you to make this practice your own/ get creative. This practice can also be used/adapted at an individual level to cultivate self-empathy as you prepare yourself for a courageous conversation.

- How are you arriving in this space today?
- Given my today's context, which principled norm or practice feels most salient for me? And/or, which one feels particularly hard to practice today or in this moment?
- What permission do I need to give myself to engage as a whole person?
- What grace do I need to give myself to engage as a whole person?
- What grace do I seek from others as I grow deepen my practice of engaging in courageous conversations?

Note: We expand and discuss each of these.

Source: Created by the authors.

Please note that we do not intend this to be an exhaustive list of norms and practices, nor do we assert that these are immediately applicable/generalizable to all contexts. Rather, what we share below, are some of the key cultural elements that we have discovered and found helpful in our praxis as social justice-focused educators and facilitators in public administration. We offer this as a working tool for DEILJ educators, practitioners, embodied social justice leaders, and facilitators. We invite you to adapt, apply, and use it in ways that will allow you to make it your own, in language/s and using vocabulary, terminology, and practices that are most appropriate for the cultural context of the group/classroom/organizational/team settings that you are participating/facilitating/managing/leading.

1 **Consent and Confidentiality:** Consent and confidentiality are foundational to building the trust and relationality necessary for courageous conversations. Consent and confidentiality are an important shared norm and agreement, as there may be information shared, for example, in a specific meeting/workshop/classroom context that one may not necessarily feel safe/willing/comfortable sharing in other groups/contexts. *However, it is important to acknowledge and recognize that even when we practice consent and confidentiality, it is not possible to guarantee 100% confidentiality and hence all shares in a collective context for DEILJ work need to be invitational and voluntary.*

   Ideas for Practice:

   a **Practicing Consent:** For example, during training, in classrooms, during meetings, if you are nominated to speak on behalf of your group, ask for consent before sharing your colleague's/peer's ideas, thoughts, and perspectives. Or invite your colleagues/peer to share it themselves.
   b **Practicing Confidentiality:** A group can share the responsibility to flag issues that are super confidential. We share only such information or experiences that are ours to share. We must keep confidential all issues of a personal or professional nature discussed in a specific context of a private meeting/workshop/classroom. We must honor the consent and confidentiality of those who may not be present and not share information about other people from outside of a given meeting space (e.g., colleagues, friends, family members, clients, students) without their prior consent.
   c **How to share with consent and confidentiality?** In a learning context, the invitation is to focus shares on what I/we are learning/discerning as an individual and a group. For example, we might say "What I/we learned from our conversations was...." While presenting/communicating on behalf of our small groups we focus on sharing – highlights, lowlights, big ideas, big questions,

additional perspectives, major and minor limitations, and concerns that emerged in discussions without naming who said what (unless with consent).

2 **Embodiment and Honoring Wholeness:** This principle recognizes that the work of liberatory social justice is both a goal and an embodied process (Bell 2016). It implies we place highest value in honoring the wholeness of our bodyminds, our personhood, and humanity. We acknowledge specific internal and external contexts in which learning/work is situated as well as our embodied lived experiences that shape our learning/work. Below we offer some practice ideas to bring embodiment and wholeness to life.

Ideas for Practice:

a **Embodied approaches:** In learning/leadership/decision-making contexts, embodiment seeks to interrupt the common practice of exploring issues of oppression within our organizations/institutions by focusing only on the cognitive and intellectual examination of oppression without inviting curiosity about and engagement with the reactions of our bodies. Embodied approaches include practices such as pausing, movement, rocking, humming, journaling, and cultivating a gentle awareness of the signs of discomfort when our learning challenges our existing assumptions, especially those that may be deeply embedded through our socialization processes.

When we cover difficult social justice topics and/or discuss manifestations of oppression in our organizational contexts, embodied practice acknowledges that our bodyminds (i.e., our nervous systems) may feel activated or disconnected due to feelings of overwhelm and lack of capacity to cope in the moment. Embodiment is an invitation to be accountable to collective while honoring our capacities and context. To move at a pace that feels accessible and sustainable for our bodyminds. To step away/step back/take time-in, if necessary, and return to learning/work when our bodyminds feel ready enough. Embodiment is an invitation to engage with clean pain, avoid hurt and harm caused by dirty pain, and be in practice of compassionate accountability and transparency with ourselves and our collective.

b **Embodied empathy:** The practice of embodied empathy is necessary to co-create a space for conversations that may feel vulnerable and require courage to show-up and speak-up.

i In moments when difficult feelings and emotions rise, the practice of embodied empathy teaches us to first pause and take the time to connect with/find our embodied anchors (such as breath, movement, objects that offer a sense connection to our bodies) to avoid disembodiment. It teaches us that our capacities to empathize with others depend on how well we can cultivate a practice of self-empathy.

ii While offering and sharing our thoughts, feelings, and perspectives the practice of self-empathy invites us to do an internal check-in and ask – "am I acting from a place of nourishment or depletion? Am I acting in alignment with my values and needs?" For example, we may use the THINK acronym and ask ourselves is information/perspective I am about to share – True, Helpful, Important, Necessary, and Kind (THINK)?[4]

iii While receiving/listening to others' thoughts, feelings, and perspectives, with which we may agree or disagree, embodied self-empathy is the practice of doing another internal check-in "how is that landing in my bodymind?" It invites us to acknowledge the feelings and emotions we are experiencing in the moment, our embodied reactions, the stories we are telling ourselves in the moment and then taking the time to pause with them. This practice can help us create a little more headspace to practice curiosity and openness, to check our assumptions, and to notice at an embodied level when shame and judgement toward self and others shows up.

c **Prioritize self-compassion and healing for justice:** The movement for healing justice and somatic abolitionism (as explored in chapter 3) teaches us that trauma is pervasive and experiencing oppression is a form of trauma bearing its short-term and long-term consequences for our bodyminds (Page and Woodland 2023; Peck 2020; Raffo 2018). It acknowledges that trauma is historical, inter-generational, persistent institutional, and personal (Menakem 2017, 2021). Therefore, an important piece of resisting oppression and working toward social justice and collective liberation is acting in commitment toward our own and collective healing journey. This is an important piece for building collective and inter-generational resilience.

In the context of courageous DEILJ conversations, the practice of prioritizing self-compassion and healing for justice teaches us and invites us to interrupt our internalized scarcity and urgency mindset, to pause, and to honor our own embodied capacities and limits in any given context. This practice means leaning into embodied empathy and giving each other, as well as ourselves, the permission to move at the pace of trust and capacity. This practice means offering trigger warnings and asking for consent before sharing information that could be heavy and/or triggering or re-traumatizing for our group/community members.

3 **Acknowledging Power Dynamics and Centering the Margins:** An acknowledgment of power dynamics and the work of centering those at the margins (i.e., those farthest away from structural power) is necessary to interrupt and dismantle reproduction of oppressive hierarchies in our social/organizational/institutional contexts. It means intentionally building the foundations and consistently doing the work of prioritizing and centering experiences, voices, and perspectives of those historically disempowered, marginalized, and minoritized within power structures.

   In times of critical conversations and emergent conflicts, this principle reminds us of and guides us toward generative - conversations, conflicts, compromises, and relationships that are anchored in mutuality, reciprocity, and respect. It means acknowledging the felt presence of multiple layers of power dynamics that may or may not be explicit. Examples of implicit or explicit power dynamics that may be operational in the context of courageous DEILJ conversations includes those related to positional power dynamics, such as, student-faculty relationships in a classroom context, supervisor-supervisee relationships in work contexts, mentor-mentee, relationships between administrator/social worker/public servant and clients/community members being served.

   It is also important to acknowledge implicit and explicit power dynamics of our social positionalities. Our current institutional and organizations systems, structures, and cultures create advantages/privileges and disadvantages/burdens based on our social identity locations. Centering the margins means both naming and acknowledging these power dynamics and building individual and organizational competence and capacity for vulnerable, courageous, and proactive efforts to share and shift the locus of power within the context specific non-dominant/marginalized groups.

4 **Compassionate and Decolonizing Accountability:** Compassionate and decolonizing accountability is an invitation for us to find ways to align practices of self-compassion as well as decolonizing accountability to strengthen solidarity for justice. Our dominant norms such binary either/or thinking, scarcity, and urgency mindsets socialize us into assuming that compassion for self can be a barrier to practice of accountability. However, spiritual and social justice leaders, scholars, and practitioners of compassion, demystify these assumptions. They teach us that compassion in general is about alleviating suffering that may be located within us or in our outer world (Neff 2021; Rosenberg 2015; Tutu and Tutu 2015; williams 2021a). Self-compassion is "compassion turned inward" (Neff 2021, 2023).

   A leading scholar of self-compassion, Kristen Neff (2023) explains that a less understood aspect of self-compassion is that it is both "tender" and "fierce." Tender self-compassion is about being present to our pain, accepting of our imperfections, comforting, and reassuring ourselves that we are not alone. Fierce self-compassion is about taking the action that we need to take to alleviate suffering. For example, sometimes, fierce self-compassion could be "saying no," setting, and maintaining boundaries. Other times, it could it be "saying yes" to ourselves and prioritizing our own needs instead of subordinating or sacrificing them for others. Fierce self-compassion could be about motivating ourselves to take action to prevent hurt or harm.

Neff's (2021, 2023) research has shown that we need to integrate and balance both tender and fierce self-compassion for wholeness and well-being. Without the balance of fierce self-compassion, our tenderness could lead to self-complacency, a lack of growth and maturing. Without the balance of tender self-compassion, fierceness alone could lead to hostile and hurtful behaviors.

In the context courageous DEILJ conversations, the practice of "compassionate and decolonizing accountability," means discerning to balance and integrate both tender and fierce elements self-compassion with our practice of accountability in ways that are decolonizing. It means that we need to cultivate self-compassion as a source of nourishment and courage to support our practice of accountability. It means that our practice of accountability must be rooted in unlearning colonial ways of being that are extractive, dominating, and exploitative. It means that we need to build relationality and solidarity across our differences to nurture the practice of authentic diversity and liberatory social justice in our organizations. Table 4.2 presents a set of developing prompts we want to offer in supporting the practice of decolonizing accountability anchored in self-compassion.

5 **Building Shame Resilience and Psychological Safety[5]:** While participating/facilitating DEILJ conversations it is important to distinguish between emotions of guilt, discomfort, shame, and unsafety. When multiple/mixed emotional experiences such as guilt, discomfort, shame, and unsafety emerge in a space held for DEILJ conversations, this practice invites us to discern and prioritize dismantling of shame and psychological unsafety (Ferraro 2019a, 2019b).

For example, in academic or organizational learning contexts, shame and psychological unsafety may show up when we are navigating conflict and disagreements. They may show up in our behaviors through wounding and dehumanizing language, name-calling, stereotyping, shaming, microaggressions, mistreatment and invalidation (gaslighting), slights, or insults. These are power-over tactics.

Building capacity for courageous DEILJ conversations involves individual and collective work toward building shame resilience and

Table 4.2 Building a Practice of Compassionate and Decolonizing Accountability

Reflective Prompts to Support a Practice of ***Decolonizing Accountability***	*Reflective Prompts to Support a Practice of* ***Self-Compassion***
I give myself permission to build my own capacity and discernment-	I give myself permission to build my own capacity and discernment-
• To center voices and perspectives that are marginalized and minoritized historically and in our current systems. • To show up and speak up against oppression with efficacy and confidence. • To listen more and speak less. • Share space: Step-up/step-back during discussions, and share airtime to listen, share perspectives, and build relationships. • To be mindful of savior complex within me and act proactively from the discipline of accountability and care. • To show up in ways that allow me to live into my values. • To contribute toward the collective goals and an inclusive experience of learning/working. • To engage in equitable reciprocity in doing the work of repair in instances of hurt and harm. • To be mindful of extractive behaviors within me and proactively cultivate generative and reciprocal relationships with my peers and colleagues.	• To give myself the gift of grace, patience, and kindness as I learn and grow my practice of DEILJ. • To acknowledge and request my access needs. • To pause, to take breaks as needed, to move, to stretch my body as needed. • To step-up and step-back based on my capacity to contribute toward collective learning/work. • To move at the pace of trust and capacity of my bodymind for learning and doing the work. • To hold myself with tenderness and care. To seek support in doing the work of repair in instances of hurt and harm. • To practice self-care and collective care with my peers/colleagues • To give and receive support to meet my own and our collective needs. • To save my emotional energy for learning/work situations that I discern to be nourishing and worthy of my energy and effort. • To protect my inner peace. To prioritize self-compassion and healing for justice.

Source: Created by the authors.

fostering psychological safety for all, particularly those who may be farthest away from social or positional power in a given context. [For more practice suggestions, refer to the following discussions on "rupture, repair, and reciprocity" (#item 6) and "constructive critiquing" (item #7)].

Guilt and discomfort may show up in courageous DEILJ conversations when we feel challenged to reckon with our privileges and advantages due to our social positionality (e.g., due to race, gender, sexuality, age, religion, caste, disability, and more). It is important to acknowledge and understand that guilt and discomfort are "normal" and expected elements of transformative adult learning and when processed from a place of (self) compassion, decolonizing accountability and support, these emotions could serve are motivators for our inner transformation, growth, and maturity (refer to Brown 2020 for difference between guilt and shame; Kluttz, Walker, and Walter 2020; Neff 2023; Morris 2017).

6 **Rupture, Repair, and Reciprocity[6]:** As humans, it is our biological need to feel connection and co-regulation, first for survival and then for living a life and for well-being. However, to meet our core need for connection, it is not a necessity for our relationships to be always in balance; rather, what we need is for our relationships to be reciprocal (Dana 2021). In moments of conflicts, tension, and rupture, building capacity for courageous DEILJ conversations means we understand and cultivate pathways to do the necessary work of repair and avoid deep suffering. As noted wisely by Deb Dana (2021), "it's only when rupture happens without repair that our longing for connection brings suffering" (p. 40).

A courageous space for DEILJ conversations necessitates that we give ourselves and others the permission to bring our whole (authentic) selves, to speak our truth, to share our perspectives. When we all bring our whole selves, there is also potential for difference of opinions and perspectives, mistakes, hurt, tension, conflict, and rupture.

Creating strong boundaries, knowing our limits, discerning what energy, ideas, thoughts "I must engage with and what I can/must ignore or let go", being intentional and mindful about our engagement with learning materials and each other as human beings, are important skills and practices we need to cultivate to create a courageous culture, where we learn to navigate mistakes that can cause hurt. When mistakes cause hurt, for example, when someone says something offensive or frames something poorly from a place of ignorance or limited understanding, that person must take responsibility and do the necessary work of repair/growth. At the same time, we need to be discerning in how we respond suitably to harm, hurt, and mistakes from a place of growth, relationality, tenderness, responsibility, and transformation, and centering needs of those who are experiencing hurt/harm.

We must give each other permission to make mistakes and make amends, learn, and grow. Many times, hurt happens because of misunderstandings, language barriers, when something (feelings, thoughts, ideas) get lost in translation or our choice of words/framing. We want to invite us to remember to start from a place of curiosity and grace, inquire and seek clarity before responding to words and actions that do not land as intended. At the same time, we must take responsibility for our own learning and feelings, and not expect (to perform or receive) emotional labor for/from others without consent and embodied capacity to educate one another.

We can build generative relationships anchored in resilience and reciprocity:

- By demonstrating our maturity as responsible adults who show up (instead of shying away) when rupture happens.
- By holding generous assumptions and practicing curiosity about each other's intentions to avoid misunderstandings, shaming, and blaming. For example, ask, "what do you mean?" "What's the point you are trying to make, I am not following."
- By using dialogues and even moments of conflict generatively as opportunities to learn about each other's differences, to build connections and transformation. Often, one-on-one private conversations serve as necessary and powerful tools to foster generative dialogues, disagreements, and potential conflicts. Private conversations may seem slower than public conversations. Yet, when practiced with intention, consent, dignity, and an acknowledgement of power dynamics, they can be deeply efficient, equitable, and effective in moving us forward, to cultivate relationships and to navigate conflicts generatively.
- By offering and receiving patience and grace.
- By taking responsibility for the impact of our words and actions and, doing the necessary work of repair when mistakes and rupture happens (brown 2020; Mingus 2019).

7 **Constructive Critiques and Humanizing Call-Outs (or Call-Ins):** Building critical analysis (we would like to refer to it as constructive curiosity) is a core skill for courageous DEILJ conversations and praxis. Critical analysis or constructive curiosity is the skill of assessing or analyzing the strengths, limitations, and growing edges of someone's work and contributions to advance knowledge and practice. Courageous DEILJ conversations need us to be vigilant of the symptoms of groupthink, to humanely call attention to mistakes, limitations, hurt and harm and use constructive critiques as growth opportunities.

Humanizing call-outs or call-ins when used in interpersonal contexts for culture change work, are invitational and do not engage in dehumanizing power-over tactics of shaming and blaming[7]. For example, in an academic/organizational learning context there will be moments where we might critique or push back on each other's contributions/perspectives/knowledge to advance the work in meaningful ways. Advancing the work of liberatory DEILJ in meaningful ways is the key piece here. When done in the service of advancing the work meaningfully and to strengthen engagement of the people involved in the work, critiques are more likely to be strengths-based, constructive, helpful, appreciated and well received. Critiques are less likely to be received well when offered from a place of deficit or bad faith and as a power-over strategy such as to put down someone or discourage engagement.

Constructive curiosity invites us to go beyond acknowledging limitations and engage with creative work of construction and imagination. We remember that all humans, including ourselves, are imperfect beings who have potential for excellence, we make mistakes, cause hurt and have limitations, and at the same time we have strengths when cultivated and nourished can help us overcome our limitations.

Ideas for Practice:

The practice of constructive critiques and humanizing callouts (or call-ins) invite us to acknowledge our shared humanity. Together they remind us that all humans, including ourselves, have limitations and imperfections. As much as possible, constructive critiques and humanizing call-outs (or call-ins) are practiced, privately, especially in the context of interpersonal conflicts, disagreements, and differences, and when power dynamics allow space for such dialogues in private before public action is taken. They are not people-focused, rather they are focused on naming the gaps in understanding/analysis/behaviors/processes/decisions/outcomes to improve them and acknowledging the hurt/harm/unmet need as a first step to do the necessary work of repair.

This is a both/and practice – to engage in courageous DEILJ conversations we need to (both) give each other permission to critique/push back on ideas and perspectives or callout (i.e., bring to light/highlight) gaps, limitations, or mistakes; and we need to support and empower each other to do so in ways that are constructive, inclusive, and humanizing (rather than shaming, exclusionary and dehumanizing). This means:

a In our critiques and call-outs (or call-ins), we practice mindful vigilance and challenge ourselves to avoid using the tactics of domination and revenge such as – public humiliation and shaming, punishing, cancelling, dehumanizing verbally or nonverbally (e.g., through body language).
b We must affirm and challenge each other with grace, consent, and dignity. We might say "I want to acknowledge your share, and may I offer a different perspective?," or "May I push back on your share?," "May I explore the perspective you offered and share a counter perspective?," or "I want to acknowledge that I know/you seem to have good intentions, and at the same your words/actions might land as hurtful. May I share how?"

c We might use "Oops" and "Ouch" to acknowledge mistakes or hurt. When we feel hurt or offended by anything said during conversations, we may acknowledge it immediately by saying "Ouch." When we realize we phrase something poorly, we may acknowledge it by saying "Oops" and circling back to rephrase it. For example, "Ouch that hurt," "Oops, I did not say it the way I meant it, I meant to say – <add your rephrased statement here>."
d We Circle Back: We commit to creating a space to circle back, to give and receive apologies, to give and receive feedback with compassion. Circling back is a useful tool/practice in moments of heat and tension when we may lack the capacity to respond in integrity with our values, with calm and compassion for self and others. Circling back allows time to process thoughts and emotions and find support and clarity to move forward with grace and compassion in moments of rupture or tension.

8 **Take Responsibility for Our Own Learning and Feelings:** In practice this means:

a We learn to listen to and honor our embodied limits and boundaries. bell hooks (1984) taught us "being oppressed means the absence of choices" (p.5). In the context of courageous DEILJ conversations, interrupting oppression could mean we give and receive permission to practice full embodied consent while navigating content and conversations. We use embodied pauses and practices to reflect and discern our YES, NO, and MAYBE. We use embodied practices to STOP, PAUSE, and RETURN, to the content and conversations based on our context and embodied (mental, emotional, spiritual) capacity. Knowing and claiming that we all have a choice, and the choices we make matters. This is a way to take responsibility for our own learning and growth.
b We do not expect ourselves or others to communicate on behalf of our/their gender identity, sexual orientation, racial groups, ethnic groups, religious groups, disability identity, and class (or the groups we perceive them to be a part of).
c We do not expect ourselves or others to perform emotional labor to educate (others or) us.
d We speak our truth. We use "*I*" statements to avoid generalization of our beliefs or opinions: "*I like your...*" "*I think...*" "*I feel...*" "*I propose...*"
e We honor reflective silence as a powerful tool to process ideas, thoughts, and feelings. In practice, this means it is okay to have moments of silence during discussions or after someone poses a question or an idea for digestion, reflection, and response. We honor reflective

silence as an opportunity to take responsibility for our own learning and feelings and avoid the urgency-based habit in our dominant culture to fill in the so-called "awkward silences." Creating space for reflective silence can allow for the emergence of sacred moments we need for internal reflection, thinking, and responding with care, curiosity, and compassion

f We distinguish between intent and impact. We acknowledge that human motivations are complex. We assume that others are communicating and acting from a place of good intent and good faith. At the same time, if our actions negatively impact others, we must take responsibility for that impact. Some defensiveness is inevitable in difficult conversations. Human desire to sanitize impact is especially common in tough and emotional conversations. However, we must acknowledge that good intentions do not sanitize bad impact. In navigating difficult conversations, we must try to share our feelings and the impact of other's words and behaviors on us; and inquire about their intentions.

9 **Practice Inclusive Communications:** This means:

a We practice inclusive language. We commit to unlearning language used to reproduce and perpetuate oppression and building a vocabulary of words for practice of inclusive language. We allow our teachers, students, peers, and colleagues to nudge us gently (if possible, privately) when we unintentionally use exclusive or offensive language. Language is constantly evolving. Therefore, it is important to have a shared responsibility to offer updates on inclusive language as it evolves within the social justice movements. (refer to sub-section "deep dive resources" for helpful tools and resources to learn more about inclusive language).

b We observe the "one mic, one voice" rule. We avoid interruptions or cross talk. Gentle interruptions with permission of the speaker could be reasonable to clarify the speaker's need and/or intention.

c We may gently nudge if someone (i.e., peers, facilitators, or colleagues) is dominating the conversation. Examples of gentle nudges:

i "I am appreciating our conversation, and I am curious and wanted to invite other group members to share their thoughts and perspectives."

ii "I am appreciating our conversation and in interest of time, I wanted to move us along to the next item."

iii "I am appreciating our conversation, and I wanted to circle back to previous point from <name of the speaker>. I think we did not consider it fully."

A Reflection Invitation: Principled Norms and Practices for Courageous Conversations

There are many ways to apply and integrate these principled norms and practices into everyday work settings, meeting contexts, learning contexts and courageous dialogues that can nurture collectives focused on transformative DEILJ change work. For a practice example, refer to table 4.1. We invite you to reflect on:

1 *What is resonating and what is causing dissonance?*
2 *Based on your reading of these norms and practices, are there any tensions or contradictions you want to name, particularly based on your lived experiences and organizational contexts?*
3 *What adaptations/changes would you make to these norms if you were to apply and integrate them in the context of the meetings/gatherings that you participate/facilitate?*
4 *How would you engage your group/team/collective to co-create courageous conversations norms and practices? How would ensure your collective has an opportunity to return to and reflect on these norms regularly?*

Summary and Key Teachings

Social equity is a core value in public administration and public service professions. As public service professionals invested in promoting social equity and liberatory justice, we continue to build on legacies of intergenerational social equity and social justice movement work. There is a growing call from social justice movements to practice solidarity to resist manifestations of oppression in public service contexts. They invite us to cultivate a liberatory praxis that seeks to transform conditions that enable oppression to persist.

To advance social equity and justice work, it is critical to continue to focus on transforming oppressive public policies and administrative procedures and protocols. However, we must also prioritize the work of building liberatory cultures. We must recognize that liberation can happen through collective efforts. Therefore, public service professionals and organizations will need to nurture collectives that share a vision for liberatory social justice and seek to follow the leadership of those most impacted by systemic inequities and injustices. Through collective efforts, we can find and implement creative, innovative, and transformative approaches to solve wicked problems posed by systemic social inequities and injustices.

However, nurturing collectives for liberatory praxis of social equity and justice is not an easy task. And an important, yet underestimated piece of this work is building individual and collective capacity to initiate and sustain courageous DEILJ conversations. Holding space for courageous DEILJ conversations is an important part of culture building to drive transformative social justice change work within public service organizations and institutions. Courageous DEILJ conversations can lead to critical and meaningful actions and relationships.

However, like any DEILJ work, facilitating courageous conversations is more than intellectual and cognitive work. It necessitates an embodied praxis of social justice leadership. It requires emotional labor, disciplined practice, and intentionality to hold space for diverse members of a collective, and to elevate and center voices and perspectives that are systemically marginalized and excluded. In this chapter, we offer nine principles as a starting point to build necessary norms and practices that can support and sustain courageous DEILJ conversations.

Deep Dive Resources [Full Citations in References)

Nurturing Collectives and Courageous DEILJ Cultures

1 brown, adrienne maree. 2020. We *Will Not Cancel Us: And Other Dreams of Transformative Justice.*
2 Menakem, Resmaa. 2017. *My Grandmother's Hands: Racialized Trauma and the Pathway to Mending Our Hearts and Bodies.*
3 ———. 2021. Resmaa Menakem — "Notice the Rage; Notice the Silence" Interview by Krista Tippett.
4 Mitchell, Sherri. 2018. *Sacred Instructions: Indigenous Wisdom for Living Spirit-Based Change. Berkeley, California: North Atlantic Books.*
5 Mingus, Mia. 2019. "The Four Parts of Accountability & How To Give A Genuine Apology." Leaving Evidence (blog). December 18, 2019.

Interrupting Shame, Building Shame Resilience, and Psychological Safety

6 Brown, Brené. 2012. "Brené Brown: Listening to Shame | TED Talk." 2012.
7 https://www.ted.com/talks/brene_brown_listening_to_shame.
8 ———. 2018. *Dare to Lead: Brave Work. Tough Conversations. Whole Hearts.*
9 ———. 2020. *Focus on Guilt Instead of Shame.* 60 Minutes.
10 Edmondson, Amy C. 2018. *The Fearless Organization: Creating Psychological Safety in the Workplace for Learning, Innovation, and Growth.*

Self-Compassion and Non-Violent Communication

11 Neff, Kristen. 2021. "Self-Compassion." Self-Compassion. 2021.
12 ———. 2023. "Fierce Self-Compassion by Kristin Neff."
13 Rosenberg, Marhsall B. 2015. *Nonviolent Communication: A Language of Life.*
14 williams, Rev angel Kyodo. 2021. Belonging: From Fear to Freedom on the Path to True Community.

Inclusive Language

15 Brown, Lydia X. 2021. "Ableism/Language."
16 GLAAD. 2022. "Glossary of Terms: LGBTQ | GLAAD." February 24, 2022. https://glaad.org/reference/terms/.
17 National Institutes of Health (NIH). 2022. "Inclusive and Gender-Neutral Language."
18 Pinsker, Joe. 2018. "The Problem with 'Hey Guys.'"

Notes

1 We acknowledge Seattle University and its mission that inspires and shapes our use of language of 'just and humane world' in this book.
2 We acknowledge Rev angel Kyodo williams for their wisdom and language focused on integrating inner change and collective change for social justice.
3 Based on J.K. Rowling's quote written for the character of Prof. Albus Dumbledore in the book and movie titled "Harry Potter and the Goblet of Fire." The original quote is "Dark times lie ahead of us and there will be a time when we must choose between what is easy and what is right" (Albus Dumbledore).
4 Different versions of THINK acronym are available online. This one resonates with us. We invite you to make it your own.
5 We acknowledge Prof. Brene Brown (refer to Brown 2012, 2018, 2020) for her profound contributions on understanding and interrupting shame and building shame resilience. We also acknowledge Prof. Amy Edmondson for her contributions to elevate the idea and framework of psychological safety in organizational contexts (refer Edmondson 2018).
6 We acknowledge Prof. Deb Dana's work on Befriending Our Nervous System using Polyvagal Theory. We borrow the language of Rupture, Repair, and Reciprocity from Chapter 3 "Longing for Connection" of her above cited book.
7 Refer to brown 2020 for nuanced reflections on cancel culture and accountability.

References

Alexander, Jennifer, and Camilla Stivers. 2020. "Racial Bias: A Buried Cornerstone of the Administrative State." *Administration & Society* 52 (10): 1470–90. https://doi.org/10.1177/0095399720921508

Alkadry, Mohamad G., and Brandi Blessett. 2010. "Aloofness or Dirty Hands?" *Administrative Theory & Praxis (M.E. Sharpe)* 32 (4): 532–56. https://doi.org/10.2753/ATP1084-1806320403

Alkadry, Mohamad G., Brandi Blessett, and Valerie L. Patterson. 2015. "Public Administration, Diversity, and the Ethic of Getting Things Done" *Administration & Society*, April. https://doi.org/10.1177/0095399715581032

Bell, Lee Anne. 2016. "Theoretical Foundations for Social Justice Education." In *Teaching for Diversity and Social Justice*, edited by Maurianne Adams, Lee Anne Bell, Diane J. Goodman, Khyati Y. Joshi, and Maurianne Adams, 3rd ed., 3–26. New York, NY: Routledge.

———. 2020. *We Will Not Cancel Us: And Other Dreams of Transformative Justice.*

Brown, Brené. 2010. "Brené Brown: The Power of Vulnerability | TED Talk." 2010. https://www.ted.com/talks/brene_brown_the_power_of_vulnerability

———. 2012. "Brené Brown: Listening to Shame | TED Talk." 2012. https://www.ted.com/talks/brene_brown_listening_to_shame

———. 2018. *Dare to Lead: Brave Work. Tough Conversations. Whole Hearts.* 1st ed. New York, NY: Random House.

———. 2020. *Focus on Guilt Instead of Shame.* 60 Minutes. https://www.youtube.com/watch?v=RSrXxqKfYwI

Brown, Lydia X. 2021. "Ableism/Language." *Ableism/Language* (blog). 2021. https://www.autistichoya.com/p/ableist-words-and-terms-to-avoid.html

Chordiya, Rashmi, and Adana Protonentis. Forthcoming. "Healing from White Supremacy Culture and Ableism: Disability Justice as an Antidote." *Journal of Social Equity and Public Administration.2 (1):* 127–52. *https://doi.org/10.24926/jsepa.v2i1.4856.*

Chordiya, Rashmi, and Larry Hubbell. 2022. "Fostering Internal Pay Equity Through Gender Neutral Job Evaluations: A Case Study of the Federal Job Evaluation System." *Public Personnel Management*, September, 00910260221124866. https://doi.org/10.1177/00910260221124866

Chordiya, Rashmi, Stephanie Dolamore, Jeannine M. Love, Erin L. Borry, Adana Protonentis, Brendan Stern, and Geoffrey Whitebread. 2023. "Staking the Tent at the Margins: Using Disability Justice to Expand the Theory and Praxis of Social Equity in Public Administration." *Administrative Theory & Praxis*: 1–26. https://doi.org/10.1080/10841806.2023.2216616

Dana, Deborah. 2021. *Anchored: How to Befriend Your Nervous System Using Polyvagal Theory.* Boulder, CO: Sounds True.

Edmondson, Amy C. 2018. *The Fearless Organization: Creating Psychological Safety in the Workplace for Learning, Innovation, and Growth.* 1st ed. Hoboken, NJ: Wiley.

Ferraro, Holly. 2019a. "(Q&A) Red Talks - Professor Holly Ferraro, Ph.D. (Winter 2019)." Seattle University, October 28. https://www.youtube.com/watch?v=LgIfHSuAxso

———. 2019b. "Red Talks - Professor Holly Ferraro, Ph.D. (Winter 2019)." Seattle University, October 28. https://www.youtube.com/watch?v=g052CP5rN5Y

Frederickson, George. 2005. "The State of Social Equity in American Public Administration." *National Civic Review* 94 (4): 31–38. https://doi.org/10.1002/ncr.117

GLAAD. 2022. "Glossary of Terms: LGBTQ | GLAAD." February 24, 2022. https://glaad.org/reference/terms/

Gooden, Susan T. 2014. *Race and Social Equity: A Nervous Area of Government.* 1st ed. Armonk, NY: Routledge.

———. 2017. "Social Equity and Evidence: Insights from Local Government." *Public Administration Review* 77 (6): 822–28. https://doi.org/10.1111/puar.12851

Harding, Vincent. 2019. Our Lives Can Be Signposts for What's Possible | Vincent Harding Interview by Krista Tippett. https://onbeing.org/programs/our-lives-can-be-signposts-for-whats-possible-vincent-harding/

hooks, bell. 1984. *Feminist Theory: From Margin to Center*. 1st edition. Boston, MA: South End Press.

Kluttz, Jenalee, Jude Walker, and Pierre Walter. 2020. "Unsettling Allyship, Unlearning and Learning Towards Decolonising Solidarity." *Studies in the Education of Adults* 52 (1): 49–66. https://doi.org/10.1080/02660830.2019.1654591

Lorde, Geraldine Audre. 1984. *Sister Outsider: Essays and Speeches*. 1st ed. Trumansburg, NY: Crossing Press.

Mastracci, Sharon. 2021. "Dirty Work and Emotional Labor in Public Service: Why Government Employers Should Adopt an Ethic of Care." *Review of Public Personnel Administration* 42 (February): 0734371X2199754. https://doi.org/10.1177/0734371X21997548

Menakem, Resmaa. 2017. *My Grandmother's Hands: Racialized Trauma and the Pathway to Mending Our Hearts and Bodies*. Illustrated ed. Las Vegas, NV: Central Recovery Press.

———. 2021. Resmaa Menakem — 'Notice the Rage; Notice the Silence' Interview by Krista Tippett. https://onbeing.org/programs/resmaa-menakem-notice-the-rage-notice-the-silence/

Mingus, Mia. 2019. "The Four Parts of Accountability & How to Give a Genuine Apology." *Leaving Evidence* (blog). December 18, 2019. https://leavingevidence.wordpress.com/2019/12/18/how-to-give-a-good-apology-part-1-the-four-parts-of-accountability/

Mitchell, Sherri. 2018. *Sacred Instructions: Indigenous Wisdom for Living Spirit-Based Change*. Berkeley, CA: North Atlantic Books.

Morris, Katie Boudreau. 2017. "Decolonizing Solidarity: Cultivating Relationships of Discomfort." *Settler Colonial Studies* 7 (4): 456–73. https://doi.org/10.1080/2201473X.2016.1241210

National Institutes of Health (NIH). 2022. "Inclusive and Gender-Neutral Language." National Institutes of Health (NIH). August 11, 2022. https://www.nih.gov/nih-style-guide/inclusive-gender-neutral-language

Neff, Kristen. 2021. "Self-Compassion." 2021. https://self-compassion.org/

———. 2023. "Fierce Self-Compassion by Kristin Neff." *Self-Compassion* (blog). 2023. https://self-compassion.org/fierce-self-compassion/

Page, Cara, and Erica Woodland. 2023. *Healing Justice Lineages: Dreaming at the Crossroads of Liberation, Collective Care, and Safety*. Berkeley, CA: North Atlantic Books.

Peck, Krysten. 2020. "What It Means to Center 'Healing Justice' in Wellness - Transform Harm." Https://Transformharm.Org/ (blog). October 1, 2020. https://transformharm.org/what-it-means-to-center-healing-justice-in-wellness/

Pinsker, Joe. 2018. "The Problem with 'Hey Guys.'" The Atlantic. August 23, 2018. https://www.theatlantic.com/family/archive/2018/08/guys-gender-neutral/568231/

Portillo, Shannon, Domonic Bearfield, and Nicole Humphrey. 2020. "The Myth of Bureaucratic Neutrality: Institutionalized Inequity in Local Government Hiring." *Review of Public Personnel Administration* 40 (3): 516–31. https://doi.org/10.1177/0734371X19828431

———. 2022. *The Myth of Bureaucratic Neutrality*. 1st ed. New York, NY, NY: Routledge.

Raffo, Susan. 2018. "What Is Healing Justice and How Would It Affect This Gathering? - Transform Harm." Https://Transformharm.Org/ (blog). December 15, 2018. https://transformharm.org/what-is-healing-justice-and-how-would-it-affect-this-gathering/

Rosenberg, Marhsall B. 2015. *Nonviolent Communication: A Language of Life*. 3rd ed. Encinitas, CA: Puddle Dancer Press.

Starke, Anthony M., Nuri Heckler, and Janiece Mackey. 2018. "Administrative Racism: Public Administration Education and Race." *Journal of Public Affairs Education* 24 (4): 469–89. https://doi.org/10.1080/15236803.2018.1426428

Stensöta, Helena. 2011. "A Public Ethics of Care for Administration and Implementation." *Western Political Science Association Annual Meeting Paper*: 1–14. https://ssrn.com/abstract=1766979

Tutu, Desmond, and Mpho Tutu. 2015. *The Book of Forgiving: The Fourfold Path for Healing Ourselves and Our World*. Reprint ed. New York, NY: HarperOne.

williams, Rev. angel Kyodo. 2021a. *Belonging: From Fear to Freedom on the Path to True Community*. Unabridged ed. Sounds True.

———. 2021b. "Reclaiming Mindfulness." Presented at the Embody Lab.

5 Cultivating a Liberatory Public Service

Lessons from Social Justice Movement Visions and Frameworks

Abstract

In this chapter, we offer an emergent framework of liberatory public service (LPS). LPS is inspired by and anchored in the teachings from critical academic scholarly work and social justice movement visions and frameworks. We explore some of the key frameworks, and visions emerging from grassroots social justice movement spaces that are focused on collective liberation and serve as building blocks of LPS. These include – Restorative Justice (RJ), Transformative Justice (TJ), Healing Justice (HJ), and Disability Justice (DJ). We discuss how each of these frameworks are deeply aligned, inextricably related, and mutually reinforce each other. We offer and reflect on the principles and praxis of an emergent LPS framework. LPS is the creative and innovative practice of nurturing diversity, equity, inclusion, and belonging in meaningful and empowering ways. LPS calls for equity and social justice approaches in public service contexts to be trauma-informed, repair and healing-oriented, and compassionately centering the margins within all our organizational functions, structures, designs, policies, procedures, leadership, and cultures.

Introduction

Liberatory public service (LPS) is the vision and practice of eliminating systemic biases and barriers in public services while simultaneously advancing a proactive politics of equity, inclusion, belonging and freedom. LPS is about investing in, centering, and advancing the work of diversity, equity, inclusion, belonging, and liberatory justice (DEILJ) in all domains of public service. These include domains of government administration, healthcare and public health, education, social services, law enforcement and public safety, emergency services, social and economic development, housing and urban development, arts and culture, and the work of nonprofit organizations.

DOI: 10.4324/9781032670669-7

LPS means that all public service work is guided by trauma-informed and healing centered (TIHC) approaches and our systems are designed with care and intentionality to honor humanity and dignity of public servants and the public they serve. LPS looks and feels like purposeful and meaningful public service work that follows the leadership of those most impacted by systemic inequities and injustices. This means our research, education, and practice proactively engage with and draw on lessons from both interdisciplinary critical academic scholarship and grassroots social justice movements.

LPS humbly recognizes that social justice movements offer frameworks, innovations, and visions for the present and future of our world. These are rooted in the lived experiences, wisdom, and resilience of multiply marginalized communities that are living with and navigating the failures of our current designs and systems (McDowell 2015). Following the leadership of those most impacted by inequities and injustices can help us not only address the failures and flaws in the designs of our current systems, but also to create, innovate, and transform our systems to meet the needs of "all means all" public (Chordiya et al. 2023).

In the following sections, we describe the context, core values, and key tenets that guide the practice of leading-edge social justice frameworks. These frameworks are rooted in the resistance and healing justice (HJ) movements led by disabled, BIPOC & LGBTQIA+ activists, organizers, leaders, and visionaries of our times. While these frameworks are innovated and reinvented to meet the liberatory needs, oppression, and complexities of our times, each of these frameworks have historical and ancestral lineages in diverse BIPOC community-led resistance movements against colonialism and settler colonialism.

The frameworks explored in this chapter are:

a **Restorative justice (RJ):** RJ is a philosophy and approach to addressing harm, violence, and conflict that prioritizes repair for and the healing of those who are experiencing harm. RJ approaches originate from many Indigenous wisdom traditions and cultural knowledge systems and focus on repairing harm, and restoring humanity, trust, and relationships. It is an alternative to traditional punitive justice systems, such as incarceration, and seeks to provide a more holistic and constructive way of dealing with harm and conflicts (Zehr 2011a, 2011b, 2015).

b **Transformative justice (TJ):** TJ is a social justice movement framework that seeks not only to respond to individual incidents of harm, violence, and conflict but also to fundamentally transform the societal conditions that give rise to violence, injustice, and harm. TJ is an alternative to traditional punitive justice systems, such as incarceration, are often practiced in community-based settings. It focuses on addressing the core causes of violence and oppression and promoting long-term transformative social change where harm and violence becomes less likely to occur (Kaba 2021b; Kaba and Hassan 2021, Nocella 2011).

c **Healing justice (HJ):** HJ is a social justice movement framework that seeks to address systemic and individual harm, particularly in marginalized and oppressed communities, by prioritizing healing, well-being, and self-determination. It recognizes that various forms of harm and oppression, such as racial injustice, economic inequality, and historical trauma, can have profound and enduring effects on individuals and communities. HJ approaches recognize that healing should extend beyond individual recovery to encompass entire communities that share common experiences of harm from oppression. It recognizes that social justice cannot be achieved without addressing the need for healing and fostering emotional, psychological, and physical well-being of individuals and communities (Page and Woodland 2023).

d **Disability justice (DJ):** DJ is a social justice framework and movement that centers the experiences and needs of people with disabilities, particularly multiply marginalized, BIPOC & LGBTQIA+ people with disabilities. The traditional disability rights framework often takes a single-identity approach and focuses on legal rights and accommodation, to address the broader issues of systemic discrimination and inequality. DJ extends disability rights based approaches and aims to develop a legal, structural, and cultural context to co-create and sustain collective access and collective liberation.

Within the framework of DJ, access needs are not shameful and the work of collective liberation centers multiply marginalized people with disabilities. We follow the leadership of multiply marginalized people with disabilities who are most impacted by systemic inequities to create greater access and equity for all. Disability is valued as diversity (not a deficit), and people with disabilities are valued as whole people, empowered, and feel a sense of inclusion and belonging. DJ recognizes that achieving justice for multiply marginalized BIPOC, LGBTQIA+ people with disabilities is inseparable from achieving justice for all marginalized communities (Sins Invalid 2019).

Re-Inventing Alternatives to Punishment Based Systems: A Context

In the United States, 1980s marked the beginning of "war on drugs" leading to mass arrests. As overt policies and practice of racism, sexism, and ableism became untenable through transformative wins of the civil rights movement of 1960s and 1970s, mass incarceration and prison-industrial complex became the new face of enduring systems of oppression.

Incarceration replaced rehabilitation. People experiencing poverty, people with visible/invisible disabilities, people in BIPOC & LGBTQIA+ communities were ensnared in the criminal punishment system (Nocella 2011).

In the 1990s, education was taken out of prisons and substituted with factory jobs that profited corporations. The 2000s, marked by the Bush administration's "war on terrorism" was characterized by war, violence, economic, and ecological crisis. The prison population grew, for the first time, to over two million in the United States, overextending the bed limit. Various forms of social control from ankle bracelets to surveillance, to questioning, to punishment, including in forms of capital punishment, continued to be used within this punishment or retribution-based approaches. This phenomenon has been named incarcerated slavery (Nocella 2011) or the "New Jim Crow" (Alexander 2020) and led to the growth of prison-industrial complex.

In this context, critical scholarship in sub-fields such as peacemaking criminology and within social justice movements led to the (re)discovery, and reinvention of alternative approaches to peacekeeping that are rooted in BIPOC cultural knowledge systems and wisdom traditions of conflict transformation and peacemaking. These approaches include RJ, TJ (Nocella 2011), HJ, and DJ (Nocella 2011; Page and Woodland 2023; Piepzna-Samarasinha 2018; Sins Invalid 2019).

The RJ, TJ, HJ, and DJ frameworks have deep lineages in Black and Indigenous approaches to nurturing community connections and interdependence, forgiveness, and accountability (Nocella 2011; Page and Woodland 2023; Piepzna-Samarasinha 2018; Sins Invalid 2019). These approaches challenge retributive or punishment-based dominant culture of society as well as within our institutions, and organizations, and in our interpersonal relationships. They also challenge the widespread systems and structures of institutionalization, associated violence, and exploitation within the prison-industrial complex.

It is important to note that RJ, TJ, HJ, and DJ, like many non-dominant wisdom traditions and cultural knowledge systems have faced invisibilization and marginalization. This marginalization is a consequence of their resistance to dominant ideologies and enduring influences of colonialism, neo-colonialism, settler colonialism, systems based in racialized capitalism (that puts profit over people and planet) and supremacy (of certain bodies and minds over others). Despite deliberate efforts to sideline these approaches, RJ, TJ, HJ, and DJ approaches to conflict transformation and human transformation continue to survive, remain resilient, and are being rediscovered and reinvented by contemporary grassroots social justice movements and critical academic scholarship.

Collectively, RJ, TJ, HJ, and DJ re-emerged as responses to center the needs and healing of the survivors and those impacted by conditions and circumstances of harm. They seek to build community-based alternatives that can replace dominant punishment-based and dehumanizing prison-industrial complex, and criminal legal system. They call upon us to divest from mass incarceration and invest in mass healing. With their focus on radical transformation, healing, repair, and accountability, RJ, TJ, HJ, and DJ have important lessons and implications for public service work all around that seeks to develop a DEILJ praxis.

In the following sub-sections, we offer a brief context and introduction to RJ, TJ, HJ, and DJ frameworks. We also share some of our reflections about the tensions and contradictions that arise from engagement with these frameworks within the context of dominant public service systems. Our dominant systems are not always intentionally designed to center collective liberation and often reproduce oppression and marginalization of BIPOC communities that RJ, TJ, HJ, and DJ intend to center.

Please note that this is not intended to be an exhaustive or even a complete discussion of these nuanced approaches and frameworks to liberatory justice work. What follows is intended to be an introduction to the key ideas, principles, and a beginning discussion on cautions and contradictions with application and integration of these frameworks in the context of public service. We hope these contribute to and advance continued courageous conversations, critical scholarship and action rooted in imagination and creation of liberatory possibilities within public service contexts.

Restorative Justice (RJ)

RJ challenges the punishment-based retributive justice system and emphasizes repairing and healing from the harm caused by violence and abuse. RJ views violence and abuse as a source of harm that must be repaired. The overall goal of RJ is to bring people together, to try to heal the whole community that was impacted directly and indirectly by an incident in which people are harmed, and to help prevent similar harm from happening again (Kaba and Hassan 2019).

The Key Principles of Restorative Justice Approach

RJ recognizes that the essential harm of violence and abuse is the loss of trust and a violation of people and relationships. The obligation is to make things right and ask, "how can this harm be repaired?" (Zehr 2011b). As a survivor and community-centered approach, at a fundamental level, the work of the RJ process is to restore trust and reclaiming the spirit and inherent humanity of the survivor/victims, and their core human needs (Zehr 2015) of safety, dignity, and belonging (Haines 2019). A fundamental obligation of individuals who caused hurt/harm is to practice accountability and demonstrate that they are trustworthy (London 2010).

RJ recognizes that punishment alone cannot restore trust in the offender or in society. It also cannot offer the healing space and support systems necessary for the restoration of victims/survivors spirit, humanity and core needs for safety, dignity, and belonging. RJ interrupts dominant punishment-based approaches that are more often than not a ritual of exclusion and dehumanization, a form of symbolic degradation that strips offenders of their membership in a "moral" community (London 2010). Instead, RJ seeks to tap into the potential of justice processes to become a ritual of inclusion and restoration (Zehr 2011a).

In practice, since the 1990s, RJ approaches have been explored as a promising alternative to punitive and exclusionary approaches used in school systems that fuel a "school-to-prison pipeline" (Adams 2023; Zehr 2015). It must be noted that like any major cultural change, embracing RJ as an organizational/institutional approach to conflict management takes time and the process can be controversial. However, when embraced wholeheartedly, school-level use of RJ approaches that invite a shift in school cultures based on norms of exclusion to one of relationality have been associated with declines in schoolwide student misbehavior, gang membership, victimization, depressive symptoms, and substance abuse (Darling-Hammond 2023).

RJ prioritizes the needs and healing of the survivor/victim. It also creates an opportunity for those who caused hurt/harm to take responsibility and make amends with the survivor and the community. Recently, there have been increasing conversations and engagement with the use of RJ approaches to address workplace violence and harm (refer to Adams 2021; Opie and Roberts 2017).

Transformative Justice (TJ)

In the late 1990s, late Ruth Morris, a visionary thinker, scholar, and leader of prison abolition and transformative justice movement, acknowledged the crucial role of RJ in shifting away from retributive systems and also challenged RJ as limiting. She argued that RJ does not go far enough to address underlying oppression and structural injustices that make harm, abuse, and violence imaginable and possible (Nocella 2011; Kaba and Hassan 2019). While restorative processes aim at transformation at the personal and interpersonal level, the politics and practice of RJ does not require or fully utilize its potential to create awareness of larger social issues and create room for transformation at the social level (Zehr 2011b).

TJ framework was developed in part due to these perceived limitations of RJ (Kaba and Hassan 2019). TJ builds on RJ and extends its boundaries to include larger social, cultural, and structural transformation as fundamental to its political approach. In that sense, TJ could be viewed as "Restorative Justice +."

TJ as a framework has its roots at the intersections of critical criminology and abolitionist social justice movements. The philosophy of critical criminology and abolitionist social justice movements is rooted in challenging domination and control of any sort (e.g., prisons, surveillance, and other forms of state and social control). It seeks to find alternatives to carceral systems and retributive or punishment-based criminal legal systems. In reflecting on distinctions between the focus or goals of retributive, restorative, and transformative approaches to justice, Howard Zehr (2011b) offers the following helpful perspectives as outlined in Figure 5.1.

The Key Principles of Transformative Justice Approach

TJ is a survivor-centered and community-led approach for responding to violence, harm, and abuse without creating more violence and/or engaging in harm reduction to lessen the violence (Generation Five 2007; Mingus 2019). TJ is liberatory in its approaches as it strives to use the conflict as an opportunity to address larger socio-political injustices and seeks to transform the structures, systems, and conditions that allow violence, oppression, domination, and harm to occur in the first place (Nocella 2011). TJ responds to violence and harm in ways that are aligned with long-term visions for preventing violence, responding to violence, and ultimately

Retributive Justice	Restorative Justice	Transformative Justice
What rule has been broken?	Who has been hurt and what are their needs?	Restorative Justice +
Who is to blame?	Who is obligated to address these needs?	What social conditions promoted the harmful behavior?
What punishment do they deserve?	Who has a "stake" in this situation & what is the process to involve them in making things right and preventing future occurrences?	What structural similarities exist between this incident and others like it?
		What measures could prevent future occurrences?

Figure 5.1 Retributive Justice vs. Restorative Justice vs. Transformative Justice

Source: Authors' adaptation of Howard Zehr's (2011b) Perspective on Retributive, Restorative and Transformative Justice Approaches

ending violence. For example, TJ asks, what would it take to not only respond to rape, but to end rape? To not only respond to domestic violence, but to end domestic violence? To end child abuse? To end bullying? To end all forms of abuse? (Mingus 2019, p.4)

TJ is grounded in non-punitive and non-violent approaches to justice and seeks to make violence unthinkable in our culture. In practice, the TJ approach requires the rigor and discipline that challenges our punitive impulses and seeks to interrupt cycles of revenge and oppression and open portals to healing, repair, and accountability (Kaba 2021a).

TJ understands that violence and harm is nuanced, and that punitive systems in our organizations and institutions are not. Mariame Kaba, a visionary thinker, educator, organizer, and leading practitioner immersed in TJ work wisely notes, punishment is not the same as transformation (Kaba and Hassan 2021). Prisons and other punitive approaches lack the nuance and understanding that violence and harm does not happen in vacuum, that it is socially located and contingent on historical, cultural, and political contexts and norms (Mingus 2019; Nocella 2011).

TJ approaches are rooted in the reality that often it is hurt people who hurt other people. In other words, we are the oppressed oppressors, colonized colonizers, and victimized offenders. TJ is grounded in the idea that survivors of harm and trauma often perpetuate the cycle of harm and trauma when trauma is not metabolized and remains unhealed. Without a nuanced understanding of harm and violence, prisons and punishment-based approaches reproduce the same forms of violence, fear, and oppression they claim to condemn (Kaba and Hassan 2021).

Therefore, in addressing and seeking to transform harm and violence, at interpersonal as well as organizational and institutional levels, responses and interventions rooted in TJ do not rely on the state systems and structures (e.g., police, prisons, the criminal legal system, immigration enforcement system, foster care system[1]). Rather TJ approaches and interventions are community-based and center the survivors/victims of harm/violence/abuse. In their interventions and responses to harm and violence, TJ approaches work to connect incidences of violence to the oppressive conditions such as capitalism, poverty, trauma, heterosexism, cis-sexism, white supremacy, (trans) misogyny, gender oppression, ableism, religious oppression, displacement, and war that create and perpetuate acts of harm and violence (Mingus 2019).

Generation FIVE is a key organization that uses TJ as an approach to end child sexual abuse. It has played an instrumental role in the development and diffusion of TJ approach. Generation FIVE identifies the goals of TJ are: (a) survivor safety, healing, and agency; (b) offender accountability and transformation; (c) community response and accountability; and (d) transformation of community and the social conditions that create and perpetuate harm, abuse, and violence – systems of oppression, exploitation, domination, and state violence. (Generation Five 2007, 26).

TJ seeks to transform and shift power within communities by creating a proactive community culture. One that is rooted in liberatory values and cultivates the practice of living into those values, building relationships and communities rooted in mutuality and solidarity. In practice, TJ seeks to build capacity and skills of community members to cultivate reciprocal and generative relationships, communication skills, bystander interventions skills to de-escalate active or "live" harm and violence in the moment, learning to express anger and other difficult emotions in ways that are constructive and incorporating self and collective healing into everyday lives of community members (Mingus 2019).

TJ interventions can take many forms based on needs and context and center the needs and healing of the impacted survivor and/or community. Most TJ interventions involve a community accountability process, wherein a few members of community work directly with the individual responsible for causing harm, aiming to hold them accountable for their actions and prevent future harm. TJ interventions may also include engaging bystanders and building community responsibility for creating conditions that provide opportunities for accountability and change. TJ is an emergent framework, and it is not perfect, however, it offers an alternative to prison and punishment-based approaches by seeking to address violence, harm and abuse in communities in ways that are generative and do not perpetuate cycles of harm, oppression, and trauma. (Mingus 2019).

Community accountability process within TJ approaches is about widening the circle of accountability and acknowledging that what happens between, for example, two people, both impacts a wider group of people and is also (in many ways) made possible by community context. It involves moving community members (bystanders) toward taking action to prevent violence from occurring, building capacities, and supporting community members to interrupt or stop violence while it is happening, and engaging in the transformation of abusive power dynamics (Generation FIVE 2007).

Overall, the TJ approaches and interventions invite us to interrogate questions such as:

1 Who has been hurt/harmed and what are their needs?
2 What social/institutional/organizational conditions and circumstances promoted the harmful behavior?
3 What structural and cultural similarities exist between this incident and others like it?
4 Who caused hurt/harm, what are their needs, and how can they be supported to practice accountability?

5 What measures could prevent future occurrences?
6 What are the skills we need to be able to prevent, respond to, heal from, and take accountability for harmful, violent, and abusive behaviors?
7 What kinds of community culture and infrastructure can we create to support more safety, transparency, sustainability, care, and connection (e.g., a network of community safe places that those in danger can use, an abundance of community members who are skilled at leading interventions to violence)?

(*Note*: Authors' adaptation of questions offered in Zehr 2011b and Mingus 2019.)

Healing Justice (HJ)

HJ was named and reinvented as a liberatory framework in early 2000s by Black, Indigenous, and People of Color, Lesbian, Gay, Bi, Trans, Queer, Intersex, and Asexual + (BIPOC & LGBTQIA+) healers and organizers in the South. The idea or innovation of HJ has roots in generations of resistance (Middleton and Page 2023). It has roots in cultural and spiritual traditions of multiply marginalized BIPOC communities around the world that used healing traditions, rituals, and practices "to address, transform, and recover from trauma, grief, violence, and crisis" (Page and Woodland 2023, 27–28).

Amidst horrific losses, grief, systemic neglect, and violence, and suffering experienced after Hurricane Katrina in 2005 and Hurricane Rita in 2005 and national attention to trauma experienced by survivors, HJ was reinvented as a liberatory framework. The Kindred Southern Healing Justice Collective (also known as Kindred Collective) was conceived in 2005. Through Kindred Collective, the Healing Justice movement framework was developed to build communal healing traditions as a long-term political strategy that seek to intervene, respond, and transform grief, trauma, and violence experienced in BIPOC communities and movement spaces.

HJ was developed by social justice movement leaders and organizers as a response to meet and center the persistent physical, emotional, psychological, environmental, and spiritual healing needs of their collectives and communities. Erica Woodland (2023b) notes, "*burnout; mental and physical health crisis; surviving interpersonal, state, and community violence; and people leaving movement all together highlight the need to include health and healing practitioners in our organizing strategies*" (pp. 219–220). Social justice movement leaders, organizers, visionaries recognized that HJ is necessary for all social justice work because we need "*healing for the sake of justice and justice for sake of healing*" (Utah and Page 2023, 183).

The Key Principles of Healing Justice Approach

HJ "seeks to intervene on generational trauma to build collective power towards resistance" (Page and Woodland 2023, 146). The three core principles of HJ framework are (a) collective trauma is transformed collectively, (b) there is no single model of care, and (c) healing strategies are rooted in place and ancestral technologies (Middleton and Page 2023, 137). Through these three principles, HJ framework recognizes the trauma of oppression experienced by marginalized people and communities is historical, inter-generational, persistent institutional, and personal.

Oppressive experiences of enslavement, colonization, domination, exclusions, genocide have happened to a people, a collective, and hence our healing strategies must be rooted in collectives, in a culture[2] (Menakem 2021). Healing strategies must be in the right relationship to the peoples, the places, the land, and ancestral technologies. HJ seeks to interrupt supremacist characteristics of domination, saviorism, paternalism and foster interdependence, and solidarity in communal care practices (Middleton and Page 2023).

Healing Justice: The Work of Reclamation and Remembrance

Page and Woodland (2023) describe HJ as the work of remembrance and reclamation. They note, forgetting – through erasure, invisibilization, and marginalization is a tool of white supremacy. It is designed to prevent the current generation of liberation workers from building on intergenerational resistance strategies of their elders and ancestors. HJ is the work of remembering that despite the intensities of inter-generational personal and collective violence happening repeatedly to the bodies and minds of their ancestors, multiply marginalized poor, Black, Indigenous, and negatively racialized People of Color have survived.

HJ is memorializing and holding in reverence this history, one that is deeply personal for multiply marginalized communities. It is honoring the history of movements for liberation that found infinite ways to always center collective care and safety strategies. HJ is multiply marginalized people and collectives reclaiming "the power, resilience, and innovation" of their ancestors, to know that "*to embody their wisdom across centuries and generations is to continue their legacy of liberation and healing*" (Page and Woodland 2023, 25–26).

Disability Justice

DJ was envisioned in 2005 as a movement framework through the work of BIPOC & LGBTQIA+ activists with disabilities including Patty Berne, Mia Mingus, Leroy Moore, Stacey Milbern, Eli Clare, and Sebastian Margaret. Collectively, they envisioned a "second wave" of disability rights movement in response to continued failure to address ableism and its intersectionality with other "isms" in policy, politics, structures, systems, cultures, and even within radical movement spaces (Berne 2020).

DJ critiques ableism and the harm and violence associated with ableism. It is distinct from disability rights – based framework that "seeks to give people with disabilities more access inside of ableist structures" and cultures (Page and Woodland 2023, 150). In describing the strengths and limitations of disability rights movement, Sins Invalid (2019, 15) notes,

> while a concrete and radical move forward toward justice for disabled people, the disability rights movement simultaneously invisibilized the lives of disabled people of color, immigrants with disabilities, disabled people who practice marginalized religions (in particular those experiencing the violence of anti-Islamic beliefs and actions), queers with disabilities, trans and gender non-conforming people with disabilities, people with disabilities who are houseless, people with disabilities who are incarcerated, people with disabilities who have had their ancestral lands stolen, amongst others.

DJ extends and deepens the disability rights movement by advocating for transformative change that replaces single-identity approaches to problem-solving with intersectional approaches. It centers and foregrounds the lived experiences and needs of BIPOC & LGBTQIA+ people with disabilities. It recognizes the vastness in disability diversity and wholeness of human beings. In its approach, DJ calls for commitment to anti-capitalist politic, cross-movement organizing, cross-disability solidarity, and collective access to move us toward collective liberation.

The ten principles of DJ framework are described in Table 5.1. We also offer our interpretations of these ten principles in relation to the practice of solidarity and what it means for public service organizations and professionals.

The framework of DJ offers us deeper insights into oppression and its intersectional effects. Through it tens principles, DJ also provides guidance for fostering liberatory and anti-oppressive practices. DJ's profoundly intersectional approach rejects scarcity based, oversimplified "either/or" stance in anti-oppression work and invites us to practice creativity and abundance mindset to achieve the goals of collective liberation (Chin 2021; Chordiya and Protonentis 2024).

DJ is inherently liberatory, urging us to move beyond merely disrupting and dismantling oppressive structures. It encourages us to engage in the constructive and creative work of realizing the world we aspire and envision (Piepzna-Samarasinha 2018, 2020). This orientation fundamentally differs from the proliferation of diversity and inclusion initiatives in recent years.

Table 5.1 10 Principles of Disability Justice

1. Intersectionality	"Simply put, this principle says that we are many things, and they all impact us. We are not only disabled, but we are also each coming from a specific experience of race, class, sexuality, age, religious background, geographical location, immigration status, and more. Depending on context, we all have areas where we experience privilege, as well as areas of oppression." (Sins Invalid 2019, 23). In the context of public service organizations, the principle of intersectionality invites us into a practice of solidarity that is anchored in recognizing differences and valuing them (not ignoring them). Intersectionality invites us to acknowledge power dynamics and to center lives, experiences, and perspectives of those who are furthest away from power.
2. Leadership of Those Most Impacted	"When we talk about ableism, racism, sexism and transmisogyny, colonization, police violence, etc., we are not looking to academics and experts to tell us what's what — we are lifting, listening to, reading, following, and highlighting the perspectives of those who are most impacted by the systems we fight against. By centering the leadership of those most impacted, we keep ourselves grounded in real-world problems and find creative strategies for resistance." (Sins Invalid 2019, 23). In the context of public service organizations, the DJ principle of following the leadership of those most impacted calls upon us to practice solidarity by shifting away from savior complex and leaning into unsettling, uncomfortable courageous praxis of deeply listening to, seeking to understand, and following the leadership of those most impacted by failures of our inequitable systems. While savior complex teaches us that as public service scholars and professionals, we are the most qualified to "save" or "fix" people and solve public problems, this DJ principle counters savior complex and invites us to lean into the humbling experience of "power-with" approaches. It teaches us that power is not zero-sum, and we can expand power by sharing it. By embracing the vulnerability and joy of co-creating, co-innovating, and leaning into community and survivor-led efforts, public service organizations can continue to find more effective and equitable approaches to solving wicked problems of society and our organizations.

(*Continued*)

Table 5.1 (Continued)

3. Anti-Capitalist Politic	"Capitalism depends on wealth accumulation for some (the white ruling class), at the expense of others, and encourages competition as a means of survival. The nature of our disabled bodyminds means that we resist conforming to 'normative' levels of productivity in a capitalist culture, and our labor is often invisible to a system that defines labor by able-bodied, white supremacist, gender normative standards. Our worth is not dependent on what and how much we can produce." (Sins Invalid 2019, 23–24). In the context of public service organizations, the DJ principle of anti-capitalist politic calls upon us to resist ableist norms of productivity and worth that are associated with what and how much we can produce. It teaches us to critically examine extractive and exploitative habits and approaches that are often justified in name of technical rationality and efficiency. Anti-capitalist politic is aligned with the ethics of care in all our decision making and our actions- care for people, care for our planet and our ecosystem. It teaches us to not take resources for granted, to unlearn singular profit-focused mindset that prioritizes narrow financial gains and justifies exploitation of mind, body, and resources. Anti-capitalist politic seeks to disrupt scarcity-based, win-lose mindset. It is about creating new possibilities and exploring alternative ways of being, surviving, and thriving that are anchored in a disciplined practice of mutuality, reciprocity, and relationality, with people and our planet.
4. Cross-Movement Organizing	"Disability justice can only grow into its potential as a movement by aligning itself with racial justice, reproductive justice, queer and trans liberation, prison abolition, environmental justice, anti-police terror, Deaf activism, fat liberation, and other movements working for justice and liberation. This means challenging white disability communities around racism and challenging other movements to confront ableism. Through cross movement solidarity, we create a united front." (Sins Invalid 2019, 24). In the context of public service organizations, the DJ principle of cross-movement organizing is a call to action rooted in solidarity. While Sins Invalid and authors of DJ principles speak directly to grassroots social justice movements and organizing, this principle has implications for public service work all around. It invites us to resist and shift away from siloed and single-issue approaches, to embracing multi-issue, multi-dimensional, and intersectional approaches to complex problem solving. It helps us recognize that systems of oppression overlap, are mutually dependent, and one form of oppression is often used to reproduce another form of oppression. This DJ principle reminds us that our freedom is tied to one another. As Rev. Martin Luther King Jr. wisely noted, "No one is free until we all are free."

(*Continued*)

Table 5.1 (Continued)

5. Recognizing Wholeness	"Each person is full of history and life experience. Each person has an internal experience composed of our own thoughts, sensations, emotions, sexual fantasies, perceptions, and quirks. Disabled people are whole people." (Sins Invalid 2019, 24). In the context of public service organizations, the DJ principle of recognizing wholeness implies we create physically and psychologically safe-enough spaces for people to take risks to arrive as their authentic selves, where access needs are requested and received with ease. Differences are not shamed or ignored, they are recognized and valued. Being authentic self does not mean there are no boundaries, rather it is a compassionate practice of self-awareness and interpersonal awareness that approaches differences with nuance, humanity, and intentionality. For example, co-creating spaces which recognize people as whole people allow bodyminds to be free, allow differences in perspectives and lived experiences, acknowledge power dynamics, center the margins, and when conflicts inevitably happen, they are used as opportunities to learn about each other's needs and differences, to grow and transform as a collective with shared vision and values.
6. Sustainability	"We learn to pace ourselves, individually and collectively, to be sustained long-term. We value the teachings of our bodies and experiences and use them as a critical guide and reference point to help us move away from urgency and into a deep, slow, transformative, unstoppable wave of justice and liberation." (Sins Invalid 2019, 24–25). In the context of public service organizations, the DJ principle of sustainability invites us to pace ourselves, individually and collectively in alignment with our long-term goals and visions. The way we interpret and understand this principle is that exploitation and oppression of bodies and minds even for good intentions or causes is not in alignment with liberatory values. There is a nuanced distinction between clean pain that comes with sacrifice that public servants often must make and has an element of consent and autonomy, and dirty pain that comes with relentless, scarcity-based, oppressive norms of working till bodies and minds are burned out. This principle invites us to reflect individually and collectively as groups and teams, how can we interrupt and resist the burnout culture? How can we foster creativity, collaboration, imagination, and innovation? What does a meaningful and sustainable pace look like and feel like for a given task, project, mission? What does nurture, and nourishment look like and feel like for diverse bodyminds – and how can we cultivate it as a daily practice? What resources and relationships must be cultivated to build a practice of collective care?

(*Continued*)

Table 5.1 (Continued)

7. Commitment to Cross-Disability Solidary	"We value and honor the insights and participation of all our community members, even and especially those who are most often left out of political conversations. We are building a movement that breaks down isolation between people with physical impairments, people who are sick or chronically ill, psych survivors and people with mental health disabilities, neurodiverse people, people with intellectual or developmental disabilities, Deaf people, Blind people, people with environmental injuries and chemical sensitivities, and all others who experience ableism and isolation that undermines our collective liberation". (Sins Invalid 2019, 25). This principle invites us to first and foremost recognize and understand that disability is diverse and nuanced. It is not a monolith and the liberatory work of centering the margins must break down isolation and foster disability diverse communities and collectives that honor differences and value all bodyminds. For example, in public service contexts, this means we break down isolation and intentionally foster disability awareness, disability identity, disability visibility, and disability collectives. It means our access and accommodation policies and procedures, our efforts towards universal design, transition support for people experiencing and navigating life changing disabilities, and all the work of creating inclusive and equitable organizations and systems must center experiences, perspectives, and needs of multiply marginalized disability diverse communities.
8. Interdependence	"Before the massive colonial project of Western European expansion, we understood the nature of interdependence within our communities. We see the liberation of all living systems and the land as integral to the liberation of our own communities, as we all share one planet. We work to meet each other's needs as we build toward liberation, without always reaching for state solutions which inevitably extend state control further into our lives." (Sins Invalid 2019, 25). This principle reminds us that as public servants working in government and nonprofit contexts, we are often deeply entrenched in systems of oppression, including white supremacy, ableism, and settler colonialism that causes harm against multiply marginalized groups. We interpret and understand that the authors of Sins Invalid are inviting a transformative justice practice rooted in mutual aid and collective care to foster interdependence, to shed the myth of individualism, and avoid over reliance on state solutions that may perpetuate harm and oppression. This principle, like others, has many implications for the public service community. One of these include finding ways to align for transformative change that disrupts oppressive policies and procedures and seeks to cultivate solidarity through practice of interdependence and mutuality anchored in trust, accountability, and relationality with communities we serve. However, many of us, as professionals and organizations may discern that deep and honest work of repair, healing, and trust building will be necessary to build the foundations for any long-term, sustainable, and intentional practice of interdependence, especially in context of multiply marginalized BIPOC communities that have experienced violence and harm from government and nonprofit organizations and actors.

(*Continued*)

Table 5.1 (Continued)

9. Collective Access	"As Black and brown and queer crips, we bring flexibility and creative nuance to our engagement with each other. We create and explore ways of doing things that go beyond able-bodied and neurotypical norms. Access needs aren't shameful — we all function differently depending on context and environment. Access needs can be articulated and met privately, through a collective, or in community, depending upon an individual's needs, desires, and the capacity of the group. We can share responsibility for our access needs, we can ask that our needs be met without compromising our integrity, we can balance autonomy while being in community, we can be unafraid of our vulnerabilities, knowing our strengths are respected." (Sins Invalid 2019, 26). This principle invites us to imagine, co-create, co-innovate, build, and sustain supportive systems that go beyond compliance-based disability accommodations and nurture favorable policies, procedures, structures, and cultural norms and practices that foster disability diversity, disability visibility and normalize collective care and collective access.
10. Collective Liberation	"We move together as people with mixed abilities, multiracial, multi-gendered, mixed class, across the sexual spectrum, with a vision that leaves no bodymind behind. This is disability justice. We honor the longstanding legacies of resilience and resistance which are the inheritance of all of us whose bodies and minds will not conform." (Sins Invalid 2019, 26). This DJ principle invites us to honor the resilience and resistance of non-conforming multiply marginalized disabled bodies and minds that challenge and invite us to dream and imagine liberatory present and futures where all people can experience embodied freedom, joy, and self-actualization. The practice of collective liberation is about finding ways to move together and leaves no bodymind behind.

Source: Excerpted from Sins Invalid, 2019. Quotes explaining the ten principles excerpted from Sins Invalid 2019 with authors' interpretations included in the table.

For example, DJ perspective applied to DEILJ contexts helps us understand that the objective is not to train organizational members to act as gracious hosts, inviting marginalized and minoritized communities to assimilate as guests. Rather, DJ through its ten principles focused on – embracing intersectionality, prioritizing leadership by the most affected, advocating for anti-capitalist politics, fostering cross-movement collaboration, acknowledging wholeness, promoting sustainability, upholding cross-disability solidarity, celebrating interdependence, facilitating collective access, and pursuing collective liberation – call upon us to share power, collectively shape the path forward, and create space for our organizations and ourselves to undergo transformation through this process (Chordiya and Protonentis 2024).

Social Justice Movement Framework: Lessons for Practice of Solidarity

Like many other scholars and practitioners, we argue that public service and public administration are professions that should be rooted in ethics of care, relationality, and interdependence (Dolamore 2021; Dolamore and Whitebread 2022; Guy, Newman, and Mastracci 2014; Meyer, Johnson III, and McCandless 2022; Stensöta 2011; Valenzuela 2017). Collectively, the social justice movement frameworks such as RJ, TJ, HJ, and DJ offer valuable lessons about building and nurturing relationships anchored in mutuality, trust, and solidarity with the communities we seek to serve.

RJ, TJ, HJ, and DJ invite us to regularly examine how we are showing up, and the impact of our practices in each space. They invite us to ask ourselves questions such as: "What is my *(personal and professional)* lineage and the lineage of my *(personal and professional public service)* practice? How am I being accountable to the people receiving my *(public service)* practice and the communities within which I am practicing? How am I holding my and my people's values?" (Middleton and Page 2023, 139; parentheses added by authors to contextualize the importance of this invitation for public service professionals.)

Social justice movement frameworks invite solidarity. For public service professionals, the practice of solidarity could mean interrupting, resisting, and transforming the legal, the structural, and the cultural mechanisms the perpetuate systemic oppression (such as within the education systems, in public utilities, welfare systems, immigration systems, licensing offices, criminal-legal systems and prison-industrial complex, healthcare, public health, and medical-industrial complex and so on).

The practice of solidarity means working to transform oppressive systems and mechanisms that overtly and covertly pathologize, dehumanize, dominate, devalue, and control the bodies and minds of multiply marginalized poor, sick and disabled, LGBTQIA+, Black, Indigenous, and negatively racialized People of Color based on socially constructed notions of whose body mind is "fit" or "unfit," "healthy" or "unhealthy," "valued" and "disposable," and useful for (re)productive labor (Page 2023c, p. 80).

RJ, TH, HJ, and DJ invite us to follow the leadership of survivors and communities that are impacted by systems of harm. The practice of solidarity could mean that we are engaging with transformation work within our spheres of influence and within the wider network of public service systems. As public servants involved in public policymaking, public administrators, public health officials, social workers, healers, health care providers, teachers, scholars, students committed to DEILJ work, we can find creative ways to co-create micro-moments and micro-movements towards inclusion, equity, belonging, justice, and freedom for all. We can create and sustain refuge from systems of oppression within everyday spaces that are within our spheres of influence.

We can nurture sanctuaries that offer "safe-enough" spaces to become potential sites of collective healing or, at the very least, that we avoid the re-traumatization and interruption of ongoing healing work of many multiply marginalized people we work with and serve. It means we can build or support building a self- and community-determined infrastructure and a culture of care (Chordiya and Protonentis 2024; Farrow 2023; Page and Woodland 2023; Sins Invalid 2019).

Care work is an essential part of public service work. It necessitates the practice of trauma-informed approaches including cultivating relationality, nurturing interdependence, autonomy, and mutuality in all internal and public facing functions, workforce development, operations of our organizations (Burnier 2003 2009; Chordiya and Protonentis 2024; Dolamore 2021; Dolamore and Whitebread 2022). Social justice movement frameworks including RJ, TJ, HJ, and DJ call upon us to embrace our superpower values of care and relationality in everyday practice of public service. As Miss Major Griffin-Gracy, a Black Trans woman warrior, powerfully notes,

> Care and resistance, have to be together and they have to work together...One of the things that I have found is when I work on different aspects of the community, like civil rights or gender justice... that it is so important to care for people you are building power with
>
> (Miss Major Griffin-Gracy quoted in Page 2023a, pp. 43–44)

A Call for Liberatory Public Service (LPS)

RJ, TJ, HJ, and DJ are social justice movement frameworks and visions that call upon communities of public service workers, care-centered practitioners involved in policymaking and administration to work toward decriminalizing and destigmatizing emotional and mental health crisis as well as crisis related to intersectional poverty. They invite us to interrogate exclusion based and punitive responses in our policymaking and administrative actions. They call upon us to disrupt and dismantle the nexus of prison-industrial complex and medical-industrial complex that we may reproduce and find ourselves entangled in, through our work, our agencies, and departments.

RJ, TJ, HJ, and DJ call upon us to be vigilant and examine whether our policies and administrative decisions and processes are care-centered and life-affirming or are they contributing toward harm, marginalization, and exploitation of the bodies and minds of sick, disabled, poor BIPOC & LBGTQIA+ populations. HJ, RJ, TJ, and DJ invite us to move toward liberatory systems and infrastructures and cultures that are rooted in genuine care, in relationality and mutuality with the public we are committed to serve. This vision and call for a liberatory public service (LPS) asks us to always pause and examine "our roles as agents of state when being asked to control or surveil bodies, families, and communities under the guise of "safety" or "for the public good or well-being," when it oftentimes can lead to irrevocable harm" (Page 2023b, p. 209).

Based on the lessons offered by various social justice movement frameworks (including RJ, TJ, DJ, and HJ) as well as critical academic scholarship (such trauma-informed approaches and intersectionality discussed in preceding chapters), we identify and describe the core values and emergent principles of LPS that can serve as a constellation of guiding stars for the future of public service. It is not intended to be "the" constellation, rather we describe this as "a" constellation that can serve us as travelers on the path of LPS.

We invite you to adapt or reinvent our offering and/or develop a whole new constellation of guiding stars of principles anchored in social justice frameworks that have served/could ideally serve to offer you the clarity and discernment you need in your own journey and practice of LPS.

Liberatory Public Service (LPS)

LPS is rooted in the core values love, courage, repair, healing, joy, efficacy, solidarity, and transformation.

LPS is a vision, a process, and a practice of creating the conditions for liberation to emerge through alignments across policy work, administrative work, structure and culture change work, and leadership praxis that serves – "*all means all*" public. It involves the systematic removal of oppressive policies, administrative and cultural barriers, one step at a time, until we collectively eliminate all forms of oppressive policies, administrative and cultural barriers.

LPS is not about simply dismantling structures or removing burdens to create a void. LPS is about replacing burdensome systems and procedures that are exclusionary, marginalizing, causing hurt and harm, with, nourishing systems, inclusive and life-affirming cultures that are rooted in collective work, shared accountability, transparency, and demonstrate care. LPS is about integrating inner and systemic transformation to foster public service that is trauma-informed, repair and healing-oriented, and compassionately centering the margins.

The Guiding Stars of Liberatory Public Service: A Constellation of Core Values and Key Principles

In our teaching, scholarship, and practice, we are discerning that to build the foundations of LPS within public service organizations, we need approaches that are trauma-informed, healing-oriented, and that compassionately centering the margins within all our organizational/institutional functions structures, designs, policies, procedures, leadership, and cultures. LPS is rooted in the core values love, courage, repair, healing, joy, efficacy, solidarity, and transformation. LPS is a vision, a process, and a practice of creating the conditions for liberation to emerge through alignments across policy work, administrative work, structure and culture change work, and leadership praxis that serves – "*all means all*" public. It involves the systematic removal of oppressive policies, administrative and cultural barriers, one step at a time, until we collectively eliminate all forms of oppressive policies, administrative and cultural barriers.

LPS is not about simply dismantling structures or removing burdens to create a void. LPS is about replacing burdensome systems and procedures that are exclusionary, marginalizing, causing hurt and harm, with, nourishing systems, inclusive and life-affirming cultures that are rooted in collective work, shared accountability, transparency, and demonstrate care. LPS is about integrating inner and systemic transformation to foster public service that is trauma-informed, repair and healing-oriented, and compassionately centering the margins.

A commitment to the values and practice of LPS necessitates that we are deeply intentional about not co-opting social justice movement frameworks in ways that are superficial, extractive, and strip them of their core values in our practices. It requires us to cultivate relationships rooted in sharing and shifting of power, a practice of transparency, accountability,

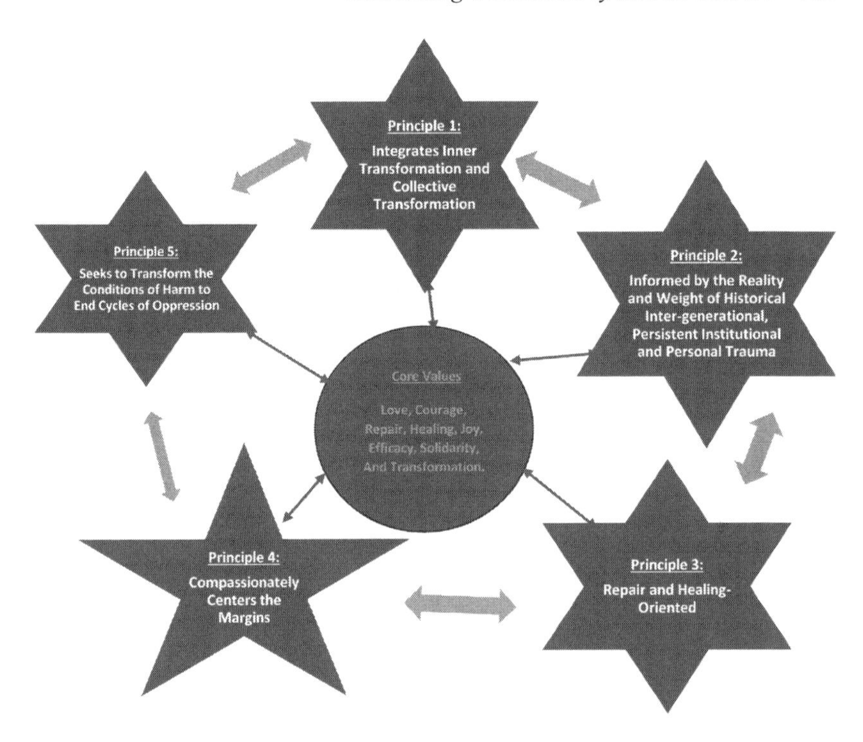

Figure 5.2 The Guiding Stars of Liberatory Public Service: A Constellation of Core Values and Principles

Source: Created by the authors. We acknowledge Resmaa Menakem's work and framing of trauma as historical, intergenerational, persistent institutional, and personal trauma. It has shaped our language for LPS's principle 2.

and solidarity with people with disabilities, BIPOC & LGBTQIA+ people led grassroots movement bases and organizations that are innovating and leading the work of RJ, TJ, HJ, and DJ (Figure 5.2).

The Five Emergent Principles of LPS

Principle 1: LPS Integrates Inner Transformation and Collective Transformation

LPS work must have both an internal and external focus to bring transformative change for social equity and justice. It necessitates interrupting cycles of harm and oppression and developing liberatory practice at both intrapersonal, interpersonal, as well as institutional and societal levels. In the words of rev. angel Kyodo williams (n.d.), "love & justice are not two. without inner change, there is no outer change; without collective change, no change matters" (for detailed discussions and guiding frameworks of building liberatory consciousness, refer to Chapter 2).

Principle 2: LPS Is Trauma Informed

LPS acknowledges the truth and weight of historical, inter-generational, persisting organizational/institutional, and personal trauma that has occurred due to oppressive public policies and administrative decisions (e.g., racialized ableist public policies and administrative burdens). Acknowledging this hard truth can also serve as helpful reminder that our current reality was/is created by a series of decisions. And we can make different decisions!

LPS invites us to consistently engage with trauma-informed approaches in our public policymaking, administrative decision-making, and culture change work that seeks to create physically and psychologically safe-enough spaces for people to belong to themselves and each other. Being trauma-informed policy makers, decision-makers, educators, learners, and practitioners does not mean we all become therapists and healers. Rather, it calls upon organizational systems, structures, cultures as well as individual leaders, educators, and practitioners engaged in public – policy, administrative, and service work – to foster a therapeutic and healing presence (for detailed discussions and guiding frameworks for trauma-informed healing centered (TIHC) public service, refer to Chapters 3 and 4).

Principle 3: LPS Is Repair and Healing-Oriented

LPS recognizes that the work of diversity, equity, inclusion, and liberatory justice (DEILJ) seeks to proactively identify, recognize, and address the historical and ongoing impacts of colonialism, settler colonialism, imperialism, racialized capitalism, and imbalanced power structures and systems within public – policy, administrative, and service contexts.

Addressing historical and ongoing harms of oppression means engaging in the vulnerable work of repairing relationships and trusts, especially with populations and communities that have been underserved, exploited, marginalized, and disenfranchised. LPS creates space for emergence of healing by finding authentic ways of telling the truth, acknowledgment of hurt and harm, making amends, transformation toward community-engaged public service that seeks to become decolonial in its approaches, and is committed to shared equity leadership (for detailed discussions and guiding frameworks of building liberatory consciousness and TIHC public service, refer to Chapters 2, 3, and preceding sections of this chapter).

Principle 4: LPS Compassionately Centers the Margins

LPS recognizes intersectionality and the need to follow the leadership and perspectives of multiply marginalized people and communities. It compassionately centers and foregrounds the needs, contexts, and experiences of people and communities multiply marginalized by the trauma of historical, inter-generational, persistent institutional, and personal disenfranchisement and othering. LPS engages in solidarity and mutuality-based politics to imagine, co-create, innovate, and implement targeted DEILJ solutions for collective liberation. LPS invites us to shift away from win-lose politics and scarcity mindsets and lean into collaborative politics of solidarity that is anchored in abundance mindset (for detailed discussions and guiding frameworks for compassionately centering the margins, refer to preceding sections of this chapter as well as the following Chapter 6).

Principle 5: LPS Seeks to Transform the Conditions of Harm to End Cycles of Oppression

LPS seeks to interrupt and end cycles of harm and oppression, including criminalizing, stigmatizing, and marginalizing public and institutional policy and administrative responses. It works to channel energy, creativity, innovativeness, and resources to build transformative policies, procedures, infrastructures, and cultures that are trauma-informed, repair and healing-oriented, community- and survivor-led, and envision a LPS (for detailed discussions and guiding frameworks for ending cycles of harm and oppression and cultivating a TIHC public service, refer to preceding sections of this chapter as well as Chapters 3 and 4).

Concluding Reflections: Need for Integrity, Accountability, and Mutuality

The practice of LPS necessitates integrity, accountability, and solidarity. Lila Watson (n.d.) notes, "*If you have come to help me, you are wasting your time. If you have come because your liberation is bound up with mine, then let us work together.*" As a starting point, the practice of LPS means we interrupt extractive, appropriative, and co-opting strategies that borrow language and practices emerging from movement spaces, without relationality and connection to the values and philosophies of their original frameworks. We must engage in the essential and continuous learning process to develop a strong and deep understanding of the core principles, values, and philosophies of liberatory movement frameworks (including RJ, TJ, HJ, and DJ). It also means we need to hold contradictions that come from working with systems that were designed to further capitalist values of profit-making and extraction at the cost of being oppressive or marginalizing to vulnerable groups. At the same time, we need to finding ways to move toward alignment with the liberatory movement visions and values.

For example, we need to be very vigilant about not misusing or appropriating the language of DJ, or TJ, if we are only focused on legal compliance and not truly working to transform systems that cause harm, and if we are not intentionally working to build collective access and collective liberation. Similarly, we need to practice vigilance to avoid co-optation of HJ to promote self-care at individual and organizational/institutional levels without addressing the need to create trauma-informed systems that support the practice of collective care, collective power, and solidarity; and without transforming systems that contribute toward reproducing persistent institutional trauma.

It is important for us to remain accountable to the base. This practice of accountability also means to move at the pace of our training, skill, growing depth, and capacity and finding ways to be transparent and accountable about that growth and maturing. LPS work is more than intellectual work, it is emotional, relational, and embodied social justice work. It requires deep and embodied self-awareness, self-connection, tender and fierce self-compassion. It challenges and empowers us to lean into our embodied wisdom and discernment, to embrace vulnerability and find embodied courage to do the right thing and live into our values. It requires us to cultivate discipline and patience, to embrace successes, to fail forward with grace and humility, to resist the norms of scarcity and urgency-mindsets in our dominant culture, and to know that there are no shortcuts to liberatory praxis.

Such practice of vulnerability and humility does not undermine our innate wisdom or make us small. Moving with vulnerability and humility is a deep practice of courage and of discerning and honoring the "*the space between what we know, what we do not yet know, and what is unknowable. It requires decentering ourselves and our ego to be open to learning, regardless of years of training and so-called expertise*" (Woodland 2023a, p. 239).

Dreaming Liberatory Public Service: An Imagination Exercise

We invite you to reflect on the above described five principles of liberatory public service (LPS) framework.

Notice and journal: (a) What is resonating? (b) What is causing dissonance? (c) What else would you add to this framework to make it you own?

We invite you identify and reflect on one area/domain that needs transformation within an organization that is familiar to you. This could be your workplace or a public/nonprofit sector organization that is familiar to you. Examples of areas needing change could be, recruitment practices or hiring and selection practices, promotion practices, or interactions with clients and communities that your organization serves, curriculum and pedagogy, learning and development practices, or budgeting and funding practices, policymaking practices or community engagement approaches.

Once you have identified a domain that needs transformation, we invite you to dream/imagine/envision: How the principles of LPS framework can be applied to support transformative change?

Based on the context of your organization, including its developmental stage (for example, there is a strong resistance to change, or the organization is at a beginning or deepening stage with the change process) in relation to liberatory social justice praxis, we invite you to reflect on:

1 What are your and your organization's areas of strength or superpowers that could serve as a starting/deepening point for application of LPS principles? For example, these could be your organization's shared mission, vision, core values, organizational community, the human resources and organization's area of expertise, the elegance of the product or service that you offer, organization's relationships with community and so on. In other words, your strengths could be rooted in the "why", the "for whom", the "what" and/or the "how" as it relates to your organization.
2 What are the areas of challenges, limitations, risks, and contradictions that will get in the way of applying LPS principles? These could be people constraints, lack of political education for liberation, resource constraints, geographical constraints, politics, contextual factors and so on.
3 Explore what other questions and contradictions must you consider in thinking about application and integration of LPS framework to you selected organizational context?
4 Within the context of your organization's change process, reflect on one or two possibilities for your organization to move forward toward alignment with LPS principles and core values? Imagine and co-create possibilities that will help your organization to move forward collectively and meaningfully and build on your existing strengths. Remember, this can be a slow process,

requiring discipline, determination, and patience, and therefore, all the effort and work matters. Be kind, be intentional, be bold in this imagination.

5 Write down the possibilities for individual and collective imagination and reflection.
6 We invite you to return to this imagine exercise, adapt it, add/change prompts as needed and make it your own, as you move toward individual/collective clarity.

Note: We invite you to make this imagination/dreaming exercise your own and adapt the prompts to meet your group/team and organizational needs. If possible, we invite you to practice this dreaming exercise in a trusted collective, learning community, or an identity-based affinity group.

Summary and Key Teachings

In this chapter, we offer an emergent framework of LPS that is inspired by and anchored in the teachings from critical academic scholarly work (such as frameworks of intersectionality and trauma-informed approaches) and social justice movement visions and frameworks (such as RJ, TJ, HJ, and DJ). The five principles of LPS introduced in this chapter are not intended to be prescriptive. Rather, they are intended to guide our collective dreams, visions, and processes toward co-creating socially just and liberatory public service in ways that are fluid, adaptive, context specific and anchored in common values and principles. The five principles of LPS invite our social justice approaches to be trauma-informed, repair and healing-oriented, and compassionately centering the margins within all our organizational functions, structures, designs, policies, procedures, leadership, and cultures.

It is important to distinguish LPS from liberal inclusion. In practice, liberal inclusion often seeks to invite people with marginalized and minoritized identities into existing systems and power structures without changing the oppressive nature of the systems. LPS is the creative and innovative practice of nurturing diversity, equity, inclusion, and belonging in meaningful and empowering ways. Through LPS we could interrupt the ongoing cycles of oppression and pause to imagine and channelize our energy and resources to co-create liberatory alternatives. In Part III of this book, we share our visions and explore potential application and integration of these five principles of LPS to address various social justice issues (including racism, white supremacy, sexism, heteropatriarchy, trans oppression, and intersectional ableism) in public service contexts.

Deep Dive Resources [Full Citations in References]

1 Page, Cara, and Erica Woodland. 2023. Healing Justice Lineages: Dreaming at the Crossroads of Liberation, Collective Care, and Safety.
2 Howard Zehr. 2015. The Little Book of Restorative Justice.
3 Kaba, Mariame. 2021b. We Do This 'Til We Free Us: Abolitionist Organizing and Transforming Justice.
4 Sins Invalid. 2019. Skin, Tooth, and Bone: The Basis of Movement Is Our People, A Disability Justice Primer.
5 brown, adrienne maree. 2017. Emergent Strategy: Shaping Change, Changing Worlds.
6 Tutu, Desmond, and Mpho Tutu. 2015. "The Book of Forgiving: The Fourfold Path for Healing Ourselves and Our World."

Notes

1 However, TJ responses may rely on or incorporate social services like counseling (Mingus 2019).
2 Chapter 3 offers a detailed discussion of trauma, including collective trauma experiences from historical, inter-generational, and persistent institutional oppression. In Chapter 3, we also discuss the importance of embodied healing and collective healing. In this chapter we continue that discussion and with an addition of healing justice perspective to it.

References

Adams, Cara. 2021. "Can Restorative Justice Be Used in Workplace Sex Harassment and Sexual Violence Cases?" National Women's Law Center. July 21, 2021. https://nwlc.org/can-restorative-justice-be-used-in-workplace-sex-harassment-and-sexual-violence-cases/

Adams, Caralee. 2023. "Schools Are Using Restorative Justice to Resolve Conflicts. Does It Work?" Washington Post, July 16, 2023. https://www.washingtonpost.com/education/2023/07/15/restorative-justice-montgomery-county-schools/

Alexander, Michelle. 2020. *The New Jim Crow: Mass Incarceration in the Age of Colorblindness*. 10th Anniversary ed. New York, NY: The New Press.

Berne, Patty. 2020. "What Is Disability Justice?" Sins Invalid. June 16, 2020. https://www.sinsinvalid.org/news-1/2020/6/16/what-is-disability-justice

brown, adrienne maree. 2017. *Emergent Strategy: Shaping Change, Changing Worlds*. Reprint edition. Chico, CA: AK Press.

Burnier, DeLysa. 2003. "Other Voices/Other Rooms: Towards a Care-Centered Public Administration." *Administrative Theory & Praxis 25* (4): 529–44.

———. 2009. "Markets No More: Toward a Care-Centered Public Administration." *Administrative Theory & Praxis 31* (3): 396–402.

Chordiya, Rashmi, and Adana Protonentis. 2024. "Healing from Intersectional White Supremacy Culture and Ableism: Disability Justice as an Antidote."

Journal of Social Equity and Public Administration 2 (1): 127–52. *https://doi.org/10.24926/jsepa.v2i1.4856.*

Chordiya, Rashmi, Stephanie Dolamore, Jeannine M. Love, Erin L. Borry, Adana Protonentis, Brendan Stern, and Geoffrey Whitebread. 2023. "Staking the Tent at the Margins: Using Disability Justice to Expand the Theory and Praxis of Social Equity in Public Administration." *Administrative Theory & Praxis*: 1–26. https://doi.org/10.1080/10841806.2023.2216616

Darling-Hammond, Sean. 2023. "Fostering Belonging, Transforming Schools: The Impact of Restorative Practices." Learning Policy Institute. https://learningpolicyinstitute.org/product/impact-restorative-practices-report

Dolamore, Stephanie. 2021. "Detecting Empathy in Public Organizations: Creating a More Relational Public Administration." *Administrative Theory & Praxis (Taylor & Francis Ltd) 43* (1): 58–81. https://doi.org/10.1080/10841806.2019.1700458

Dolamore, Stephanie, and Geoffrey Whitebread. 2022. "Recalibrating Public Service: Valuing Engagement, Empathy, Social Equity, and Ethics in Public Administration." *Public Integrity 24* (4–5): 375–86. https://doi.org/10.1080/10999922.2021.2014223

Farrow, Keynon. 2023. "A House Is a Temple: How Dance Music Culture Became a Refuge in the HIV/AIDS Epidemic." In *Healing Justice Lineages: Dreaming at the Crossroads of Liberation, Collective Care, and Safety*, edited by Cara Page and Erica Woodland, 106–12. Berkeley, CA: North Atlantic Books.

Generation Five. 2007. "Towards Transformative Justice: A Liberatory Approach to Child Sexual Abuse and Other Forms of Intimate and Community Violence." http://www.generationfive.org/downloads/G5_Toward_Transformative_Justice.pdf

Guy, Mary E., Meredith A. Newman, and Sharon H. Mastracci. 2014. *Emotional Labor: Putting the Service in Public Service.* 2nd ed. London: Routledge.

Haines, Staci. 2019. *The Politics of Trauma: Somatics, Healing, and Social Justice.* Illustrated edition. Berkeley, California: North Atlantic Books.

Kaba, Mariame. 2021a. "The Sentencing of Larry Nassar Was Not 'Transformative Justice.' Here's Why." In *We Do This 'Til We Free Us: Abolitionist Organizing and Transforming Justice*, edited by Tamara K. Nopper, 58–62. Chicago, IL: Haymarket Books.

Kaba, Mariame. 2021b. *We Do This 'Til We Free Us: Abolitionist Organizing and Transforming Justice.* Edited by Tamara K. Nopper. Chicago, IL: Haymarket Books.

Kaba, Mariame, and Shira Hassan. 2019. *Fumbling Towards Repair: A Workbook for Community Accountability Facilitators.* Illustrated ed. Project NIA.

Kaba, Mariame, and Shira Hassan. 2021. "From 'Me Too' to 'All of Us': Organizing to End Sexual Violence Without Prisons." In *We Do This 'Til We Free Us: Abolitionist Organizing and Transforming Justice*, edited by Tamara K. Nopper, 41–48. Chicago, IL: Haymarket Books.

London, Ross D. 2010. *Crime, Punishment, and Restorative Justice: From the Margins to the Mainstream.* Boulder, CO: Lynne Rienner Publishers.

McDowell, Ceasar. 2015. "Democracy from the Margins | Ceasar McDowell | TEDxIndianaUniversity." TEDx Talks. https://www.youtube.com/watch?v=irkqd0q9a9k&ab_channel=TEDxTalks

Menakem, Resmaa. 2021. Resmaa Menakem — 'Notice the Rage; Notice the Silence' Interview by Krista Tippett. https://onbeing.org/programs/resmaa-menakem-notice-the-rage-notice-the-silence/

Meyer, Seth J., Richard Greggory Johnson III, and Sean McCandless. 2022. "Meet the New Es: Empathy, Engagement, Equity, and Ethics in Public Administration." *Public Integrity 24* (4–5): 353–63. https://doi.org/10.1080/10999922.2022.2074764

Middleton, Tamika, and Cara Page. 2023. "Conjuring the Roots of Healing Justice in the Southeast." In *Healing Justice Lineages: Dreaming at the Crossroads of Liberation, Collective Care, and Safety*, edited by Cara Page and Erica Woodland, 130–41. Berkeley, CA: North Atlantic Books.

Mingus, Mia. 2019. "Transformative Justice: A Brief Description." *Transform Harm* (blog). January 11, 2019. https://transformharm.org/transformative-justice-a-brief-description/

Nocella, Anthony J. II. 2011. "An Overview of the History and Theory of Transformative Justice." *Peace & Conflict Review* 6 (1): 1–10.

Opie, Tina, and Laura Morgan Roberts. 2017. "Do Black Lives Really Matter in the Workplace? Restorative Justice as a Means to Reclaim Humanity." *Equality, Diversity and Inclusion: An International Journal 36* (8): 707–19. https://doi.org/10.1108/EDI-07-2017-0149

Page, Cara. 2023a. "Blackprints for Freedom." In *Healing Justice Lineages: Dreaming at the Crossroads of Liberation, Collective Care, and Safety*, edited by Cara Page and Erica Woodland, 39–49. Berkeley, CA: North Atlantic Books.

———. 2023b. "Dismantling the Medical Industrial Complex: Building Power for Collective Care." In *Healing Justice Lineages: Dreaming at the Crossroads of Liberation, Collective Care, and Safety*, edited by Page, Cara, and Erica Woodland, 209–18. Berkeley, CA: North Atlantic Books.

———. 2023c. "Roots of the Medical Industrial Complex." In *Healing Justice Lineages: Dreaming at the Crossroads of Liberation, Collective Care, and Safety*, edited by Page, Cara, and Erica Woodland, 72–81. Berkeley, CA: North Atlantic Books.

Page, Cara, and Erica Woodland. 2023. *Healing Justice Lineages: Dreaming at the Crossroads of Liberation, Collective Care, and Safety*. Berkeley, CA: North Atlantic Books.

Piepzna-Samarasinha, Leah Lakshmi. 2018. *Care Work: Dreaming Disability Justice*. Vancouver: Arsenal Pulp Press.

Sins Invalid. 2019. "Skin, Tooth, and Bone: The Basis of Movement Is Our People, A Disability Justice Primer." https://www.sinsinvalid.org/skin-tooth-and-bone

———. n.d. "10 Principles of Disability Justice — Sins Invalid." Accessed July 27, 2023. https://www.sinsinvalid.org/blog/10-principles-of-disability-justice. http://ebookcentral.proquest.com/lib/seattleu/detail.action?docID=7179053

Stensöta, Helena. 2011. "A Public Ethics of Care for Administration and Implementation." *Western Political Science Association Annual Meeting Paper*, 1–14. https://ssrn.com/abstract=1766979

Tutu, Desmond, and Mpho Tutu. 2015. "The Book of Forgiving: The Fourfold Path for Healing Ourselves and Our World." Reprint edition. New York, New York: HarperOne.

Utah, Adaku, and Cara Page. 2023. "A Constellation of Healing Justice and Liberation: Sites of Practice in New York City." In *Healing Justice Lineages: Dreaming at the Crossroads of Liberation, Collective Care, and Safety*, edited by Cara Page and Erica Woodland, 179–86. Berkeley, CA: North Atlantic Books.

Valenzuela, Matias. 2017. "King County's Journey in Institutionalizing Equity and Social Justice." Public Administration Review. https://kingcounty.gov/~/media/elected/executive/equity-social-justice/2017/PAR2017ArticleValenzuela-KCJourneyInInstitutionalize.ashx?la=en

Watson, Lilla. n.d. "About." *Lilla: International Women's Network (blog). n.d. https://lillanetwork.wordpress.com/about/*

williams, Rev. angel Kyodo. n.d. "Angel Kyodo Williams 'Love and Justice Are Not Two. without Inner Change, There Can Be No Outer Change; without Collective Change, No Change Matters.'" n.d. https://angelkyodowilliams.com/

Woodland, Erica. 2023a. "Return to Spirit: Lineage, Integrity and Accountability." In *Healing Justice Lineages: Dreaming at the Crossroads of Liberation, Collective Care, and Safety*, edited by Cara Page and Erica Woodland, 234–43. New York, NY: North Atlantic Books.

———. 2023b. "Why We Organize Practitioners." In *Healing Justice Lineages: Dreaming at the Crossroads of Liberation, Collective Care, and Safety*, edited by Page, Cara, and Erica Woodland, 219–23. Berkeley, CA: North Atlantic Books.

Zehr, Howard. 2011a. "Justice as a Restoration of Trust." Eastern Mennonite University. *Zehr Institute for Restorative Justice* (blog). February 8, 2011. https://emu.edu/now/restorative-justice/2011/03/10/restorative-or-transformative-justice/

———. 2011b. "Restorative or Transformative Justice?" Eastern Mennonite University. *Zehr Institute for Restorative Justice* (blog). March 10, 2011. https://emu.edu/now/restorative-justice/2011/03/10/restorative-or-transformative-justice/

———. 2015. *The Little Book of Restorative Justice: Revised and Updated.* 2nd ed. Intercourse, PA: Good Books.

6 Diffusion of DEILJ Innovations in Public Service

Abstract

In this chapter, we explore frameworks that can guide public service professionals in operationalizing the normative DEILJ values, especially at institutional and organizational levels. This chapter is intended to address some of "the how" questions or questions related to change management work in DEILJ contexts. Specifically, we explore three selected theoretical frameworks that could help us strategically develop, diffuse, and sustain DEILJ-change effort at both individual and collective (e.g., community or organizational/institutional) levels. These are: (1) Everett Roger's (2003) the Diffusion of Innovation (DOI) theory, (2) Taylor Cox's (2001) Organizational Change Model for Diversity, (3) powell, Menendian, and Ake's (2019) Targeted Universalism or Equity 2.0 approach. Some of the key teachings offered in this chapter focus on the importance of taking an integrated change management approach anchored in organization's core values, the necessity of aligning management systems, the importance of shared leadership approaches, coalition building work, and collaboration (and solidarity) across various levels of organizations to effect and diffuse DEILJ-focused change.

Introduction

Public service is an applied field. One of the key explorations of diversity, equity, inclusion, and liberatory justice (DEILJ) praxis in public service contexts therefore focuses on finding meaningful ways to operationalize and implement the normative justice values and principles: "the how" piece.

In Chapter 2, we explored Barbara Love's (2018) Liberatory Consciousness framework and Bobbie Harro's (2018) Cycle of Liberation that can guide us in inner transformation work that purposefully interrupts cycles of oppression and move us toward liberatory social justice. In Chapter 5, we offered a liberatory public service framework with an intent to distill

DOI: 10.4324/9781032670669-8

some of the key teachings and principles of social justice-focused scholarship and practice. We hope these and other frameworks explored so far have offered you adequate clarity about the normative values that are important to the practice of DEILJ work.

For example, from an LPS perspective, these normative values include the importance of trauma-informed healing-centered (TIHC) public service, restorative justice and repair work, transformative justice, and the need to transform the conditions that make harm possible in the first place, the role of communities, and collectives for DEILJ work, and the importance of following the leadership of those most impacted by social injustices and inequities.

In this chapter, we shift gears and explore frameworks that can guide public service professionals in operationalizing the normative DEILJ values, especially at institutional and organizational levels. In other words, this chapter is intended to address some of "the how" questions in relation to change management work and to advance diffusion of innovative ideas, frameworks, and practices in DEILJ contexts. We seek to highlight and underscore that creativity, imagination, and innovation are not restricted to domains of science and technology. Rather, creativity, imagination, and innovation are at the core of social and organizational change management work related to DEILJ. We hope that the interdisciplinary policy and administrative change management frameworks explored in this chapter will help us in our approaches to diffusing DEILJ innovations.

To answer "how questions," we explore three theoretical frameworks that could help us strategically develop, diffuse, and sustain DEILJ-change effort at both individual and collective (e.g., community or organizational/institutional) levels. These are: (1) Everett Roger's (2003) the Diffusion of Innovation (DOI) theory, (2) Taylor Cox's (2001) Organizational Change Model for Diversity, (3) powell et al.'s (2019) Targeted Universalism (TU) or Equity 2.0 approach.

We hope the theoretical frameworks covered in this chapter offers introductory ideas about how to advance DEILJ-change process and practice, including addressing concerns and resistance to change. The key questions we explore include:

1 How can we diffuse DEILJ innovations (i.e., ideas, practices, and approaches) across organizational levels? What are the key elements of DOI framework and how are they relevant for DEILJ-change processes? Our intention is that the interpretative ideas based on Rogers (2003) DOI framework offered in this chapter serve both type of change initiatives – those that are led by top leadership and management and those that are led by bottom-up change initiatives (e.g., student initiatives, employee initiatives, community initiatives).

2 How can we integrate DEILJ-change initiatives across organizational functions, operations, and culture? In other words, what are the key strategies that must align to integrate and institutionalize DEILJ-change work? Cox's (2001) diversity and culture change model offer insights to respond to these questions.
3 How can we approach equity work in ways that are consistent and considerate of the needs of diverse populations we seek to serve? How can we approach equity work with a universal goal in mind and that is flexible and adaptive in its targeted strategies. We hope powell et al.'s (2019) TU framework offers insights to respond to these questions. TU approach allows us to be creative in approaching equity work and co-create many possibilities to meet the specific needs of the populations we intend to serve.

It is important to note that these are not intended to be step-by-step guides, neither are these the only frameworks to approach DEILJ-change work. We have found these three frameworks to be helpful in thinking about DEILJ-focused change work. We invite you to connect the dots between these three frameworks and other change management frameworks that you have come across, that resonate with you, and/or you have meaningfully applied in your change management praxis. We do not offer these as either/or approaches, rather each of these frameworks have key teachings, ideas, and insights that align with each other, and they can collectively serve as helpful approaches for strategic work of implementing and institutionalizing DEILJ-change work that centers the margins. An understanding of these three frameworks can help us affect external or collective change for DEILJ in systematic and structured ways at organizational, institutional, or societal levels.

In the following sections, we offer an overview for each of these frameworks, their key tenets followed by a discussion of interpretative understandings and reflections on how these frameworks could serve the public service community in envisioning and operationalizing organizational and institutional level change work for DEILJ praxis.

Diffusion of Innovation Theory

The DOI theory was developed by Everett Rogers in 1962. This theory explains how new ideas, technologies, products, or practices spread through a social system over time. This theory is widely used in fields such as sociology, communication studies, marketing, agriculture, and public health to understand the adoption and acceptance of innovations by individuals and groups. The theory outlines the stages as well as the factors that influence the rate of adoption of innovations.

In the context of DEILJ-change work, the theory of DOI can serve organizational leaders and change agents in promoting DEILJ ideas, practices, and approaches. We think the DOI framework can help us examine and understand how change works, especially at larger societal and institutional levels. However, we want to note that DOI is a process, a tool, if you will, and like other scientific inventions, depending on who is using it, it can bring either positive or negative change. Not all innovations are necessarily helpful and desirable; some may be harmful, inefficient, and undesirable for individuals and social systems (Rogers 2003). For example, think about the ongoing diffusion of anti-trans bills, anti-DEI bills, or banned books across several states in the United States. We want to make this important acknowledgment and invite you to hold these contradictions about using a change management tool as we dive into the key tenets of DOI theory.

The Key Tenets of Diffusion of Innovation (DOI) Theory and Implications for DEILJ Praxis

Innovation is an "idea, practice, or object that is perceived as new by an individual or other unit of adoption" (Rogers 2003, p. 12). Note that by this definition, perception matters and "a perceived" newness of an idea, practice, or an object by an adopting individual or other units of adoption (such as a group, an organization) can count as innovation. Adoption refers to the process through which an individual or group decides to accept and use an innovation.

The process of DOI is a social change process in which "an innovation *is communicated* through certain channels over time and among members of a social system" (Rogers 2003, p. 5, emphasis added by authors). DOI may be planned, or they could involve a spontaneous spread of new ideas, behaviors, and objects within a social network of a given social system. While some new ideas diffuse at a faster rate, other ideas have a slower adoption rate and move quite incrementally. Furthermore, innovations spread in planned or spontaneous manners *from network of one social system to a network of another social system* – that is, one person, one team, one organization, one collective, one locality, one state, one nation at a time (Rogers 2003).

From a DEILJ-change perspective, an innovation could mean new ideas, practices, and approaches that serve in advancing DEILJ-focused change work. Given that DEILJ work is often inspired, guided, and led by social movements and organizing work, DEILJ-change work, even in the contexts of organizations and institutions, could be led by top leadership and/or it could be driven by bottom-up leadership and collective actions at various stages of the change process.

In public service contexts, DEILJ innovations can be applied in the domains of:

1 Public policy making (e.g., use of housing first policy as a policy approach to solve the housing crisis).
2 Administrative decision-making (e.g., use of race and social equity consciousness approaches in organizational goal setting and management practices).
3 Procedural developments (e.g., removing administrative and access burdens in procedures to foster procedural justice).
4 Structural development (e.g., using equitable and inclusive job evaluation techniques in pay structures, building gender neutral bathrooms, integrating accessibility tools in software and other designs, building accessible ramps, and building elevators, adding curb-cuts to sidewalks).
5 Cultural development (e.g., the development of social equity as a foundational pillar of public administration, the growing calls for social justice and climate justice as core values of organizational practice).

In Chapter 5, we offer a DEILJ innovation, a framework, which we named "Liberatory Public Service" or LPS. LPS approach is inspired and guided by social justice movement frameworks such as Restorative Justice (RJ), Transformative Justice (TJ), Disability Justice (DJ), and Healing Justice (HJ) as well as interdisciplinary critical academic scholarship such as frameworks of liberatory consciousness, intersectionality, and trauma-informed approaches. LPS focuses on advancing DEILJ work by prioritizing inner transformation and collective transformation to promote trauma-informed, repair and healing-centered public service that compassionately centers the margins. LPS seeks to transform the conditions that allow forms of oppression to exist and persist.

A Reflection Opportunity: Diffusion of DEILJ Innovation

In the following sections, we will describe the key tenets of various frameworks that can support and guide collective transformation for DEILJ. As you explore these frameworks, we invite you to reflect on:

a *LPS or another DEILJ innovation (e.g., critical race theory, queer theory, intersectionality framework, trauma-informed practice, RJ, TJ, HJ, or DJ framework) that resonates with you to guide the core values, principles, and practice of an organization's social justice-focused change work.*
b *We invite you to imagine/envision diffusion of LPS or another DEILJ innovation in organizational/team/community contexts. How can organizational leaders and change agents approach their DEILJ diffusion work? What challenges and resources can they expect?*

Diffusion of Innovation: What Gets in the Way?

As in case of any innovation change work, getting a new idea, practice, process, or an object adopted, even when it has demonstrated obvious advantages, is difficult. Consider our experience with COVID-19 pandemic as it relates to adoption of masks and COVID-19 vaccines. Consider voting behaviors. Consider the diffusion of digital innovations such as the internet or the adoption rate of recycling practices or use of bicycles. Even everyday behaviors of brushing and flossing teeth twice a day or washing hands with soap for 20 seconds or exercising our bodies or practicing mindfulness. As public service professionals, many of us are already deeply familiar with the challenging process of diffusion of an innovation. You may recognize that both individual behaviors and systemic and structural challenges can hinder the adoption of an innovative idea, behavior, or object.

As we seek to identify factors that get in the way of DOI and behavioral change in contexts where we act as change agents, we must avoid individual blame bias and develop a keen understanding of system-blame. Individual-blame bias refers to assumptions that hold an individual responsible for their problems, rather than considering the role of the system of which the individual is a part.

How we define a social problem, determines our approach to solving it, and a common error in change work is to overemphasize individual blame while underestimating system-blame. System-blame refers to holding a system responsible for the problems involving individual members of the system (Rogers 2003). It is important to note that both individuals and systems must work in tandem for meaningful change to occur.

A Reflection Opportunity: Individual and Systemic Barriers in Diffusion of Innovation

We invite you to think about examples of innovative ideas, behaviors, and approaches introduced within your teams and organizations using the following prompts. Consider journaling your reflections using key words, sentences or phrases using the accompanying reflection box:

i *Think of one DEILJ-focused innovative idea, practice, or approach introduced in your teams and organizations. Write it down. Examples may include adoption of practices related to use of pronouns, or consistent participation in voluntary learning opportunities about social and racial justice matters in relation to your work or starting employee resource groups.*

ii *Now that you have identified an innovation, we invite you to think about how well the adoption of an innovative idea, practice, or approach is going. This will be subjective (not an empirical response)* *and from your perspective. To avoid generalization of your opinions, we invite you to use "I" statements such as "I think the <innovation> is (or is not) going so well <explain your reasons>."*

iii *For the final prompt, we invite you to think about individual as well as systemic or structural and cultural factors that are helpful or hinder the diffusion of innovation within your team or organization. Here, it is important to be mindful of individual-blame bias or attribution error wherein we overestimate the blame on individuals and do not analyze systemic or structural barriers that may be getting in the way of adoption behaviors of individuals. Be sure to think about system blame that is about systemic and structural barriers that impede the progress in diffusion of innovative idea, behavior or object related to DEILJ-change work. System-blame could also include dominant cultural paradigms and learnings, it could be experiences of historical, inter-generational, persistent institutional, and personal trauma resulting from oppression. It could also be a culture rooted in fear, insecurity and scarcity-mindset, with retaliatory consequences for challenging the status quo.*

iv *Journal your observations.*

Reflection Box for Journaling: Individual and Systemic Barriers in Diffusion of Innovation

Role of a Social System in Diffusion of Innovation

The DOI occurs within the boundary of a social system. A social system is a set of interrelated units or members, that is, individuals, informal groups, organizations, and/or subsystems. The structure of a social system influences the diffusion process of innovation in several ways. For example, an important role is played by norms of a social system in DOI. Norms define a range of accepted or tolerable behaviors. Norms serve as a guide or standard for established behavior patterns that members are expected to perform. For example, religious norms are found to play an important role in diffusion of family planning and other social innovations (Rogers 2003).

ROLES OF CHANGE AGENTS, CHANGE AGENT AIDES, AND OPINION LEADERS

In addition to norms of a social system, opinion leaders, change agents, and change agent aides significantly influence DOI. In the context of social change work, change agents seek to influence target audience's innovation decisions in a direction deemed desirable by a change agency. Applied to the DEILJ context, we imagine that the change agencies could be a social organization, a student organization or organizational executive leadership office. Similarly, change agents can encompass both top leadership and management as well as those leading change from grassroots social movements or bottom-up change within organizations.

In the following paragraphs, we explore the implications of DOI theory for public service organizational contexts where there exists a commitment from top leadership and management to invest in DEILJ-change efforts. However, as we have noted, DEILJ-change work in organizational contexts, can often be led by bottom-up efforts from students, employees, and communities. In bottom-up change scenarios, change agents are likely to be students, employees and community organizations seeking change and, the target population for change may be organizational leadership across different levels, especially including those at the top executive and management levels.

DOI research suggests that to establish trust with their diverse client base, change agents collaborate with change agent aides who typically share similar backgrounds and contexts as the clients/target population for change. These aides engage with clients to influence their innovation decisions (Rogers 2003).

Opinion leaders are individuals who have a significant influence on the adoption and acceptance of new ideas, technologies, products, or practices within a social system. Opinion leaders are typically early adopters who are respected, trusted, and perceived as knowledgeable by their peers. They play a crucial role in spreading information, shaping perceptions, and encouraging others to adopt innovations (Rogers 2003).

For example, in the context of organizational and institutional DEILJ innovation, consider a university working to disseminate an innovative approach, such as incorporating a racial equity and justice focus into the curriculum for all university programs. The university's change agents, including those from the president's and provost's office, may collaborate with change agent aides (such as department and program chairs and deans) from each department or school/college who share similarities in backgrounds and contexts with potential adopters (i.e., faculty members) within each department or school. Furthermore, alongside change agent aides like department chairs and program chairs, faculty members who are respected, trusted, and perceived as knowledgeable by their peers in the department could assume the role of early adopters and opinion leaders in the diffusion of a curriculum with a racial equity and justice focus.

Thus, from a DOI theory perspective, it is important for DEILJ-change agent/s (e.g., an executive leader or a team member of diversity and inclusion office) working within an organization's broader context to collaborate closely with opinion leaders and change aides within specific departments or teams. Opinion leaders and change agent aides within the same social system (e.g., a department or a team) share individual, technical, professional, contextual, and cultural similarities, and understandings with potential adopters. Hence, they are likely to influence change in ways that change agents may not.

Innovativeness and Adopter Categories

Innovativeness is the degree to which (i.e., how soon or how late) an individual or a unit adopts a new idea, practice, or approach compared to other members of a given social system. Based on their innovativeness (i.e., how soon or how late they adopt an innovation) the members of a social system are classified into five broad adopter categories. Within diffusion research and practice, these adopter categories are referred to as: (1) innovators, (2) early adopters, (3) early majority, (4) late majority, and (5) laggards (Rogers 2003). Figure 6.1 represents adopter categories and their percentages based on existing DOI research.

Innovators are enterprising and daring. Typically, DOI research shows that innovators constitute 2.5% of the target population. They are interested in new ideas, which lead them into broader social networks that extend beyond their local peer networks. They are willing to take risks and be the first to try the innovation. They help "launch the new idea in the system by importing the innovation from outside the system's boundaries" (Rogers 2003, p. 283).

Early adopters have the highest degree of opinion leadership in most systems. They constitute 13.5% of the target population. Respected by

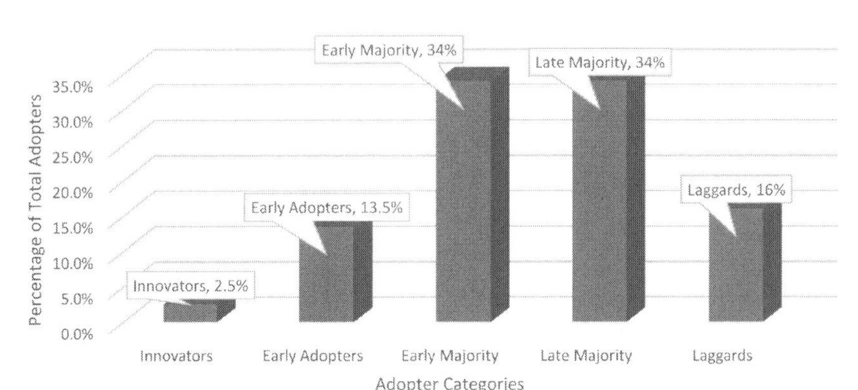

Figure 6.1 Successful Innovation Adopter Categories and Respective Percentages: Based on Everett Roger's Diffusion of Innovation Theory

Source: Adapted from Rogers 2003.

their peers, they serve as a role model for many other members of a social system. They need to make judicious innovation-decisions to maintain their credibility, respect, and central position in the communication network of the system. By adopting an innovation, early adopters who are influential opinion leaders, prompt the critical mass of potential adopters (Rogers 2003).

The early majority are deliberate in their willingness to adopt an innovation. They typically need to observe the evidence that the innovation works before they are willing to adopt it, hence, their innovation-decision period is relatively longer. They make up about one-third (34%) of all members of a system and their unique position between the very early and the relatively late adopters makes them an important link in the diffusion process (Rogers 2003).

The late majority adopt innovation just after the majority has tried it. Like the early majority, the late majority also constitute one-third (34%) of the target population. Members who constitute the late majority are skeptical and cautious about the new idea. To appeal to the late majority members of the system and make them feel safe enough to adopt an innovation, uncertainties associated with the new idea must be removed. Peer pressure must be strong enough to motivate their adoption, and the weight of system norms must favor the innovation (Rogers 2003).

Laggards value traditions and are the last members of the social system to adopt an innovation. They constitute 16% of the target population. Laggards tend to be suspicious of innovations and change agents. The innovation-decision process is relatively lengthy as they often lack resources for risk taking and need certainty that a new idea will not fail before they can adopt it. To convince laggards, an important point of reference is the past. They often make decisions based on what has been done previously and interact primarily with others who also have relatively traditional values (Rogers 2003).

There are at least four important points we would like to emphasize about innovative behaviors and adopter categories from a DEILJ-change perspective. First, it is important to remember the significance of skills such as patience, vulnerability, and courage throughout diffusion of DEILJ innovation process. These skills and qualities help us avoid scarcity and urgency mindset when thinking about DEILJ change and, enable us to practice empathy and compassion toward ourselves and others. These skills help us deepen our discernment that some members are slower to adopt DEILJ innovations based on their readiness and the system's capacity to support their needs throughout the adoption process.

Second, it is important to avoid individual bias and instead, be curious about systemic and structural factors contributing to late adoption. It invites us to decode resistance to change with an abundance and curiosity mindset, challenging change agents to view *resistance as a form of feedback* that may reveal important needs, concerns, and limitations about the change process and/or outcomes (Ford and Ford 2009; Rogers 2003).

Third, most individuals, particularly those in the early and late majority categories, rely on subjective evaluations conveyed by peers who have already adopted the innovation. Effective communication is crucial in this social process (Rogers 2003). And fourth, any major change effort, such as DEILJ effort is a collective effort, requiring a shared leadership approach, coalition building work, and collaboration (and solidarity) across various levels of organizations. This includes collaboration among change agents, change agent aides, opinion leaders, and early majority adopters.

The Key Factors that Influence the Rate of Adoption of Innovation

Diffusion research has identified five perception-based characteristics of innovations that shed light on the varying rates of adoption. These characteristics encompass perceptions regarding the innovation's (1) relative advantage, (2) compatibility, (3) complexity, (4) trialability, and (5) observability.

Before discussing these five factors, it is important to acknowledge their value in providing insights into individual-level perceptions that influence adoption decisions. However, it is essential to recognize their limitations in terms of systemic- and structural-level analyses. In other words, these five characteristics do not offer sufficient information about systemic factors that impact an individual's adoption of innovation. Systemic factors include access to necessary resources, information, and support systems.

This limitation is inherent in diffusion research itself (Rogers 2003). Nonetheless, we believe that these five factors are intuitive and may prove relevant to the diffusion of DEILJ innovations within our collectives and organizations, and particularly help with understanding the determinants of individual-level innovation adoption (Rogers 2003).

First, a relative advantage is the degree to which an innovation is perceived to be better than the idea, practice, or approach it supersedes. For example, why should potential adopters invest in changing their behaviors or practices? Why should they care or why it matters? How does a given DEILJ innovation help to create better outcomes for those impacted, compared to the idea, practice or approach it supersedes?

Second, compatibility is the degree to which an innovation is perceived to be compatible with the values, experiences, and needs of the potential adopters. At a fundamental level, the task of the change agent and their aides/allies is to help potential adopters notice how the innovation is compatible with the values, experiences, and/or needs. Here, it is important to note, diffusion research shows that "an idea that is incompatible with the values and norms of a social system will not be adopted as rapidly as an innovation that is compatible. The adoption of an incompatible innovation often requires the prior adoption of a new value system, which is a relatively slow process" (Rogers 2003, p. 15).

We think the preceding quote from Rogers (2003) offers an important piece of instruction for diffusion of DEILJ innovation work. An organization's culture audit might reveal that the current cultural norms and value systems do not align with the direction or vision of DEILJ innovation. Pushing for change efforts without doing the necessary work of value alignment before, during, and after the introduction of a DEILJ change can lead to superficial and/or performative DEILJ work. Based on the information gathered through the culture audit process, DEILJ-change agents might find the need to prioritize DEILJ-focused communication, programming, priming and culture-change work prior to introduction of change. Furthermore, change agents and their aides/allies will need to focus on continued culture change work during and after change initiative has been implemented to ensure its long-term adoption, sustainability, adaptability, and effectiveness. For example, we are often focused on creating new policies or structures without prioritizing and resourcing necessary communication and cultural foundations to ease the implementation and adoption of the policies and structures.

The third factor influencing the rate of adoption of innovation is complexity. Complexity is the degree to which the innovation is difficult to understand and use. Simpler innovations that are easier to understand and practice are adopted more easily than those that require adopters to develop new skills and understandings. Given the nuances and complexities of DEILJ work, the third factor of keeping the innovations simple and/or easy to practice presents an important contradiction. Probably, this is one of the key factors that hinders DEILJ work, as people tend to avoid mental and emotional complexities and the associated discomfort.

For example, a key skill involved in DEILJ work is to build capacity for courageous conversations. Based on our experiences and discernments, we are finding our way to navigate this contradiction with small but bold experiments, creating spaces for learning and development that honor agency, choice, and meaningful pace for individuals and groups, offering examples of successes and rewards to motivate and nourish peoples' bodyminds and spirits in sustaining DEILJ work.

We invite you to reflect on this challenge and opportunity individually and in collectives/groups and explore possibilities to move forward given your contexts. It does not have to be perfect, and we must be open, adaptive and learn to fail forward. This is hard and nuanced work. It requires collective imagination, inspiration, self-determination, motivation, discipline, persistence, and practice. The nature of the challenge itself could be inspiring for people to engage in the work of culture change, especially, if the above two factors related to relative advantage (factor one) and values and needs alignment (factor two) are fulfilled. How can we co-create persuasive visions and nourishing systems that make the work of DEILJ focused change (even when it could be complex) meaningful, engaging, joyful, and pleasurable for potential adopters?

Fourth, trialability is the extent to which the innovation could be tested or experimented with on a limited basis (e.g., with a trial period option) before making a commitment to adopt. "An innovation that is trialable represents less uncertainty to the individual who is considering it for adoption, as it is possible to learn by doing" (Rogers 2003, p. 16).Fifth, observability is the extent to which the innovation provides tangible results. The likelihood of adoption increases as it gets easier for potential adopters to tangibly experience (or see) the results of an innovation. The visibility of an innovation stimulates peer discussion of a new idea within a diffusion network as interested friends, neighbors, colleagues, community members of an adopter often request innovation evaluation information about it.

From our perspectives, the fourth and fifth factor applied to the context of DEILJ change work implies that are we offering people choices, agency, self-determination, examples of meaningful and tangible change outcomes and successes, and creating a supportive environment for people to navigate vulnerabilities of DEILJ work. For example, organizations and DEILJ change agents can co-create, facilitate, and sustain empowered communities of practice, learning communities, identity-based affinity groups, one-on-one or group consultations, and DEILJ labs to provide spaces for potential adopters to test ideas, experiment, explore, and gain clarity about the innovation.

The DOI scholarship suggests, "These five qualities of innovations are the most important characteristics (determinants) of innovations in explaining the rate of adoption. Innovations that are perceived by individuals as having greater relative advantage, compatibility, trialability, and observability and less complexity will be adopted more rapidly than other innovations" (Rogers 2003, pp. 16–17).

In addition to these five attributes of innovation, diffusion research also shows that re-invention or in other words, adaptation, or customization of an innovation to suit the needs and context of the adopters is an important factor that contributes toward sustainability of an innovation (Rogers 2003). Re-invention is important to avoid a standardized, one-size-fits-all template for innovation and to allow creativity in adapting the innovation (i.e., ideas, practices, protocols, and processes) to meet the cultural and contextual needs of the adopting social system.

An Invitation to Pause and Reflection: Diffusion of Innovation Theory

We invite you to pause here and notice what you need. Take one or more deep breaths if they are accessible, connect with your body, move, hydrate, and take care of your needs. We invite you to return to this reflection and the rest of the chapter when you feel able and ready.

When you return, if you are able and willing, we invite you to notice and journal your reflections using the following suggested prompts. As you respond/return to these prompts, prioritize and focus on prompts that resonate with you in this moment and move at a pace that feels kind and nourishing.

Suggested Reflection Prompts

1 *What is your understanding of the key tenets or principles of diffusion of innovation theory?*
2 *Which theoretical ideas, principles, and research findings (or our interpretations and reflections) based on diffusion research resonate for you? Which ones are causing dissonance?*
3 *In what ways can diffusion of innovation theory and research be helpful/relevant for diffusion of DEILJ innovations? Please offer examples/specific ideas.*
4 *Based on diffusion research findings discussed in this chapter, what challenges and opportunities can we expect with diffusion of DEILJ innovations?*

Key Take-Aways From Diffusion of Innovation for DEILJ Praxis

The theory, practice, and research built on the DOI framework offers us several valuable insights on how we can diffuse DEILJ innovations at individual, organizational, institutional levels and beyond. One of the most important takeaways from DOI theory and research is that successful DEILJ innovations (i.e., ideas, practices, and approaches) – with success measured by the rate of adoption – are likely to follow an incremental growth curve. Some members of a social system (e.g., an organization or a team or a locality) adopt an innovation sooner, while others may need more time.

Diffusion research has consistently shown support for the following pattern where innovators (2.5%) and early adopters (13.5%) are quick to adopt an innovation, constituting an important 15% of the critical mass of the target population necessary for wider DOI. Members who constitute the early majority (34%) are an important link for wider DOI, followed by late majority (34%) and laggards (16%) who are last to adopt an innovation (Rogers 2003). From a future research perspective, it is important to empirically test if this typical adoption rate and these categories are also generalizable and valid for DEILJ-focused innovations. However, based on existing diffusion research we can hypothesize that similar patterns may hold true for DEILJ innovation adoptions.

Diffusion research offers important lessons into the individual factors that influence adoption rates of innovation. These include access to resources, risk taking capacity, perceived relative advantage of innovation, and compatibility with individual's values, needs, and experiences. It also reveals important information about systemic and structural factors that affect adoption rates. These include resource constraints, inequities, design issues as well as cultural norms, values, and beliefs.

Furthermore, diffusion research emphasizes the distinct roles played by different members of a social system in the DOI, including change agents, opinion leaders, and change agent aides. It teaches us to be mindful of individual blame bias, especially when advocating for change and prompts us to focus carefully, creatively, and critically at system-blame that may reveal structural, design, and systemic factors that hinder individual adoption of DEILJ innovation. It teaches us the value of reinvention or adaptation of the original innovation, enabling members of a social system to customize the innovation to align with their contexts, needs, values, and cultures.

In the next section, we discuss Taylor Cox's (2001) organizational change model for diversity. Cox's (2001) model can help DEILJ-change workers to identify important cultural change elements for successful and sustainable diffusion of DEILJ innovations within organizations.

Cox's (2001) Organizational Change Model for Diversity

In their book on "Creating Multicultural Organizations," Taylor Cox Jr. (2001) developed and described a model for organizational cultural change as a strategy to cultivate and sustain organizational diversity. Cox's (2001) model serves as a helpful framework in thinking about DEILJ-change work especially at organizational and institutional levels because it invites us to strategize change work in an integrated manner.

Often organizations limit their DEILJ-change work to the level of awareness training and educational programming. However, such effort can become superficial and performative without a follow-through and integration with wider organizational functions and goals. Cox (2001) identified five key elements that must interact with one another as we design and develop DEILJ-change strategies. These are: (1) leadership, (2) research and measurement, (3) education, (4) alignment of management systems, and (5) follow-up. In the following paragraphs, we describe these five main elements of Cox's (2001) change model for work on diversity as well as offer our adaptation to it. This model is highlighted in Figure 6.2.

The first and most important element for organizational and institutional DEILJ-change effort is leadership. Leadership is the fuel that drives the change effort, supplies members of an organization with motivation, direction, inspiration, clarity, direction, and vision for change. It is an essential ingredient for developing and sustaining DEILJ-change efforts (Cox 2001). Building upon the DOI theory, in the context of DEILJ work, various leadership roles such as change agents, opinion leaders, change agent aides, and other culturally appropriate leadership roles will be needed at across organizational levels.

The second element is research and measurement, which are essential for operationalizing data informed DEILJ-change efforts (Cox 2001). A common understanding in the domain of organizational performance measurement is "what gets measured gets done." Research and measurement are core elements of DEILJ-change efforts and can help organizational leaders and community members make evidence-based decisions about DEILJ priorities and directions. It can help assess the organizational culture, climate, and environment regarding DEILJ change, identify sources of support, and engage with feedback and resistance to change efforts in meaningful ways.

While there is immense scope and value in using existing literature, cross-learning, borrowing, and adapting existing contributions and promising practices from similar organizations or within a given policy and administrative domain (e.g., K-12 education, higher education, or information technology or public health and so on), efforts should be invested to contextualize research design and measurements to meet the unique needs, strengths, and challenges of an organization. Mixed methods and

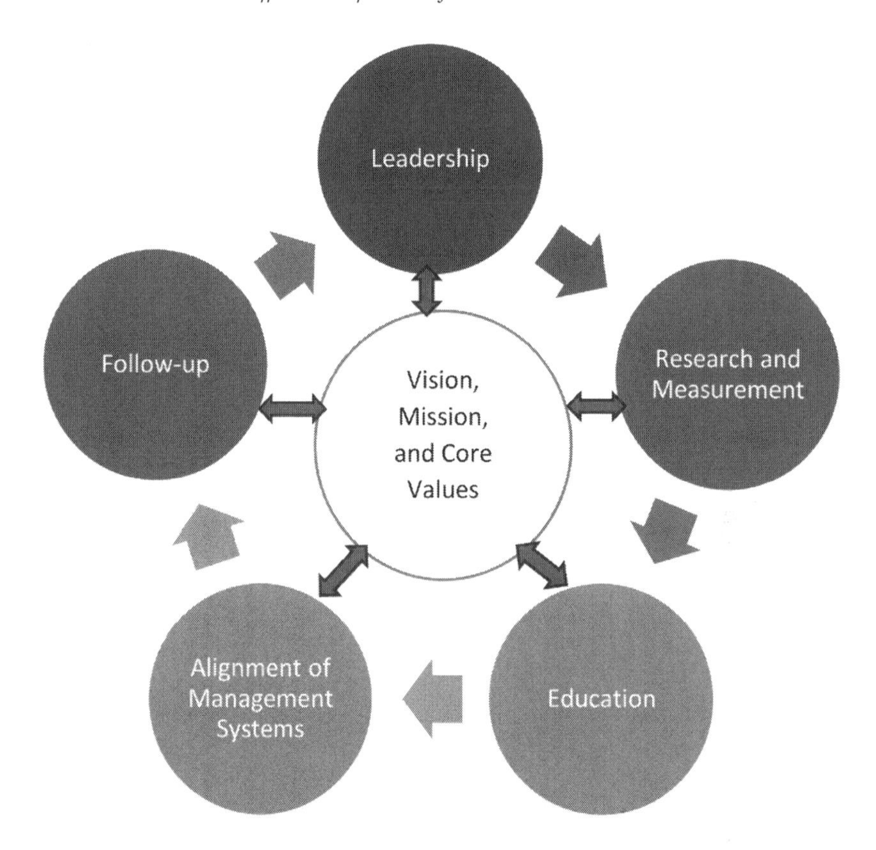

Figure 6.2 Author's Adaptation of Cox's (2001) Organizational Change Model for Diversity

Source: Adapted from Cox (2001).

qualitative research designs and measurements are important for understanding the nuanced complexities related to DEILJ-change work.

The third element is education. The idea is to shift away from ad hoc, check-in-the-box training culture and gear toward cultivating an organizational culture of learning and development (Cox 2001). The culture of learning and development adopts multiple pedagogies and methods, including mentoring, coaching, affinity group work, workshops, and facilitating courageous DEILJ conversations. Often the vibrant energy of an organization's culture of learning and development becomes palpable when its members learn to use a common language and develop norms and practices that create a safe environment for them to be courageous with each other and express their authentic perspectives. Thus, building a culture of learning and development through education is a critical ingredient for individuals and organizations to develop and grow in their DEILJ journeys.

The fourth element is alignment of management systems. For DEILJ-focused change work to be sustainable, it must be infused within all operations of an organization (Cox 2001). In the absence of alignment of DEILJ efforts across all management systems and operations, DEILJ work can become siloed and fade out.

Alignment of management systems does not require every organizational member to become a DEILJ expert, however, it does create room for shared norms, practices, and shared equity leadership to emerge. Different organizational members are invited and supported at individual and collective levels to integrate DEILJ values within their functional and decision-making domains, processes and tasks, and spheres of influence. For example, these include making budgetary decisions or hiring decisions or decisions about product and service delivery. Organizational effort to align and infuse DEILJ values within all management systems could demonstrate the strength of its commitment beyond superficial or performative levels. Ideally, alignment of management systems enables and sets in motion a long-term, steady, well-paced, incremental process of diffusion of DEILJ innovation.

The fifth and final element is follow-up. It creates structured room for continuous loop learning. It is linked closely with the research and measurement component and helps make informed, evidence-based decisions about what is working, and what is not. This component involves implementing change efforts, tracking development, establishing accountability for results, gathering the learnings along the way, and recycling them to make change efforts more focused and precise (Cox 2001).

Overall Cox's (2001) model demonstrates and recognizes that DEILJ-change process like any innovation is an iterative process. We learn as we grow, and we grow as we learn – this is the practice of constantly innovating and engaging in DEILJ-change process. In addition to these five important elements identified by Cox (2001), for public service community, we add a sixth component, namely "organizational vision, mission, and values." By anchoring all five elements to the core of "organizational vision, mission, and values," we gain the strength, clarity, and purpose required for the continuous and sometimes challenging path of DEILJ-change journey.

A Reflection Opportunity: Organizational Change Model for DEILJ work

We invite a pause to check-in with yourself. Connect with your breath and bodymind. Move, stand, stretch, hydrate, and take care of yourself as you engage with this learning experience. When you feel ready, we invite you to reflect on the following prompts. Focus on an organization that is familiar to you, it may or may not be your workplace.

1 *How does the integrated organizational change model for DEILJ proposed by* Cox (2001) *compare to the DEILJ developments that have taken place within your organization thus far?*
2 *Using the model as a guide, what are your organization's greatest strengths and most glaring weaknesses?*
3 *Identify and describe your organization's core values. To what extent is the DEILJ work in your organization shaped by and shaping organizational core values.*

Key Take-Aways From Cox's (2001) Organizational Change Model for DEILJ Praxis

The most important take-away from Cox's (2001) organizational change model for DEILJ praxis is the need to recognize and internalize that DEILJ-change work necessitates an integrated approach and a shared equity leadership praxis. For DEILJ innovations to be sustainable and meaningfully diffused throughout an organization, courageous leadership will be necessary at all levels of an organization.

DEILJ-change work will necessitate purposeful and meaningful research designs and measurements that are suited for the needs and contexts of an organization and its members. Through multiple modalities for education, organizations will need to foster a culture of learning and development. Integral to this change process will be the need for alignment of all management systems and organizational functions to operationalize DEILJ values, a follow-up component to maintain accountability, transparency, growth, and innovativeness. Finally, we also propose that all these five important elements must be anchored within organizational vision, mission, and values to offer members clarity and purpose as they navigate through the difficulties and uncertainties of DEILJ-change work.

Next, we discuss TU or Equity 2.0 as an approach which can help DEILJ-change workers to innovate targeted strategies to collectively solve complex social problems. TU shifts us away from disparity-based approaches in equity work and invites us to focus on achieving universally identified goals (or needs). It seeks to meet these universal goals with targeted strategies that are developed to meet unique needs and contexts of diverse members of the given social system. The objective is to help everyone move toward the universal goal.

Targeted Universalism (TU)

TU is a "goal-oriented" approach to equitable public policy and practice. TU distinguishes universal goals from universal strategies. It aims to replace "one-size-fits all" universal strategy approach with needs and context-based targeted strategies that help to achieve universal goals for all members of the given population. TU is also distinct from targeted approaches that focus on specific sub-population of marginalized populations without addressing intersectionality. TU approach involves establishing universal goals for all groups within the boundaries of given jurisdiction and development of targeted strategies to achieve those universal goals for "all means all" public.

"Universal" refers to the area within a policymakers' jurisdiction. The scope or unit of analysis and implementation for TU framework could be at a meso- to macro level – including an organization, a department, a city, a county, a state, a nation state, and so on (powell et al. 2019). In the next sub-section, we discuss the five broad steps of TU approach.

The Five-Step Process for Developing Targeted Universalism (TU) Approaches

As step one, TU approach starts with a *clear and concrete articulation of "a universal goal."* A universal goal is a meta goal or goal of goals. It is based upon a broadly shared recognition of societal problems and collective aspiration to improve societal development with regard to a universally acknowledged need within a given unit or policy jurisdiction (e.g., an organization, a department, a municipality, a county, a state, a nation-state, or at a global level) (powell et al. 2019). Examples of universal goals or meta goals may be fostering student belonging and success in an educational organization, or creating an organizational environment where all employees have a sense of belonging and can contribute meaningfully to advance organization's vision and mission, or ensuring food justice and housing justice for all members of a given local community.

Step two in TU framework involves *assessing the general population's performance relative to the universal goal.* To continue with the example of student learning experience, this step involves measuring and assessing the overall student population for their current experiences of belonging and success. Step three focuses on identifying groups and places that are performing differently with respect to the universal goal. It can be done by disaggregating the performance data gathered based on social demographic and other locations (e.g., geographical, programmatic, department level, and so on) for the sub-groups.

In the student learning experience example, step three would involve disaggregating information about student belonging and success based on social demographic and other characteristics of the student or employee populations. Identifying how various groups and places are performing differently with respect to the universal goal is an important step from an intersectionality perspective. Disaggregated data can inform an intersectional analysis of the equity problem and thus, help to develop intersectional solutions.

However, it is important to remember that we can only disaggregate data to the extent that social demographic and other relevant information is available. Gathering intersectional social identity-focused data depends on organizational culture where people feel safe to reveal their identities. For example, we cannot simply expect people to disclose their racial identity, disability identity, sexual orientation, or gender identity, particularly if their social group is marginalized and subjected to stigma and prejudice in the context of an organization. Trust building and maintaining reciprocal relationships are important systemic factors that influence the accuracy of information gathered and analyzed at this stage (Sabharwal and Chordiya forthcoming).

Step four focuses on *assessment and understanding of the structures* that support or impede each group or community from achieving the universal goal. This step helps us reach the source of the problem/need and directly informs the strategies that will emerge in the next step (powell et al. 2019). Again, trust and relationships with groups and communities involved is an important factor. Without the support and insights of those impacted by the issue, it is difficult to accurately assess support structures and unique barriers to achieving universal goals.

Finally, step five involves *development and implementation of targeted strategies* for each group to reach the universal goal. This final step demonstrates TU's emphasis on moving away from "one size fits all" approach and development and implementation of a range or set of strategies to advance all groups toward the universal goal. Thus, TU approach necessitates creating many possibilities to move different population sub-groups toward the universal goal by taking into account their unique contexts and needs. This step recognizes that each group is located differently within existing power structures and hence the needs and circumstances of some groups may be more acute and extreme than others due to systematic exclusion. Unique lived experiences of target populations should guide the decision-making process and change agents must follow the leadership of those most impacted by the problems (powell et al. 2019).

Reflections on the Challenges and Opportunities in Implementation of Targeted Universalism

The implementation of targeted strategies may necessitate various prioritization decisions. This includes assessing the systemic harms caused by different systems of oppression and the need to plan for immediate, intermediate, and long-term relief, harm-reduction, repair, and healing. It is crucial to consider and weigh the structural and systemic barriers that different groups face in achieving universal goals. Priority should be given to those experiencing the most acute barriers when making decisions about the equitable distribution of resources. This approach helps prevent the perpetuation of harm and inequities.

This does not mean that those who face relatively fewer barriers are excluded. As we have explored in discussions offered in Chapter 5 focused on disability justice, healing justice, restorative justice, and transformative justice, designs and solutions developed for those most impacted by problems often work for most (if not all) members of the community or at least include a variety of solution options that may create a win-win situation for all. For example, consider curb-cuts developed for wheelchair users that have helped to create greater access for most types of movements on the streets. This step may involve continuous conversations, negotiations, generative engagement in conflicts, generative compromises, and consideration of multiple and sometimes conflicting access needs while making decisions about resource prioritization and allocations.

Policy makers and public administrators, when confronted with ethical dilemmas regarding resource allocation, may frequently opt for beginning with a group for whom the existing systems and structures are designed to work effectively (often, people/groups in the middle). However, such an approach often gives priority to the groups that benefit from the system while neglecting those who are marginalized and minoritized within the existing systems and problem-solving approaches.

TU rejects narrow, "one-size-fits-all" approaches to problem-solving that do not consider the inclusion of diverse needs and contexts, particularly for traditionally excluded and marginalized populations. TU creates room for many possibilities, multiple innovations, and technologies (i.e., problem-solving approaches) to co-exist. It could be understood as an emergent approach to problem-solving that creates room for agility, adaptability, cross-learning, and reinvention of innovations to create targeted solutions to meet unique needs and contexts of the specific groups and sub-groups within a target population[1].

With its focus on targeted strategies as a problem-solving approach to meet universal needs, TU creates room for change agents to approach problem-solving with a sense of humility, openness, co-creativity, collaborative, and inclusive spirits. TU invites us to trust the wisdom that lies at the margins, wisdom of those who are already navigating ways to work with failures of the system. It is not to minimize ethical dilemmas faced by public servants; rather the invitation is to collectively explore and co-create DEILJ innovations that can help us better navigate and find alternatives to dominant approaches to problem-solving that often neglect the needs of multiply marginalized groups.

When marginalized and minoritized populations take a central role in our range of problem-solving strategies, we are more likely to address the systemic causes of the issue and eliminate them. Neglecting marginalized groups often leads to superficial, quick-fix solutions that perpetuate oppression and inequities. Consider how our collective response to COVID-19 could have been different if, instead of marginalizing, denying, and ignoring, we had employed targeted strategies that prioritized the needs and contexts of older individuals, disabled individuals, people with pre-existing health conditions, geographically marginalized urban and rural populations, those with limited financial resources, and racially marginalized individuals with intersectional identities. What if we acknowledged, embraced, and treated social problems as "our problems" rather than "their problems"?

Caveats for Application and Integration of Targeted Universalism

While it is beyond the scope of this chapter to offer a deeper and a more nuanced understanding of the complexities and contradictions involved in application of TU framework, we would like to acknowledge a few important caveats and invite our readers to refer to the original TU primer authored by john a. powell, Stephen Menendian and Wendy Ake (2019).

First, TU approach to equity cannot necessarily resolve political disagreements about whether a social/public need exists and/or whether it must be addressed through public policy response. Nonetheless, when there is widespread consensus regarding an inequity or a specific set of needs, and a policy response is deemed necessary, targeted universalism can serve as a valuable approach for collaboratively developing sustainable and equitable solutions to address the issue. In essence, reaching a consensus or addressing disagreements related to a particular "universal" need or problem and implementing policy and administrative responses are inherently political decision-making processes (powell et al. 2019).

However, from our experience, there are different tools and approaches that can shape/inform the political process of evidence-based decision-making to agree upon a universal goal for any given jurisdiction. For example, evidence to identify universal goals or meta-goals can be gathered using independently conducted mixed methods needs assessment studies that may include inclusive and equitably designed surveys, focused groups, and interviews with diverse stakeholders, particularly those who are most impacted by inequities related to the given problem.

Second, all the five steps of TU approach emphasize making evidence-based or data-informed decisions. While gathering these data, authors of TU approach emphasize the need to embrace the non-linearity of this process as well as the need to use mixed methods approaches to engage diverse communities insights and perspectives throughout the processes (powell et al. 2019).

Third, and very importantly, TU emphasizes a focus on universal goals and moving different groups and sub-groups to the universal goal as a measure of success. It cautions against and resists a disparity-based approach that merely measures outcomes or success by comparing performance or outcomes for those in marginalized groups with those who are in the dominant groups. TU's focus on universal goals means that a goal or success is not simply about closing disparities between different groups, rather it is to bring all groups closer to the universal goal.

For example, in the context of student belonging and success in educational contexts, the goal is not to attain a level of belonging and student success for BIPOC students equal to that of their white peers. Rather the aim is to achieve a universally defined goal of belonging and student success for all students (such as students identifying as white, BIPOC, and those located within various sub-groups of white and BIPOC students based on the intersectionality of their race with disability, gender, age, sexual orientation, access to income and/or financial resources, and including other context specific social identities and individual factors). The universal goal can be attained for all students by using targeted, needs and context-based strategies for various (intersecting) sub-groups of BIPOC and white students.

Finally, TU approach calls for shifting power, building trust, and relationality while engaging with diverse communities, particularly those who have been excluded and marginalized within existing power structures and systems. A core assumption of targeted universalism approach is the need to center the margins. By centering those who are most impacted by inequities or those farthest from universal goals, TU calls for equity approaches that are designed for the margins (powell et al. 2019).

TU seeks to interrupt the decision-making and planning process that attends to the margins as an afterthought. Rather it invites us to empower and follow the leadership of those on the margins throughout the decision, planning, and implementation process. Such an approach to creating meaningful inclusion and belonging will help to find co-creative, innovative, nuanced, sustainable, and promising solutions to social and economic problems (Chordiya et al. 2023; McDowell 2015; powell et al. 2019; Sabharwal and Chordiya Forthcoming; Sins Invalid 2019).

Case Study 6.1: Targeted Universalism in Action: Addressing the Housing Crisis in King County

Intentions and Acknowledgments: We want to acknowledge that this is a very brief narrative for a case study focused on housing crisis and targeted universalism. Our intention for including this case study is merely illustrative to demonstrate what the process of targeted universalism may look like using King County's approach as case study. Offering a nuanced and critical understanding of King County's approach to solving housing crisis is beyond the scope and intention of this case study. Similarly, we invite you to refer to the targeted universalism primer to understand the critical nuances of using this approach to equity work.

The Case Study

King County, which includes the city of Seattle, located in the state of Washington, has experienced a rapid increase in housing costs, making it increasingly unaffordable for many residents. Consequently, rates of those experiencing homelessness have risen, and it has disproportionately affected multiply marginalized communities including Black, Indigenous, and People of Color, LGBTQIA+ individuals, people with disabilities, and low-income households. The county recognized the need for a comprehensive and equitable solution to these interconnected issues.

King County's approach to addressing housing crisis demonstrates various alignments with the Targeted Universalism approach to equity work. King County's public housing policies are based in the principle that housing is a basic, universal human right. The universal goal in King County is to ensure stable, affordable, and safe housing for all residents, regardless of their background or circumstances. The county conducted an in-depth analysis to identify disparities and inequities within its housing system. Data revealed that certain communities disproportionately experienced homelessness and housing instability.

To address these disparities, the county adopted targeted strategies that focused on specific populations and neighborhoods most affected by the housing crisis. These strategies included:

a **Affordable Housing Initiatives:** Implementing policies and incentives to increase the supply of affordable housing units.
b **Anti-Displacement Measures:** Implementing measures to prevent the displacement of vulnerable communities due to gentrification.

c **Support Services:** Offering support services such as mental health counseling, substance use treatment, and job training for individuals experiencing homelessness.
d **Rental Assistance Programs:** Expanding rental assistance programs to prevent eviction and experience of homelessness.

Throughout the process, the county administrators and public servants sought to actively engage with affected communities and involved them in the decision-making process. Community engagement helped shape policies and interventions to ensure they were culturally sensitive and responsive to the needs of different groups. The county continuously engaged in data collection and analysis to assess the impact of interventions and course-correct or adapt strategies as needed. Some of the key markers of result and impact include significant improvements in housing stability, increase in the availability of affordable housing units, and building relationships and empowering community members to foster an equitable and inclusive approach to solving the housing crisis.

Yet, given the complexity of housing crisis and systemic, intergenerational, and persistent institutional experiences of oppression and trauma from oppression; the fulfilment of universal goal of ensuring stable, affordable, and safe housing for all residents remains a long-winding road for King County.

Case Study 6.1: Suggested Discussion Questions:

1 What about targeted universalism approach is resonating with you? What is causing dissonance?
2 In this case study, which key principles of targeted universalism approach can be observed in action?
3 How can the principles of targeted universalism be applied to other social issues beyond housing? We invite you to explore this question with an example.
4 What are the opportunities/benefits of using targeted universalism approach to equity work?
5 What challenges might one anticipate in using targeted universalism approach?

Sources: City of Seattle Office of Housing, 2023; powell et al. 2019; Regional Affordable Housing Task Force, 2018.

Summary and Key Teachings

In this chapter, we explore the frameworks that can guide public service professionals in operationalizing the normative DEILJ values, especially at institutional and organizational levels. The three theoretical frameworks covered in this chapter are intended to inform and guide DEILJ-change agents to develop, diffuse, and sustain DEILJ-change effort at both individual and organizational/institutional levels.

These are: (1) Everett Roger's (2003) the DOI theory, (2) Taylor Cox's (2001) Organizational Change Model for Diversity, (3) powell et al.'s (2019) Targeted Universalism or Equity 2.0 approach. Some of the key teachings offered in this chapter focus on the importance of taking an integrated change management approach anchored in organization core values, the necessity of aligning management systems, the importance of shared leadership approaches, coalition building work, and collaboration (and solidarity) across various levels of organizations to effect DEILJ-focused change. Another key teaching explored in this chapter is related to application of equity frameworks such as TU that seeks to shift away from disparity-based and one-size-fits-all approaches. TU invites us to set universal goals and co-create many innovative possibilities to achieve the universal goal across various sub-groups of population using context-based and needs based targeted strategies.

Deep Dive Resources [Full Citations in References]

1 powell 2019 (an interview on targeted universalism)
2 powell et al. 2019. Targeted Universalism Primer
3 Rogers 2003. Diffusion of Innovations
4 Cox 2001. A Strategy for Meeting the Challenge.

Note

1 For those familiar with emergent strategy approach, we want to note: in this sense, targeted universalism is aligned with emergent strategy approaches and elements, particularly, the element of "creating many possibilities". To learn more about the framework of emergent strategy refer to brown 2017.

References

brown, adrienne maree. 2017. *Emergent Strategy: Shaping Change, Changing Worlds*. Reprint edition. Chico, CA: AK Press.

Chordiya, Rashmi, Stephanie Dolamore, Jeannine M. Love, Erin L. Borry, Adana Protonentis, Brendan Stern, and Geoffrey Whitebread. 2023. "Staking the Tent at the Margins: Using Disability Justice to Expand the Theory and Praxis of

Social Equity in Public Administration." *Administrative Theory & Praxis* 0(0): 1–26. https://doi.org/10.1080/10841806.2023.2216616
City of Seattle Office of Housing. 2023. "Housing - Housing | Seattle.Gov." City of Seattle Office of Housing. 2023. https://www.seattle.gov/housing
Cox, Taylor Jr. 2001. "A Strategy for Meeting the Challenge." In *Creating the Multicultural Organization: A Strategy for Capturing the Power of Diversity*, 1st ed. San Francisco, CA: Jossey-Bass.
Ford, Jeffrey D., and Laurie W. Ford. 2009. "Decoding Resistance to Change." *Harvard Business Review* 87 (4): 99–103.
Harro, Bobbie. 2018. "Cycle of Liberation." In *Readings for Diversity and Social Justice*, edited by Maurianne Adams, Warren J. Blumenfeld, D. Chase J. Catalano, Keri Dejong, Heather W. Hackman, Larissa E. Hopkins, Barbara Love, Madeline L. Peters, Davey Shlasko, and Ximena Zuniga, 4th ed., 627–34. New York, NY: Routledge.
Love, Barbara J. 2018. "Developing a Liberatory Consciousness." In *Readings for Diversity and Social Justice*, edited by Maurianne Adams, Warren J. Blumenfeld, D. Chase J. Catalano, Keri Dejong, Heather W. Hackman, Larissa E. Hopkins, Barbara Love, Madeline L. Peters, Davey Shlasko, and Ximena Zuniga, 4th ed., 610–15. New York, NY: Routledge.
McDowell, Ceasar. 2015. "Democracy from the Margins | Ceasar McDowell | TEDxIndianaUniversity." TEDx Talks.
powell, john a. 2019. Podcast: Targeted Universalism, with john a. powell | Othering & Belonging Institute Interview by Marc Abizeid. https://belonging.berkeley.edu/podcast-targeted-universalism-john-powell
powell, john a., Stephen Menendian, and Wendy Ake. 2019. "*Targeted Universalism: Policy & Practice*." Berkeley, CA: Haas Institute for a Fair and Inclusive Society at UC Berkeley. file:///C:/Users/chordiyarash/Downloads/targeted_universalism_primer.pdf
Regional Affordable Housing Task Force. 2018. "Final Report and Recommendations for King County, WA." King County, WA.
Rogers, Everett M. 2003. *Diffusion of Innovations*. 5th ed. New York, NY: Free Press.
Sabharwal, Meghna, and Rashmi Chordiya. Forthcoming. "Doing Equity Work 'Equitably': A Need for Intersectional Approaches." In *Achieving Social Equity: From Problems to Solutions*, edited by Mary E. Guy and Sean A. McCandless, 2nd ed. Irvine, CA: Melvin & Leigh, Publishers.
Sins Invalid. 2019. "Skin, Tooth, and Bone: The Basis of Movement Is Our People, A Disability Justice Primer." https://www.sinsinvalid.org/skin-tooth-and-bone

Part III

Liberatory Public Service Approach

Applications and Integrations

Intentions and Objectives

In Part III, we offer our visions and reflections on potential applications and integrations of the liberatory public service (LPS) framework and its key principles. We reflect on how LPS approach can inform social justice praxis to interrupt and end cycles of oppression, and foster liberatory justice in specific contexts including:

a Racism and white supremacy (Chapters 7 and 8)
b Sexism, heteropatriarchy, and trans oppression (Chapter 9)
c Intersectional ableism (Chapter 10)

We also share reflections on the future of LPS and next steps for action (Chapter 11).

Our objective is to explore each of these manifestations of oppression from a historical, legal, structural, and cultural perspective. We intend to deepen an intersectional analysis of these various manifestations of oppression. Through our analysis we also seek to demonstrate how these various manifestations of oppression are operationalized at individual and institutional/organizational levels and within various domains of public administration and policy making.

We continue to reflect on promising social justice approaches that can support and guide the development of individual and organizational capacities for an LPS praxis. While we are limited by our scope to examine all the major manifestations of oppression, our intention and hope is that the following chapters offer teachings and perspectives that will be of service to you in diversity, equity, inclusion, and liberatory justice (DEILJ) contexts that are beyond those covered in this book.

DOI: 10.4324/9781032670669-9

7 Unravelling Racism and Moving Toward Racial Justice

Part I

Abstract

This chapter is Part I of the two-part chapter series that focus on unravelling racism and moving toward racial justice in public service. In this chapter, we explore the concepts of racism and white supremacy, examining how they are operationalized through process of racialization, white institutionalized spaces, and white supremacy culture. We also offer a historical context of racism in the United States using sociological frameworks that explain logics of settler colonialism and white supremacy. This chapter demonstrates that racialized oppression is embedded deeply into the systems, structures, and cultures that are shaped by process of racialization and implicit and explicit norms of white supremacy. Racialized oppression is persistent, durable, and mutating. Consequently, the progress toward achieving racial and social justice has persistently encountered resistance from overt and covert manifestations of white supremacy, both historically and in contemporary times. We also explore and highlight that the work of resisting oppression and building racial and social justice movements for freedom and liberation is continued across generations. Solidarity across movements and diverse racial groups with an intersectional understanding of differences in our lived experiences, contexts, and needs, is an antidote to racialized oppression and, a key to ensuring long-lasting and transformative progress toward racial and social justice.

An Acknowledgment of Heavy and Potentially Triggering Content

We want to acknowledge that any reading or discussion of racism and white supremacy is heavy and can be triggering. As you move through this chapter, we invite you to honor your embodied reactions and move at a pace that feels accessible and manageable for your bodymind. We invite gentleness and compassion for self and others. We invite you to move your body in ways that allow you to feel settled; and to find places and

DOI: 10.4324/9781032670669-10

times that are nourishing and comforting as you process the content of this chapter and this book.

An Introduction: What Is Racism and White Supremacy?

The construct of "race" is a social invention, one that was innovated to perpetuate cycles of oppression and to maintain and expand the power of the ruling class. Race is not rooted in biology. It is a socially constructed concept, and it shapes and is shaped by social, cultural, historical, economic, and institutional factors.

Racism is a form of oppression rooted in the deeply embedded ideology that asserts the superiority of the white racial group over negatively racialized 'others,' such as Black, Indigenous, and People of Color (BIPOC) (Bell et al. 2016; Menakem 2017, 2019). Racism is a tool to perpetuate white supremacy. White supremacy is a form of oppression that places value or devalues, humanizes, or dehumanizes bodyminds in ways that reinforce a racial hierarchy of power and control. The system of white supremacy impacts everyone, distributing varying levels of harm and violence across different individuals and groups, with certain groups, particularly white racialized groups, benefiting from its structures and culture, by design, whether or not they intend to do so (Okun 2023). It is maintained through our systems and shapes our dominant societal, institutional, and organizational cultures.

It is important to reflect on and understand that while the system of white supremacy is designed to benefit the white racialized groups, for example, through access to dominant power structures, resources, infrastructure, leadership, cultural dominance, decision-making authority, and by normalizing standards and norms that center whiteness or white privilege; it has negative consequences for even the white racialized group. Many white-bodied, and BIPOC thinkers, scholars, movement leaders have reflected on the negative impact of white supremacy on white people and envisioned what it could mean to be free from all forms of supremacy, including white supremacy.

The system of white supremacy prevents the white majority groups from reckoning with the fact that we have only one planet, one core humanity and that our lives and humanity are interconnected with one another. The system of white supremacy (like other forms of supremacy) thrives on ignorance fear, scarcity, and urgency mindsets, preventing white people to have access to their full range of humanity, creativity, kindness, collaboration, and collective visioning of liberation. For example, by excluding, othering, and marginalizing negatively racialized groups of BIPOC communities within the United States and around the world, the system of white supremacy impacts our entire social, economic, (geo) political, and environmental ecosystem through win-lose, power-over, fear and scarcity-based approaches to human conflicts.

It seeks to desensitize inherent humanity and bonds of kinship among white people and their BIPOC kins. The system of white supremacy is interconnected with other forms of supremacy, it reinforces and reproduces other forms of supremacist ideologies and continued oppression based on gender, color, ethnic, religious, national, geographical, abled-ness that impact all humanity, including white racialized groups. Ideologies and systems rooted in white supremacy allows for perpetuation of systemic groupthink behaviors at a structural and cultural level and it prevents us from moving toward the vision of collective liberation and freedom for all. It prevents us, including the advantaged white racialized group from exploring the full potential of collective visioning, collective imagination, collaboration and recognition of shared humanity and shared planet as we seek to find our way through and solve complex macro-level problems that affect all humanity.

To heal from harms of racism and white supremacy, we must begin with an understanding and critical awareness of how they are operationalized. In the next section, we discuss how racism and white supremacy are operationalized through our institutions and organizations, including public service contexts. The ideas and discussions offered below are based on critical race scholarship. They might resonate or cause dissonance, they might affirm or challenge your existing assumptions, and/or they might spark new ideas and reflections within you. We invite you to lean into your curiosity, patience, openness, and mindful noticing of what is emergent for you as you engage with the following materials.

How Is Racism and White Supremacy Operationalized?

Scholars of racialized organizations and white institutional spaces have shed light on how racism and white supremacy are operationalized within our organizations through structured and cultural ways that maintain racialized systems and advantage white racial groups.

Racialization is a complex, multi-layered, and multi-faceted socially constructed process by which individuals and groups of peoples are assigned racial categories such as, Black, Indigenous, Asian, Latine/x, Hispanic, and White (Gonzalez-Sobrino and Goss 2019). Racialization involves assigning these socially constructed racial categories to individuals and groups based on physical characteristics, ancestry, cultural markers, or social perceptions, leading to the creation of racial hierarchies, stereotypes, prejudices, and discrimination (Omi and Winant 2014).

Public administrators and the administrative state have had a significant, yet often overlooked, role in interpreting and implementing government policies that either prevented negatively racialized groups from accessing state programs or maintained their unequal status based on racialization throughout American history. The deeply embedded and intricate socio-cultural and political process of racialization has a profound impact on shaping public policies and practices. This influence is evident in various areas, including employment, education, public services, welfare benefits, and the criminal legal system (Pandey et al. 2022).

Racial disparities are evident in citizenship services, determines who holds authority and privilege, and access to systems of power and resources. Race plays a pivotal role in who is included and who is excluded, who gets a seat at the decision-making table, whose voices and perspectives are elevated, and whose experiences are marginalized. It also influences how benefits, resources, and opportunities are distributed.

In the context of the United States, the process of racialization has been systematically ingrained throughout its history. This process has privileged and advantaged people assigned to the "white" racial group, while simultaneously marginalizing those assigned to Black, Indigenous, and other negatively racialized People of Color (Mills 1997; Ray, Herd, and Moynihan 2022). Racism and white supremacy find their expression through the mechanisms of racialization and white institutionalized spaces.

White institutionalized spaces encompass more than the demographic realities, that is, historical exclusion and current inclusion of people of color within our institutions and organizations. These spaces persist not only due to racialized geographic segregation (i.e., persistence of majority white neighborhoods, and majority BIPOC neighborhoods, lineages of administrative policies and practices such as redlining), but also through covert and normalized organizational and institutional structures, practices, cultural norms, and power hierarchies. The historical and contemporary power structures within institutions have been deeply shaped by racism. Simultaneously, ingrained white logics, discourses, and ideologies exert a pervasive influence on the everyday racialized practices, norms, and values of these organizations. All these mechanisms work in concert to disproportionately channel the resources of these institutions toward white individuals (Moore 2020; Ray 2019).

Our dominant organizational cultural norms also play a major role in preservation of white institutionalized spaces. Tema Okun has identified a set of 15 characteristics that prevail across our organizations as dominant cultural norms, values, and practices. Okun (2023) attributed them as characteristics of white supremacy culture. The reflection invitation below outlines these 15 characteristics for examining white supremacy culture. Okun (2023) defines white supremacy culture as:

> The widespread ideology baked into the beliefs, values, norms, and standards of our groups (many if not most of them), our communities, our towns, our states, our nation, teaching us both overtly and covertly that whiteness holds value, whiteness is value. It teaches us that Blackness is not only valueless but also dangerous and threatening. It teaches us that Indigenous people and communities no longer exist, or if they do, they are to be exoticized and romanticized or culturally appropriated as we continue to violate treaties, land rights, and humanity. It teaches us that people south of the border are "illegal." It teaches us that Arabs are Muslim and that Muslim is "terrorist." It teaches us that people of Chinese and Japanese descent are both indistinguishable and threatening as the reason for Covid. It pits other races and racial groups against each other while always defining them as inferior to the white group.
>
> (pp.4–5)

A Reflection Invitation: Examining White Supremacy Culture

Okun (2023) identifies and describes 15 specific norms, values, and behaviors through which white supremacy culture permeates in our structures, institutions, and societies. These are briefly outlined in the following section. We strongly encourage you to refer to the detailed description offered in referenced source (Okun 2021, 2023). We invite you to reflect on these norms and respond to following prompts in an order that feels helpful to you.

a Identify which of these characteristics make up the dominant norms, values, and behaviors of your organizational/team culture.
b Notice your embodied reactions to your own observations.
c Critically analyze whether and how these cultural norms contribute toward oppression? Who benefits from these norms and who is disadvantaged?
d Which of these norms might have you internalized? How might they be affecting your well-being and of those around you? How might you cultivate embodied practices that can help to counter and unlearn these internalized norms and behaviors. For example,

to counter a constant sense of urgency, one might cultivate awareness of heartrate, breath, and take intentional steps to slow down and pace oneself.

The 15 Characteristics of White Supremacy Culture: A Brief Outline (For Detailed Descriptions of these Characteristics and their Antidotes, refer to Okun 2021, 2023)

1 Perfectionism- hinders appreciation for one's own and others' work, often focusing on inadequacies and mistakes rather than learning from them. We can counter perfectionism by fostering a practice and a culture of appreciation, embracing mistakes as learning opportunities, and separating individuals from their errors to encourage growth.
2 A sense of urgency- prioritizing quick actions over careful decision-making and long-term planning, often sacrificing potential allies or interests for immediate outcomes.
3 Defensiveness and/or denial- is a structural barrier, aiming to safeguard existing power dynamics, resist criticism, impede the exploration of new ideas, and divert energy towards preserving rather than addressing underlying issues of racism.
4 Quantity over quality- prioritizes quantifiable outputs and outcomes, emphasizing numerical achievements at the expense of qualitative elements such as relationship quality, democratic decision-making, conflict resolution and emotional understanding.
5 Worship of the written word- Emphasizes written communication, written proofs and written documentation even when they are full of lies, have misinformation, inaccuracy, and create racialized administrative burdens for impacted people who did not have a say in the creation of written forms or documents that they have to comply to receive access to resources. It also means overlooking other ways of sharing information and assessment of writing and communication skills and expression by white standards.
6 The belief in one "right" way- This mindset insists there is only one correct approach, viewing alternative methods as inferior. Encouraging flexibility and openness to diverse paths and many possibilities can foster a more inclusive and adaptable organizational culture.
7 Paternalism- assumes decision-making clarity for those in power, while assuming those without it often lack insight into

the process. Encouraging transparency and inclusive decision-making can address these dynamics.

8 Either/or binary thinking- categorizes things as good/bad, right/wrong, lacking a both/and perspective, leading to oversimplification and conflict. Encouraging creation of many possibilities, diverse options, and avoiding rushed decisions can counteract this tendency.
9 Power hoarding- occurs when those in authority resist sharing power and believe that they alone have the organization's best interest at heart. Encouraging power-sharing, valuing diverse perspectives, and embracing change can address this behavior.
10 Fear of open conflict- people in charge fear conflicts and avoid addressing uncomfortable issues, often blaming individuals for bringing them up. Encouraging open communication, practicing conflict resolution, and revisiting resolved conflicts can help.
11 Individualism- manifests as a lack of teamwork, with individuals preferring to solve problems alone, seeking individual recognition, and valuing competition over cooperation.
12 Progress defined as more- emphasizes success through growth and expansion, often overlooking the associated costs and impacts. To counteract this, a long-term perspective, considering the broader consequences that encompass both financial and non-financial costs must be considered.
13 The right to profit- reinforces societal divisions, favoring a few at the cost of the majority. These ideologies prioritize financial gain over human well-being, perpetuating inequalities and exploitation, particularly along racial and class lines.
14 Objectivity- involves the belief in a neutral perspective, often dismissing emotions, embodied reactions, and favoring linear thinking. To counter this, develop embodied practices, recognize diverse viewpoints, be open to and build capacity to constructively engage with discomfort, and acknowledge the validity of different perspectives and lived experiences, use "I" statements to create room for different perspectives, and hold space for multiple truths, and even contradictions to co-exist.
15 The right to comfort- belief that those in power deserve emotional and psychological comfort, often scapegoating those causing discomfort. It is important to embrace discomfort as crucial for growth, expanding one's understanding of systemic issues, and avoiding personalizing every situation.

Based on Okun (2021, 2023).

Public servants are bound by a code of ethics that underscores their commitment to serving individuals of all races, cultures, and backgrounds as equals. However, racism is deeply entrenched within the realms of public service. There is a need to adopt a new ethical approach in public administration, one that not only acknowledges the historical legacy of racism but also recognizes its enduring and harmful impacts on people of color (Stark, Heckler, and Mackey 2018). When race is not discussed openly and meaningfully with intentionality, it becomes a nervous area of the government, impeding the progress toward achieving racial equity in public services (Gooden 2014).

In the next section, we offer a historical account of racism in the United States. We discuss the logics of white supremacy and settler colonialism as these critical frameworks help to contextualize and understand the history of racism in the United States.

Racism in the United States: A Historical Context

In the United States, race is pivotal to social organization (Omi and Winant 2014). It is important to delve into the history of race and racism as "the next generation of public service professionals will need to recognize and validate the history and experiences of historically marginalized groups in ways that have been previously unacknowledged" (Lopez-Littleton and Blessett 2015, p. 5).

The Indigenous peoples of this land, Latine/x peoples, Black peoples, and Asian peoples have a complex and varied history in the United States. Racism affects the various negatively racialized groups in distinct and interconnected ways. However, even when there are benevolent intentions about promoting cross-racial alliances to resist racial injustice, it is important to avoid lumping of all forms of racism together (Glenn 2015). Such an approach eludes critical differences between racial groups and their unique histories of oppression and resistance (Smith 2012).

Building a decolonizing solidarity for racial justice necessitates fostering skills and capacity to work with nuance and complexity of different lived experiences. The concepts and logics of white supremacy and settler colonialism can help us understand the nuanced implications of racism and racialization for diverse groups of communities of color.

Sociologists have brought to light how racial, gender, class, and sexual identity formation in the United States is shaped by a range of political, economic, and social projects determined by the logic of settler colonialism and white supremacy. White supremacy and settler colonialism are not historical events, neither are they enacted in one singular fashion. Rather, like racism, white supremacy and settler colonialism are ongoing structures that shape our dominant policies, systems, and cultures (Glenn 2015).

The Logics of White Supremacy

[Content Warning: Emotionally Heavy Material] Smith (2012) argues that in the context of the United States, the key pillars of white supremacy include the logic of genocide, the logic of slaveability/anti-Black racism, and the logic of Orientalism. The logic of genocide holds that Indigenous peoples must disappear and must always be disappearing to enable non-Indigenous peoples' claim to land. We can observe this logic manifest throughout the history of the United States, where policy and administrative efforts were made to eliminate the embodied and cultural existence of tribal societies and nations. This logic continues into the present day, as efforts persist to marginalize and render invisible the enduring presence of Indigenous peoples and tribal nations.

The logic of slaveability/anti-Black racism renders Black people as inherently enslaveable. This logic has remained consistent and persistent through legal, structural, and institutional racism throughout the history of the United States. It has manifested in forms of explicit slavery and sharecropping systems that regard Black people as permanent property of the state. It persists in the present times through systems linked to the prison-industrial complex (Smith 2012).

The term and concept of "Orientalism" was developed by Edward Said (1978). "Orientalism" is used to describe the processes used by the West to define itself as a superior civilization by constructing itself in opposition to an "exotic," "mysterious," but inferior "Orient." The logic of orientalism marks certain peoples or nations as inferior and imagined as permanent foreign threats to well-being of empire.

For example, the logic of orientalism is manifested in anti-immigration movements in the United States and their institutionalized consequences that target immigrants of color. Furthermore, irrespective of how long immigrants of color reside in the United States, they generally become targeted as foreign threats, particularly during crisis and wartime (Sabharwal, Becerra, and Oh 2022). It is used to justify the United States being in a constant state of war to protect itself from its enemies. It is also used to justify the logics of slavery and genocide to maintain the United States' power to fight constant wars (Smith 2012).

The Logics of Settler Colonialism

Settler colonialism is distinct from classic colonialism. Classic colonialism aims to extract resources from colonized lands and peoples to benefit the *metropole*. On the other hand, "settler colonialism destroys to replace" (Wolfe 2006, p. 388). The objective of settler colonialism is to acquire land and gain control of resources so that the colonists can permanently settle and transform the new colony into "home" (Glenn 2015).

[Content Warning: Emotionally Heavy Material] To realize these objectives, settler colonialism uses the logic of elimination. Settlers seek to eliminate the Indigenous peoples of the land. Elimination is carried out through genocide, forced removal from territories desired by white settlers, confinement of Indigenous peoples to reservations outside the boundaries of white settlement. It is also enacted through biological and cultural assimilation that seeks to destroy Indigenous culture and replace it with settler culture (Glenn 2015).

In the context of the United States, the project of settler colonialism has been driven by the impulse to gain control over land, bodies, and labor. It has been institutionalized through the logic of private property. Land, bodies, and labor are turned into private property that can be bought, exploited, and sold by white settlers. These logics affect Black, Indigenous, and other negatively racialized People of Color throughout the history of the United States and endures into present times (Glenn 2015).

In the following sub-sections, we discuss some of the key historical events and laws that institutionalized the logics of settler colonialism and white supremacy. We also discuss their impact on white settlers and negatively racialized groups in the United States. The following discussion of historical context is not intended to be exhaustive. Rather, the objective for offering this context with an illustrative timeline (outlined in Table 7.1) and discussion is to offer a glimpse into how deeply ingrained racism is within the government policies, structures, and cultures.

A historical context of racism also helps us recognize the inter-generational nature of the work of resistance against systems of oppression. Historical context helps us develop a hindsight of oppression and of the continued intergenerational movements for social justice and liberation. It helps us understand that our current work of social justice and liberation falls on an arc, a continuum of a long history of movement for freedom and justice for all and, it has a future too. As Ruby Sales, the wise and legendary, embodied and spiritual social justice leader notes, "I think that one of the things that theologies *(and all forms of embodied social justice work)* must have is, hindsight, insight, and foresight. That is complete sight. And I think that fragmentation really shatters that sight, and it says that it's not an "I" sight, it's a "we" sight." (Sales, 2016, p.9; parentheses added by authors').

A Reflection Invitation: Historical Context of Racism in the United States

As you go through the following historical context of racism in the United States, we gently remind you to move at a pace that feels accessible to your bodymind. If the content feels overwhelming or triggering, the invitation is to stop and return when you have embodied capacity to process the content. As you process the content take deep breaths, move, hydrate, and find space, time, and place that can offer you support and nourishment.

Our histories are intertwined and painful. As painful as they are, we must remember these histories, resist erasure and fragmentation, learn to respect the pain, and remember that transformation is possible. We do not have to repeat our histories, we can find other possibilities, we can make other choices, and we can leave behind evidence of transformation, solidarity, and healing for our future generations. If we are willing to build capacity to metabolize our individual and collective pain, trauma and suffering, there is a possibility waiting for us, to move toward collective healing and transformation.

Suggested reflection prompts as you review through following discussions on historical context:

1 *As you will review, pause, and notice, what is resonating and what is causing dissonance for you?*
2 *Notice, if you can observe logics of white supremacy and settler colonialism manifest through the historical events (described below)?*
3 *Reflect on the characteristics of social justice and liberation work. Notice how social justice and liberation that seeks to resist racist oppression is resilient, inter-generational and necessitates a communal solidarity.*
4 *Finally, we invite you to take pauses and imagine what the practice of racial solidarity and racial justice means to you. You may consider your involvement in organizations, communities, and volunteer activities? In what ways do your social identities as well as the strengths of your communal culture and communal resilience, shape, inform, and strengthen your racial and social justice praxis?*

A Brief History of Indigenous Peoples and Tribal Nations in the United States

[Content Warning: Emotionally Heavy Material] The history of Indigenous Peoples in the United States is a complex and an extensive tale that spans thousands of years and encompasses a multitude of tribes and tribal nations. It is a story of survival, resilience, and continued struggle for freedom and liberation in the face of immense adversities.

Before the arrival of Europeans, Indigenous peoples had flourishing cultural traditions, languages, and ways of life. However, the impact of European colonization, since the 16th century, anchored in settler colonial and white supremacist logics of elimination, brought significant and lasting harm and trauma from racialized oppression to Indigenous peoples' lives. European colonization introduced diseases, violence, and displacement of Indigenous communities and entire tribal nations (Brave Heart n.d.; Krawec 2022; Zinn 2015).

We can observe the settler colonial logic of elimination throughout the history of the United States that resulted in the loss of millions of Indigenous lives. Indigenous people and tribal nations experienced immense harms, historical, intergenerational, and personal trauma, and sufferings due to forced removals from their ancestral lands, violated treaties, and massacres like the Wounded Knee Massacre in 1890. In the devastating Wounded Knee Massacre, the U.S. soldiers indiscriminately fired on Lakota men, women, and children killing an estimated 150 to 300 Native Americans (Krawec 2022).

The Indian Removal Act of 1830 forcibly relocated tens of thousands of Native Americans from the Southeast to what is now Oklahoma. This tragic experience is known as the Trail of Tears (refer to Blackhawk 2008; Brown 2007; Dunbar-Ortiz 2014; Edmunds 1995; Ehle 2011). The U.S. government established reservations for Indigenous nations, often on less desirable lands. Subsequently, the Dawes Act of 1887 was enacted to break up communal land ownership, leading to the division of reservations into individual allotments. All this resulted in the loss of millions of acres of tribal land (Krawec 2022).

In addition to the loss of land, the policies of forced assimilation implemented by the federal government also had devastating consequences for Indigenous children, families, and communities. Indigenous children were frequently taken from their families and sent to boarding schools, where they were forbidden from speaking their native languages and compelled to adopt European American customs and values (Krawec 2022).

Some efforts have been made by the U.S. federal government to address these harms and trauma from historical and inter-generational racialized oppression. However, the challenges posed by the white supremacist and settler colonial logic of elimination continue to affect Indigenous peoples and tribal nations in the United States. Consequently, the resistance movement for social justice goes on into present times.

For example, in the realm of adoption rights of the Native American community, the June 2023 Supreme Court decision upheld a 1978 Indian Child Welfare Act (ICWA). ICWA is a federal statute that aims to preserve the ties between Native American adoptees and their tribes and traditions. The case involved a dispute between a white foster couple and five tribes regarding the adoption of a Native American child, challenging the law's preference for Native families based on race. This decision recognizes Congress' authority in Native American child welfare. The 1978 law upheld by the 2023 Supreme Court decision sought to recognize and address the legacy of harm and abuse to Native American children, hundreds of thousands of whom had been separated from their tribes to be raised by families with no connection to their culture (VanSickle 2023).

In the 1950s, Native Americans were encouraged to leave reservations, where they had been segregated, and move to urban areas. The Bureau of Indian Affairs assisted families in finding their first home and employment. However, the relocation subsidy provided to Native American families was minimal, resulting in many of them residing in lower-income neighborhoods. These urban neighborhoods often faced issues like overcrowding, inadequate garbage collection, and limited access to public services such as water and sewer systems. These conditions led to the development of slum-like living conditions (Fixico 2000). Even today, Native Americans are subjected to significant environmental pollution, ranking among the worst in the United States (Bullard and Johnson 2000; Vickery and Hunter 2016).

Despite these immense challenges, Indigenous cultures and traditions have endured and are resilient. Indigenous organizing and activism have played a crucial role in achieving significant legal and political victories, including the Indian Citizenship Act of 1924, the Indian Child Welfare Act of 1978, and the Native American Graves Protection and Repatriation Act of 1990. Today, there are over 570 federally recognized tribal nations in the United States, each with its own unique history, culture, and governance. Indigenous communities and tribal nations persist in their efforts to secure and protect cultures, languages, sacred sites, self-governance, land rights, social and climate justice while simultaneously facing ongoing challenges posed by settler colonialism, anti-Indigenous, anti-Black racism, and white supremacy.

A Brief History of Black People in the United States

[Content Warning: Emotionally Heavy Materials] The history of Black people in the United States is profoundly complex. Black history is a significant account that spans centuries of challenges, resilience, and continued movement toward freedom and liberation. It is a tale of endurance, strength, and the pursuit of freedom and equality in the face of immense adversity.

The first recorded arrival of enslaved Africans in English North America was in 1619 in Jamestown, Virginia. They were forcibly brought to America, separated from their families, homes, and communities, and suffered through deep trauma of oppression and inhumane treatment as they were forced into a life of bondage (Jones 2019).

By institutionalization of settler colonial and white supremacist logics of slaveability, anti-Blackness, and private property regimes, enslaved

Black people were treated as property. They endured physical and emotional harm and abuse as their bodyminds, and labor were exploited to build settler colonies on Indigenous/tribal lands and promote racialized capitalism. During the long period of chattel slavery, which lasted approximately 250 years from 1619 to 1865, Black people endured unimaginable suffering and trauma without access to fundamental human rights, citizenship rights, or freedoms (Blackhawk 2020; Jones 2019).

In the 19th century, led by prominent abolitionists such as Frederick Douglass, Harriet Tubman, and Sojourner Truth, the abolitionist movement gained momentum as Black people and white allies fought to end slavery. They highlighted the moral injustice of treating humans as property and worked tirelessly to bring about its abolition. The Emancipation Proclamation, issued during the Civil War in 1863, declared enslaved people in Confederate territory free. The eventual victory of the Union led to the 13th Amendment in 1865, formally abolishing slavery throughout the United States (Blackhawk 2020).

After the Civil War, the Reconstruction era aimed to secure civil rights and political representation for formerly enslaved individuals. African Americans actively participated in politics, holding elected positions, and working toward social and economic progress. However, as we have explored in Chapter 2, oppression is persistent and mutating. In this context, racialized oppression persisted through emergence of white supremacist groups, leading to the implementation of Jim Crow laws.

Jim Crow laws enforced racial segregation and institutionalized discrimination, denying Black people access to education, employment, and public spaces (refer to Alexander 2020; Baldwin 1963; Coates 2015; Kendi 2019; Wilkerson 2020). Despite the abolition of slavery, for over a century, spanning from 1865 to 1965, Black individuals and communities in the United States continued to be deprived of their basic human rights. As oppression endured, the resistance to oppression and movement for freedom and liberation also continued.

In the mid-20th century, the Civil Rights Movement reignited the fight for racial equality. Led by prominent figures such as Rev. Martin Luther King Jr., Bayard Rustin, Rosa Parks, Malcolm X, and Fannie Lou Hamer, activists from diverse social backgrounds fought against segregation, voter suppression, and systemic racism. Through nonviolent protests, marches, and acts of civil disobedience, they garnered public support and brought attention to the cause of racial equality and the need for social equity. Landmark achievements like the Civil Rights Act of 1964 and the Voting Rights Act of 1965 prohibited racial discrimination and secured crucial civil rights protections.

However, despite these hard-fought victories, racial disparities and discrimination persist and serve as a stark reminder for the continued movement for racial and social justice. This includes areas such as education, employment, healthcare, housing, access to clean water, breathable air, nutritious food, and physical and emotional safety for all people (Lopez-Littleton 2016). As discussed in chapter 5, the ongoing efforts toward liberation of Black people are led by grassroots movements such as Black Lives Matter, Healing Justice, Disability Justice and through cross-movement organizing and solidarity.

Collectively, contemporary racial and social justice movements led by Black and Brown people focus on abolition of the harmful prison-industrial complex and medical-industrial complex that continues to enact the logics of slaveability/anti-Blackness and dehumanize bodyminds of marginalized and minoritized peoples. The movements seek to replace these oppressive logics with liberatory logics that invest in marginalized communities and end cycles of harm and anti-Black oppression. These include advocacy and organizing for equitable opportunities in education, housing, healthcare, and the economy, and challenging systemic barriers that perpetuate racial inequalities (Black Lives Matter n.d.).

Creating lasting transformative change for racial and social justice requires collective commitment and creating many possibilities for actions rooted in solidarity from individuals, communities, and across public service organizations. Such a solidarity will be necessary to build a society where all individuals are truly equal and have equal opportunities to realize their full potential.

A Brief History of Hispanic and Latine/x[1] People in the United States

The history of Hispanic and Latine/x people in the United States is characterized by countless achievements and the profound impact of individuals and communities of Hispanic and Latin American heritage. It highlights the rich and diverse cultural, historical, economic, political, and social contributions of Latine/x and Hispanic communities and emphasizes the need for solidarity to achieve racial and social justice.

Hispanic and Latine/x peoples' history in the United States dates to the 16th century, when the Spanish first began colonizing what is now Mexico and the American Southwest. After Mexico gained independence from Spain in 1821, Mexican residents continued to live in the northern territories of Mexico. However, the Mexican-American War of 1846–1848 led to the annexation of much of Mexico's northern territories by the United States- 55% of Mexico's territory, including the present-day states Texas, California, Nevada, Utah, New Mexico, most of Arizona and Colorado, and parts of Oklahoma, Kansas, and Wyoming (Castillo and Griswold 1992; National Archives and Records Administration 2016). The war and subsequent annexation resulted in the displacement, deportation, and marginalization of many Mexican residents. The Treaty of Guadalupe Hidalgo, which ended the war, promised to protect the property and civil rights of Mexicans in the newly acquired territories, but this promise was often ignored in practice (Castillo and Griswold 1992).

Mexican Americans established communities in the newly acquired territories, maintaining their cultural traditions, and contributing to the development of the American Southwest. However, they also faced discrimination and land dispossession. Mexican Americans faced significant discrimination and segregation throughout the 20th century, including being barred from public schools and segregated into low quality, under resourced schools (refer to Martinez 1994; Padilla 2008; Rosales 1997).

In the 1940s and 1950s, Mexican Americans began to organize for civil rights, including through the founding of organizations such as the League of United Latin American Citizens (LULAC) and the Mexican American Legal Defense and Educational Fund (MALDEF) (Marquez 1987, 1989; O'connor and Epstein 1984). Hispanic and Latine/x communities were active participants in the broader civil rights movement of the 1960s. Leaders like Cesar Chavez and Dolores Huerta organized the United Farm Workers (UFW) to fight for better working conditions for farm laborers (Public Broadcasting Service 2013).

During the Chicano Movement of the 1960s and 1970s, Mexican Americans advocated for greater political representation, civil rights, educational opportunities, and cultural recognition. The movement led to important victories, such as the establishment of ethnic studies programs in universities and the appointment of Juliet Villareal Garcia, the first Mexican American Woman as the college President of a U.S. university.

Florida, New Mexico, and California were the first states to send Hispanic representatives to Congress. Since the 1960s, there has been an increase in Hispanic members in the U.S. Congress due to population growth, stronger Hispanic organizations, and expanded voter participation. The Congressional Hispanic Caucus was formed in 1976 to address Hispanic needs.

The immigration of Hispanic and Latine/x peoples to the United States has continued, with significant migration from countries such as Mexico, Puerto Rico, the Dominican Republic, Cuba, El Salvador, Colombia, Guatemala, and others. This has led to a diverse Latine/x population with a wide range of cultural backgrounds and languages. The future promises further growth in Hispanic/Latine/x representation, reflecting their rising population. By 2050, Hispanics/Latine/x peoples are expected to become the largest minority population in the United States, comprising approximately 29% of the total population (currently at 19%) (Passel and Cohn 2008).

Throughout the U.S. history of settler colonialism and expansion into the Southwest as well as the current times, Hispanic and Latine/x communities continue to be affected by issues related to racism in immigration, education, health care access, and economic disparities. At the same time the history of Hispanic and Latine/x people in the United States is also marked by resilience, cultural richness, and contributions to the nation's social, cultural, economic, and political landscape.

A Brief History of Asian People in the United States

Asian people in the United States[2] have a diverse and dynamic history, spanning several centuries. It is shaped by settler colonial and white supremacist logics of racialization and super-exploitation. While the history of Asian Americans in the United States is marked by significant contributions to the economy, history, culture, and society, settler colonial, and white supremacist logics have caused invisibilization of Asian American contributions and treatment as perpetual "aliens."

Asian people in the United States have been subjected to widespread institutionalized restrictions and exclusions. For example, the Chinese were the first immigrant group subject to exclusion, first through the Page Act of 1875 and the Chinese Exclusion Act of 1882 and then through the Immigration Act of 1924 that extended exclusion to cover other Asian peoples. During World War II, Japanese communities were forcibly removed from their homes and placed in internment camps, many of them were U.S. citizens (refer to Lee 2019; Sabharwal et al. 2022).

The Philippines, which was as a U.S. colony from 1898 to 1946, led to Filipino migration to the United States. The new waves of migration of Asian Americans in the United States were often a result of U.S. conflicts and wars in South-East Asia (e.g., Vietnam War 1955-1975). In the 1970s, the United States admitted many refugees from Vietnam, Cambodia, and Laos due to conflicts in Southeast Asia. This influx of refugees formed new and diverse Asian American communities. The South Asian immigration in the United States began in late 19th and early 20th centuries, however, it was severely limited due to restrictive immigration policies at the time. The immigration of South Asians in the United States increased in late 20th century after the restrictive and discriminatory immigration quotas based on nationality were eliminated by the Immigration and Nationality Act of 1965.

However, the settler colonial and white supremacist logics of racialization and "orientalism" that treat immigrants (including citizens) of color as foreign threats continue to play out especially during crisis and conflicts. For example, Asian communities became targets of hate crime and violence during the COVID-19 pandemic in the United States.

These hate crimes are not new and have been experienced by Asian immigrants throughout the history of the United States (Sabharwal et al. 2022), and, it is important to resist normalization of hate crimes against people of color.

Today, the Asian community is the United States is diverse and vibrant. It plays a vital role in shaping the country's social, cultural, and economic landscape. However, some of the key struggles facing the Asian people include stereotypes and prejudices, discrimination, invisibilization, alienation, and underrepresentation in leadership roles (Min 2019).

Despite an intense and traumatizing history of racialized oppression, Indigenous people, Hispanic/Latine/x people, Black people, and Asian people in the United States have remained resilient and made significant contributions to the formation of American economy, culture, and society. Today, though communities of color continue to face discrimination and marginalization they also continue to be on the frontlines and are among those leading social and climate justice movements.

A Reflection Invitation: Timeline of Key Events and Laws Impacting Racial Rights

Table 7.1 provides a broad timeline of key events and laws impacting racial rights in the United States. This table is not intended to provide an exhaustive description of the racial history in the United States. Rather it is intended to be illustrative. We also acknowledge that these historical events are not mere historical facts and are lived, embodied experiences of people and have contributed to immense historical, intergenerational, and spiritual trauma. These are heavy, painful, and triggering and therefore we invite you to prioritize self-compassion and healing for social justice. As has been our approach throughout this book, we invite you to process this content and the suggested reflection prompts at a pace that feels meaningful, compassionate, and accessible to your bodymind.

1. *What are your embodied reactions to the information presented in Table 7.1. If you are able and willing, journal these reactions on a piece of paper. No need to analyze them, we invite you to simply practice noticing.*
2. *What else are you noticing? Are there any themes you can identify across this timeline?*
3. *What other important events and laws would you add to this table?*
4. *What are the lessons that public service workers and DEILJ students, scholars, and practitioners can draw from this history?*

Table 7.1 A Broad Timeline of Key Events and Laws Impacting Racial Rights in the United States

Pre-1492:

- **Before European Arrival:** Indigenous peoples, tribes, and nations have lived on the American continent for thousands of years with diverse cultures, languages, and societies.

Late 15th Century–Early 16th Century

- **1492:** Christopher Columbus arrives in the Americas, leading to the eventual colonization and displacement of Indigenous populations by European powers.
- **1565:** Saint Augustine brings the first European settlement to the United States, introducing Catholicism and the Spanish language in Florida.
- **1598:** New Mexico is settled by the Spanish – making it the largest and oldest Spanish settlement in the Southwest.

17th Century

- **1619:** The first enslaved Africans are brought to the English colony of Virginia, marking the beginning of slavery in the English colonies.

18th Century

- **1776:** The Declaration of Independence is adopted, asserting the principle that "all men are created equal," even as slavery continues.

Early 19th Century

- **1808:** The international slave trade is banned, but slavery itself continues to grow in the Southern United States.
- **1830:** The Indian Removal Act is signed into law, leading to the forced removal of Indigenous tribes from their ancestral lands, most notably the forced removal of the Cherokee Nation, known as the Trail of Tears.
- **1848:** The Treaty of Guadalupe Hidalgo ends the Mexican-American War and cedes a significant portion of Mexican territory to the United States, including what is now Texas, California, Nevada, Utah, New Mexico, most of Arizona and Colorado, and parts of Oklahoma, Kansas, and Wyoming. Mexican residents in these areas become U.S. citizens, but their civil rights are often restricted.

Mid-19th Century

- **1850:** Foreign Miners' Tax is imposed by California, targeting Chinese miners ($20/month) to discourage Chinese immigration.
- **1861–1865:** The American Civil War is fought, primarily over issues of slavery and states' rights.
- **1862:** Anti-Coolie Act passed in California to impose a tax on Chinese immigrants and protect white laborers.
- **1863:** President Abraham Lincoln issues the Emancipation Proclamation, which declares the freedom of enslaved people in Confederate-held territory.
- **1865:** The Thirteenth Amendment to the U.S. Constitution is ratified, officially abolishing slavery throughout the United States.

(*Continued*)

Table 7.1 (Continued)

- **1865:** The tradition of Juneteenth originates in Texas to celebrate the end of slavery after news of the Emancipation Proclamation reached Galveston.
- **1865:** Black codes are enacted in form of state laws and local ordinances, after the Civil War, aimed at limiting the civil rights and liberties of African Americans and to regulate every aspect of the lives of Black people.
- **1865:** Ku Klux Klan is established in Pulaski, Tennessee, as a secret society terrorizing Black communities.

Late 19th Century

- **1866:** Civil Rights Act of 1866 enacted, defining citizenship, and affirming equal protection under the law.
- **1867–1877:** Reconstruction era begins, aimed at rebuilding the country, ending Confederate secession, and countering slavery and efforts are made to provide citizenship rights and voting rights to formerly enslaved people.
- **1868:** 14th Amendment ratified, granting citizenship and equal protection to all persons born or naturalized in the United States.
- **1868:** Burlingame Treaty is signed, establishing diplomatic relations between the United States and China. It recognized the importance of Chinese immigrants to development of the American West and their right to travel, reside and engage in commerce.
- **1870:** 15th Amendment is ratified, granting African American men the right to vote.
- **1882:** Chinese Exclusion Act is signed into law, prohibiting Chinese laborers from immigrating for 10 years.
- **1885:** Tape v. Hurley case in California Supreme Court challenges segregation in public schools.
- **1887:** The Dawes Act is passed, allowing for the allotment of reservation lands to individual Native Americans, resulting in the loss of millions of acres of tribal land.
- **Late 1800s:** The U.S. government enacts policies of forced assimilation, including the establishment of Indian boarding schools aimed at erasing Indigenous cultures and languages.
- **1890:** Separate Car Act is passed in Louisiana, requiring racial segregation on trains.
- **1890s:** Jim Crow Laws reestablished black codes and limited rights for Black people in the American South. These laws are designed to institutionalize racial segregation and maintain white supremacy.
- **1892:** Geary Act is passed, extending Chinese Exclusion Act and imposing residency permits on Chinese residents.
- **1893:** Fong Yue Ting v. United States upholds the Geary Act, allowing arrest and deportation of Chinese without residency permits.
- **1896:** Plessy v. Ferguson Supreme Court decision upholds racial segregation under "separate but equal" doctrine.
- **1898:** Wong Kim Ark v. U.S. ruling grants citizenship to anyone born in the United States.

(*Continued*)

Table 7.1 (Continued)

Early 20th Century

- **1907:** Gentlemen's Agreement imposed significant restrictions on Japanese immigrants.
- **1915–1960s:** The Great Migration sees millions of African Americans move from the rural South to the urban North in search of better economic opportunities and to escape racial violence.
- **1910–1940s:** Mexican immigration increases significantly due to labor demands, particularly in agriculture and railroads.
- **1917:** "Asiatic Barred Zone" is implemented in 1917 and the Immigration Act of 1917 continues the broader trend of imposing severe immigration restrictions (e.g., literacy tests, creates inadmissible categories, and barring immigration) for countries from Asia-Pacific regions.
- **1920s:** The Mexican Repatriation program results in the forced deportation of hundreds of thousands of Mexicans and Mexican Americans, including many U.S. citizens, during the Great Depression.
- **1921:** Emergency Quotas Act is established to impose numerical restrictions on immigrants, reducing immigration from Southern and Eastern Europe.
- **1924:** Johnson-Reed Immigration Act of 1924 further restricts quotas and effectively prohibits immigration from Asia.
- **1924:** The Indian Citizenship Act grants U.S. citizenship to all Indigenous peoples born in the United States.
- **1943:** The Magnuson Act effectively repealed the Chinese Exclusion Act of 1882 and its various amendments. It opens Chinese immigration and permits naturalization.

Mid-20th Century

- **1950s–1960s:** The federal government's termination policy seeks to dissolve tribal governments and assimilate Native Americans into mainstream society.
- **1952:** Immigration and Nationality Act of 1952 upholds the national origins quota system.
- **1954:** The Supreme Court decision in Brown v. Board of Education declares that racial segregation in public schools is unconstitutional, overturning Plessy v. Ferguson.
- **1955:** Rosa Parks' refuses to give up her bus seat in Montgomery, Alabama, sparking the civil rights movement.
- **1955–1968:** The Civil Rights Movement gains momentum, leading to the end of legal segregation and the passage of the Civil Rights Act of 1964 and the Voting Rights Act of 1965.
- **1960s:** The Chicano Movement advocates for civil rights and social justice for Mexican Americans and emphasizes cultural pride.
- **1957:** Civil Rights Act of 1957 establishes the U.S. Commission of Civil Rights and the Civil Rights Division within the Department of Justice and empowers federal prosecutors to protect voting rights.
- **1963:** The Equal Pay Act of 1963 is signed into a federal law and aimed at addressing wage disparities based on gender.
- **1964:** Title VII of the Civil Rights Act is passed, prohibiting employment discrimination based on race, color, religion, national origin, and sex.

(*Continued*)

Table 7.1 (Continued)

- **1965:** The Hart-Cellar Act, also known as Immigration and Nationality Act of 1965, abolishes the federal quota system and opens the door to large-scale immigration based on skills and family ties.
- **1965:** The Voting Rights Act of 1965 enforced the 15th Amendment to the Constitution and is signed into a law 95 years after the amendment was ratified. It outlawed the discriminatory voting practices adopted in many southern states after the Civil War, including literacy tests as a prerequisite to voting.

Late 20th Century

- **1960s–1970s:** Affirmative action policies are implemented to address historical racial discrimination and promote equal opportunities.
- **1970s:** A period of activism and the American Indian Movement (AIM) advocates for greater recognition of Native American rights and issues.
- **1972:** Title IX of the Education Amendments is signed into law, prohibiting gender discrimination in federally funded educational institutions.
- **1980s–1990s:** The crack cocaine epidemic disproportionately impacts African American communities, leading to harsh drug sentencing laws.
- **1986:** Immigration Reform and Control Act of 1986 makes it illegal for employers to knowingly hire unauthorized individuals and grants legal status to most undocumented immigrants who entered the country before January 1, 1982.

21st Century

2000s:

- **2001:** September 11 attacks lead to increased discrimination and profiling of individuals perceived as Muslim or from Middle Eastern region.
- **2005:** Hurricane Katrina exposes racial disparities in disaster response and recovery efforts in New Orleans.
- **2008:** Barack Obama is elected as the first African American President of the United States.

2010s:

- **2012:** Trayvon Martin, a Black teenager, is fatally shot by George Zimmerman in Florida, sparking protests and discussions about racial profiling and self-defense laws.
- **2014:** The Black Lives Matter movement emerges in response to the killings of Michael Brown in Ferguson, Missouri, and Eric Garner in New York City by police officers.
- **2017:** The "Unite the Right" rally in Charlottesville, Virginia, results in violence and the death of Heather Heyer, as white supremacists, and counter-protesters clash.

2020s:

- **2020:** The COVID-19 pandemic exposes and exacerbates racial health disparities in the United States, with Black, Indigenous, and negatively racialized communities of color disproportionately affected.
- **2020:** The murder of George Floyd, an unarmed Black man by a police officer Derek Chauvin in Minneapolis leads to global protests and renewed calls for police reform and racial justice.

(*Continued*)

Table 7.1 (Continued)

- **2021:** The conviction of former police officer Derek Chauvin for the murder of George Floyd is seen as a landmark moment in the fight against police brutality.
- **2022–2023:** Texas, Florida, and other legislatures eliminate funding for DEI (Diversity, Equity, and Inclusion) programs in Texas public schools.
- **2019–2023:** The first CROWN Act (Creating a Respectful and Open World for Natural Hair Act) is passed in 2019 in California, and since, more than 20 states have moved to pass a similar legislation. In 2022, a national version of the CROWN Act is passed the U.S. House but failed in the Senate.
- **2023:** The Supreme Court strikes down affirmative action in institutions of higher education.

Invitation to Pause

We invite you to pause here. Take two or more deep breaths, move your body in ways that feel comforting and soothing. If you are able and willing, find a comfortable place and body position (seated/lying down) to reflect on pieces of information shared in this timeline. Notice what is emerging for you at an embodied level. Journal your embodied responses and reactions. Simply notice.

Acknowledgement

We would like to credit and acknowledge Ms. Aurora M. Becerra who is currently a doctoral student at the University of Texas at Dallas for her the support and research assistance in co-developing this table with us.

Sources (Full Citations in References)

1 Daniels 2021. “Explore 100 Years of Immigration History with The Times Archive.”
2 Gressman 1952. “The Unhappy History of Civil Rights Legislation.”
3 Gabrielle Hays. 2023. “When CROWN Acts Stall in States, Cities Step in to Ban Hair Discrimination.”
4 Howard Zinn. 2015. *A People’s History of the United States*, 5th ed.
5 Klarman. 2004. *From Jim Crow to civil rights: the Supreme Court and the struggle for racial equality.*
6 Krawec, Patty. 2022. *Becoming Kin: An Indigenous Call to Unforgetting the Past and Reimagining Our Future.*
7 Public Broadcasting Service. 2013. “Timeline of Latino American History.”
8 Mitchell, Sherri. 2018. Sacred Instructions: Indigenous Wisdom for Living Spirit-Based Change.
9 National Archives and Records Administration. 2016. “The Treaty of Guadalupe Hidalgo.”

Summary and Key Teachings

This chapter is Part I of the two-part chapter series that focus on unravelling racism and moving toward racial justice in public service. In this chapter, we explored the concepts of racism and white supremacy and how they are operationalized through process of racialization, white institutionalized spaces, and white supremacy culture. We also developed a historical context of racism in the United States using sociological frameworks that explain logics of settler colonialism and white supremacy.

The historical timeline of racism demonstrates that racialized oppression is embedded deeply into the systems, structures and cultures shaped by process of racialization and white supremacy. Racialized oppression is persistent, durable, and mutating; in other words, the progress toward racial and social justice has historically and into present times has continued to face movement backlash in forms of overt and covert white supremacy (we discuss these characteristics of oppression in Chapter 2). Therefore, the work of resisting oppression and building social justice movements for freedom and liberation continues across generations.

Resistance work as is demonstrated through the key events in historical timeline of racism reveal that racial and social justice work is not a sprint, not a marathon, it is an inter-generational relay. Racism and white supremacy pits one racial group against another to hinder progress toward racial equality. Solidarity across movements and diverse racial groups is an antidote to racialized oppression and key to ensure long-lasting and transformative progress toward racial and social justice.

In the next chapter, we continue this discussion and examine manifestations of racism and white supremacy in contemporary organizational/institutional contexts. We will also reflect on potential applications of liberatory public service (LPS) framework to interrupt intersectional racism and move us toward racial justice in public service.

Deep Dive Resources [Full Citations in References]

1 Glenn, Evelyn Nakano. 2015. "Settler Colonialism as Structure: A Framework for Comparative Studies of U.S. Race and Gender Formation."
2 Okun, Tema. 2023. "White Supremacy Culture Characteristics."
3 Moore, Wendy Leo. 2020. "The Mechanisms of White Space(s)."
4 Ray, Victor, Pamela Herd, and Donald Moynihan. 2022. "Racialized Burdens: Applying Racialized Organization Theory to the Administrative State."
5 Krawec, Patty. 2022. Becoming Kin: An Indigenous Call to Unforgetting the Past and Reimagining Our Future.

Notes

1 Latina/e/o/x refers to people from Latin America, emphasizing cultural ties, while Hispanic refers to people from Spanish-speaking countries, emphasizing language connection. Latinx/e is a gender-inclusive term. See for more information on the terminology: https://www.bu.edu/articles/2022/why-is-latinx-still-used-if-hispanics-hate-the-term/

2 "Asian" is an umbrella term used for a group of 22 million Asians that currently live in the United States and comprised of at least 22 ethnic groups with "Chinese, Indian, Filipino, Vietnamese, Korean and Japanese – accounted for 85% of all Asian Americans as of 2019" (Budiman and Ruiz 2021).

References

Alexander, Michelle. 2020. *The New Jim Crow: Mass Incarceration in the Age of Colorblindness*. New York, NY: The New Press.

Baldwin, James. 1963. *The Fire Next Time*. New York, NY: The Dial Press.

Bell, Lee Anne, Michael S. Funk, Khyati Y. Joshi, and Marjorie Valdivia. 2016. "Racism and White Privilege." In *Teaching for Diversity and Social Justice*, edited by Maurianne Adams, Lee Anne Bell, Diane J. Goodman, and Khyati Y. Joshi, 3rd ed. New York, NY: Routledge.

Black Lives Matter. n.d. "Policy." *Black Lives Matter Impact Report*. n.d. https://impact.blacklivesmatter.com/policy/.

Blackhawk, Ned. 2008. *Violence Over the Land: Indians and Empires in the Early American West*. Cambridge, MA: Harvard University Press.

Blackhawk, Ned. 2020. "The Iron Cage of Erasure: American Indian Sovereignty in Jill Lepore's These Truths." *The American Historical Review* 125(5): 1752–1763. https://doi.org/10.1093/ahr/rhaa515

Brave Heart, Maria Yellow Horse. n.d. "The Return to the Sacred Path: Reflections on the Development of Historical Trauma Healing." https://www.ihs.gov/sites/telebehavioral/themes/responsive2017/display_objects/documents/slides/historicaltrauma/htreturnsacredpath0513.pdf

Brown, Dee. 2007. *Bury My Heart at Wounded Knee: An Indian History of the American West*. New York, NY: Macmillan.

Budiman, Abby, and Neil G. Ruiz. 2021. "Key facts about Asian Americans, a diverse and growing population." *Policy Commons*. https://policycommons.net/artifacts/1526590/key-facts-about-asian-americans-a-diverse-and-growing-population/2214830/

Bullard, Robert D., and Glenn S. Johnson. 2000. "Environmentalism and Public Policy: Environmental Justice: Grassroots Activism and Its Impact on Public Policy Decision Making." *Journal of Social Issues* 56(3): 555–578. https://doi.org/10.1111/0022-4537.00184

Coates, Ta-Nehisi. 2015. *Between the World and Me*. New York, NY: Spiegel & Grau..

Castillo, Del, and Richard Griswold. 1992. *The Treaty of Guadalupe Hidalgo: A Legacy of Conflict*. Norman, OK: University of Oklahoma Press.

Daniels, Nicole. 2021. "Explore 100 Years of Immigration History With The Times Archive." *The New York Times*. Accessed May 19, 2021.

Dunbar-Ortiz, Roxanne. 2014. *An Indigenous Peoples' History of the United States, Vol. 3*. Boston, MA: Beacon Press.

Edmunds, R. David. 1995. "Native Americans, New Voices: American Indian History, 1895-1995." *The American Historical Review* 100(3): 717–740. https://doi.org/10.2307/2168602

Ehle, John. 2011. *Trail of Tears: The Rise and Fall of the Cherokee Nation*. New York, NY: Anchor.

Fixico, Donald Lee. 2000. *The Urban Indian Experience in America*. Albuquerque, NM: UNM Press.
Glenn, Evelyn Nakano. 2015. "Settler Colonialism as Structure: A Framework for Comparative Studies of U.S. Race and Gender Formation." *Sociology of Race and Ethnicity* 1(1): 52–72. https://doi.org/10.1177/2332649214560440
Gonzalez-Sobrino, Bianca, and Devon R. Goss. 2019. "Exploring the Mechanisms of Racialization Beyond the Black–White Binary." *Ethnic and Racial Studies* 42(4): 505–510. https://doi.org/10.1080/01419870.2018.1444781
Gooden, Susan T. 2014. *Race and Social Equity: A Nervous Area of Government*. New York, NY: Routledge.
Gressman, Eugene. 1952. "The Unhappy History of Civil Rights Legislation." *Michigan Law Review* 50(8): 1323–1358. https://doi.org/10.2307/1284416
Hays, Gabrielle. 2023. "When CROWN acts stall in states, cities step in to ban hair discrimination." *PBS NewsHour*. July 3. https://www.pbs.org/newshour/nation/when-crown-acts-stall-in-states-cities-step-in-to-ban-hair-discrimination
Jones, Nicole Hannah. 2019. "The 1619 Project." *The New York Times*, August 14, 2019, sec. Magazine. https://www.nytimes.com/interactive/2019/08/14/magazine/1619-america-slavery.html, https://www.nytimes.com/interactive/2019/08/14/magazine/1619-america-slavery.html
Kendi, Ibram X. 2019. *How to Be an Antiracist*. New York, NY: Random House Publishing Group.
Klarman, Michael J. 2004. *From Jim Crow to Civil Rights: The Supreme Court and the Struggle for Racial Equality*. New York, NY: Oxford University Press.
Krawec, Patty. 2022. *Becoming Kin: An Indigenous Call to Unforgetting the Past and Reimagining Our Future*. Minneapolis, MN: Broadleaf Books.
Lee, Erika. 2019. *America for Americans: A History of Xenophobia in the United States*. Basic Books.
Lopez-Littleton, Vanessa, and Brandi Blessett. 2015. "A Framework for Integrating Cultural Competency into the Curriculum of Public Administration Programs." *Journal of Public Affairs Education* 21 (4): 557–574. https://doi.org/10.1080/15236803.2015.12002220
Lopez-Littleton, Vanessa. 2016. Critical dialogue and discussions of race in the public administration classroom. *Administrative Theory & Praxis*, 38(4): 285–295. https://doi.org/10.1080/10841806.2016.1242354
Marquez, Benjamin. 1989. "Organizing the Mexican-American Community in Texas: The Legacy of Saul Alinsky." *Review of Policy Research* 9(2): 355–373. https://doi.org/10.1111/j.1541-1338.1989.tb01130.x
Marquez, Benjamin. 1987. "The Politics of Race and Class: The League of United Latin American Citizens in the Post-World War II Period." *Social Science Quarterly* 68(1): 84. https://doi.org/10.2307/448359
Martinez, Oscar J. 1994. *Border People: Life and Society in the US-Mexico Borderlands*. Tucson, AZ: University of Arizona Press.
Menakem, Resmaa. 2017. *My Grandmother's Hands: Racialized Trauma and the Pathway to Mending Our Hearts and Bodies*. Illustrated ed. Las Vegas, NV: Central Recovery Press.
Menakem, Resmaa. 2019. Francesca Maximé - ReRooted - Ep. 13 – Resmaa Menakem – Be Here Now Network 2022 Interview by Francesca Maximé. https://beherenownetwork.com/francesca-maxime-rerooted-ep-13-resmaa-menakem/

Mills, Charles W. 1997. *The Racial Contract.* Ithaca, NY: Cornell University Press.

Min, Pyong Gap. 2019. "Major Issues Relating to Asian American Experiences." In *Race and Ethnic Conflict: Contending Views on Prejudice, Discrimination, and Ethnoviolence*, 195. https://doi.org/10.4324/9780429497896-19

Mitchell, Sherri. 2018. *Sacred Instructions: Indigenous Wisdom for Living Spirit-Based Change.* Berkeley, CA: North Atlantic Books.

Moore, Wendy Leo. 2020. "The Mechanisms of White Space(s)." *American Behavioral Scientist* 64 (14): 1946–1960. https://doi.org/10.1177/0002764220975080

National Archives and Records Administration. 2016. "The Treaty of Guadalupe Hidalgo." *National Archives.* August 15, 2016. https://www.archives.gov/education/lessons/guadalupe-hidalgo.

O'connor, Karen, and Lee Epstein. 1984. "A Legal Voice for the Chicano Community: The Activities of the Mexican American Legal Defense and Educational Fund, 1968-82." *Social Science Quarterly* 65(2): 245. https://doi-org.libproxy.utdallas.edu/10.1002/9781119168577.ch17

Okun, Tema. 2021. "White Supremacy Culture: Still Here." WHITE SUPREMACY CULTURE. 2021. https://drive.google.com/file/d/1XR_7M_9qa64zZ00_JyFVTAjmjVU-uSz8/view.

Okun, Tema. 2023. "White Supremacy Culture Characteristics." WHITE SUPREMACY CULTURE. https://www.whitesupremacyculture.info/characteristics.html

Omi, Michael, and Howard Winant. 2014. *Racial Formation in the United States*, 3rd ed. New York, NY: Routledge. https://doi.org/10.4324/9780203076804

Padilla, Amado M. 2008. "Social Cognition, Ethnic Identity, and Ethnic Specific Strategies for Coping With Threat Due to Prejudice and Discrimination." In *Motivational Aspects of Prejudice and Racism*, 7–42. New York, NY: Springer New York.

Pandey, Sanjay K., Kathryn Newcomer, Leisha DeHart-Davis, Jasmine McGinnis Johnson, and Norma M. Riccucci. 2022. "Reckoning With Race and Gender in Public Administration and Public Policy: A Substantive Social Equity Turn." *Public Administration Review* 82(3): 386–395. https://doi.org/10.1111/puar.13501

Passel, Jeffrey S., and D. D'Vera Cohn. 2008. *US Population Projections, 2005-2050.* Washington, DC: Pew Research Center.

Public Broadcasting Service. 2013. "Timeline of Latino American History." Latino Americans. https://www.pbs.org/latino-americans/en/timeline/

Ray, Victor. 2019. "A Theory of Racialized Organizations." *American Sociological Review* 84 (1): 26–53. https://doi.org/10.1177/0003122418822335

Ray, Victor, Pamela Herd, and Donald Moynihan. 2022. "Racialized Burdens: Applying Racialized Organization Theory to the Administrative State." *Journal of Public Administration Research and Theory*, January. https://doi.org/10.1093/jopart/muac001

Rosales, F. Arturo. 1997. *Chicano! The History of the Mexican American Civil Rights Movement.* Houston, TX: Arte Publico Press.

Sabharwal, Meghna, Aurora Becerra, and Seongdeok Oh. 2022. "From the Chinese Exclusion Act to the COVID-19 Pandemic: A Historical Analysis of "Otherness" Experienced by Asian Americans in the United States." *Public Integrity* 24(6): 535–549. https://doi.org/10.1080/10999922.2022.2120292

Said, Edward W. 1978. *Orientalism*. New York: Pantheon Books.
Sales, Ruby. 2016. Ruby Sales — Where Does It Hurt? Interview by Krista Tippett. https://onbeing.org/programs/ruby-sales-where-does-it-hurt/.
Smith, Andrea. 2012. “Indigeneity, Settler Colonialism, White Supremacy.” In *Racial Formation in the Twenty-First Century*, 66–90. California, USA: University of California Press. https://www.calfac.org/sites/main/files/file-attachments/andy_smith_indigeneity_settler_colonialism_white_supremacy.pdf
VanSickle, Abbie. 2023. “Supreme Court Upholds Native American Adoption Law.” *The New York Times*, June 15. https://www.nytimes.com/2023/06/15/us/supreme-court-native-american-children-tribes.html
Vickery, Jamie, and Lori M. Hunter. 2016. “Native Americans: Where in Environmental Justice Research?.” *Society & Natural Resources* 29(1): 36–52. https://doi.org/10.1080/08941920.2015.1045644
Wilkerson, Isabel. 2020. *Caste: The Origins of Our Discontents*. New York, NY: Random House.
Wolfe, Patrick. 2006. “Settler Colonialism and the Elimination of the Native.” *Journal of Genocide Research* 8(4): 387–409. https://doi.org/10.1080/14623520601056240
Zinn, Howard. 2015. *A People’s History of the United States*. Reissue ed. New York, NY: Harper Perennial.

8 Unravelling Racism and Moving Toward Racial Justice

Part II

Abstract

This chapter is Part II of the two-part chapter series that focus on unravelling racism and moving toward racial justice in public service. In this chapter, we examine the manifestations of institutionalized racism and white supremacy at micro, meso, and macro levels. We also examine these manifestations in key areas of public policymaking and administrative implementation such as workplaces, education, policing, voting rights, housing, finance, and healthcare. We conclude this two-part chapter series with reflections on how the principles of liberatory public service (LPS) framework can serve to interrupt intersectional racism and move us toward racial justice in public service. Efforts toward advancing racial justice from an LPS perspective must seek to interrupt and transform the conditions that allow intersecting racial inequities to persist. This chapter emphasizes that an LPS approach requires divesting from systems of racialized oppression and investing in systems that advance a decolonizing solidarity and are pro-Black, pro-Indigenous, and pro-People of Color. LPS approach requires investment in goals and systems that seek inclusion, equity, justice, and liberation of "all means all" people. LPS approach to racial justice work at any level (e.g., systemic, institutional, organizational, or individual) and in any domain (e.g., education, housing, policing, or workplace) of public policymaking and administration requires that we shift power and follow the leadership of multiply marginalized people of color who are most impacted by injustices.

An Acknowledgment of Heavy and Potentially Triggering Content

We want to continue to offer this acknowledgment that any reading or discussion of racism and white supremacy is heavy and can be triggering. As you move through this chapter, we invite you to honor your embodied reactions and move at a pace that feels accessible and manageable for your bodymind. We invite gentleness and compassion for self and others. We

DOI: 10.4324/9781032670669-11

invite you to move your bodies in ways that can allow you to feel settled; to find places and times that are nourishing and comforting as you process the content of this chapter and this book.

Manifestations of Racism

Critical race theory (CRT) provides a powerful framework for understanding and analyzing the intricate relationship between systemic, structural, and institutional racism. CRT when applied to public service contexts, helps us recognizes that racism is not simply a matter of individual prejudice or discriminatory actions of an individual public service professionals. Rather, racism and white supremacy are deeply embedded within the fabric of society and upheld by longstanding structures, processes, and cultural norms that influence law making, public policymaking, and implementation through public administrative systems (Blessett and Gaynor 2021; Riccucci 2022).

CRT challenges conventional ideas and myths of neutrality, objectivity, and technical rationality in public administration (Blessett and Gaynor 2021; Chordiya and Protonentis 2024; Portillo, Humphrey, and Bearfield 2022). CRT invites and facilitates a shift toward a discipline and practice that acknowledges the historical context of racialized oppression, centers the voices, perspectives, and lived experiences of marginalized communities, and places racial justice at the forefront as a significant priority that demands meaningful action (Blessett and Gaynor 2021; Martínez Guzmán, Jordan, and Joyce 2023; Riccucci 2022).

In the following sub-sections, we continue our examination of racism, especially in terms of its contemporary manifestations at individual/interpersonal (i.e., micro levels), institutional/organizational (i.e., meso levels), and systemic, structural, and cultural levels (i.e., macro levels).

Racism at a Micro Level: Individual and Interpersonal Racism

At a micro level, individual and interpersonal racism could manifest through internalized subordination or internalized domination. Internalized racism is produced and maintained through cycle of socialization that seeks to perpetuate systems and society built on foundations of racist and white supremacist ideologies.

Internalized racial subordination could be experienced, for example, when people with minoritized identities are made to feel[1] they are not enough (e.g., by biased performance standards and evaluations), that they cannot succeed (e.g., due to lack of support and resources), and that they do not belong (e.g., due to exclusionary and oppressive cultural norms and practices). These experiences are often mis-labeled as "imposter syndrome" where marginalized people, and people of color are made to feel like imposters and persistently doubting themselves. Scholars and practitioners are interrupting the pervasive ideas of imposter syndrome highlighting that these feelings of self-doubt are not about individual flaws. Rather the patterns of persisting self-doubt or feelings of being an imposter among marginalized groups reveal the inequities and flaws in our dominant systems, structures and cultures that were not originally designed for people of color and individuals with marginalized identities (Tulshyan and Burey 2021).

Internalized domination can manifest through overtly racist behaviors such as use of racist jokes, or racial slurs. Internalized domination can also manifest in covert or subtle ways. This includes behaviors embedded in savior complex or paternalistic racism, such as when people of dominant racial identity place individualized blame and try to "fix" or "save" the racialized "others." Other manifestations of internalized domination include unexamined racial stereotypes, prejudices, gaslighting, racial microaggressions, and implicit biases based on people's race and ethnicity.

Racism at Meso Level: Institutional and Organizational Racism

W. E. B. Du Bois is credited as one of the first scholars to introduce concepts of systemic, structural, and institutional racism (Braveman et al. 2022). Du Bois (1899) observed how racial discrimination became entrenched within various sectors of society, leading to its self-perpetuation. The racialized social system is operationalized at institutional levels (e.g., racialized laws – explicit or implicit), at organizational levels (e.g., wage differentials in workplaces), and at individual levels (e.g., in-group favoritism, prejudiced racial attitudes and behaviors, and implicit biases) (Ray 2019).

Institutional racism means that people of different races are treated differently and unequally in the institutions they use, like public safety, education, housing, healthcare, financing, delivery of citizen services etc. Institutionalized racism means that people of different races have different opportunities, both materially and politically, for example, because of discrimination in the workplace, education, housing, employment, and medical care. This is especially true in America, where the history of racism has created an association between race and socioeconomic status (SES) (Rivera and Ward 2017).

In the context of public administration, emerging concepts, and frameworks such as racialized organizations (Ray 2019) and racialized administrative burdens (Ray, Herd, and Moynihan 2022) help to examine institutionalized and organizational racism. Racialized burden explains how administrative burdens (i.e., learning costs, psychological costs, and compliance costs) involved in interactions with the administrative state often have racialized logics (Moynihan, Herd, and Harvey 2015; Ray et al. 2022).

According to Ray et al. (2022), racialized burdens represent a form of administrative practice that not only perpetuates but also normalizes racial inequalities within public services. These practices simultaneously perpetuate unequal treatment while masking discrimination because bureaucratic actors can claim they are "just following the rules." Racialized burdens take shape through rules that are intentionally designed (though possibly with deniability) or facially neutral rules that disproportionately disadvantage and harm marginalized racial groups.

Administrative burdens can perpetuate racial inequality through covert, facially neutral procedures, and rules, especially when more explicit forms of racial bias in policies or administrative practices become illegal, politically untenable, or culturally unacceptable. For instance, some bureaucratic rules may require specific identification papers that are harder for certain racial or ethnic groups to get. This puts them at a disadvantage. Also, bureaucratic red tape can slow down or even stop marginalized people from accessing essential services and resources, making existing inequalities worse (Ray et al. 2022).

The burden on Black people, Indigenous people, and People of Color (BIPOC) comes from a history of racism and unfair treatment in society's institutions. Past policies, like redlining and exclusion in education, housing, and jobs, have left an enduring disadvantage for BIPOC communities. Additionally, racialized administrative burdens intersect with other forms of discrimination, like disability-based, gender-based, and class-based biases. This creates even more disadvantages for people with multiple marginalized identities, thus perpetuating the cycle of inequality and making it harder for multiply marginalized BIPOC individuals to fully participate in social, economic, and political life (Ray et al. 2022).

Racism at Macro Level: Systemic, Structural, and Cultural Racism

Banaji, Fiske, and Massey (2021, p. 2) define systemic racism as the "processes and outcomes of racial inequality and inequity in life opportunities and treatment. Systemic racism permeates a society's (a) institutional structures (practices, policies, climate), (b) social structures (state/federal programs, laws, culture), (c) individual mental structures (e.g., learning, memory, attitudes, beliefs, values), and (d) everyday interaction patterns (norms, scripts, habits)." Systemic racism is thus deeply embedded within a society's structures and manifested in racial disparities in opportunities and outcomes. It can arise at different levels and can occur unintentionally or without our awareness of its existence and/or practice. Its power lies in its integration into a systematic framework of racial differentiation and discrimination that controls and decides opportunities and outcomes over generations. Racism reflects the biases of the powerful, while the biases of the less influential have little significance (Fiske 1993).

Systemic racism is a type of racism that involves entire systems (e.g., political, legal, economic, healthcare, school, and criminal legal systems), as well as the structures that uphold these systems (e.g., laws, policies, institutional practices, and entrenched norms). Berry-James et al. (2021, p. 5) note that "Segregation, as facilitated by discriminatory practices and supported by systemic racism, creates vulnerabilities adversely affecting communities of color." The enduring impact of systemic racism particularly in BIPOC communities, has created a disproportionate vulnerability that increases the risk of premature death during crises like COVID-19, Flint Water crisis, Hurricane Katrina, Hurricane Harvey among others (Gaynor and Wilson 2020).

The racial threat theory can help to explain the systemic differences across racial lines. The theory was developed by sociologist Hubert Blalock (1967) and posits that an increase in the number of Black people is perceived by white people as a challenge to their social and economic positions, leading to harsher criminal sanctions. There are three types of racial threat – economic, political, and symbolic – all aimed at reducing the power of people of color. By applying the concept of racial threat to areas such as education, criminal legal system, housing, health, and so on, we can better understand how dominant groups may feel threatened and use policymaking as a form of state control. This highlights the need to recognize and address the impact of systemic racism on marginalized communities in all aspects of society.

In summary, systemic racism stems from deeply entrenched unjust systems that sustain past discriminatory practices, policies, laws, beliefs, and logics of (settler) colonialism and white supremacy. It perpetuates racial inequities, socioeconomic disparities, and adverse health outcomes for BIPOC communities. Even when explicit discriminatory measures are no longer in effect, systemic racism persists covertly, through dominant structures (laws, policies, institutional practices) and cultures (norms, values, beliefs, and taken-for-granted assumptions). Table 8.1 provides definition and examples of the various types of racism.

Table 8.1 Racism Terms and Examples

Term	*Definition*	*Examples*
Individual/ Interpersonal Racism	Personal beliefs and attitudes toward other races that affect the way a person treats people of color.	A person believing in white supremacy, telling, or laughing at a racist joke, sharing a racist post on social media.
Internalized Racism	When members of racialized communities internalize domination or subordination through cycle of socialization into white supremacy and racialization that tells the story of who is valued and who is not, who belongs and who does not.	Black students believing that they are not good at Math. White people believing they are better than people of color and need to lead the world and "save" or "fix" people of color. Generally believing in the stereotypes and prejudices perpetuated in the society.
Institutional and Organizational Racism	Policies or behaviors within an organization intended to discriminate against people of color.	A hiring manager disqualifies candidates based on their names, citing a discriminatory logic of "cultural fit."
Systemic Racism	Perpetuated discrimination within a system that was founded on racist principles or practices.	A social work department lacks diversity and representation of people of color among staff, especially in leadership roles, despite organizational mission to serve communities of color.
Structural and Cultural Racism	Racialized structures and cultural values in a society are so ingrained in daily life that they are taken for granted and seen as "the way things are."	A judge gives a lengthier sentence to a person of color than a white person with the same charges.

Source: Authors' adaptation of USC Suzanne Dworak-Peck 2021; Bell et al. 2016

Unveiling Institutional Racism in Key Public Policy and Administrative Areas

In this section, using some of the key areas of public policymaking and administration we describe how racism persists in our institutions and organizations.

Workplace

In workplace contexts, institutional racism permeates organizational structures, human resources practices, politics, symbolism, management, and leadership, leading to underrepresentation and racial stratification within departments, teams, and agencies (Heckler and Starke 2020). Unexamined organizational cultures can foster microaggressions, exhibit lack of support, hostility, and pose risks to minoritized racial groups and the communities they are meant to serve (Medina and Azevedo 2021; Riccucci 2015; Sue 2010). Statements like "We can't find qualified Latinx candidates" or "You can speak good English for an Asian," or "You are not like the Black women I know" are microaggressions that one experiences at work. Workplace racism can be toxic, contribute to hurt and harm to minoritized employees. It can lead to burnout, lower job satisfaction, and mental stress (Washington 2022).

The theory and practice of representative bureaucracy (discussed in detail in Chapter 1) highlights that representation of BIPOC civil servants in public bureaucracies matters and forms a crucial pillar of social equity. We know that recruitment and hiring play a paramount role in every job, determining who enters and who remains excluded. They serve as initial measures to ensure that our workforce reflects the diverse populations we serve. However, recruitment of people with minoritized and marginalized identities does not guarantee their retention. Furthermore, even successful recruitment and hiring of minoritized and marginalized people of color continues to be a challenge for many organizations. Biased hiring processes continue to persist under the garb of bureaucratic neutrality (Portillo et al. 2022).

Portillo et al. (2022) shed light on the persistence of the myth of bureaucratic neutrality in public administration and its historical and institutional lineages. An examination of myth of bureaucratic neutrality reveals racialized, ableist, and gendered nature of our organizational systems. These biased organizational systems and structures shape the processes (e.g., evaluation and selection criteria) and decisions related to who is hired, promoted, developed, and retained in our organizations. To provide an example, Case 8.1 highlights the myth of merit in academia in the US.

For example, Lardy (2023) highlights notable disparity in representation of people of color at senior-level positions in the U.S. federal government. Their findings reveal that even though people of color constituted

47% of full-time, entry-level (GS 1-9) employees, their representation dropped to 33% in senior-level positions (GS 13-15). The gap further widened within the Senior Executive Service (SES), where only 23% of all career SES members were people of color (Lardy 2023). Similarly, an examination of data from the Federal Employee Viewpoint Survey indicated that women belonging to racially underrepresented groups face hurdles in advancing to supervisory roles and experience a decreased sense of inclusion in their work environments (Nelson and Piatak 2021).

In 2013, Dr. Kecia Thomas and colleagues, identified a phenomenon that has a negative impact on the career trajectories of Black women. Thomas et al. (2013) found that early in their careers, women of color received valuable support and mentorship from their managers and mentors, often white males, who were eager to train, mentor, and develop them. However, as these women gained competence and confidence in their roles, their mentors' attitudes often shifted.

Dr. Thomas and her colleagues coined the term "Pet to Threat" to describe this workplace phenomenon. Their research shows that women of color were initially viewed as likable and trainable newcomers who can be molded and guided. However, as they advanced in their positions and began to assert their earned influence and authority, their increased agency was perceived as a threat to the dominant culture predominantly led by white males. Just as these women were on the verge of making significant progress in their careers, they found themselves losing the support and access to career-building opportunities they had once enjoyed (Stallings 2020). Overall, these experiences contribute toward a toxic workplace culture and issues of retention.

Case Study 8.1: The Myth of Merit in Academia

The Case of Kathleen O. McElroy at Texas A&M University

Texas A&M University made headlines with its announcement of hiring Dr. McElroy to revive the journalism program, generating excitement among students, faculty, and alumni. McElroy, a Texas A&M graduate, and experienced journalist was appointed as the program's director with tenure. Her expertise in news media and race made her a suitable candidate for building a curriculum that addressed delivering news to underserved audiences and expanding the program's offerings.

Soon after the signing ceremony, A&M employees informed McElroy about the concerns raised by constituents within the system regarding her background and work on diversity and inclusion.

Behind-the-scenes negotiations altered the terms of her job, leading to revised offers that excluded tenure and emphasized at-will employment. After several rounds of alterations to the terms of her appointment, each round further limiting the terms, Dr. McElroy rejected the offer. The situation occurred against the backdrop where schools are preparing for a new state law to go in effect in coming months that bans offices, programs, and trainings related to diversity, equity, and inclusion in Texas public universities. The scrutiny faced by McElroy highlighted the complexities of navigating issues related to race and the limitations imposed by political circumstances.

The case study underscores the challenges faced by universities in promoting diversity, equity, and inclusion amidst political debates and changing legal frameworks. It reveals the tensions arising from contrasting ideologies and differing perceptions of diversity-related initiatives. The controversy surrounding McElroy's appointment exemplifies the ongoing struggle to reconcile diverse perspectives and create inclusive environments within academic institutions.

Implications

The case study raises important questions about the ability of universities to foster a climate of diversity and inclusion. It highlights the need for institutions to navigate the tensions between promoting equitable practices and complying with legal restrictions. The experiences of McElroy, a Black woman with a distinguished career, demonstrate the ongoing barriers faced by marginalized individuals in academia. It was not too long ago when a similar decision was made by the University of North Carolina (UNC), which decided to withhold tenure from Nikole Hannah-Jones, a Pulitzer Prize winning journalist involved in the 1619 Project after facing criticism from conservative groups. The 1619 Project is an initiative by The New York Times Magazine that examines the historical impact of slavery on the United States. The university's decision raised concerns about academic freedom and the influence of political pressure on tenure decisions. These and several such cases serve as a reminder of the imperative to continue advocating for inclusive hiring practices, despite the challenges and resistance encountered.

Suggested Discussion Questions

1 In the hiring decision regarding Kathleen O. McElroy at Texas A&M University, in what ways were the concerns about her

background and work on race, diversity and inclusion, indicative of the myth of bureaucratic neutrality?
2 What implications does McElroy's experience have for the broader issue of diversity, equity, and inclusion in academia, particularly considering recent legal developments such as the U.S. Supreme Court's ruling in *SFFA v. UNC et al.* (2023) that ended use of affirmative action in college admissions?
3 What steps could academic institutions take to address the challenges and barriers faced by racially marginalized individuals in hiring processes?
4 How can universities navigate compliance with legal restrictions, such as censorship of books, and bans on diversity, equity, and inclusion initiatives that contradict the university's mission and values of promoting and supporting diversity, equity, and inclusion?
5 What lessons can be learned from this case study to improve the recruitment and retention of BIPOC marginalized and minoritized students, staff, and faculty members in higher education institutions?
6 How can universities and/or organizations create a more inclusive and supportive environment for multiply marginalized BIPOC individuals, ensuring that they have the necessary support and protection to thrive in their positions?

Sources: McGhee 2023; Robertson 2021

Education

Education in the United States has a long history of intertwining with issues of race, leading to significant legal and social implications. Affirmative action (AA) is a prominent public policy designed to combat racial discrimination and promote representation of historically marginalized racial groups in areas such as college admissions, employment, and government contracts. Originating in the 1960s civil rights movement, AA gained national attention through executive orders issued by Presidents Kennedy and Johnson, a response to systemic discrimination and inequalities faced by racial and ethnic minorities, women, and other disadvantaged groups.

The Supreme Court has played a crucial role in shaping AA policies through key cases. *Regents of the University of California v. Bakke* (1978) determined that racial quotas in college admissions were unconstitutional, but universities could consider race as one of many factors. *Grutter v. Bollinger* (2003) upheld the use of race-conscious admissions policies, emphasizing the educational benefits of diversity. *Fisher v. University of Texas at Austin* (2013 and 2016) further affirmed the consideration of race as part of a holistic admissions process.

However, the *Students for Fair Admissions v. University of North Carolina, et al.* (2023) ruling by the Supreme Court put an end to AA in institutions of higher education effectively ending race-conscious admission policies. The court ruled that the admission policies at Harvard and University of North Carolina violated the 14th amendment that guarantees equal protection to all under the law. Supporters of the ban argue that AA is no longer necessary to create educational opportunities for marginalized communities given its existence for close to half a century. Nevertheless, studies consistently show enduring disparities between white students and students of color in terms of achievement gaps, harsher/more frequent use of disciplinary practices for students of color, racialized stereotypes in teacher attitudes and beliefs, high school completion rates, and overall psychological well-being (Milner IV 2013; Rutherford and Meier 2020).

Previous state-level AA bans starting in 1990s, such as in the states of California, Texas, Washington, Florida, Arizona, Georgia, and others have shown that race-neutral or color-blind admissions are ineffective at improving racial equity in institutions of higher education. For example, Long and Bateman's (2020) study revealed persistent declines in the share of underrepresented minorities among students admitted to and enrolling in public flagship universities in the states that eliminated AA policies.

For example, in the state of California, prior to Proposition 209, passed in 1996, Black applicants to the University of California (UC) system had an admission rate six percentage points lower than the overall rate, while Latinx applicants were admitted above the average rate. However, by 2019, Black students were admitted to the UC system at a rate 16 percentage points lower than the overall rate, and Latinx students were admitted 6 percentage points below the overall rate (Long and Bateman 2020).

These results imply that alternative policies and administrative decisions have fallen short in replacing the equitable representation opportunities created by race-conscious AA. The nationwide ban on AA is likely to exacerbate existing disparities and reverse the progress that has been achieved thus far. As a society, we have not reached a point where we can disregard social identities such as race, gender, color, and disability, in any aspect of our lives, including education.

From the perspective of intersectionality of race and class, recent research reveals differential impacts of families' SES on the achievement gaps between Black and white students. The findings suggest that socioeconomic advantage does not necessarily benefit Black children in the same way as white children, and socioeconomic adversity does not impose equivalent disadvantages on white children as it does on Black children.

Both low-income and high-income Black families in the United States face cumulative disadvantages that contribute to the achievement gaps observed among Black and white students (Henry et al. 2020).

Historical, systemic, institutional factors such as reduced social and cultural capital, limited wealth accumulation for high-income Black families, and economic strain, extreme neighborhood poverty all play a role in these disparities. Addressing these challenges requires a comprehensive approach that tackles systemic barriers and promotes economic empowerment, improved neighborhood conditions, and comprehensive support systems for Black families to create a more equitable educational system. These disparities highlight the unique privileges and constraints that intersect with race and SES, shaping children's learning experiences and emphasizing the need to consider this intersection when addressing educational inequities (Henry et al. 2020).

The intersection of education and race in the United States continues to be an ongoing and complex topic. Inequities in K-12 education can have long-lasting impacts on an individual's life, affecting the college they are admitted to, the opportunities they receive, and the social and cultural capital they accumulate through their networks. The academic achievement gap that exists is a consequence of historical, interpersonal, systemic, structural, and institutional racism faced by communities of color. These inequities multiply and create early disadvantages that can persist throughout a person's life.

Policing

[Content Warning: Emotionally Heavy Materials] The 2020 Black Lives Matter movement gained national attention following the killings of George Floyd, Breanna Taylor, and countless other innocent lives brought renewed attention to issues of police violence and racial inequality. Black people, while comprising 13% of the U.S. population, accounted for 25% of those fatally shot by the police (Nix and Shjarback 2021). There is a greater awareness and recognition among the public that institutional racism exists in policing, even though it is supposed to protect citizens. This is because public killings of Black people are a very clear example of how the criminal legal system fails to protect Black people.

The persistent institutional and personal harm, violence and trauma experienced by Black and brown people can be attributed to various factors within police departments. These include – administrative practices, policies, chains of command, levels of scrutiny, and both formal and informal messaging. These systemic elements contribute to the creation of unequal treatment and outcomes, as seen in incidents where excessive use of force exemplifies the unchecked discretion and limited oversight of front-line officers.

Scholars like Glaser (2015) and Headley (2020) have highlighted how these unjust outcomes are deeply entrenched in systems marked by racism and white supremacy. To address these issues, it is imperative for public administrators to approach their roles with ethics of care, respect, and a commitment to reevaluating and reshaping the social contract. This involves ensuring that public policies benefit all members of society, rather than favoring only the privileged few (Berry-James et al. 2021). Recognizing racialized police violence as a failure of public governance is imperative for public administration to actively engage in addressing complex and wicked issues.

Overall, law enforcement is seen more positively by white people than by people of color. White people are more likely to view the police positively overall, while Black people are more likely to report problems with police killings. In *Terry v. Ohio* (1968), the Supreme Court established the reasonable suspicion doctrine, which allows law enforcement to stop someone based on a suspicion that a crime is happening or about to happen. This doctrine, in conjunction with other rulings, allows law enforcement to do more policing that is likely to result in racial profiling of people of color. Black, Indigenous, and negatively racialized People of Color are more likely to experience police contact than white people. Often, law enforcement services are not equitable, and Black people are more likely to be racially profiled and stopped, searched, arrested, and killed in greater numbers than white people (Berry-James et al. 2021).

In recent times, a burgeoning movement led by transformative justice, healing justice and disability justice activists and leaders has emerged and focus on transforming systems, structures, and cultures to end harm and violence against people of color, including police violence. For example, these grassroots movements seek to reallocate funding from police departments to social services programs. This involves channeling resources toward initiatives like mental health resources, affordable housing programs, and community outreach (Kaba 2021a). The rationale behind this shift is the understanding that issues such as mental health crises and homelessness, which police are often called upon to deal with, are better handled by experts with specialized training in those fields (Cummins 2023; Spolum et al. 2023).

By redirecting funds away from law enforcement and toward social services, certain jurisdictions endeavor to promote greater equality and justice for underprivileged communities. However, we must remain vigilant of logics of settler colonialism, white supremacy and racialization that permeate most (if not all) of our current systems, structures, and cultures. Hence any transformative effort at ending police violence needs to follow the leadership of those most impacted by injustices. Such efforts also necessitate envisioning and creating systems that are pro-Black, pro-Indigenous, and pro-People of Color.

Political Disenfranchisement

Political disenfranchisement (voter suppression and gerrymandering) is an important historical and contemporary manifestation of systemic and institutional racism. The legal right for all men to vote was secured in 1870, but during the nearly 100-year era of Jim Crow laws, Black people were kept from voting in many states through violent intimidation and selectively applied laws.

In 1965, the Voting Rights Act (VRA) was passed to provide the racial minority groups the right to vote. However, this has been a point of contention in the American democracy. Even in 2021, many states recently passed or were considering legislation disproportionately restricting the voting rights of people of color and changing voting procedures (Shah and Smith 2021). Other forms of political disenfranchisement include gerrymandering, the deliberate redrawing of electoral district boundaries to favor the political party in power. This makes some people's votes count less than others', depriving them of full representation.

To safeguard the fundamental right to vote and achieve universal access to voting rights for all individuals in America, The Lewis Voting Rights Advancement Act is currently being considered. This proposed legislation, named after the late Congressman and civil rights icon John Lewis, seeks to restore key provisions of the VRA of 1965, which were diluted by a Supreme Court ruling in 2013. If passed, the Act would bolster federal oversight of elections in states with a history of discriminatory voting practices, offering greater protection for minority voters. Collectively, these actions reflect a growing recognition that addressing systemic inequities in society requires transformative measures (Brennan Center for Justice 2023).

Housing and Finance

Homeownership is often seen as a pathway to the American dream and the accumulation of inter-generational wealth. However, the benefits from homeownership have not been shared equally. The Joint Center for Housing Studies of Harvard University reports that between 2015 and 2019, nationally, 71.7% of white households owned homes compared to 41.7% of Black households, 46.8% of Hispanic households, 56.7% of Native American households, and 59.4% of Asian American households (Hermann 2023). The U.S. Department of Treasury (2022) reports that the Black-White gap in homeownership rates was the same in 2020 as it was in 1970, just two years after the passage of the Fair Housing Act of 1968, which sought to end racial discrimination in the housing market.

Racial preferences have existed throughout American history, favoring white individuals and families, and perpetuating systemic and institutionalized inequalities. For example, evidence of institutionalized racial bias can be witnessed from the early days of European settlers replacing indentured servants with African slaves, to government policies that caused displacement of Indigenous peoples and tribal nations from their ancestral homelands, to policies and programs that bestowed preferential treatment upon white people, like the Homestead Act distributing millions of acres of western land to individual settlers, as well as discriminatory immigration and citizenship policies. It is evident that racial biases have profoundly influenced American politics, public policies, the administrative state, and society at large (Lui 2006). Jim Crow laws further cemented these racialized preferences, reserving the best opportunities and resources for white people. Even in more recent times, policies like redlining and unequal access to mortgages have contributed to the racial wealth gap (Herring and Henderson 2016).

Predatory financial services disproportionately target communities of color, perpetuating systemic racism that affects many aspects of their lives, including their ability to obtain loans and own homes. This leads to significant disadvantages for people of color in accessing good loans and achieving success in life (Gentry and Cook-Davis 2021), as highlighted in Case Study 8.2. Even in segregated communities where mainstream banking services are available, people of color often must pay extra for these services, creating additional obstacles for them.

An example of systemic racism in lending is the discriminatory practices of banks that use race and ethnicity data to decide whether to provide loans, as demonstrated by the guidelines used by the Home Owners' Loan Corporation in the 1930s. Additionally, payday lenders and check cashing services charge high fees and interest rates that are particularly burdensome for people of color, who are often charged more than their white counterparts (Engel and McCoy 2008).

Case Study 8.2: "Whitewashing" for a Home Loan

In a recent lawsuit case filed by a Black couple, the courts settled a lawsuit under the federal housing discrimination. The couple won the lawsuit against a real estate appraiser who they accused of giving their home a low value because of their race.

In 2016, Paul Austin and Tenisha Tate-Austin saw a listing for a house in Marin City, CA that was worth $550,000, and they decided to buy it. A few years later, they embarked on a series of major upgrades, and to help pay for the work, they decided to refinance their mortgage.

Ms. Janette Miller was hired by the lender to inspect the home and come up with a new valuation that would determine whether the Austin's would qualify for a loan. Miller's appraisal concluded that the home was worth $995,000. When they applied for a mortgage refinance a year ago, the house they were buying appraised at $1,450,000. The Austins were disappointed when they received the new appraisal for their loan, which was much lower than their original appraisal.

The Austins decided to "whitewash" their house. They removed family photos and artwork, books, hair products and anything else that might indicate that a Black family lived there. They also asked a white friend to be present at the house and greet the appraiser as if she were the homeowner and to display some of her family photos in the house. The Austins were not home during the appraisal. The new appraiser found that the house is worth nearly half a million dollars more than the estimate Miller gave.

A lot of Black Americans are calling out the housing appraisal process as discriminatory because they feel that the appraisal was done unfairly because of their race. Homes of comparable quality and with similar amenities are worth 23% less (averaging $48,000 per home, resulting in cumulative losses of $156 billion) in majority Black neighborhoods compared to those with minimal or no Black residents (Perry, Rothwell, and Harshbarger 2018).

Suggested Discussion Questions

1 What impact do you think the Austins' experience will have on the wider conversation about systemic racism in the housing industry?
2 In what ways do you think unconscious bias can affect home appraisals?
3 How can the appraisal process be improved to ensure that it is fair and unbiased?
4 Do you think that the settlement in this case will deter future instances of discriminatory appraisals? Why or why not?

Source: Romo (2023).

Healthcare

In the realm of healthcare, it is essential to acknowledge the historical and ongoing trauma caused by racial discrimination and biased treatment experienced by poor people, and multiply marginalized people of color. The U.S. history is replete with historical and institutional racism in the medical and public health institutions.

[Content Warning: Emotionally Heavy Materials] Some of the key historical events that have shaped experiences of medical trauma for people of color, include the pseudo-scientific conceptualization of race and creation and perpetuation of the logics of white supremacy and eugenics by medical practitioners and biologists. It includes the unethical, brutal, and inhumane medical experimentation carried out by white male doctors and medical practitioners on enslaved Black kids, girls, men, and women.

It includes the practices of involuntary (non-consensual) sterilization and hysterectomies operated on Black and women of color by doctors and medical practitioners as well as the Tuskegee Syphilis Study sponsored by the U.S. Public health Service. It includes health disparities experienced by Indigenous peoples and tribal nations due to land loss, displacements, cultural devastation, environmental injustices. And it includes ongoing neglect of medical needs and health hazards experienced by people of color caused by overt and covert racist policies and administrative decisions (Feagin and Bennefield 2014). These negative experiences and the resulting distrust and continuing disparities in access to quality healthcare impact Black, Indigenous, Latinx, Hispanic, and Asian communities (Zhu and Wright 2020).

The devastating impact of COVID-19 on communities of color can be directly linked to the racialized beliefs and values embedded in public policy and administration that sanctioned inequitable systems of housing, education, employment, healthcare, environment, and infrastructure. For example, Indigenous communities on reservations are generally rural, remote, or both, with little to no supporting infrastructure. Distance to healthcare, lack of health insurance, and lack of facilities affected access to care and treatment for COVID-19-infected family members in Indigenous communities (Solomon et al. 2022). Structural racism through decades of disinvestment and racist policies in multiple sectors, which deepened socioeconomic and health inequality in minoritized populations largely contributed to the outsized share of COVID-19 infection and mortality burden experienced by Indigenous, Black, and Hispanic/Latinx communities in the United States (Holden et al. 2022).

Racial and ethnic minorities consistently experience worse health outcomes compared to white racial groups, even when SES is considered. Barriers to health care access, social determinants of health, systemic racism and discrimination, cultural and language barriers, and historical trauma contribute to these disparities. Systemic racism has far-reaching consequences on people's health, as it increases their exposure to harmful conditions and restricts their access to resources that promote well-being. Economic disadvantages and racial segregation contribute to poorer health outcomes by exposing individuals to detrimental factors like air pollution, toxic waste, and inadequate housing conditions, such as the presence of lead and mold (Wright II, Dolamore, and Berry-James 2022).

Discrimination in housing prevents people from accessing healthy living environments, while limited resources and opportunities, such as education and healthcare, further undermine their health. Additionally, the chronic stress caused by financial strain, where individuals face daily challenges with insufficient financial resources, negatively impacts their well-being (Braveman et al. 2022). Thus, health disparities cannot be studied in isolation, it is a result of intersection of economic, historical, social, political disadvantages accrued over time. Comprehensive efforts are needed to address these systemic issues and promote health equity for marginalized communities.

Action and Change for Racial Justice: A Liberatory Public Service Perspective

We now turn to reflections on action and change to advance racial justice in public service contexts from a liberatory public service (LPS) perspective. As discussed in detail in Chapter 5, the LPS framework is inspired by teachings from inter-generational social justice movements led by multiply marginalized Black, Indigenous, and negatively racialized People of Color. These include Restorative Justice, Transformative Justice, Healing Justice, and Disability Justice movement frameworks.

LPS invites us to dream, to reimagine and re-envision our current systems. LPS calls upon us to engage in the work of radically transforming our current organizational and institutional systems. At the same time it invites us to maintain a steady momentum for transformative change work that is aligned with values of compassionate, humane, and sustainable change work.

LPS is rooted in the core values of love, courage, repair, healing, joy, efficacy, solidarity, and transformation. The five emergent principles of LPS seek to approach public service and social justice work from a trauma-informed, repair and healing-oriented lens that compassionately centers the margins within all our organizational functions structures, designs, policies, procedures, leadership, and cultures. These principles are:

- *Principle 1: LPS integrates inner transformation and collective transformation.*
- *Principle 2: LPS is trauma informed.*

- *Principle 3: LPS is repair and healing oriented.*
- *Principle 4: LPS compassionately centers the margins.*
- *Principle 5: LPS seeks to transform the conditions of harm to end cycles of oppression.*

Ideas for Application and Integration of LPS Perspective

LPS principle one implies that any work toward racial justice must integrate inner transformation and collective transformation. For example, any organizational or institutional transformation work toward development of racial justice policies and infrastructures is incomplete without individual transformation of members of the organization, especially those in leadership roles and those with closest access to power and resources.

However, it is important to note that while external resources and motivations play a critical role, any individual transformation work requires a strong intrinsic motivation for it to be sustainable. As discussed in detail in Chapter 2, individual transformation work may follow the path of building liberatory consciousness (Love 2018) or cycle of liberation (Harro 2018) that seek to unlearn racialized and biased socialization and learn new behaviors and actions rooted in racial justice and solidarity. Individual transformation means we identify and seek to internalize the transformative and liberatory values that resonate with us. For example, individual transformation entails the work of unlearning and learning to match our behaviors, our decisions, and our actions (not just our words) in ways that demonstrate courage and commitment to racial justice.

Organizational and institutional transformation implies replacing racialized systems (i.e., policies, procedures, structures, and cultures) with systems that are pro-Black, pro-Indigenous, and pro-People of Color. For example, individuals, institutions, and organizations may critically examine how they are invested in perpetuating white supremacy cultural norms such as urgency and scarcity-based mindsets, paternalism, and power-over approaches (discussed in Chapter 7 and Okun 2023) in their hiring and promotion, leadership behaviors, investment policies, and other programs. Organizations may explore counter cultural norms, practices, and values systems such as intersectionality, honoring wholeness, sustainability, and following the leadership of those most impacted by inequities to support the work of liberatory racial justice (e.g., refer Chordiya and Protonentis 2024; Sins Invalid 2019).

Among some of the immediate and intermediate steps, organizations may foster culture of continued learning and practice (or learning and development) for racial justice with a sincere intent to transform racialized systems. A culture of learning and practice is different from a training culture that is driven by compliance (Chordiya and Protonentis 2024). Learning and practice for racial justice necessitates creating strong containers to facilitate courageous and nourishing conversations for racial justice (we invite you to refer/return to Chapter 4 for an example of principled agreements for racial justice conversations).

Learning and practice opportunities to cultivate racial justice perspectives can be integrated across organizational structures and functions. Racial equity tools such as white and BIPOC mutual support groups can be used to support collective transformation efforts that are anchored in trust, mutuality, and relationality. (However, it is important to avoid performative actions or misuse of affinity groups or mutual support groups to maintain the status quo.)

Mutual support groups or any other such collectives such as racial and social justice committees or communities of practice or learning and development groups that are tasked with the responsibility of bringing individual and organizational transformation must be invested into, empowered, and supported to guide wider organizational transformation work. Investment, empowerment, and support are necessary to prevent further hurt and harm and exploitation of labor of people involved in advancing racial justice work. It might be worthwhile to explore non-capitalist ways to invest, empower, and support people leading racial justice work. Depending on organizational contexts the complexities of challenges and risks may vary. LPS invites leaning into collective creativity and innovation, and shared equity leadership models to figure out the complexities of prioritization, channeling investments, and support essential to sustain racial justice work.

LPS principles two and three imply that racial justice work must be approached from trauma-informed perspectives and must center the work of repair and healing. The implementation of LPS principles two and three requires sustained effort, focusing on developing embodied social justice leadership and relationships grounded in solidarity. This approach aims to cultivate collective courage, capacity, and resources to recognize the historical, inter-generational, persistent institutional, and personal harm and racialized trauma that our institutions and organizations may have played a role in.

We acknowledge that in the contexts of historical, inter-generational, persistent institutional, and personal trauma from systemic, governmental, and institutional racism and white supremacy, repair work is political, complicated, messy, and necessitates collective desire and effort to move forward. However, a lack of large-scale societal and national repair work need not become a barrier in the path of individual, organizational, and institutional repair work. Individuals, organizations, and institutions committed to repair can find numerous large- and smaller-scale examples across the world where repair work has been successful and transformative (e.g., refer to Tutu and Tutu 2015).

Acknowledgment of hurt and harm and telling the truth are among the important pieces in doing the work of repair and moving toward healing. However, truth-telling must be followed by necessary work to make amends, repair relationships and trust with people and communities that have been hurt, harmed, and traumatized by our institutions and organizations.

As we explored in Chapter 7, throughout the history of racism in the United States, there have been many occurrences of broken treaties, broken trust, and betrayal. Like any human endeavor, repair work cannot be perfect and can be in fact messy. However, it is important that repair work anchored in LPS is carried out with intentionality and seeks to avoid re-traumatization of individuals and communities experiencing harm. It necessitates a commitment to live up to the promises of repair with transformative and actionable changes that seek to end cycles of hurt and harm.

Repair work – whether it is individual, interpersonal, or organizational – is deeply vulnerable. It is not linear and is filled with uncertainty. It requires patience, a depth of emotional maturity and a profound sense of compassion for self and others. However, having clarity that doing the work of repair is the right thing to do and must be done to move us forward in the direction of decolonizing solidarity, can be nourishing and sustain our commitment to liberatory praxis. As Rosa Parks has powerfully noted "*I have learned over the years that when one's mind is made up, this diminishes the fear; knowing what must be done does away with fear.*"

The work of repair is decolonizing by nature, as true repair means we do not expect forgiveness from those we have hurt and harmed, rather, we do the right thing of going through the process of asking for forgiveness from others and ourselves. Genuine apologies acknowledge the hurt and harm and demonstrate sustainable and meaningful actions that can mend the hurt and ensure that the harm is not repeated (Tutu and Tutu 2015).

While the long-term work of repair and healing relationships may seem daunting, there are immediate and intermediate steps that individuals, organizations, and institutions can take to build capacity for deeper repair work. For example, the immediate and intermediate steps may include cultivating an organizational culture for trauma-informed practice (we discuss these in detail in Chapter 3). Such a practice recognizes that trauma of racial oppression is historical, inter-generational, persistent institutional and personal. That trauma impacts our bodyminds and we need to build organizational cultures of care and compassion.

Trauma-informed practice recognizes that we must make every effort to avoid re-traumatization and to support individual or communal healing work (e.g., when people and communities are in grief and processing grief). Organizations and institutions can work to create trauma-informed policies (e.g., health care policies, leave policies, pay equity policies), procedures (e.g., access and accommodation processes), structures, and practices (e.g., in our meetings, our gathering, and in service delivery).

As discussed in detail in Chapter 3, the principles of trauma-informed practice include cultivating physical, emotional, and psychological safety in the organizational environment for both staff and communities we serve. It includes establishing trustworthiness and transparency, building peer support and collaboration, empowerment through sharing power and following the leadership of those most impacted by injustices and inequities, so their perspectives and choices are centered in decision-making processes. It includes practicing awareness, cultivating sensitivity toward cultural and historical contexts of diverse staff and communities we serve, and building strength-based and resilience-focused approaches to move wider organizational and racial justice work forward.

LPS principles four and five are guided by values of intersectionality and seek to compassionately center those who are multiply marginalized by systems of oppression. They seek to transform the conditions that allow racialized and other intersecting oppressions to persist. In practice this means perspectives and voices of those who are most impacted by intersectional racialized systems of oppression and harm such as people with disabilities, older as well as young people, low-income communities, LGBTQIA+ people, women and BIPOC communities are invited to decision-making tables, empowered, and valued. It is more than setting up advisory committees or inviting a BIPOC consultant to facilitate difficult conversations. LPS invites us to always ask "who is at the table," "who needs to be at the table," "who else needs to be at the table?" "what are we doing to shift power and follow the leadership of those most impacted by intersectional racial injustices?"

The practice of LPS principles in creating BIPOC affirming cultures requires a will and intrinsic motivation from those who are closest to power and resources to share power and resources. It necessitates alignment with voices and perspectives emerging from social justice and climate justice movements that are asking us to divest from systems that are causing hurt and harm to people and planet; and invest in sustainable systems of care and nurture to meet fundamental human needs and rights, foster well-being, and achieve collective liberation from all forms of oppression.

Summary and Key Teachings

In this chapter, we explored how racism and white supremacy are forms of oppression that exhibit clear and concrete patterns of operating at macro or systemic (broad legal, structural, and cultural) level, meso or institutional and organizational levels, and at micro or individual and interpersonal levels. Racism and white supremacy are oppressive tools used to create and sustain settler colonialism in the United States and globally. In the context of the United States the historical lineages of racism and white supremacy date back to 15th and 16th centuries when European settlers arrived and marked the beginning of the persistent settler colonial project.

These historical lineages continue to persist through logics of racialization and white supremacy operationalized across institutions and organizations and through dominant societal culture. In the context of public policy and public administration, logic of racialization impacts relationship between the racialized "others" and the administrative state, including in the domains of workplace, housing, healthcare, education, and policing. For example, these are operationalized in the forms of racialized administrative burdens, myth of bureaucratic neutrality, and have consequences such as racialized socioeconomic disparities, all of which impact the lives and livelihoods of multiply marginalized people of color.

Efforts toward advancing racial justice from an LPS perspective must seek to interrupt and transform the conditions that allow intersecting racial inequities to persist. An LPS approach requires divesting from systems of racialized oppression and investing in systems that advance a decolonizing solidarity and seek inclusion, equity, justice, and liberation of all people.

LPS approach to racial justice work at any level (e.g., systemic, institutional, organizational, or individual) and in any domain (e.g., education, housing, policing, or workplace) of public policymaking and administration requires that we shift power and follow the leadership of multiply marginalized people of color who are most impacted by injustices. When multiply marginalized people and communities of color are empowered and centered in social equity and justice work, we are likely to think-through public problems holistically, from multiple dimensions, and in nuanced ways. Thus, we are likely to have better and inclusive solutions to existing problems, better designs, better infrastructures, better and inclusive cultures, better systems that include and benefit everyone and more mature democratic societies (Chordiya et al. 2023).

Deep Dive Resources [Full Citations in References]

Articles and Books

1. Chordiya, Rashmi, and Adana Protonentis. 2024. "Healing from White Supremacy Culture and Ableism: Disability Justice as an Antidote."
2. Kaba, Mariame. 2021a. We Do This 'Til We Free Us: Abolitionist Organizing and Transforming Justice.

3 Suarez, Cyndi, and Dax-Devlon Ross. 2022. "When Blackness Is Centered, Everybody Wins."

Podcast Interviews

4 Menakem, Resmaa. 2019. Francesca Maximé - ReRooted – Ep. 13 – Resmaa Menakem – Be Here Now Network 2022 Interview by Francesca Maximé. https://beherenownetwork.com/francesca-maxime-rerooted-ep-13-resmaa-menakem/.
5 Kaba, Mariame. 2021b. Harm, Punishment, and Abolition with Mariame Kaba — Finding Our Way Podcast Interview by Prentis Hemphill. https://www.findingourwaypodcast.com/individual-episodes/s2e12.

Note

1 We intentionally use the language of "made to feel" rather than "feel" to highlight the systemic nature of racism perpetuated through internalized subordination.

References

Banaji, Mahzarin R., Susan T. Fiske, and Douglas S. Massey. 2021. "Systemic Racism: Individuals and Interactions, Institutions and Society." *Cognitive Research: Principles and Implications* 6(82): 1–21. https://doi.org/10.1186/s41235-021-00349-3

Bell, Lee Anne, Michael S. Funk, Khyati Y. Joshi, and Marjorie Valdivia. "Racism and white privilege." In Teaching for diversity and social justice, edited by Lee Anne Bell, and Maurianne Adams, 3rd ed., 133–181. New York, NY: Routledge,

Berry-James, RaJade M., Brandi Blessett, Rachel Emas, Sean McCandless, Ashley E. Nickels, Kristen Norman-Major, and Parisa Vinzant. 2021. "Stepping Up to The Plate: Making Social Equity a Priority in Public Administration's Troubled Times." *Journal of Public Affairs Education* 27(1): 5–15. https://doi.org/10.1080/15236803.2020.1820289

Blalock, Hubert M. Jr 1967. "Status Inconsistency, Social Mobility, Status Integration and Structural Effects." *American Sociological Review* 32(5): 790–801. https://doi.org/10.2307/2092026

Blessett, Brandi, and Tia Sherèe Gaynor. 2021. "Race, Racism and Administrative Callousness: Using Critical Race Theory for a Race-Conscious Public Administration." *Public Integrity* 23(5): 455–458. https://doi.org/10.1080/10999922.2021.1967011

Blessett, Brandi, Tia Sherèe Gaynor, Matthew Witt, and Mohamad G. Alkadry. 2016. "Counternarratives as Critical Perspectives in Public Administration Curricula." *Administrative Theory & Praxis* 38(4): 267–284. https://doi.org/10.1080/10841806.2016.1239397

Braveman, Paula A., Elaine Arkin, Dwayne Proctor, Tina Kauh, and Nicole Holm. 2022. "Systemic and Structural Racism: Definitions, Examples, Health Damages, And Approaches To Dismantling: Study Examines Definitions, Examples,

Health Damages, and Dismantling Systemic and Structural Racism." *Health Affairs* 41(2): 171–178. https://doi.org/10.1377/hlthaff.2021.01394

Brennan Center for Justice. 2023. *The John Lewis Voting Rights Advancement Act.* Accessed March 12, 2023. https://www.brennancenter.org/our-work/research-reports/john-lewis-voting-rights-advancement-act

Chordiya, Rashmi, and Adana Protonentis. 2024. "Healing from Intersectional White Supremacy Culture and Ableism: Disability Justice as an Antidote." *Journal of Social Equity and Public Administration* 2 (1): 127–52. https://doi.org/10.24926/jsepa.v2i1.4856.

Chordiya, Rashmi, Stephanie Dolamore, Jeannine M. Love, Erin L. Borry, Adana Protonentis, Brendan Stern, and Geoffrey Whitebread. 2023. "Staking the Tent at the Margins: Using Disability Justice to Expand the Theory and Praxis of Social Equity in Public Administration." *Administrative Theory & Praxis* 0(0): 1–26. https://doi.org/10.1080/10841806.2023.2216616

Cummins, Ian. 2023. "'Defunding the Police': A Consideration of the Implications for the Police Role in Mental Health Work." *The Police Journal* 96(2): 230–244. https://doi.org/10.1177/0032258X211047795

Du Bois, William Edward Burghardt. 1899. *The Philadelphia Negro: A Social Study*. No. 14. Published for the University. https://doi.org/10.2307/j.ctv327fwjk

Engel, Kathleen C., and Patricia A. McCoy. 2008. "From Credit Denial to Predatory Lending: The Challenge of Sustaining Minority Homeownership." In *Segregation: The Rising Costs for America*, edited by James H. Carr and Nandinee K. Kutty, 1st ed., 81–124. New York, NY: Routledge.

Feagin, Joe, and Zinobia Bennefield. 2014. "Systemic Racism and U.S. Health Care." *Social Science & Medicine* 103(February): 7–14. https://doi.org/10.1016/j.socscimed.2013.09.006

Fisher v. University of Texas, 570 U.S. 297 (2013). https://www.loc.gov/item/usrep570297/

Fisher v. University of Texas, 579 U.S. 365 (2016). https://supreme.justia.com/cases/federal/us/579/14-981/

Fiske, Susan T. 1993. "Controlling Other People: The Impact of Power on Stereotyping." *American Psychologist* 48(6): 621. https://doi.org/10.1037/0003-066X.48.6.621

Gaynor, Tia Sherèe, and Meghan E. Wilson. 2020. "Social Vulnerability and Equity: The Disproportionate Impact of COVID-19." *Public Administration Review* 80(5): 832–838. https://doi.org/10.1111/puar.13264

Gentry, Katie, and Alison Cook-Davis. 2021. "A Brief History of Housing Policy and Discrimination in Arizona." *Morrison Institute for Public Policy*, November. https://morrisoninstitute.asu.edu/sites/default/files/a-brief-history-of-housing-policy-and-discrimination-in-arizona-nov-2021.pdf

Glaser, Jack. 2015. *Suspect Race: Causes and Consequences of Racial Profiling.* USA: New York, NY: Oxford University Press.

Grutter v. Bollinger, 539 U.S. 306 (2003). https://www.loc.gov/item/usrep539306/

Harro, Bobbie. 2018. "Cycle of Liberation." In *Readings for Diversity and Social Justice*, edited by Maurianne Adams, Warren J. Blumenfeld, D. Chase J. Catalano, Keri Dejong, Heather W. Hackman, Larissa E. Hopkins, Barbara Love, Madeline L. Peters, Davey Shlasko, and Ximena Zuniga, 4th ed., 627–34. New York, NY: Routledge.

Headley, Andrea M. 2020. "Race, Ethnicity, and Social Equity In Policing." In *Achieving Social Equity: From Problems to Solutions*, edited by Mary Guy and Sean McCandless, 1st ed., 82–97. Irvin, CA: Melvin & Leigh Publishers.

Heckler, Nuri, and A. Starke. 2020. "At the Intersection of Identities." In *Achieving Social Equity: From Problems to Solutions*, edited by Mary Guy and Sean McCandless, 1st ed., 53–64. Irvin, CA: Melvin & Leigh Publishers.

Henry, Daphne A., Laura Betancur Cortés, and Elizabeth Votruba-Drzal. 2020. "Black–White Achievement Gaps Differ by Family Socioeconomic Status From Early Childhood Through Early Adolescence." *Journal of Educational Psychology* 112(8): 1471. https://doi.org/10.1037/edu0000439

Hermann, Alexander. 2023. "In Nearly Every State, People of Color Are Less Likely to Own Homes Compared to White Households." *Joint Center for Housing Studies of Harvard University*. Accessed February 8, 2023. https://www.jchs.harvard.edu/blog/nearly-every-state-people-color-are-less-likely-own-homes-compared-white-households

Herring, Cedric, and Loren Henderson. 2016. "Wealth Inequality in Black And White: Cultural and Structural Sources of the Racial Wealth Gap." *Race and Social Problems* 8: 4–17. https://doi.org/10.1007/s12552-016-9159-8

Holden, Tobias M., Melissa A. Simon, Damon T. Arnold, Veronica Halloway, and Jaline Gerardin. 2022. "Structural Racism and COVID-19 Response: Higher Risk of Exposure Drives Disparate COVID-19 Deaths Among Black and Hispanic/Latinx Residents of Illinois, USA." *BMC Public Health* 22(1): 312. https://doi.org/10.1186/s12889-022-12698-9

Kaba, Mariame. 2021a. *We Do This 'Til We Free Us: Abolitionist Organizing and Transforming Justice*. Chicago, IL: Haymarket Books.

Kaba, Mariame. 2021b. Harm, Punishment, and Abolition with Mariame Kaba — Finding Our Way Podcast Interview by Prentis Hemphill. Accessed 2022. https://www.findingourwaypodcast.com/individual-episodes/s2e12

Lardy, Brandon. 2023. "A Revealing Look at Racial Diversity in the Federal Government." Accessed March 23, 2023. https://www.ourpublicservice.org

Long, Mark C., and Nicole A. Bateman. 2020. "Long-Run Changes in Underrepresentation After Affirmative Action Bans in Public Universities." *Educational Evaluation and Policy Analysis* 42(2): 188–207. https://doi.org/10.3102/0162373720904433

Love, Barbara J. 2018. "Developing a Liberatory Consciousness." In *Readings for Diversity and Social Justice*, edited by Maurianne Adams, Warren J. Blumenfeld, D. Chase J. Catalano, Keri Dejong, Heather W. Hackman, Larissa E. Hopkins, Barbara Love, Madeline L. Peters, Davey Shlasko, and Ximena Zuniga, 4th ed., 610–615. New York, London: Routledge.

Lui, Meizhu. 2006. *The Color of Wealth: The Story Behind the US Racial Wealth Divide*. New York, NY: The New Press.

Martínez Guzmán, Juan Pablo, Meagan M. Jordan, and Philip G. Joyce. 2023. "Towards Inclusive Public Administration Systems: Public Budgeting from the Perspective of Critical Race Theory." *Public Administration*. https://doi.org/10.1111/padm.12956

McGee, Kate. 2023. "Texas A&M Recruited a UT Professor to Revive Its Journalism Program, Then Backtracked after 'DEI Hysteria.'" The Texas

Tribune. July 11, 2023. https://www.texastribune.org/2023/07/11/texas-a-m-kathleen-mcelroy-journalism/.

Medina, Pamela S., and Lauren Azevedo. 2021. "Latinx COVID-19 Outcomes: Expanding the Role of Representative Bureaucracy." *Administrative Theory & Praxis* 43(4): 447–461. https://doi.org/10.1080/10841806.2021.1910411

Menakem, Resmaa. 2019. Francesca Maximé - ReRooted - Ep. 13 – Resmaa Menakem – Be Here Now Network 2022 Interview by Francesca Maximé. Accessed 2022. https://beherenownetwork.com/francesca-maxime-rerooted-ep-13-resmaa-menakem/

Milner, H. R. IV 2013. "Why Are Students of Color (Still) Punished More Severely And Frequently Than White Students?." *Urban Education* 48(4): 483–489. https://doi.org/10.1177/0042085913493040

Moynihan, Donald, Pamela Herd, and Hope Harvey. 2015. "Administrative Burden: Learning, Psychological, and Compliance Costs in Citizen-State Interactions." *Journal of Public Administration Research and Theory* 25(1): 43–69. https://doi.org/10.1093/jopart/muu009

Nelson, Ashley, and Jaclyn Piatak. 2021. "Intersectionality, Leadership, And Inclusion: How Do Racially Underrepresented Women Fare In The Federal Government?." *Review of Public Personnel Administration* 41(2): 294–318. https://doi.org/10.1177/0734371X19881681

Nix, Justin, and John A. Shjarback. 2021. "Factors Associated With Police Shooting Mortality: A Focus on Race and A Plea For More Comprehensive Data." *PLoS One* 16(11): e0259024. https://doi.org/10.1371/journal.pone.0259024

Okun, Tema. 2023. "White Supremacy Culture Characteristics." *WHITE SUPREMACY CULTURE.* Accessed 2023. https://www.whitesupremacyculture.info/characteristics.html

Perry, Andre, Jonathan Rothwell, and David Harshbarger. 2018. "The Devaluation of Assets In Black Neighborhoods." Library Catalog: www.brookings.edu

Portillo, Shannon K., Nicole Humphrey, and Domonic A. Bearfield. 2022. *The Myth of Bureaucratic Neutrality: An Examination of Merit and Representation.* New York, NY: Taylor & Francis.

Ray, Victor, Pamela Herd, and Donald Moynihan. 2022. "Racialized Burdens: Applying Racialized Organization Theory to the Administrative State." *Journal of Public Administration Research and Theory*, 139–152. https://doi.org/10.1093/jopart/muac001

Ray, Victor. 2019. "A Theory of Racialized Organizations." *American Sociological Review* 84(1): 26–53. https://doi.org/10.1177/0003122418822335

Regents of *University of California v. Bakke*, 438 U.S. 265 (1978). https://www.loc.gov/item/usrep438265/

Riccucci, Norma M. 2015. "Diversity and Cultural Competency." In *Public Personnel Management: Current Concerns, Future Challenges*, edited by Norma M. Riccucci, 5th ed., 58–67. New York, NY: Routledge. https://doi.org/10.4324/9781315663036-10

Riccucci, Norma M. 2022. *Critical Race Theory: Exploring Its Application to Public Administration.* Cambridge, UK: Cambridge University Press.

Rivera, Mario A., and James D. Ward. 2017. "Toward an Analytical Framework For The Study Of Race And Police Violence." *Public Administration Review* 77(2): 242–250. https://doi.org/10.1111/puar.12748

Robertson, Katie. 2021. "Nikole Hannah-Jones Denied Tenure at University of North Carolina." *The New York Times, May 20, 2021, sec. Business. https://www.nytimes.com/2021/05/19/business/media/nikole-hannah-jones-unc.html.*

Romo, Vanessa. 2023. "Black Couple Settles Lawsuit Claiming Their Home Appraisal Was Lowballed Due to Bias." NPR, March 9, 2023, sec. Race. https://www.npr.org/2023/03/09/1162103286/home-appraisal-racial-bias-black-homeowners-lawsuit

Rutherford, Amanda, and Kenneth J. Meier. 2020. "The Common Denominator: Persistent Racial Gaps in the Administration of Policy. In *Race and Public Administration*, edited by Amanda Rutherford and Kenneth J. Meier, 1st ed., 1–15. New York, NY: Routledge.

Shah, Paru, and Robert S. Smith. 2021. "Legacies of Segregation and Disenfranchisement: The Road From Plessy to Frank and Voter ID Laws in the United States." *RSF: The Russell Sage Foundation Journal of the Social Sciences* 7(1): 134–146. https://doi.org/10.7758/rsf.2021.7.1.08

Sins Invalid. 2019. "Skin, Tooth, and Bone: The Basis of Movement Is Our People, A Disability Justice Primer." https://www.sinsinvalid.org/skin-tooth-and-bone.

Solomon, Teshia G. Arambula, Rachel Rose Bobelu Starks, Agnes Attakai, Fatima Molina, Felina Cordova-Marks, Michelle Kahn-John, Chester L. Antone, Miguel Flores, and Francisco Garcia. 2022. "The Generational Impact of Racism on Health: Voices From American Indian Communities." *Health Affairs* 41(2): 281—288. https://doi.org/10.1377/hlthaff.2021.01419

Spolum, Maren M., William D. Lopez, Daphne C. Watkins, and Paul J. Fleming. 2023. "Police Violence: Reducing the Harms of Policing Through Public Health–Informed Alternative Response Programs." *American Journal of Public Health* 113(S1): S37–S42. https://doi.org/10.2105/AJPH.2022.307107

Stallings, Erika. 2020. "When Black Women Go from Office Pet to Office Threat." *ZORA* (blog). Accessed January 16, 2020. https://zora.medium.com/when-black-women-go-from-office-pet-to-office-threat-83bde710332e

Students for Fair Admissions v. University of North Carolina, et al. (2023) *https://www.oyez.org/cases/2022/21-707*

Suarez, Cyndi, and Ross Dax-Devlon. 2022. "When Blackness Is Centered, Everybody Wins: A Conversation with Cyndi Suarez and Dax-Devlon Ross." *Non Profit News | Nonprofit Quarterly* (blog). April 28, 2022. https://nonprofitquarterly.org/when-blackness-is-centered-everybody-wins-a-conversation-with-cyndi-suarez-and-dax-devlon-ross/

Sue, Derald Wing. 2010. "Microaggressions, Marginality, and Oppression." In *Microaggressions and Marginality: Manifestation, Dynamics, and Impact*, edited by *Derald Wing Sue*, 1st ed., 3–24. Hoboken, NJ: John Wiley & Sons.

Terry v. Ohio, 392 U.S. 1 (1968). https://www.loc.gov/item/usrep392001/

Thomas, Kecia M., Juanita Johnson-Bailey, Rosemary E. Phelps, Ny Mia Tran, and Lindsay Johnson. 2013. "Women of color at midcareer: Going from pet to threat." In *The psychological health of women of color: Intersections, challenges, and opportunities, edited by Lilian Comas-Diaz and Beverly Greene*, 1st ed., 275–286. New York, NY: Guilford Press.

Tulshyan, Ruchika, and Jodi-Ann Burey. 2021. "Stop Telling Women They Have Imposter Syndrome." *Harvard Business Review,* February 11, 2021. https://hbr.org/2021/02/stop-telling-women-they-have-imposter-syndrome

Tutu, Desmond, and Mpho Tutu. 2015. *The Book of Forgiving: The Fourfold Path for Healing Ourselves and Our World.* Reprint ed. New York, NY: HarperOne.

USC Suzanne Dworak-Peck, School of Social Work. 2021. "How to Explain Structural, Institutional and Systemic Racism." *USC-MSW* (blog). October 26, 2021. https://msw.usc.edu/mswusc-blog/how-to-explain-structural-institutional-and-systemic-racism/

Washington, Ella F. 2022. "Recognizing and responding to microaggressions at work." Harvard Business Review. https://hbr.org/2022/05/recognizing-and-responding-to-microaggressions-at-work. May 10, 2022. Accessed July 3, 2023

Wright, James E. II, Stephanie Dolamore, and RaJade M. Berry-James. 2022. "What the Hell Is Wrong With America? The Truth About Racism and Justice for All." *Journal of Public Management & Social Policy* 29(1): 2. https://digitalscholarship.tsu.edu/jpmsp/vol29/iss1/2

Zhu, Ling, and Kenicia Wright. 2020 "Public Administration and Racial Disparities in Health and Health Care: Toward New Health Inequality Research." In *Race and Public Administration*, edited by Amanda Rutherford and Kenneth J. Meier, 1st ed., 68–97. New York, NY: Routledge.

9 Interrupting Sexism, Heteropatriarchy, and Trans Oppression

Moving Toward LGBTQIA+ and Gender Justice

Abstract

In this chapter, we explore Lesbian, Gay, Bisexual, Transgender, Queer, Intersex, Asexual + (LGBTQIA+) and gender justice with an intersectional lens. We focus on how sexism, heteropatriarchy, and trans oppression are interconnected and reinforce each other. We examine key terms, historical contexts, and various feminist perspectives advocating for equitable and compassionate public service. One of the key teachings of this chapter is to encourage intersectional thinking in public service, moving away from binary views on gender. We offer reflections based on core values and principles of liberatory public service (LPS) to advance the work of LGBTQIA+ and gender justice. LPS approaches to LGBTQIA+ and gender justice, recognize that sexism, heteropatriarchy, and trans oppression have consequences for all. LPS approaches seek to counter binary assumptions by deepening our understanding of gender diversity and diverse sexualities. LPS is the practice of advancing policies, procedures, structures, and cultural norms within our organizational, team, classroom, and community contexts that are anchored in gender affirming values. LPS teaches us to approach DEILJ and public service work focused on intersectional issues related to LGBTQIA+ and gender justice from trauma-informed and repair and healing-oriented lens that centers those who are most impacted by harm and violence.

An Acknowledgment of Heavy and Potentially Triggering Content

We want to acknowledge that any reading or discussion of sexism, heteropatriarchy, and trans oppression is heavy and can be triggering. As you move through this chapter, we invite you to honor your embodied reactions and move at a pace that feels accessible and manageable for your bodymind. We invite gentleness and compassion for self and others. We invite you to move your body in ways that can allow you to feel settled; to find places and times that are nourishing and comforting as you process the content of this chapter and this book.

DOI: 10.4324/9781032670669-12

We also want to acknowledge that this is a somewhat long and dense chapter. In this chapter, we take a holistic, intersectional approach in our analysis and writing as best as we can. We also cover several key concepts and terminologies, theoretical frameworks, a historical timeline, policy and administrative areas, and offer an LPS perspective on action and change. We invite you to take your time and encourage you to read this chapter in two, three or more intervals, to allow time and headspace for your bodymind to digest and process the content.

Introduction: A Need for Intersectional Analysis

In this chapter, we take an intersectional approach to examining issues of sexism, heteropatriarchy, and trans oppression in public service contexts. We resonate with Catalano and Griffin's (2016) approach to align our social justice teaching, learning, and practice approaches to respond to the calls from contemporary social justice and intersectional feminist movements. Social justice and intersectional feminist movements highlight the importance of interrupting binary thinking and understanding. They invite us to lean into the nuance and complexities of intersectionality and address power dynamics across systems of oppression.

As we demonstrate through this chapter, sexism, heteropatriarchy, and trans oppression are deeply interconnected systems of oppression that depend on perpetuation of orthodox binary approaches and norms about gender and sexuality. These binary approaches do not match the lived realities of human life across space and time. We seek to interrupt binary thinking in public service contexts and emphasize the need to shift away from single-issue thinking to intersectional thinking in our approaches to solving social inequities and injustices.

Binary thinking and divisiveness are tools of oppression. Intersectional thinking and solidarity are tools of liberation. We cannot solve the problems of patriarchy (i.e., male dominance) without addressing heterosexism (i.e., heterosexual dominance) and trans oppression (i.e., prejudice against transgender and gender non-conforming people), because they overlap with each other, and vice versa. For example, women's issues include issues of trans women and LGBTQIA+ women; similarly, LGBTQIA+ issues include issues of cisgender and transgender people, trans issues include issues of LGBTQIA+ people (Catalano and Griffin 2016). Furthermore, it is important to recognize that all of these issues intersect with other "isms" including racism, ableism, ageism, religious oppression, and more.

We acknowledge that intersectional analysis may seem too complex and daunting at times, especially if we are new to it and need to develop more practice with it. We, therefore, want to invite curiosity and remind you to practice grace, self-compassion, and patience with self and others. We invite you to find a pace that feels meaningful, achievable, and sustainable to learn and practice approaches offered in this book, including intersectionality. We invite you to start with and focus on policy and administrative context and jurisdiction and identify intersectionality among individual and group demographic characteristics of populations that you seek to serve. The targeted universalism approach explored in chapter 6 offers an operational framework to put principles of intersectionality into practice (for more discussion on intersectionality and targeted universalism, refer to Sabharwal and Chordiya, Forthcoming).

The goal of this book, as well as this chapter, is to demonstrate that we can use intersectionality as a prism to analyze public problems and social inequities related to sexism, heteropatriarchy, and trans oppression. (Crenshaw 2020). It may take some time to learn how to use this prism and we can always get better at it. However, an intersectional analysis can help us think about a public service problem whether it is housing, or healthcare or emergency management or immigration or workplace related from many dimensions. Problem-solving approaches that apply an intersectional lens can help us identify nuanced, multi-layered, and multi-dimensional nature of the structural causes and contributing factors of the problem we seek to solve. Intersectional approaches can help us acknowledge the context and the needs of the diverse populations, create many possibilities with targeted and long-lasting solutions that are likely to benefit all people we intend to serve (Sabharwal and Chordiya, forthcoming).

Intersectional analysis can help us build solidarity. It can help us move beyond win-lose, scarcity-based approaches to problem-solving and resource allocation to a win-win, collaborative, and abundance mindsets (Sabharwal and Chordiya, Forthcoming). In the next section, we highlight the importance of inclusive language with a focus on gender and sexuality. We also offer description of key terminology and guidelines for an inclusive language practice.

Guidelines for Inclusive Language and Key Terminology

Language is power. Using inclusive language that seeks to honor humanity, dignity, and respect for people of all gender identities and sexual orientations is key to cultivating diversity, equity, inclusion, and liberatory justice (DEILJ) in public service. In Table 9.1, we define and describe inclusive language guidelines for some key terminologies we will be using in this chapter, including meaning of sexism, heteropatriarchy,

Table 9.1 Key Terminology and Guidelines for LGBTQIA+ and Gender Inclusive Language[1]

Gender and Gender Identities

- "Sex" refers to biological characteristics based on reproductive, anatomical, and genetic traits (e.g., male, female, intersex). "Sexual" refers to sexual identity, attraction, behavior, and related physiological and psychological processes (e.g., sexual orientation, sexual minority, sexual health).
- Sex at Birth refers to the process of assigning sex to infants when they are born. Infants are assigned a sex, either "male" or "female," based on the visible external features of their anatomy, and this information is recorded on their birth certificate as an "M" or an "F." It's important to recognize that the human body's development is a complex and multifaceted process, and sex is not exclusively determined by anatomy, nor is it strictly confined to a binary classification. It's worth noting that up to 1.7% of individuals may be born with intersex traits. Additionally, it's essential to understand that a person's body can be medically transitioned in ways that can fundamentally change the sex they were originally assigned at birth.
- Gender refers to the social, cultural, and psychological attributes, roles, and behaviors associated with being male, female, or non-binary, as defined by a particular society or culture. It encompasses a complex interplay of personal identity, expression, and societal expectations. Gender is distinct from biological sex, which is based on physical and anatomical characteristics. Gender is a more fluid and multifaceted concept. It is socially constructed and can vary across cultures and throughout history. Gender is influenced by cultural, historical, and individual factors.
- Gender identity refers to a person's deeply held, internal understanding and perception of their own gender. It is a fundamental part of one's self-concept and may align with the sex assigned at birth (cisgender) or differ from it (transgender). Gender identity is how individuals personally and emotionally identify themselves in terms of being a man, a woman, genderqueer, or nonbinary. It is important to understand that gender identity is not visible to others. You cannot look at someone and "see" their gender identity.
- Gender expression refers to the external manifestation of an individual's gender identity, encompassing the way a person presents themselves to others and the outward expression of their gender. This expression includes various aspects of appearance, behavior, clothing, grooming, and other visible characteristics. Gender expression is a personal and cultural matter and may vary significantly from one person to another and across different societies. Some people choose to express their gender in ways that align with societal expectations, while others may challenge or transcend these norms by adopting gender expressions that are non-conforming or unconventional. It is important to note that gender expression is separate from gender identity, which is an individual's internal understanding of their own gender.
- Cisgender refers to individuals whose gender identity corresponds with the sex assigned to them at birth. This can be abbreviated as "cis" (cisgender). While the term "cisgender" may not be widely recognized by the general population, it is frequently used by younger generations and transgender individuals. The word "cisgender" can also be abbreviated to "cis," but we recommend doing so only after initially using and defining the term "cisgender" for your audience. "Cisgender" is written without a hyphen, and it does not require the addition of "-ed" at the end.

(*Continued*)

Table 9.1 (Continued)

- "Transgender" or "trans" refers to individuals who identify with a gender different from the one assigned at birth. The term "transgender" is preferred over "transgendered," which is outdated and implies a point in time when someone "became" transgender, not aligning with the experiences of most transgender people. "Trans" and "transgender" are adjectives that should be treated like other adjectives (e.g., "trans man," "trans woman," "transgender person"). It is considered outdated to use "transgender" as a noun ("he is a transgender").
- Nonbinary is an adjective used by individuals who perceive their gender identity and/or gender expression as diverging from the traditional binary gender labels of "man" and "woman." While some nonbinary individuals also identify as transgender and align with the transgender community, others may not. Nonbinary serves as an umbrella term encompassing a wide array of gender identities and expressions. It is important to always ask people what words they use to describe themselves.
- "Two Spirit" is a term used by some Indigenous people to describe their sexual, gender, and/or spiritual identity as having both masculine and feminine spirits. This is a term only used by the Indigenous people of what is now called North America and should not be used by non-Indigenous people, even those who identify as non-binary.
- Gender affirmation and transition refers to the journey that individuals embark on to align their gender expression and/or physical characteristics with their lived gender identity. This is a multifaceted process that unfolds over an extended period, and the specific steps taken in the transition process will differ for each person.

  - Gender affirming care and transitions can include social transition (telling friends, family, coworkers, using different name, different pronouns, gender expression); legal transition (changing name and/or sex marker on documents like driver's license, passport, social security records, bank accounts); medical transition (hormone replacement therapy and/or one or more surgical procedures).
  - It is important to emphasize and understand that being transgender is not contingent on physical appearance or medical interventions. A person can identify as transgender from the moment they recognize that their gender identity does not align with the sex they were assigned at birth. Some transgender individuals may choose not to pursue any gender-affirming steps, while others may desire to transition but face barriers like financial constraints, underlying health conditions, or concerns about potential consequences from family members or employers with anti-trans attitudes.
  - The terms "gender affirmation," "transition," or "transitioning" should be used instead of "transgendering," "sex change," "the surgery," or "pre-operative/post-operative."

- Intersex is a term (an adjective) used to describe an individual (an intersex person) who is born with one or more inherent sex characteristics, such as genitals, internal reproductive organs, and chromosomes, that fall outside of binary conceptions of male or female physiology. It is important not to confuse having an intersex trait with being transgender. However, intersex individuals are assigned a sex at birth, which is often either male or female. This decision is made by medical providers and parents/guardians, and this sex assignment may not necessarily align with the child's gender identity.

(*Continued*)

Table 9.1 (Continued)

- The term "hermaphrodite" is an outdated, offensive, and inaccurate term when applied to humans. It should not be used.

- Use pronouns that align with a person's gender identity. The best practice is to ask for someone's pronouns. English binary pronouns are "he/him" and "she/her," and some people use nonbinary pronouns like "they/them." When writing about a hypothetical person, use "they" as the singular pronoun to avoid making assumptions about an individual's gender.

  - Avoid saying "preferred pronouns." Everyone uses pronouns, and as they are about one's lived gender, not a preference. Simply say pronouns. As in "Please consider putting your pronouns in your email signature," or "I use he/him. What pronouns do you use?"

- Misgendering refers to addressing someone, especially a transgender or gender diverse person, using names, pronouns or language that doesn't align with their gender identity. This can include "deadnaming" or using the former name of a trans person who has chosen a new name that better aligns with their identity, using incorrect pronouns, microaggressions in the form of invasive questions, or more overt harassment and confrontation. We want to note that while accidental misgendering is a common and usually forgivable mistake, persistent and unrepentant misgendering can is unacceptable harassment and inappropriate for the workplace and in public.

Sexual Orientation and LGBTQIA+ terminology

- Sexual orientation is the scientifically accurate term for a person's enduring physical, romantic, and/ or emotional attraction to another person. Sexual orientations encompass a range of identities, including heterosexual (straight), lesbian, gay, bisexual, queer, asexual, and other orientations.

  - Use "sexual orientation" instead of "sexual preference." Sexual orientation refers to an individual's sexual identity, while "preference" suggests that non-heterosexuality is a choice, which is often used to discriminate against the LGBQA+ community. Measures of sexual orientation include sexual identity (how one identifies themselves), sexual attraction (who a person is sexually attracted to) and sexual behavior (with whom a person has sexual intercourse) (Meyer and Millesen 2022).
  - Gender identity and sexual orientation are not the same. Cisgender, transgender, nonbinary, intersex people have sexual orientations, and they may be straight, lesbian, gay, bisexual, queer, asexual, aromantic, pansexual, and more.

- LGBTQIA+ stands for lesbian, gay, bisexual, transgender, queer/questioning, intersex, and asexual, with the "+" added in recognition of all non-straight, non-cisgender identities including genderfluid, nonbinary, and pansexual. In community engagement or pride contexts, use LGBTQIA+.
- Lesbian is a term used to describe a woman who is romantically, emotionally, and sexually attracted to other women. Some lesbians may choose to identify as gay (adjective) or as gay women. Avoid describing lesbians as "homosexuals." The term "lesbian" can serve as both a noun and an adjective. Inquire about how individuals prefer to describe themselves before using labeling their sexual orientation.

(Continued)

Table 9.1 (Continued)

- Gay is an adjective used to describe an individual whose enduring physical, romantic, and/ or emotional attractions are toward people of the same sex (e.g., gay man, gay people). Some women may use the term "gay women" and others may use "lesbian." Avoid describing gay people as "homosexuals"; it is an outdated term and considered derogatory and offensive by many lesbian and gay people.
- Bisexual, Bi, Bi+: An adjective used to characterize an individual who can experience physical, romantic, and/or emotional attraction to individuals of multiple genders, not necessarily simultaneously, uniformly, or to the same extent. The "bi" in bisexual encompasses genders both alike and distinct from one's own gender. Avoid suggesting that bisexuality is limited to attraction to men and women, as this does not accurately represent the term. Also, refrain from using a hyphen in the word "bisexual."
- "Queer" is a term that has evolved and been reclaimed within the LGBTQ+ community to describe a diverse range of non-heteronormative sexual orientations. Typically, those who identify as queer may find terms like lesbian, gay, and bisexual to be too limiting or associated with cultural meanings that don't fully represent their experiences. However, it's important to note that the term isn't universally accepted even within the LGBTQ community and may be considered offensive, so caution should be exercised when using it to describe someone's orientation, unless they've self-identified as such or in a direct quote. The "Q" in LGBT often stands for queer, but in a setting of support, particularly for youth, it may signify "questioning." Always seek to understand how individuals prefer to describe their sexual orientation before applying labels.
- Asexuality is a sexual orientation characterized by a lack of sexual attraction to others or a low or absent interest in sexual activity. Asexual individuals may experience romantic attraction, emotional connections, and the desire for non-sexual forms of intimacy. Demisexual is a sexual orientation that falls within the asexual spectrum. Demisexual individuals experience sexual attraction only after forming a deep emotional or romantic connection with someone.
- The terms trans, transgender, and intersex identities are described above in this table.

Sexism, Heteropatriarchy and, Trans Oppression.

- "Heteronormative" refers to the cultural and societal norms that are based in binary assumptions of gender and sexuality. Heteronormativity assumes and prioritizes heterosexuality as the standard or default sexual orientation. It is the belief that heterosexuality is the norm, and it often involves the expectation that individuals should conform to traditional gender roles and engage in opposite-sex relationships. Heteronormativity marginalizes or overlooks non-heterosexual orientations and relationships, contributing to the invisibility and stigmatization of LGBTQIA+ individuals and identities (Catalano and Griffin 2016; hooks and Cox 2014; McDonald 2015).

(*Continued*)

Table 9.1 (Continued)

- "Cisnormative" refers to societal norms that are based in binary assumptions of gender and sexuality. Cisnormativity assumes and prioritizes cisgender identities as the standard or default gender identity. It is the belief that individuals should identify with the same gender as the sex assigned to them at birth, and it often involves the expectation that gender identity aligns with traditional binary notions of male and female. Cisnormativity marginalizes or overlooks transgender and gender-diverse individuals, leading to discrimination and a lack of recognition of fluid, nonbinary, and diverse gender identities that do not fall within the cisgender identities (Catalano and Griffin 2016; hooks and Cox 2014; McDonald 2015).
- "Sexism" is a form of systemic oppression. It refers to ingrained prejudice, discrimination, or bias based on a person's sex or gender, typically against women or those who do not conform to traditional gender roles. Sexism can manifest in various forms, including unequal treatment, stereotypes, limited opportunities, and unequal power dynamics. It is deeply rooted in societal structures and can impact individuals in many ways, such as in the workplace, education, and social interactions (Catalano and Griffin 2016).
- "Heteropatriarchy" refers to a societal system characterized by the dominance of heterosexual norms and male authority. It combines "hetero" (referring to heterosexuality) and "patriarchy" (referring to a social system where men hold primary power and authority). Heteropatriarchy enforces and privileges heterosexuality as the norm, while reinforcing traditional gender roles and inequalities. This system often marginalizes non-heterosexual and gender-diverse individuals, cis and trans women (henceforth, women) and LGBTQ+ communities (Catalano and Griffin 2016; hooks and Cox 2014; McDonald 2015).
- Trans oppression refers to discrimination, marginalization, and harm experienced by transgender and gender-diverse individuals. This can include various forms of discrimination, such as prejudice against transgender people in social contexts, workplace contexts, a lack of legal protection, lack of access to healthcare, and acceptance in society. Trans oppression reflects the systemic and societal barriers that transgender individuals face, often stemming from cisnormative and heteronormative expectations and structures (Catalano and Griffin 2016).

It is important to recognize and understand that sexism, heteropatriarchy, and trans oppression intersects with each other and with other forms of oppression including racism, ableism, classism, and religious oppression with the effect of multiply marginalizing individuals who are disadvantaged by more than one system of oppression.

Sources: American Psychological Association 2022; Catalano and Griffin 2016; GLAAD 2022; hooks and Cox 2014; McDonald 2015; Meyer and Millesen 2022; National Institutes of Health 2022.

Note: Before applying any labels, inquire about the terms individuals prefer to describe their sexual orientation, gender identity, and gender expression. Capitalize these terms only when used at the beginning of a sentence, except within acronyms.

and trans oppression. We offer deep dive resources for inclusive language practice at the end of the chapter. Since the language is constantly evolving, we invite you to update your vocabulary by regularly visiting the detailed guidelines offered in deep dive resources.

Serving "All Means All" Public: Diverse Feminist Calls for Equitable, Inclusive, and Care-Centered Public Service

The diverse feminist perspectives collectively offer an inclusive and comprehensive understanding of gender and sexuality issues and the continued struggle for equality. They help us recognize that no single approach can address the multifaceted and multilayered nature of oppression and privilege, and the need to advocate for the inclusion of all voices in the feminist movement. These feminist perspectives include (but are not limited to) – intersectional feminism, Black feminism, Indigenous feminism, Chicana feminism, Queer feminism, Transfeminism, and Ecofeminism. A growing body of public administration literature is elevating, amplifying, and exploring the applications and integrations of varied feminist perspectives.

In this section, we explore some of early as well as contemporary feminist perspectives within public administration scholarship. We highlight the key themes emerging from applications of diverse feminist perspectives to public service contexts. We seek to amplify their visions and calls for transforming public service to become equitable, inclusive, and care-centered in service of "all means all" public.

Please note, this discussion is intended to offer a brief introduction and we acknowledge that it is by no means complete or adequate. We invite you to explore the different feminist perspectives, study them, including with the help of deep dive resources offered at the end of this chapter, and continue to reflect on their applications and integrations in public service context.

Early Feminist Perspectives: A Call for Care-Centered Public Administration

Many of the early scholars and practitioners in the field of public administration questioned its hyper masculine nature (Heckler 2022; Burnier 2007, 2021; Shields 2017). They recognized that public service work is care work and it requires approaches anchored in values of nurturing, collaboration, love, building bridges, breaking down hierarchies, sympathetic understanding which encompasses an active form of listening, democratic and participatory cooperation, and inclusion (Burnier 2007, 2021; Guy 2000; Shields 2017, 2022).

For example, Jane Addams, the first woman to win the Nobel Peace Prize in 1931, and the founder of the field of social work, challenged the male-dominated view of city authority and civic management (Shields 2006, 2022). She challenged the male view of the city as a citadel and advocated for a feminine perspective of the city as a household in need of continuous housekeeping, cleanliness, and care to address problems systematically. This approach shifted the focus from a militaristic and defensive stance, contributing to the improvement of late 19-century Chicago (Shields and Soeters 2017). Heavily influenced with Addams works, Camilla Stivers (2000, p. 100) rightly argued that "city government should be thought of not as a business but as a kind of homemaking, devoted to creating the conditions under which residents could live safely and in relative comfort."

Challenging the Myth of Gender-Neutral Organizations

Feminist scholar Joan Acker (1990) challenged the myth of gender-neutrality in organizations. Acker (1990) argued that organizations are not gender neutral. Rather, gender is a fundamental feature that shapes the designs, structures, cultures, procedures, and day-to-day management of organizations, such that the gendered nature of organizations favors men and masculinity over women and femininity.

> Acker (1990) powerfully notes, "abstract jobs and hierarchies, common concepts in organizational thinking, assume a disembodied and universal worker. This worker is actually a (white, cisgender, heteronormative, non-disabled) man; (cisgender, heteronormative, non-disabled) men's bodies, sexuality, and relationships to procreation and paid work are subsumed in the image of the worker."
>
> (p. 139; intersectional interpretations are offered by authors in the added parentheses)

In public service contexts, the gendered nature of organizations, manifests through bureaucratic hierarchies and over emphasis on traditionally masculine values of technical rationality, efficiency, and effectiveness and without balancing feminist and anti-oppressive values of equity, inclusion, belonging, care, and relationality that are essential to performance of public service jobs (Alkadry, Blessett, and Patterson 2015; Blessett et al. 2019; Guy, Newman, and Mastracci 2014; Stivers 1993).

Many feminist voices and perspectives on gender and sexuality matters, particularly, from feminists of color, and LGBTQIA+ feminists have traditionally been marginalized, devalued, and excluded from mainstream organizational scholarship and practice, perhaps because they seek to disrupt the "status quo." These include intersectional feminism and queer feminism (or queer theory) perspectives that expose the racialized, cisnormative, heteronormative, and gendered patterns pervasive in our society and our organizations. They reveal how these patterns are biased toward multiply advantaged groups with dominant social identities (such as white, cisgender, straight, non-disabled men). Collectively, they call for the need to interrupt oppressive power dynamics embedded within our organizations that reinforce these biased patterns.

Adding diverse and marginalized feminist perspectives to organizational scholarship and practice will help us get closer to the goals of serving "all means all" public. In the next few paragraphs, we briefly explore intersectional feminism and queer feminism perspectives and their applications for public service contexts. We invite you to add many other diverse feminist perspectives to this discussion.

Intersectional Feminism: Centering the Lives of Multiply Marginalized People

Intersectional feminism has deep historical lineages within social justice and liberatory movements, and particularly Black Feminist Thought (Blessett 2023). The term "intersectionality" was coined and popularized by Kimberlé Crenshaw, an American scholar and legal theorist. Crenshaw introduced the concept of 'intersectionality' in her seminal 1989 essay "Demarginalizing the Intersection of Race and Sex: A Black Feminist Critique of Antidiscrimination Doctrine, Feminist Theory, and Antiracist Politics." In this essay, she articulated the idea that women of color experience a unique form of oppression that cannot be fully understood by examining racism and sexism separately.

Since the publication of Crenshaw's (1989) path-making work, intersectionality has become a fundamental framework in feminist and social justice movements. It has been expanded upon and applied to various aspects of identity, such as sexuality, class, disability, and more, to better understand and address the complex dynamics of privilege and oppression that affect individuals with multiple intersecting identities. Intersectional feminism places the experiences of individuals facing multiple, simultaneous forms of oppression at the forefront. Its goal is to delve into the depths of inequalities and explore the connections between them within a specific context (Bearfield 2009; Blessett 2023; Crenshaw 1989; Diggs 2022; Hancock 2011; United Nations Women 2020).

Intersectional feminism applied to public service contexts is an invitation and practice of courage to disrupt status quo by centering lives of multiply marginalized people. It is a call to include counter-narratives about a field that has predominantly been presented in a white-centric, cisnormative and heteronormative manner. Intersectional feminist approaches to public service means recognizing the vital contributions of multiply marginalized Black women and people of color in shaping the United States, its institutions, and culture. It means shifting the focus of public service policies, structures, cultures, and procedures, away from multiply advantaged, white-centric perspectives, and place the field within its proper historical, political, and economic context (Blessett 2023).

Queer Feminism: Going Beyond Binaries and Challenging Normativity in Public Service

Queer feminism often referred to as queer theory, is an academic and activist perspective within feminism that challenges and redefines traditional understandings of gender, sexuality, and identity. It emerged in the late 20th century and has played a crucial role in expanding the scope of feminist analysis.

The term Queer theory was first used by Teresa de Lauretis (1991) in her essay titled *Queer Theory: Lesbian and Gay Sexualities An Introduction*. Queer theory challenges traditional understandings of gender, sexuality, and identity. It emerged as a response to limitations in conventional theories and seeks to deconstruct binary categories and question societal norms. Influenced by scholars like Michel Foucault and Judith Butler, queer theory examines power dynamics, discourse, and performativity. It emphasizes the political and social aspects of queerness as an identity and explores how intersecting factors like race and class shape experiences (Larson 2021; McDonald 2015).

Applied to public service contexts, queer feminism (or queer theory) challenges binary norms of gender sexuality, including in our policymaking, administrative procedures, structures, and culture. It challenges traditional cultural norms that are based on binary (cisnormative, heteronormative) assumptions of gender and sexuality (refer Table 9.1 for descriptions of terminology). It invites us to develop a more inclusive, fluid, dynamic, and nuanced understanding of gender and sexuality that matches the reality of human diversity, our lived realities and experiences. Like intersectional feminism, queer feminism recognizes that experiences of oppression and privilege are influenced by multiple intersecting factors, including race, class, disability, and more (Larson 2021; Lorde 2007; McDonald 2015).

Public administration scholars have highlighted the need to elevate queer visibility in public service contexts. Queering public administration is in its infancy and, we are beginning to see a few studies use this theory in policing, nonprofits, and managerial contexts (Larson 2021). Through a queer lens, we interrogate and deconstruct societal notions of "normativity" or in other words, what is deemed "normal" or typical. This process can lead to the development of novel organizational models that better align with the objectives and aspirations of marginalized groups. By viewing organizations through the framework of queer theory, we can envision more equitable and inclusive institutions. This transformation occurs as we challenge the prevailing narratives and "normative" ideas that shape and influence our thinking (Meyer and Millesen 2022).

A Reflection Invitation: Historical Context of Struggle for Gender and LGBTQIA+ Equality in the United States

In Table 9.2, we offer a brief timeline of some of the key moments and legislation impacting gender and LGBTQIA+ equality in the United States. This table is not intended to provide an exhaustive description of the gender and LGBTQIA+ history in the United States. Rather it is intended to be illustrative. We also acknowledge that these historical events are not mere historical facts and are lived, embodied experiences of people and have contributed to immense historical, inter-generational, and spiritual harm and trauma. These can be heavy and triggering and therefore we invite you to prioritize self-compassion and healing for social justice. As has been our approach throughout this book, we invite you to process this content and suggested reflection prompts at a pace that feels meaningful, compassionate, and accessible to your bodymind.

Suggested Reflection Prompts

1 *As you review the below historical timeline, pause and notice, what is resonating and what is causing dissonance for you? What else would you add to this timeline?*
2 *What else are you noticing? Are there any themes you can identify across this timeline?*
3 *What other important events and laws would you add to this table?*
4 *What are the lessons that public service workers and DEILJ students, scholars, and practitioners can draw from this history?*

Table 9.2 Timeline of Some of the Key Moments and Legislation Impacting Gender and LGBTQIA+ Equality in the United States

1800s and Early 1900s:

- **1848:** The Seneca Falls Convention marks the beginning of the women's suffrage movement and calls for women's right to vote, initiating the fight for gender equality.
- **1849:** Harriet Tubman escaped using the Underground Railroad in 1849, which was a network of escape routes and safe houses built by Black and white abolitionists. She eventually returned to the South using this network and helped dozens of enslaved people escape to the North.
- **1851:** A formerly enslaved worker turned abolitionist and women's rights activist, Sojourner Truth delivers her famous address "Ain't I a Woman?"
- **1865:** The 13th Amendment abolishes slavery, a significant step toward racial equality.
- **1868:** The 14th Amendment grants citizenship and equal protection to all persons, a crucial constitutional change.
- **1869:** Susan B. Anthony and Elizabeth Cady Stanton form the National Woman Suffrage Association, which campaigns for women's right to vote.
- **1869:** Wyoming becomes the first state to grant women the right to vote, setting a precedent for women's suffrage.
- **1886:** Two-Spirit, We'wha, a Zuni Native American from New Mexico, meets with President Grover Cleveland.
- **1909:** The National Association for the Advancement of Colored People (NAACP) was formed as a multi-racial organization in 1909.
- **1920:** The 19th Amendment grants women the right to vote nationwide, a major milestone for gender equality.
- **First Wave Feminism and Suffrage Movement:** This wave focuses on women's suffrage and legal rights, laying the foundation for future feminist movements.

Mid-20th Century:

- **1954:** Brown v. Board of Education desegregates schools, challenging racial segregation.
- **1955:** Black seamstress Rosa Parks refuses to give up her seat to a white man on a bus in Montgomery, Alabama. The move helped launch the civil rights movement.
- **1960:** Ella Baker organized the first Student Nonviolent Coordinating Committee (SNCC) conference at Shaw University in North Carolina.
- **1960:** The Food and Drug Administration (FDA) approves the first commercially produced birth control pill in the world.
- **1963:** The Equal Pay Act becomes a law prohibiting sex-based wage discrimination between men and women performing the same job in the same workplace.
- **1964:** The Civil Rights Act becomes a law. Title VII of the Act prohibits employment discrimination based on race, color, religion, national origin, and sex.
- **1964:** Rep. Patsy Mink became the first woman of color and the first Asian American woman to serve in the U.S. Congress.

(*Continued*)

Table 9.2 (Continued)

- **1965:** The Voting Rights Act is passed addressing voting barriers, especially for African Americans.
- **1966:** Wilma Rudolph becomes the first American woman to win three gold medals in track and field during the Summer Olympics.
- **1968:** The Fair Housing Act is passed prohibiting housing discrimination, fostering housing equality.
- **Second Wave Feminism:** This wave broadens the focus to reproductive rights, workplace discrimination, and gender roles.

1970s:

- **1972:** Title IX of the Education Amendments becomes a law prohibiting sex-based discrimination in education, promoting gender equity in education.
- **1972:** Shirley Chisholm becomes the first Black woman elected to the U.S. House of Representatives.
- **1973:** Roe v. Wade legalizes abortion, affirming women's reproductive rights.
- **1973:** Yuri Kochiyama, a Japanese American activist, campaigns for reparations for Japanese Americans who were interned during World War II.
- **1977:** The Combahee River Collective Statement is published by Black feminists. The collective emphasizes the intersectionality of oppression based on race, sexuality, class, and gender. They advance the movement for equality and social justice with an intersectional lens.

1980s:

- **1984:** Geraldine Ferraro becomes the first woman to be a major party's nominee for Vice President.
- **Third Wave Feminism:** This wave embraces intersectionality and diversity, expanding the feminist movement.

1990s to Present:

- **1993:** Toni Morrison becomes the first Black woman to win the Nobel Prize in Literature.
- **1993:** The Family and Medical Leave Act is signed into law, providing unpaid leave for employees to care for newborns, newly adopted children, or ill family members.
- **1993:** "Don't Ask, Don't Tell" allows LGBTQ+ military service, ending a ban.
- **1994:** The Violence Against Women Act (VAWA) was signed into law by President Clinton. This legislation provides funding to support survivors of domestic violence, sexual assault, rape, stalking, and other forms of gender-based violence.
- **1996:** The Defense of Marriage Act was passed. It defined marriage as only between a man and a woman for purposes of Federal law.
- **2003:** Lawrence v. Texas decriminalizes same-sex sexual activity, a crucial step toward LGBTQ+ rights.
- **2005:** Condoleezza Rice becomes the first Black woman to serve as U.S. Secretary of State.
- **2009:** Sonia Sotomayor becomes the first Latina Supreme Court Justice.
- **2007:** U.S. Rep. Nancy Pelosi (D-Calif.) becomes the first female speaker of the House. In 2019, she reclaims the title, becoming the first lawmaker to hold the office two times in more than 50 years.

(*Continued*)

Table 9.2 (Continued)

- **2010s to Present:** The third wave of feminism emphasizes consent, diversity, and LGBTQ+ rights, advancing the feminist movement.
- **2010:** The Patient Protection and Affordable Care Act is signed into law, requiring health insurance plans to cover preventive services for women without copays, including contraception. Section 1557 prohibits discrimination based on all protected groups including sex (including pregnancy, sexual orientation, gender identity, and sex characteristics).
- **2010:** "Don't Ask, Don't Tell" is repealed, allowing openly LGBTQ+ individuals to serve in the U.S. military, a milestone for LGBTQ+ military rights.
- **2013:** The ban on women serving in combat positions is lifted by the U.S. military. Women serve in combat roles, breaking gender barriers in the military.
- **2013:** The Supreme Court rules in United States v. Windsor that the federal government must recognize same-sex marriages in states where they are legal.
- **2015:** Obergefell v. Hodges legalizes same-sex marriage, a landmark ruling for LGBTQ+ rights. Supreme Court overturned section 3 of Defense of Marriage Act (1996) which prevented the federal government from recognizing any marriages between gay or lesbian couples for the purpose of federal laws or programs, even if those couples are considered legally married by their home state.
- **2016:** Hillary Clinton becomes the first woman to receive a presidential nomination from a major political party.
- **2016:** Obama's guidance on transgender restroom use demonstrates support for transgender rights.
- **2016:** The Department of Defense announces that it will allow transgender individuals to serve openly in the U.S. military.
- **2019:** Trump administration placed a ban on transgender individuals from serving openly in the military, the policy was overturned by the Biden administration in 2021.
- **2020:** Bostock v. Clayton County prohibits LGBTQ+ employment discrimination, a significant step toward LGBTQ+ workplace equality.
- **2021:** Kamala Harris becomes the first Black and South Asian female Vice President, making history in U.S. politics.
- **2021:** Deb Haaland assumed the role of Secretary of the Interior and is the first Native American to serve as a Cabinet Secretary for a U.S. president. She is a member of the Pueblo of Laguna and a 35th generation New Mexican.
- **2021:** President Joe Biden's executive orders address LGBTQ+ rights, reaffirming the commitment to LGBTQ+ equality.
- **2022:** In Dobbs v. Jackson Women's Health Organization (2022), the Supreme Court overturned Roe v. Wade (1973), ending constitutional protection for reproductive rights.
- **Bathroom Bills:** States have drafted and passed "bathroom bills" that require individuals to use public restrooms that match the sex assigned at birth rather than their gender identity.

Sources: Gay, Lesbian, and Straight Education Network (GLSEN n.d.), History.com Editors (2022), Library of Congress (2022), National Park Service (2021), National Women's History Museum n.d.; Our Family Coalition and One Archives Foundation (n.d.), U.S. Department of Interior (2021).

Unveiling Institutionalized Sexism, Heteropatriarchy, and Trans Oppression in Key Public Policy and Administrative Areas

Gender and sexual-orientation-based discrimination persists in many sectors, including employment, housing, healthcare, and public services. These forms of discrimination are systemic and embedded in the legal, cultural, and structural systems. In this section, we delve into the persistent discrimination that LGBTQIA+ individuals and women encounter and suggest strategies to create inclusive workplaces and societies.

Sexual Harassment and Gender-Based Violence

Title VII of the Civil Rights Act of 1964 serves as a legal safeguard against workplace discrimination, extending its protection to include all forms of harassment whether verbal or physical, that result in a hostile or intimidating work environment. However, sexual harassment and gender-based violence against women and LGBTQIA+ people are pervasive in workplace, public spaces, and other settings. It is important to understand that sexual harassment and gender-based violence can take various shapes and intensities and cause severe physical, emotional, and psychological harm and trauma for victims/survivors.

Sexual harassment can be categorized into two main types – quid pro quo and creating a hostile work environment. Quid pro quo is the most overt form of sexual harassment, occurring when a supervisor or an individual in a position of authority demands sexual favors from an employee in exchange for benefits like promotions, salary raises, specific job assignments, and more. Creating a hostile work environment refers to a situation in which unwelcome sexual conduct, derogatory comments, or advances create an intimidating, offensive, or hostile atmosphere in the workplace making it difficult for employees to perform their jobs without fear (Elias 2022; Johnson and Otto 2019).

Gender-based violence against women and LGBTQIA+ people manifest in various forms including hate crimes, intimate partner violence, domestic violence, sexual assault, human trafficking. For women, gender-based violence is often entrenched in power imbalances, misogyny, and gender norms. Furthermore, for LGBTQIA+ people, gender-based violence often also stems from deep-seated and prejudicial gender and sexuality norms entrenched in binary either/or assumptions. It is important to recognize that LGBTQIA+ individuals often face intersectional discrimination, where their experiences of sexual harassment and gender-based violence are influenced by both their gender identity and sexual orientation (Etaugh 2020).

[Content Warning: Emotionally Heavy Materials] The violence against multiply marginalized trans people and LGBQIA+ people are deeply pervasive and yet, often invisibilized and neglected in policy and administrative decisions. The 2015 U.S. Transgender Survey data highlights the challenges transgender individuals confront, with high rates of harassment, assault, and violence. A survey of 27,715 individuals across the United States and its territories indicated 46% of transgender people were verbally harassed, while 9% faced physical attacks linked to their transgender identity. Close to half (47%) of respondents reported experiencing sexual assault at some point in their lives (James et al. 2016).

This distressing trend was even more pronounced among respondents of color, particularly Black respondents, with 53% experiencing lifetime sexual assault. Vulnerable groups, including those engaged in sex work (72%), individuals experiencing homelessness (65%), and respondents with disabilities (61%), reported significantly higher rates of sexual assault. Moreover, more than half of the respondents (54%) reported experiencing different forms of intimate partner violence, which ranged from coercive control to physical harm (James et al. 2016).

Sexual harassment is closely tied to notions of toxic masculinity, including gender norms associated with suppression of vulnerable emotions, including sadness, and feeling afraid, that can be perceived as weakness, while emphasizing aggression and dominance. Toxic masculinity is also characterized by cisnormativity, and heteronormativity, and objectification of women's bodies.

Marginalized groups are often at greater risk of experiencing sexual harassment. Marginalized communities, including women, girls, boys, LGBTQIA+ individuals, and people of color, frequently experience daily instances of sexual harassment in educational, play, domestic, workplace, and public settings. In our dominant (cis and hetero-normative) patriarchal culture, men are often socialized to assert their masculinity by engaging in toxic, dominating behaviors, contributing to perpetuation of oppressive gender hierarchies. This harassment, justified as "masculine entitlement," can be linked to men's concerns about failing to conform to societal gender expectations. To combat this, it's crucial to interrupt the learned behavior of sexual harassment early on and promote liberatory masculinity ideals, such as masculinity that is not rooted in domination (Baptist and Coburn 2019, p. 116).

#HowIWillChange, a response to #MeToo, aimed to engage men and boys in discussing their role in rape culture. Analyzing 3,182 tweets PettyJohn et al. (2019) categorized three groups: (a) users committed to dismantling rape culture, (b) users resisting change, and (c) users hostile to change. The committed group advocated self-reflection on toxic masculinity, educating the next generation, and promoting gender equality. The resistant group used "not all men" arguments, while the hostile group vehemently opposed change, criticizing men who supported #HowIWillChange movement by implying they were sexually incompetent. These findings provide insights into men's barriers to participation and potential support for change. Focusing on prevention initiatives to engage with children from an early age and recognizing the pervasive impact of hegemonic masculinity in our society is essential.

In summary, cis-normative and hetero-normative patriarchy perpetuates the oppression experienced by women and LGBTQIA+ individuals, promoting the dominance of hegemonic masculinity, characterized by attributes such as being male, white, heterosexual, strong, objective, and rational, while subordinating femininity, associated with being female, non-white, non-heterosexual, weak, emotional, and irrational (Johnson and Otto 2019; Wright 2013). Gender and sexuality intersect with other "isms", including racism, ableism, and ageism, all of which collectively uphold privileges for white, non-disabled, and middle-aged individuals, and hinder efforts to bring about broader social structural changes (Acker 2006).

Workplace Discrimination

Organizations play a pivotal role in shaping societal and gender norms, affecting employees of diverse gender and sexual identities. These norms give rise to numerous workplace challenges, often metaphorically depicted as the "glass ceiling," "glass walls," "glass cliffs," and "sticky floors," limiting opportunities and reinforcing biases (Heckler 2022).

Glass ceiling refers to invisibilized and normalized barriers to career and leadership advancement; glass walls represent barriers that confine women to certain agencies traditionally considered "feminine" in nature. Glass escalators illustrate gender-based occupational segregation where men in female-dominated roles are rapidly promoted to leadership positions compared to women. Sticky floors, conversely, keep women and people with marginalized identities in low-level positions and hinder their pursuit of top management roles. While "glass cliff," describes the phenomenon where women and people with marginalized identities may be intentionally placed in leadership roles associated with higher risks of negative consequences (Sabharwal 2015).

Cisnormativity, heteronormativity, and gendered norms are pervasive in organizational structures, cultures, and practices. From seemingly benign happy hours and networking gatherings to pay structures such as job evaluations (that are used to determine a job's value to the organization), gender and sexuality norms contribute toward disparate impact (i.e., discriminating impact) on women, LGBTQIA+ individuals and other marginalized groups. These contribute toward pervasive organizational problems of pay inequity, occupational segregation, and restricted career mobility (D'Agostino et al. 2022; Chordiya and Hubbell 2023).

Many theoretical and empirical studies have revealed that the concept of a gender-neutral workplace is a misconception, affecting all employees, especially women and LGBTQIA+ individuals, as they navigate multiple roles in their personal and professional lives (Acker 1990). For example, studies have shown that despite structural accommodations, such as child-care programs, in absence of inclusive organizational cultures, women encounter the motherhood penalty, hindering their career advancement and contributing to their turnover intentions. Furthermore, LGBQ+ individuals, including same-sex couples and transgender individuals, face unique family-related challenges and pressures to conform to traditional gender norms, exposing the fallacy of a gender-neutral workplace (Chordiya 2019; Dietert and Dentice 2009; Elias et al. 2018).

Organizational cultures often reinforce traditional masculine traits, impacting how employees perceive themselves, their opportunities, and their chances of promotion. This dynamic applies to both women and LGBTQIA+ individuals (Heckler 2022). The deeply ingrained historical masculinity affects individual, organizational, and societal levels. At the individual level, it enforces an expectation of an "appearance of control" and tough, "macho" qualities, particularly for men. Women working in male-dominated organizations often feel compelled to conform to these ideals, leading to the manifestation of aggressive behaviors (Guy 2017).

Men who deviate from these norms may face repercussions, risking being seen as deficient in leadership qualities and trustworthiness. Additionally, at the structural level, gendered imagery persists, exemplified by institutions like the Department of Homeland Security, which employs patriotic, heroic, and masculine visuals to gain support. This trend is also evident in fields like law enforcement, where officers are trained to exhibit "unemotional" characteristics (Guy 2017).

Gendered biases also extend to how employee's contributions to the organization are evaluated and in the distribution of rewards (Chordiya and Hubbell 2023). Gender biases result in women earning less than their male counterparts, even with similar qualifications and experience. Women and LGBTQIA+ individuals perceived as more feminine face heightened scrutiny for infractions or failures (Bishu, Guy, and Heckler 2019). The lack of policies supporting employees with families, including same-sex couples, adds to these challenges. Discrimination persists due to varying legal safeguards in different regions, fueling negative preconceptions and stereotypes that harm the well-being of LGBTQIA+ employees. Recognizing the intersectional impact of cisnormativity, heteronormativity, patriarchy, and gendered biases is vital to dismantling workplace barriers and ensuring equal opportunities for everyone.

Public administration research reveals that gender-related biases and occupational segregation are pervasive in public service organizations (Guy

2017). Guy (2017, p. 50) aptly notes that "Jobs are segregated by gender largely due to the emotive demands of the work." Certain professions, like social work, 911 dispatch calling, teaching, and customer service, require caring and nurturing skills, often referred to as emotional labor. Despite the essential nature of these roles, they tend to receive lower wages and fewer benefits compared to traditionally male-dominated professions.

One significant reason for this wage disparity is the traditional perception of these professions as "women's work," leading to their undervaluation and underpayment. This gender bias is especially clear when male workers in these fields are considered more competent and deserving of higher salaries than their female colleagues (Guy 2017). Moreover, the emotional labor involved in these roles, which entails managing the emotions and well-being of others, is frequently not recognized as real labor and, as a result, often goes uncompensated (Chordiya and Hubbell 2023; Guy 2017).

Transgender individuals, often contend with traditional gender norms within public service organizations, leading to gender harassment (Carpenter, Eppink, and Gonzales 2020). Legal disputes related to organizational policies for transgender employees have highlighted the necessity for comprehensive policies that address transition processes, inclusivity, harassment prevention, and restroom use within government agencies (Elias 2017). A study by Elias (2017) on a federal government workplace transition offers insights for future policies, emphasizing the need for leadership in government and nonprofit organizations to establish inclusive, gender affirming, policies and designate points of contact for workplace gender transitions and related issues.

When organizational theories fail to consider the role of gender and sexuality, they overlook how leadership styles, procedures, and rewards often reflect traditional masculine assumptions, perpetuating discrimination against women, LGBTQIA+ and other marginalized groups. This lack of gender consideration, referred to as "gender blindness," suppresses femininity by treating masculinity as the norm (Acker 1990; Stivers 2000). Researchers must recognize and examine the role of gender and sexuality in organizations to comprehend and address how sexual orientation and gender differentiation and inequality manifest in the workplace (Bishu et al. 2019; McDonald 2015). Similarly, to foster a truly inclusive work environment, organizational leadership must actively work toward creating fair and inclusive environments, acknowledging the unique challenges faced by groups marginalized by their gender identities and sexual orientation.

Housing Discrimination

Housing discrimination disproportionately affects BIPOC communities, women, LGBTQIA+ people (including young LGBTQIA+ people), creating additional barriers to secure stable housing and economic well-being

(Carpenter et al. 2020; Wilson et al. 2019). Housing affordability data reveals that LGBTQIA+ adults face a 15% higher risk of poverty compared to cisgender heterosexual adults, even after accounting for factors like age, race, urban residence, employment, language, education, and disability (Wilson et al. 2019). When it comes to homeownership, the ownership rate among LGBTQIA+ adults is 49.8%, a notable contrast to the 70.1% of non-LGBTQIA+ individuals in 35 states (Conron 2019). Building on discussions offered in chapter 8, we want to acknowledge that the homeownership gap is more pronounced among LGBTQIA+ people and BIPOC communities, further exacerbating inequities for people experiencing homelessness.[2]

In stark contrast to rate of homeownership, there are approximately 1.6–2.8 million LGBT youth experiencing homelessness in the United States, giving rise to a wicked problem since it is ill-defined and is interconnected with several other causes (Norman-Major 2018). The Fair Housing Act protects individuals from discrimination in various housing-related activities, such as renting, buying, applying for a mortgage, or seeking housing assistance. It also extends additional protections to federally assisted housing. The law prohibits discrimination based on race, color, national origin, religion, familial status, disability, and sex (including gender, gender identity, and sexual orientation). However, despite this law, we continue to see discrimination experienced by LGBT individuals.

Utilizing a randomized matched-pair email correspondence test involving 6,490 distinct property owners across 94 cities in the United States, Schwegman (, 2019) found that same-sex couples, especially same-sex male couples and minority same-sex couples, face greater challenges when it comes to accessing rental housing in the United States. Compared to heterosexual couples, same-sex male couples receive fewer responses to rental inquiries, while no clear discrimination is observed against same-sex female couples. However, the study reveals subtle discrimination against same-sex Black male couples compared to Black heterosexual couples. Discrimination is also present against Black and Hispanic couples, irrespective of sexual orientation, in comparison to White couples.

The Schwegman (2019) study highlights that being part of multiple stigmatized groups amplifies the discrimination experienced by individuals. Specifically, same-sex couples who are also racial minorities receive fewer responses compared to both same-sex White male couples and heterosexual individuals of the same race.

Despite LGBTQIA+ youth and young adults (YYA) making up approximately 10% of the overall youth and young adult population, they are significantly overrepresented among YYA experiencing homelessness, comprising an estimated 20%–40% of this population (Shelton, 2023). LGBTQIA+ who are experiencing homelessness confront unique obstacles such as violence and victimization based on their sexual orientation, gender identity, and expression.

Housing discrimination against LGBTQIA+ individuals are fueled by various factors, including family rejection of LGBTQIA+ youth, obstacles in accessing shelters, harassment by housing providers, challenges encountered by LGBTQIA+ elders, mortgage lender discrimination against same-sex couples, and intersectional discrimination. This multifaceted problem necessitates comprehensive, multidimensional changes in housing policies and infrastructure to foster equity and inclusivity for all (such as, approaches rooted in targeted universalism framework discussed in chapter 6).

Additionally, it's crucial to note that LGBTQIA+ youth and young adults experiencing homelessness exhibit elevated rates of substance abuse, engagement in the sex industry, mental health issues, and experiences of victimization compared to their heterosexual and cisgender counterparts. These disparities emphasize the need for a holistic approach to address the housing crisis and its associated challenges for the LGBTQIA+ community. To ensure housing access for LGBTQIA+ individuals, we must eliminate barriers, fund anti-discrimination programs, and provide inclusive training for relevant staff (Romero, Goldberg, and Vasquez 2020).

Health Disparities

[Content Warning: Emotionally Heavy Materials] Across various gender and sexual identity groups, widespread health disparities prevail, reflecting a disconcerting pattern of discrimination within medical settings. Women, racialized minorities, and LGBTQIA+ individuals and youth contend with a myriad of health disparities. These include elevated rates of mental health issues, vulnerability to substance abuse, and obstacles in accessing equitable, inclusive, and adequate healthcare. Additionally, the fear of rejection and non-acceptance by family and peers places LGBTQIA+ youth at a heightened risk of experiencing depression, anxiety, and even suicidal thoughts and attempts (Fredriksen-Goldsen et al. 2014; Russell and Fish 2016).

LGBTQIA+ individuals confront ongoing health care disparities. They report negative interactions with health care professionals, including anti-LGBTQIA+ prejudice and unequal treatment. This issue is further compounded by the prevalence of heteronormative preferences among health care providers. Notably, transgender individuals face additional hurdles, including being denied medical care, which significantly contributes to the health disparities present within the LGBTQIA+ community (Bonvicini 2017).

For instance, studies have shown that even when transgender men are typically younger, they face an elevated risk of experiencing multiple chronic health conditions compared to their cisgender counterparts.

(Hoy-Ellis and Fredriksen-Goldsen 2016). Transgender women experience social exclusion, characterized by lower marriage rates, greater likelihood of living alone, and reduced family size. This isolation correlates with adverse health outcomes, such as poorer mental and general health and higher disability rates. These dual challenges underline the complex health and social disparities faced by transgender individuals (Fredriksen-Goldsen et al. 2014). Transgender youth face several policy, structural and cultural barriers to healthcare, with some states banning gender-affirming care for those under 18, resulting in negative health and legal consequences. Gender-affirming care encompasses social support and medical interventions, which research highlights as crucial for mental health and overall well-being (ACLU 2023; Abreu et al. 2022; Tordoff et al. 2022).

[Content Warning: Emotionally Heavy Materials] Intersex people are a severely marginalized and ignored community. Intersex individuals often endure unnecessary medical procedures in childhood, including during infancy, without their consent, to conform with gender norms. These unnecessary medical procedures can lead to physical discomfort, emotional distress, and various long-term issues. The misconception that biological sex is solely binary adds to their isolation and stress (GLAAD n.d.; Intersex Justice Project n.d.; Wall 2021).

To address these challenges, intersex individuals and their families require comprehensive information, peer support, and mental health resources. Medical professionals should guide them to supportive communities and respect their autonomy, waiting until they can make informed decisions about medical procedures rather than pressuring parents to make irreversible choices on their behalf (GLAAD n.d.; Intersex Justice Project n.d.; Wall 2021).

In a first national health study of intersex adults in the United States conducted in 2018 by Rosenwohl-Mack et al. (2020), 43% rated their physical health as fair/poor, 53% reported fair/poor mental health, and prevalent diagnoses included depression, anxiety, arthritis, and hypertension. Difficulties with every day and cognitive tasks were reported by one-third and over half of the participants. These findings highlight the complex health challenges faced by intersex adults and emphasize the need for targeted support and interventions.

To enhance healthcare for women, BIPOC, and LGBTQIA+ individuals, it is vital to respect patients' agency and self-determination, eliminate stereotypes and stigmatization, involve patients in decision-making, address health disparities, provide non-judgmental care, and expand access to equitable and inclusive health care resources. Furthermore, addressing the unique health care needs of bisexual individuals within the LGBTQIA+ community is essential, considering their disproportionate health disparities despite being the largest subgroup within the LGBTQIA+ community

(Human Rights Campaign Foundation n.d.). Supportive policies must consider the key elements of care and support for transgender children and youth, non-binary individuals, intersex people, women and people of color, and individuals of diverse sexual and gender identities.

Invitation to Pause and Reflect

We invite you to pause here. If it feels accessible, take one or more deep breaths, hydrate your body, move your body, soothe your body in ways that feel kind and compassionate.

If/when you feel ready, take a few moments to notice. Notice what is emerging for you based on the discussions offered so far. What sensations and feelings are your feeling? Notice.

Is there a sense of resonance or dissonance, overwhelm or calm or mixed sensations, confusion or clarity, validation, or challenge? Just notice. Take your time with this pause and reflection. We invite you to return to the next section when you feel ready and resourced in your body mind.

Action and Change for Gender and LGBTQIA+ Justice: A Liberatory Public Service Perspective

In this section, we envision action and change for gender and LGBTQIA+ justice from a liberatory public service (LPS) perspective. We invite you to read these reflections alongside LPS-focused ideas and visions described in Chapter 5 (the key tenets of LPS framework), toward the end of Chapter 8 (section on LPS perspectives for racial justice), and in subsequent Chapter 10 (section on LPS perspectives for disability justice). These reflections build on each other and their practice is intrinsically aligned and mutually dependent. We think many of the ideas, practices, and strategies for action and change offered in Chapters 5, 8, 9, and 10 can be applied across various contexts of DEILJ work that are discussed in this book and beyond. We invite you to make these ideas and practices your own and adapt them to your individual and collective/organizational priorities, contexts, and needs.

LPS Principles and Core Values

To offer a quick refresher, the framework of LPS is rooted in the core values of love, courage, repair, healing, joy, efficacy, solidarity, and transformation. The five emergent principles of LPS seek to approach public service and DEILJ work from a trauma-informed, repair and healing-oriented lens that compassionately centers the margins within all our organizational functions structures, designs, policies, procedures, leadership, and cultures. These principles are:

- *Principle 1: LPS integrates inner transformation and collective transformation.*
- *Principle 2: LPS is trauma informed.*
- *Principle 3: LPS is repair and healing oriented.*
- *Principle 4: LPS compassionately centers the margins.*
- *Principle 5: LPS seeks to transform the conditions of harm to end cycles of oppression.*

Reflections on Application and Integration of LPS Perspective

In the preceding sections of this chapter, we highlight that gender and sexuality-based discrimination and harm continues to persist in many sectors, including workplace, housing, health care, and public services. In the following section, we expand and reflect on the application on the LPS framework to foster gender and LGBTQIA+ justice.

Consequences for All

An LPS approach recognizes that systems of oppression have consequences for all. Discrimination and harm based on sexuality and gender identities have dehumanizing impacts not only for those experiencing oppression more directly and intensely but for all members of our organizations and society.

Continued cycles of gender and sexuality-based harm and violence signify that we continue to live, play, and work in organizations and societies where all human lives, bodies, and minds do not have equal value. The negative consequences of this type of dominating and divisive logic of oppression may not seem to be immediately clear to those in dominant groups. However, with some time, patience, and critical examination of these forms of oppression, we can discern and learn to recognize that even those with dominant identities and favored by our current systems are not immune from harm and discrimination based on these logics of oppression.

Challenging heteronormativity, cisnormativity, and gendered biases takes act of courage, especially in current climate where risks of movement backlash and interpersonal retaliation are real. However, it is important to recognize that the risks and harm from retaliatory consequences for those in dominant groups and those in marginalized groups are different. Again, systems of oppression make it so.

LPS invites us, especially those in dominant positions, to make time, space, and resources to undertake proactive steps toward inner transformation and collective transformation. This work may look like building self and collective efficacy, courage, and skills including those related to conflict management, nonviolent communication, bystander action, and community accountability.

LPS, invites all, especially, those of us who are in dominant groups to dream, to build courage and capacities to respond to the following set of prompts:

Freedom:

"In what ways do I benefit from living in a just and humane world?" "In what ways do I benefit from social justice, liberation, and freedom movements that are often led by multiply marginalized, BIPOC, LGBTQIA+ and disability communities?" "How can I be a part of solution and collective transformation to achieve freedom and liberation for all?"

Solidarity:

"How can I share some of the weight of liberatory work, so my peers, colleagues, friends who identify as women and LGBTQIA+ individuals, especially those further marginalized by racialized and ableist norms, will not have to carry all the burden of creating a just world?" "How can I be an ally rooted in accountability and solidarity?" "How can I decenter myself, my discomfort, my struggles with what feels like an unsettling process of inner transformation, and make space for healing and affirmation of my kin with marginalized identities?" "How might me decentering my dominant identities contribute to my own healing?"

Compassionate and Decolonizing Accountability[3]:

"How can I co-create and sustain spaces and collectives that will help me, guide me, nourish me, and keep me honest and accountable as I engage with the liberatory work?" "How can I unlearn my internalized oppression?" "How can I internalize new values, habits, and behaviors that align with my identity and principles of justice? " "How can I be an affirming friend, colleague, partner, parent, sibling in this world?" "What are my superpowers and how can I use them for constructive, positive, and transformative change towards collective liberation?" "What else must I know, experience, and understand to discern that my liberation and freedom is tied to collective liberation?"

Affirming Organizational Cultures

At organizational and institutional levels, an LPS approach to transformation for gender and LGBTQIA+ justice means replacing cisnormative, heteronormative, gender-based systems (i.e., policies, procedures, structures, and cultures) with systems that are pro-women, pro-LGBTQIA+ people, and centers those multiply marginalized because of their racial, age, and disability identities. For example, individuals, institutions, and organizations may audit, critically examine, and seek to interrupt and transform cisnormative, heteronormative, and gendered biases in their hiring and promotion procedures, pay structures, workplace benefits, leadership behaviors, and other programs.

COUNTERING BIASES: CREATING A CULTURE OF LEARNING AND PRACTICE FOR JUSTICE AND INCLUSION

Organizations may foster a culture of continued learning, development, and practice for intersectional gender and LGBTQIA+ justice with a sincere intent to transform biased systems. As we have emphasized previously in this book, a culture of learning and development is different from a training culture that is driven by compliance.

For example, a culture of learning and development, applied to context of healthcare, will require health care providers to prioritize building trauma-informed practices, cultural competences and sensitivity in their interactions and care for women and LGBTQIA+ clients and patients, including with an intersectional understanding of harms from marginalization due to racial, gender, age, disability and class locations. This includes recognizing and addressing the unique health challenges and disparities they face. Education and practice programs should enhance health care providers' understanding of women and LGBTQIA+ health needs and promote inclusive practices.

Insufficient cultural competence and a lack of women and LGBTQIA+ inclusion focused learning and practice within the workplace contribute to challenges. This issue is particularly pronounced in regions that lack legal protections against discrimination based on sexual orientation and gender identities. These contribute toward heightened experiences of biases during hiring, and promotion decisions, and even termination without legal recourse.

Even in areas with legal safeguards, the persistence of a discriminatory organizational culture creates a hostile work environment characterized by harassment and exclusion. These challenges stem from an enduring historical backdrop of gender-related stereotypes that foster negative preconceptions. Within such an environment, women and LGBTQIA+ employees frequently encounter the distressing use of incorrect pronouns, along with the propagation of hurtful jokes and comments. These practices, driven by stereotypes and biases, significantly affect the mental and physical well-being of women and LGBTQIA+ individuals, compelling them to conceal their authentic identities. This concealment arises out of fear – a fear rooted in the pervasive threat of discrimination and mistreatment from colleagues and superiors who often lack the cultural competence to navigate LGBTQIA+ issues effectively (DiPadova-Stocks, Ehrlich, and Cowley 2021).

Trauma-Informed Healing-Oriented Approaches

Advancing gender and LGBTQIA+ justice from trauma-informed and healing-oriented approaches means that repair and healing are centered as core needs of public servants and communities they serve. It includes practice of cultivating physically, emotionally, and psychologically safe-enough organizational environment for both staff and communities.

Trauma-informed and healing-oriented approaches are important to increase representation and visibility of women, BIPOC, and LGBTQIA+ people across organizational levels. These include cultivating gender and sexuality affirming organizational cultures, policies, and practices that can play a big role in supporting marginalized people to arrive as their authentic selves and feel a sense of belonging.

As we have discussed in previous chapters, trauma-informed principles include taking steps to establish trustworthiness and transparency, building peer support and collaboration, empowerment through sharing power and following the leadership of those most impacted by gender and sexuality-based injustices and inequities so their perspectives and choices are centered in decision-making processes. It means practicing awareness and cultivating sensitivity toward cultural and historical contexts of diverse staff and communities we serve. It means building strength-based and resilience-focused approaches as organizations seek to meet the needs of their staff and the communities they serve. The work of translating these principles of trauma-informed healing-oriented practices to unique contexts and needs of your organization and teams needs patience, creativity, a mindset of play and curiosity, and most importantly collective imagination.

Centering the Needs of Those Impacted by Harm and Interrupting Cycles of Oppression

LPS invites public service organizations to explore restorative justice and transformative justice approaches that compassionately center the needs of those most impacted by harm and trauma of gender- and sexuality-based discrimination and harm. Furthermore, LPS invites to transform the systems (i.e., policies, procedures, structures, and cultures) that contribute toward gender- and sexuality-based discrimination and harm.

To dream a little bit here, an LPS approach applied to public service contexts may include inviting restorative and transformative justice scholars and practitioners and exploring alternatives to punishment-based systems to workplace violence. As we have noted previously in Chapter 5, punishment-based systems are not feminist, and not necessarily transformative in meeting the needs of accountability, repair, and healing of those harmed. Building on teachings offered by transformative justice framework, which is one of the key building blocks of LPS framework, the invitation is to explore possibilities of community-based approaches to prevent harm and practice repair, healing, and accountability in moments of tension and conflicts.

For example, in workplace or educational contexts, LPS invites us to explore how can community-based approaches help to prevent sexual and gender-based harassment and harm. It invites us to explore what would a system of reporting incidences of harm look like if we center the needs of victims and survivors? How can we follow the leadership of the community and survivors to create systems of accountability, repair, and healing? Can we create flexible and adaptive enough systems to meet the emergent needs and demands of changing times, contexts, and possibilities? How would we measure the effectiveness of the systems in meeting the needs of multiply marginalized communities? What other questions must we ask? Who must ask these questions?

Summary and Key Teachings

In this chapter, we explore LGBTQIA+ and gender justice with an intersectional lens, focusing on how sexism, heteropatriarchy, and trans oppression are interconnected and reinforce each other. We also examined key terms, historical contexts, and various feminist perspectives advocating for equitable and compassionate public service. Furthermore, we highlighted the systemic oppression women and LGBTQIA+ individuals face in areas like the workplace, housing, and healthcare due to the intersections of gender, race, class, and sexuality.

One of the key teachings of this chapter is to encourage intersectional thinking in public service, moving away from binary views on gender. By adopting intersectionality as a prism for analyzing public issues related to sexism, heteropatriarchy, and trans oppression, we can develop more effective and inclusive solutions that benefit everyone we serve.

We offer reflections based on core values and principles of LPS to advance the work of LGBTQIA+ and gender justice. LPS approaches to LGBTQIA+ and gender justice, recognize that sexism, heteropatriarchy, and trans oppression have consequences for all. LPS is the practice of advancing policies, procedures, structures, and cultural norms within our organizational, team, classroom, and community contexts that are anchored in gender affirming values. LPS approaches seek to counter binary assumptions by deepening our understanding of gender diversity and diverse sexualities. It focuses on undertaking both inner transformation and collective transformation work. LPS teaches us to approach DEILJ and public service work focused on LGBTQIA+ and gender justice from trauma-informed and repair and healing-oriented lens that centers those who are most impacted by harm and violence.

Deep Dive Resources [Full Citations in References]

Inclusive Language Guidelines

1 American Psychological Association. 2022. "Gender."
2 GLAAD. 2022. "Glossary of Terms: LGBTQ | GLAAD."
3 Intersex Justice Project. n.d. https://www.intersexjusticeproject.org/

Diverse Feminist Perspectives

4 **Article:** Meghna Sabharwal and Rashmi Chordiya. Doing Equity Work 'Equitably': A Need for Intersectional Approaches.
5 **Book:** McCann, Carole, Seung-kyung Kim, and Emek Ergun, eds. 2020. Feminist Theory Reader.
6 **Podcast Interview:** Wall, Sean Saifa. 2021. Breaking Binaries and Intersex Justice with Sean Saifa Wall Interview by Prentis Hemphill. Finding Our WayPodcast. https://www.findingourwaypodcast.com/individual-episodes/s2e8.

Transformative Justice

7 Generation Five. 2007. "Towards Transformative Justice: A Liberatory Approach to Child Sexual Abuse and Other Forms of Intimate and Community Violence." http://www.generationfive.org/downloads/G5_Toward_Transformative_Justice.pdf.
8 Haines, Staci. 2019. The Politics of Trauma: Somatics, Healing, and Social Justice.

Notes

1 For more examples, suggestions, and guidance, please refer to inclusive language resources offered at the end of this chapter.
2 There has been a growing movement among activists, organizers, and advocates for social change, urging the use of terms like "houseless," "unhoused," "unsheltered," or "housing insecurity" instead of "homeless." Nevertheless,

due to the lack of a consensus, we use the phrase "experiencing homelessness" instead of merely "homeless." This choice emphasizes that individuals are going through a particular circumstance rather than being solely defined by it.

3 For detailed description, refer to Chapter 4.

References

Abreu, Roberto L., G. Tyler Lefevor, Kirsten A. Gonzalez, Manuel Teran, and Ryan J. Watson. 2022. "Parental Support, Depressive Symptoms, and LGBTQ Adolescents: Main and Moderation Effects in a Diverse Sample." *Journal of Clinical Child & Adolescent Psychology*: 1–16. https://doi.org/10.1080/15374416.2022.2096047

Acker, Joan. 1990. "Hierarchies, Jobs, Bodies: A Theory of Gendered Organizations." Gender & Society 4(2): 139–158. https://doi.org/10.1177/089124390004002002

Acker, Joan. 2006. "Inequality Regimes: Gender, Class, and Race in Organizations." *Gender & Society*, *20*(4): 441–464. https://doi.org/10.1177/0891243206289499

ACLU. 2023. "Mapping Attacks on LGBTQ Rights in the U.S. State Legislatures." American Civil Liberties Union. https://www.aclu.org/legislative-attacks-on-lgbtq-rights?impact=health

Alkadry, Mohamad G., Brandi Blessett, and Valerie L. Patterson. 2015. "Public Administration, Diversity, and the Ethic of Getting Things Done:" *Administration & Society*. https://doi.org/10.1177/0095399715581032

American Psychological Association. 2022. "Gender." https://apastyle.apa.org/style-grammar-guidelines/bias-free-language/gender

Baptist, Joyce, and Katelyn Coburn. (2019) "Harassment in Public Spaces: The Intrusion on Personal Space." *Journal of Feminist Family Therapy*, 31(2-3): 114–128. https://doi.org/10.1080/08952833.2019.1634178

Bearfield, Domonic A. 2009. "Equity at the Intersection: Public Administration and the Study of Gender." *Public Administration Review* 69 (3): 383–386. https://doi.org/10.1111/j.1540-6210.2009.01985.x

bell hooks and Laverne Cox in a Public Dialogue at The New School. 2014. https://www.youtube.com/watch?v=9oMmZIJijgY

Bishu, Sebawit G., Mary E. Guy, and Nuri Heckler. 2019. "Seeing Gender and Its Consequences." *Journal of Public Affairs Education* 25(2): 145–162. https://doi.org/10.1080/15236803.2018.1565039

Blessett, Brandi, Jennifer Dodge, Beverly Edmond, Holly T. Goerdel, Susan T. Gooden, Andrea M. Headley, Norma M. Riccucci, and Brian N. Williams. 2019. "Social Equity in Public Administration: A Call to Action." *Perspectives on Public Management and Governance* 2 (4): 283–299. https://doi.org/10.1093/ppmgov/gvz016

Blessett, Brandi. 2023. "Black Women Been Knew: Understanding Intersectionality to Advance Justice." *Journal of Social Equity and Public Administration* 1 (2): 42–50. https://doi.org/10.24926/jsepa.v1i2.5034

Bonvicini, Kathleen A. 2017. "LGBT Healthcare Disparities: What Progress Have We Made?" *Patient Education and Counseling* 100(12): 2357–2361. https://doi.org/10.1016/j.pec.2017.06.003

Burnier, DeLysa. 2021. "Embracing Others With "sympathetic Understanding" and "affectionate Interpretation:" Creating a Relational Care-Centered Public Administration." *Administrative Theory & Praxis* 43, (1): 42–57. https://doi.org/10.1080/10841806.2019.1700460

Burnier, DeLysa. 2007. "Gender and Public Administration." In *Encyclopedia of Public Administration and Public Policy*, 821–823. New York, NY: Routledge. https://doi.org/10.1081/e-epap2-162

Carpenter, Christopher S., Samuel T. Eppink, and Gilbert Gonzales. 2020. "Transgender Status, Gender Identity, and Socioeconomic Outcomes in the United States." *ILR Review* 73(3): 573–599. https://doi.org/10.1177/0019793920902776

Catalano, D. Chase J., and Pat Griffin. 2016. "Sexism, Heterosexism, and Trans Oppression: An Integrated Perspective." In *Teaching for Diversity and Social Justice*, 183–211. New York, NY: Routledge.

Chordiya, Rashmi. 2019. "Are Federal Child Care Programs Sufficient for Employee Retention? Critical Examination from a Gendered Perspective." *The American Review of Public Administration* 49 (3): 338–52. https://doi.org/10.1177/0275074018804662.

Chordiya, Rashmi, and Larry Hubbell. 2023. "Fostering Internal Pay Equity Through Gender Neutral Job Evaluations: A Case Study of the Federal Job Evaluation System." *Public Personnel Management* 52(1): 25–47. https://doi.org/10.1177/00910260221124866

Conron, Kerith. 2019. "Financial Services and the LGBTQ+ Community: A Review of Discrimination in Lending and Housing." Testimony before the Subcommittee on Oversight and Investigations. https://williamsinstitute.law.ucla.edu/wp-content/uploads/Housing-and-Lending-Testimony-Oct-2019.pdf

Crenshaw, Kimberle. 1989. "Demarginalizing the Intersection of Race and Sex: A Black Feminist Critique of Antidiscrimination Doctrine, Feminist Theory and Antiracist Politics." *University of Chicago Legal Forum*, (1). https://chicagounbound.uchicago.edu/uclf/vol1989/iss1/8

Crenshaw, Kimberle. 2020. She Coined the Term 'Intersectionality' Over 30 Years Ago. Here's What It Means to Her Today Interview by Katy Steinmetz. TIME. https://time.com/5786710/kimberle-crenshaw-intersectionality/

D'Agostino, Maria, Helisse Levine, Meghna Sabharwal, and Al C. Johnson-Manning. 2022. "Organizational Practices and Second-Generation Gender Bias: A Qualitative Inquiry into the Career Progression of US State-Level Managers." *The American Review of Public Administration* 52(5): 335–350. https://doi.org/10.1177/02750740221086605

De Lauretis, Teresa. 1991. "Queer Theory: Lesbian and Gay Sexualities an Introduction." *Differences* 3 (2): iii–xviii.

Dietert, M., and D. Dentice. 2009. "Gender Identity Issues and Workplace Discrimination: The Transgender Experience." *Journal of Workplace Rights*, 14(1): 121–140. https://doi.org/10.2190/WR.14.1.g

Diggs, Nicole Schnequa. 2022. "Intersectionality of Gender and Race in Governmental Affairs." In *Handbook on Gender and Public Administration*, edited by Patricia M. Shields and Nicole M. Elias. London, UK: Edward Elgar Publishing.

DiPadova-Stocks, Laurie N., Donna M. Ehrlich, and Brian J. Cowley. 2021. "The Authoritative Sway of Artificial Boundaries of Sexual Orientation: An Ethical Imperative for Public Administration." *Public Integrity* 23(6): 555–572. https://doi.org/10.1080/10999922.2020.1843867

Elias, Nicole M. 2022. "Beyond Binary Treatment of Gender in Public Administration and Policy." In *Handbook on Gender and Public Administration*, edited by Patricia M. Shields and Nicole M. Elias, 1st ed., 103–114. London, UK: Edward Elgar Publishing.

Elias, Nicole M., Rana Lynn Johnson, Danny Ovando, and Julia Ramirez. 2018 "Improving Transgender Policy for a More Equitable Workplace," *Journal of Public Management and Social Policy* 24(2): 53–81. https://digitalscholarship.tsu.edu/jpmsp/vol24/iss2/7

Elias, Rishel Nicole M. 2017. "Constructing and Implementing Transgender Policy for Public Administration." *Administration & Society* 49(1): 20–47. https://doi.org/10.1177/0095399716684888

Etaugh, Claire. 2020. "Prevalence of Intimate Partner Violence in LGBTQ Individuals: An Intersectional Approach." In *Intimate Partner Violence and the LGBT+ Community: Understanding Power Dynamics*, 11–36. Cham: Springer International Publishing. https://doi.org/10.1007/978-3-030-44762-5_2

Fredriksen-Goldsen, Karen I., Jane M. Simoni, Hyun-Jun Kim, Keren Lehavot, Karina L. Walters, Joyce Yang, Charles P. Hoy-Ellis, and Anna Muraco. 2014. "The Health Equity Promotion Model: Reconceptualization of Lesbian, Gay, Bisexual, and Transgender (LGBT) Health Disparities." *American Journal of Orthopsychiatry* 84(6): 653–663. https://doi.org/10.1037/ort0000030

Gay, Lesbian, and Straight Education Network (GLSEN). n.d. "LGBTQ History Timeline Reference." https://lgbtqhistory.org/lgbt-rights-timeline-in-american-history/

Generation Five. 2007. "Towards Transformative Justice: A Liberatory Approach to Child Sexual Abuse and Other Forms of Intimate and Community Violence." http://www.generationfive.org/downloads/G5_Toward_Transformative_Justice.pdf

GLAAD. n.d. https://glaad.org/

GLAAD. 2022. "Glossary of Terms: LGBTQ | GLAAD." https://glaad.org/reference/terms/

Goldsen, Karen I. Fredriksen, Meghan Romanelli, Charles P. Hoy-Ellis, and Hailey Jung. 2022. "Health, Economic and Social Disparities Among Transgender Women, Transgender Men and Transgender Nonbinary Adults: Results From a Population-Based Study." *Preventive Medicine* 156: 106988. https://doi.org/10.1016/j.ypmed.2022.106988

Guy, Mary E. 2000. "The Amazing Miss Burchfield." *Public Administration Review* 60(1): 6–19.

Guy, Mary. 2017. "Mom Work Versus Dad Work in Local Government." *Administration & Society* 49(1): 48–64. https://doi.org/10.1177/0095399716641989

Guy, Mary E., Meredith A. Newman, and Sharon H. Mastracci. 2014. *Emotional Labor: Putting the Service in Public Service*. 2nd ed. London, UK: Routledge.

Haines, Staci. 2019. *The Politics of Trauma: Somatics, Healing, and Social Justice*. Illustrated ed. Berkeley, CA: North Atlantic Books.

Hancock, Ange-Marie. 2011. *Solidarity Politics for Millennials: A Guide to Ending the Oppression Olympics*. Springer. https://doi.org/10.1057/9780230120136

Heckler, Nuri. 2022. "Managing Masculinity in Public Organizations." In *Handbook on Gender and Public Administration*, edited by Patricia M. Shields and Nicole M. Elias, 1st ed., 85–102. London, UK: Edward Elgar Publishing. https://doi.org/10.4337/9781789904734.00014

Heckler, Nuri. 2022. "Public Administration and Social Equity: Catching Up to Jane Addams." In *The Oxford Handbook of Jane Addams*, edited by Shields, Patricia M., Maurice Hamington, and Joseph Soeters. UK: Oxford University Press. https://doi.org/10.1093/oxfordhb/9780197544518.013.41

History.com Editors. 2022. "Women's History Milestones: A Timeline." *HISTORY*. https://www.history.com/topics/womens-history/womens-history-us-timeline

Hoy-Ellis, Charles P., and Karen I. Fredriksen-Goldsen. 2016. "Lesbian, Gay, & Bisexual Older Adults: Linking Internal Minority Stressors, Chronic Health Conditions, and Depression." *Aging & Mental Health* 20(11): 1119–1130. https://doi.org/10.1080/13607863.2016.1168362

Human Rights Campaign. n.d. *Health Disparities Among Bisexual People*. https://www.hrc.org/resources/health-disparities-among-bisexual-people

Intersex Justice Project. n.d. https://www.intersexjusticeproject.org/

James, S. E., J. L. Herman, S. Rankin, M. Keisling, L. Mottet, and M. Anafi (2016). The Report of the 2015 U.S. Transgender Survey. Washington, DC: National Center for Transgender Equality.

Johnson, C. P. García, and Kathleen Otto. 2019. "Better Together: A Model for Women and LGBTQ Equality in the Workplace." *Frontiers in Psychology* 10(272): 1–17. https://doi.org/10.3389/fpsyg.2019.00272

Larson, Jackson O. 2021. "From Stasis to Ecstasy: Tracing Bernard of Clairvaux's" Queer" Influence on French Gothic Art."

Library of Congress. 2022. "Patsy Takemoto Mink, First Woman of Color in Congress." Web page. *Library of Congress, Washington, D.C. 20540 USA*. https://www.loc.gov/item/event-403767/patsy-takemoto-mink-first-woman-of-color-in-congress/2022-05-04/

Lorde, Audre. 2007. *Sister Outsider: Essays and Speeches*. Reprint ed. Berkeley, CA: Crossing Press.

McCann, Carole, Seung-kyung Kim, and Emek Ergun, eds. 2020. *Feminist Theory Reader*. 5th ed. New York, NY: Routledge.

McDonald, James. 2015. "Organizational Communication Meets Queer Theory: Theorizing Relations of 'Difference' Differently." *Communication Theory* 25 (3): 310—329. https://doi.org/10.1111/comt.12060

Meyer, Seth, and Judith Millesen. 2022. "Queer up Your Work: Adding Sexual Orientation and Gender Identity to Public and Nonprofit Research." *Journal of Public and Nonprofit Affairs* 8 (1): 145–156. https://doi.org/10.20899/jpna.8.1.145-156

National Institutes of Health (NIH). 2022. "Sex, Gender, and Sexuality." *National Institutes of Health (NIH)*. https://www.nih.gov/nih-style-guide/sex-gender-sexuality

National Park Service. 2021. "Yuri Kochiyama (U.S. National Park Service)." https://www.nps.gov/people/yuri-kochiyama.htm

National Women's History Museum. n.d. "Women in Civil Rights Movement." *National Women's History Museum*. https://www.womenshistory.org/new-timelines

Norman-Major, Kristen. 2018. "Thinking Outside the Box: Using Multisector Approaches to Address the Wicked Problem of Homelessness Among LGBTQ Youth." *Public Integrity* 20(6): 546–557. https://doi.org/10.1080/10999922.2017.1325999

Our Family Coalition, and One Archives Foundation. n.d. "LGBTQ Rights Timeline in American History » Teaching LGBTQ History." *TEACHING LGBTQ HISTORY Instructional Resources for California Educators, Students, & Families*. https://lgbtqhistory.org/lgbt-rights-timeline-in-american-history/

PettyJohn, Morgan E., Finneran K. Muzzey, Megan K. Maas, and Heather L. McCauley. (2019). "# HowIWillChange: Engaging Men and Boys in the# MeToo Movement." *Psychology of Men & Masculinities* 20(4): 612–622. https://doi.org/10.1037/men0000186

Romero, Adam P., Shoshana K. Goldberg, and Luis A. Vasquez. 2020. "LGBT People and Housing Affordability, Discrimination, and Homelessness." Williams Institute. https://escholarship.org/content/qt3cb5b8zj/qt3cb5b8zj.pdf

Rosenwohl-Mack, Amy, Suegee Tamar-Mattis, Arlene B. Baratz, Katharine B. Dalke, Alesdair Ittelson, Kimberly Zieselman, and Jason D. Flatt. 2020. "A National Study on the Physical and Mental Health of Intersex Adults in the US." *PLoS One* 15(100): e0240088. https://doi.org/10.1371/journal.pone.0240088

Russell, Stephen T., and Jessica N. Fish. 2016. "Mental Health in Lesbian, Gay, Bisexual, and Transgender (LGBT) Youth." *Annual Review of Clinical Psychology* 12: 465–487. https://doi.org/10.1146/annurev-clinpsy-021815-093153

Sabharwal, Meghna. 2015. "From Glass Ceiling to Glass Cliff: Women in Senior Executive Service." *Journal of Public Administration Research and Theory* 25 (2): 399–426.

Sabharwal, Meghna, and Rashmi Chordiya. (Forthcoming). "Doing Equity Work 'Equitably': A Need for Intersectional Approaches." In *Achieving Social Equity: From Problems to Solutions*, edited by Mary E. Guy and Sean A. McCandless, 2nd ed. Irvine, CA: Melvin & Leigh, Publishers.

Schwegman, David. 2019. "Rental Market Discrimination Against Same-Sex Couples: Evidence from a Pairwise-Matched Email Correspondence Test." *Housing Policy Debate* 29(2): 250–272. https://doi.org/10.1080/10511482.2018.1512005

Shelton, J. (2023). "LGBTQ+ People and Homelessness." In *The Routledge Handbook of Homelessness*, edited by Joanne Bretherton and Nicholas Pleace, 1st ed. New York, NY: Routledge. https://doi.org/10.4324/9781351113113-17

Shields, Patricia M. 2022. "Peace Weaving and Positive Peace." San Marcos, TX: City of San Marcos Library. https://hdl.handle.net/10877/16187

Shields, Patricia, ed. 2017. *Jane Addams: Progressive pioneer of Peace, Philosophy, Sociology, Social Work and Public Administration*. Cham, Switzerland: Springer International Publishing AG https://doi.org/10.1007/978-3-319-50646-3

Shields, Patricia M. 2006. "Democracy and the Social Feminist Ethics of Jane Addams: A Vision for Public Administration." *Administrative Theory & Praxis* 28 (3): 418–443.

Shields, Patricia M., and Joseph Soeters. 2017. "Peace Weaving: Jane Addams, Positive Peace, and Public Administration." *The American Review of Public Administration* 47 (3): 323–339.

Stivers, Camilla. 2000. *Bureau Men, Settlement Women: Constructing Public Administration in the Progressive Era*. Lawrence: University Press of Kansas.

Stivers, Camilla. 1993. "Reflections on the Role of Personal Narrative in Social Science." *Signs* 18 (2): 408–425.

Tordoff, Diana M., Jonathon W. Wanta, Arin Collin, Cesalie Stepney, David J. Inwards-Breland, and Kym Ahrens. 2022. "Mental Health Outcomes in Transgender and Nonbinary Youths Receiving Gender-Affirming Care." *JAMA Network Open* 5(2): e220978–e220978. https://doi.org/10.1001/jamanetworkopen.2022.0978

U.S. Department of Interior. 2021. "Secretary Deb Haaland." https://www.doi.gov/secretary-deb-haaland

United Nations Women. 2020. "Intersectional Feminism: What It Means and Why It Matters Right Now." *UN Women – Headquarters*. https://www.unwomen.org/en/news/stories/2020/6/explainer-intersectional-feminism-what-it-means-and-why-it-matters

Wall, Sean Saifa. 2021. Breaking Binaries and Intersex Justice with Sean Saifa Wall Interview by Prentis Hemphill. Finding Our WayPodcast. https://www.findingourwaypodcast.com/individual-episodes/s2e8

Wilson, D. M Bianca., Bouton, J. A., Bouton, Badgett, M. V., Lee, Macklin, L. Moriah. 2019. "LGBT Poverty in the United States Trends at the Onset of COVID-19." Williams Institute. https://williamsinstitute.law.ucla.edu/wp-content/uploads/LGBT-Poverty-COVID-Feb-2023.pdf

Wright, Tessa. 2013. "Uncovering Sexuality and Gender: An Intersectional Examination of women's Experience in UK Construction." *Construction Management and Economics* 31(8): 832–844. https://doi.org/10.1080/01446193.2013.794297

10 Countering Intersectional Ableism and Moving Toward Disability Justice

Abstract

In this chapter, we explore disability as a fact of life and a core human experience. We invite an understanding of disability as deeply diverse, profound, nuanced, and intersectional. We emphasize that ableism is a system of oppression that is based in anti-disability shaming, stigma, and prejudice against disabled bodyminds. We hope to advance the dialogue within public service community to acknowledge our disabled present and future, to destigmatize disability, to challenge, interrupt, and counter ableism and to advance the work of liberatory public service (LPS) that is deeply aligned, inspired, and grounded in the principles of disability justice (DJ). We extend the call from DJ movement builders to center lives, experiences, and leadership of multiply marginalized disabled BIPOC and LGBTQIA+ people in all aspects of public service work. This chapter unequivocally recognizes that – we may potentially experience a majority disability future, however, our current dominant systems continue to be ableist. Therefore, we need to create counter systems in public service contexts that are firmly rooted in values and principles of DJ. We acknowledge that creating and diffusing transformative systems rooted in DJ is not easy, it requires deep vulnerability and courage, and it is necessary part for creating an LPS.

An Acknowledgment of Heavy and Potentially Triggering Content

We want to acknowledge that any reading or discussion of ableism and its intersectionality is heavy and can be triggering. As you engage with this chapter, we invite you to honor your embodied reactions and move at a pace that feels accessible and manageable for your bodymind. We invite gentleness and compassion for self and others. We invite you to move your bodies in ways that can allow you to feel settled; to find places and times that are nourishing and comforting as you process the content of this chapter and this book.

DOI: 10.4324/9781032670669-13

Introduction

Disability is a fact of life. We all have familiarity with disability. We all are likely to experience disability temporarily or in the long term. We are all likely to know someone or love someone or care for someone who has a disability – a child, a sibling, an elder, a friend, a peer, a colleague, a neighbor, a community member (World Health Organization and The World Bank, 2011).

We all also have familiarity with ableism. Ableism is a form of oppression that assumes non-disability as a norm and non-disabled bodyminds as a normative standard. Ableism is based in anti-disability shaming, stigma, and prejudice of bodyminds, one that seeks to prevent disabled people from being whole people, from surviving, from thriving, and being free.

As public service professionals working across policy domains (e.g., healthcare, housing, education, public safety, public transit, and others), we are often tasked with formulating and implementing public policies that impact lives of disability diverse communities. We are responsible for leading and managing administrative procedures and their outcomes. We are tasked to ensure delivery of public services across disability diverse communities in an equitable and caring manner. Therefore, like other forms of identities and linked oppressions, it is crucial for us to continuously develop and deepen a nuanced understanding of disability diversity and intersectional ableism. For an authentic practice of social equity and liberatory justice, it is critical that we are listening to, engaging with, and following the leadership of those most impacted by inequities, including multiply marginalized people with disabilities (Chordiya et al. 2023).

Ableism as a form of systemic oppression has legal, structural, and cultural consequences. Because ableism is so deeply permeated in our dominant systems, without a critical examination, it remains hidden and normalized. And despite our individual good intentions, when public policies, administrative procedures, and our cultural norms continue to be biased by ableist assumptions, the impact of our work can cause harm to disabled people,[1] and hinder progress toward achieving the goals of social equity and liberatory justice. In this chapter, we hope to advance the dialogue within public service community to acknowledge our disabled present and future, to destigmatize disability, to challenge, interrupt, and counter ableism and to advance the work of liberatory public service (LPS) that is deeply aligned, inspired, and grounded in the principles of disability justice (DJ). (Note: For an introduction of DJ and its ten principles, please refer to Chapter 5 and we will circle back to these in the Action and Change section of this chapter.)

Public Service in the Context of Disabled Present and Future

We write this book and this chapter in the context of mass grief and ongoing consequences of the COVID-19 pandemic, multiple horrifying wars in different parts of our world, and amidst alarming rate of human-caused climate catastrophes. (***Pause.*** *Breathe.)* We invite a pause here – to breathe, allow these words to land in your bodymind, and care for your bodymind as you acknowledge with us these heavy realities of our world.

These crises have revealed that in our present and our future, many of us and people we care about, including members of our families, our classrooms, our teams, our organizations, our communities, our societies will likely experience disability. In the future, it's probable that a majority of individuals will experience some form of disability (Piepzna-Samarasinha 2022). Even, in our present times, 15% of the global population and 27% of people in the United States identify as people with disabilities (Center for Disease Control and Prevention 2023; The World Bank 2022).

As public servants we are often at the forefront of responding to crisis and serving the public as they navigate painful and even traumatic life changes, including, those related to mass disabling events life COVID-19 pandemic, or other crises. Therefore, as we serve people with disabilities and disability-diverse communities, it is important for us to discern and differentiate between the experience of becoming disabled and the experience of living life as a disabled person. Becoming disabled, for example, due to illness or an injury can be profoundly life changing, it can be a traumatic experience, and associated with pain. However, living life as a disabled person need not be traumatic – it can be every bit as rich and joyful as living a non-disabled life if we foster an infrastructure and a culture that favors collective access, collective care, where people's access needs are met with ease (rather than shame and stigma).[2]

As public servants, we have the power and the responsibility to counter ableism in our systems. We must respond to calls to practice solidarity toward making DJ a reality, in our present and future public service systems. In such a reality, irrespective of the cause of disability, and experiences of becoming disabled, the public servants and the public our organizations serve – our students, our staff, our patients, our clients, our community members– can navigate public service systems and life without re-traumatization and with joy, care, and support for their access needs. As Leah Lakshmi Piepzna-Samarasinha, a DJ leader, thinker, teacher, movement builder, and a visionary, wisely prophesized in her book "The Future Is Disabled" (2022) – our future is likely going to disabled, however, our current dominant systems continue to be ableist. Therefore, we need to create counter systems in public service contexts that are rooted in values and principles of DJ.

Invitation to Pause and Reflect

We invite you to pause here, breathe and move in ways that feel accessible for your bodymind. If you are able and willing, reflect on this preceding claim. Notice, what is resonating, what is causing dissonance? If you are able and willing, we invite you to imagine a present or future public service that is supportive of access and care needs of disability-diverse groups and communities. What does such a public service system look like and feel like?

What Is Disability?

The Americans with Disabilities Amendments Act (ADA), initially enacted in 1990 and later amended in 2008, defines a person with a disability as someone who has a physical impairment or a mental health condition that significantly restricts one or more major life activities, possesses a documented history of such an impairment, or is perceived as having such an impairment (Collier 2016, p. 1). The World Health Organization and World Bank Group's World Report on Disability (2011) characterizes disability as an intrinsic aspect of human life and underscores its universality. The United Nations Convention on the Rights of Persons with Disabilities (CRPD) emphasizes that disability arises from the interaction between individuals with impairments and attitudinal and environmental obstacles that impede their full and equitable participation in society alongside others (World Health Organization and World Bank Group, 2011, p. 4).

We would like to ground our discussions around disability, ableism, and DJ in a felt and powerful understanding of disability offered by Adana Protonentis (2021). Protonentis (2021) notes:

> Disability is a vast, flexible, nuanced, and complex human reality. Disability can be temporary or permanent. One can be born with it or acquire it. It is hugely diverse and there are infinite ways that it can be experienced and there is powerful magic in that. Because that diversity of experience is our doorway into insight and innovation.
>
> Disability brings our bodies and minds back into the conversation. It helps us remember that we are human. That our bodies and minds can and will change over time. That our capacity will shift over time. It is a socially constructed identity and is one an individual can choose. It's a culture and a community. It's a difference, not a deficit. It can and does impact all of us. It cuts across race, gender, class, religion, ethnicity, and every other facet of identity that one can think of. It is a universal, profoundly human experience.
>
> (At about 9 minutes in the talk)

Invitation to Pause

If you are able and willing, we invite you to pause here, to breathe into this quote and reflect. Allow these words to land in your bodymind.

Experience of disability is not a binary, rather disability is extremely diverse and nuanced. The experience of disability is shaped by the embodied experiences and conditions of our bodyminds, our socialization, our environments including our legal, structural, political, economic, social, and cultural systems, and our many intersectional social identities.

Disability is multi-dimensional, somewhat complex, requires deep understanding and discernment. It cannot always be strictly categorized as visible/apparent or invisible/non-apparent, permanent, or temporary, it may or may not be associated with experience of chronic pain and illness. However, it is an intrinsic part of human difference and never a deficit. Disability is fluid and expansive; it is dynamic, and it can be experienced in many ways. Disability can be both a descriptive and political identity. The experience of disability, and an individual's relationship with their disability identity – that is, whether a person chooses to self-identify and politically claim their identity as a person with disability in one or more context and spaces – at its core, is complex, dynamic, diverse, fluid, and intersectional (arielle 2019; Forber-Pratt 2021; Mingus 2011; Ostiguy, Peters, and Shlasko 2016; Protonentis 2021; World Health Organization and The World Bank 2011).

For example, a trans woman of color with non-apparent disability may choose not to reveal her disability identity in a workplace setting where she may feel discriminated against, isolated, and marginalized due to her intersectional experiences with oppressive systems and prejudice. Sometimes, people with disabilities, especially those with multiply marginalized identities may choose not to reveal their disability identity and may find taking that risk of "coming out" to be dangerous as their survival in an ableist system might depend on denying it or hiding it when possible (Mingus 2011).

Organizations that seek to cultivate disability pride and disability visibility as counters to ableism will need to develop a systems analysis and examine what are the physical, emotional, psychological, and spiritual conditions that must be cultivated for people with multiply marginalized identities to feel safe-enough to take the risks to be vulnerable, to be their whole, authentic selves, to belong. The system of ableism and its harmful and traumatizing legacies contribute toward heightened hesitancy in claiming disability as a political identity, especially in marginalized communities. Initiatives to embrace disability pride and encourage open discussion of disability within organizations necessitate an acknowledgment of and sustained, intentional effort to address the harm and trauma caused by intersectional ableism (Chordiya and Protonentis 2024, Forthcoming).

Understanding Disability: Models of Disability

There are many ways to understand disability. And it is important to recognize that as public servants, involved in policymaking, administrative decision-making, and day-to-day offering of public services, how we understand disability shapes our perspectives and approaches to addressing ableism in our systems. Our conceptualization of disability also informs and influences our approaches to fostering disability affirming diversity, equity, inclusion, and liberatory justice (DEILJ) in public service contexts.

For example, when we regard disability only as a "medical problem," defined by physical or mental traits of the individual, a common response is to try to change or "fix" people through medical or rehabilitative treatments. Such an approach is called a medical model of disability, and it can become harmful and oppressive when people with disabilities are denied choice, agency, and self-determination. The medical model of disability can cause harm when excessive power and control is vested in the hands of service providers, policy makers, and administrators, without accountability toward the people they serve.

Liberatory DEILJ praxis involves consistently reflecting on and finding alignment in "who do our organization seek to serve?" and "who should our organization be most accountable to?" (Kindred Leaders 2021). In the medical model of disability, a major power dynamic exists between organizations/people who offer service (i.e., "professionals" and "experts") and those who receive services (clients, patients, customers with disabilities). Such power dynamics hinder the practice of integrity and accountability toward those we seek to serve.

The medical model of disability becomes oppressive due to its ableist assumptions that view disability as a deficit and something to be "fixed" to meet ableist standards of health, fitness, and beauty. While preventing disability and finding cures for harmful or life-threatening health conditions or diseases such as cancer, diabetes, COVID-19 are critical and life-saving responsibilities for medical and public health professionals, it is important to discern when treatments and cures lead fulfillment of safety, care, and access needs, and when those pursuits cross the line into ableism.

For example, disability rights activists and advocates emphasize that human differences related to dwarfness, deafness, autism are core aspects of our diversity, and we must not confuse them as diseases. As such, our public policy, administrative, and service focused response to these disabilities should not be about prevention and cure, rather it needs to be focused on inclusion, access, and care (Stramondo 2021).

Disability rights activists and advocates invite us to invest in systems that can serve to meet the access needs of disability diverse populations. These include investment in innovation and provisioning of equitable and affordable services, assistive and adaptive technologies, and care infrastructure and culture at a large scale, so when people become disabled, their experience of disability need not be a traumatic one (Piepzna-Samarasinha 2022; Stramondo 2021).

For example, instead of insisting on rehabilitating a person using a cane or a wheelchair to conform with ableist and often white supremacist norms and standards of health, fitness, beauty, and wellness; what if service providers and systems listened to and honored the embodied access needs of persons with disabilities and helped to create ease for them without attaching stigma to use of assistive and adaptive technologies (Piepzna-Samarasinha 2022). Many of us with vision-related access needs, use assistive technologies including eyeglasses and contact lenses. While vision-related assistive tools such as eyeglasses and contact lenses are more normalized and destigmatized in many societies, the stigma around use of assistive tools in many aspects of disability persists. What if we supported and created systems where many types of assistive and adaptive technologies were embraced with pride and support rather than shamed and stigmatized?

In contrast to the medical model, the social model approaches disability as a social construction and a result of societal barriers and discrimination. The social model helps us recognize stigma and marginalization as central factors impeding the life chances of people with disabilities, their lived experiences, including in the contexts of work, studies, and play (Ostiguy et al. 2016).

Consider when environmental obstacles are removed and access needs are met with ease, for example, environments where American Sign Language (ASL) is one of the default languages or ASL interpretation is easily accessible for D/deaf and hard of hearing people. Consider, where modes of written communication are compatible with screen reader software and braille materials are available as a norm; where environments have built-in, structured time and space for rest and restoration and the ease it can create for everyone, especially, for people with chronic pain, or people needing access to sensory spaces and soft spaces, low lighting spaces, spaces that are less stimulating. By viewing disability as a difference, rather than an individual deficit, the social model of disability emphasizes systems-blame, and serves to advance effective analysis, policy change, culture change, and procedural justice. It works to remove barriers, promote access, foster inclusion, and affirm disability rights as basic human rights (Chordiya and Protonentis, Forthcoming ; Ostiguy et al. 2016; Shakespeare 2006).

Our understanding of disability continues to evolve. A newer, more current biopsychosocial model of disability seeks to go beyond viewing disability as simply a medical condition or a social construction. It integrates and offers a more balanced and comprehensive understanding of disability as an interplay of biological, psychological, and social factors that shape the social and embodied experiences of disability (World Health Organization and The World Bank 2011).

The biopsychosocial model recognizes that experience of disability cannot be compartmentalized simply as a medical condition (e.g., chronic pain, mental health condition, or an impairment) or a social and environmental experience (e.g., experience of disability discrimination due to environmental barriers). It understands disability to be a biological, psychological, emotional, and an embodied experience as well as interaction with social factors and much more. It is a both/and approach that helps us recognize (as we have noted previously) that while the experience of becoming disabled can be traumatic (e.g., due to injury or illness), living life a person with disability need not be a traumatic experience. Disabled people can live rich lives filled with joy, support, care, inclusion, and belonging – if one's care and access needs are met with ease. (Chordiya and Protonentis Forthcoming; Piepzna-Samarasinha 2018, 2022; Stramondo 2021). In the next section, we dive a bit deeper into understanding the systemic nature of ableism and its intersectionality with other "isms."

Ableism

Ableism is a system of oppression that is biased against bodyminds of people with disabilities and regard bodyminds of non-disabled people as a normative standard guiding decision, behaviors, and (in) actions. Lydia X. Brown notes, "ableism is an entire system of thinking and doing that hurts disabled people" (Brown 2017b, at 10 minutes 28 seconds). Ableism or bias against people with disabilities shows up in our public policies, administrative procedures, structures, protocols, practices, and cultural norms.

For example, systemic ableism is revealed through Ugly Laws that persisted across several American cities between 1860s and 1970s, and legally prohibited people with "unsightly or disfiguring" disabilities from appearing in public (Schweik 2010; Thompson 2021). It is revealed through Supreme Court cases such as *Buck v. Bell*, that granted constitutional approval for the involuntary or forced sterilization of people with disabilities (Institute on Disabilities, Temple University 2021; Wolfe 2023).

The systemic nature of ableism is revealed through the fact that it was not until enactment of Education for All Handicapped Children Act (EAHCA) of 1975, now known as the Individuals with Disabilities Education (IDEA), that children with disabilities received legal protection to receive equal access in public schools alongside their non-disabled peers (for a detailed historical account of persisting systemic ableism and movement for disability rights and DJ in the United States refer to Institute on Disabilities, Temple University 2021; Nielsen 2013; Schweik 2010; Sins Invalid 2019; Washington State Governors Office of the Education Ombuds 2020). Furthermore, this equal access to education is not always guaranteed in practice, and ableist inequities in public education systems are magnified during times of crises such as the COVID-19 pandemic where students with disabilities faced disproportionate burdens to receive education (e.g., refer to Protonentis, Chordiya, and ObeySumner 2021). Talila L. Lewis (2022) defines ableism as:

> a system of assigning value to people's bodies and minds based on societally constructed ideas of normalcy, productivity, desirability, intelligence, excellence, and fitness. These constructed ideas are deeply rooted in eugenics, anti-Blackness, misogyny, colonialism, imperialism, and capitalism. This systemic oppression leads to people and society determining people's value based on their culture, age, language, appearance, religion, birth, or living place, "health/wellness", and/or their ability to satisfactorily re/produce, "excel" and "behave". You do not have to be disabled to experience ableism.
>
> (p. 1)

Invitation to Pause

If you are able and willing, we invite you to pause here, to breathe into this quote and reflect. Allow these words to land in your bodymind.

As noted in Lewis's (2022) definition, it is important to recognize that while ableism often has most intense and marginalizing consequences for people with disabilities, it impacts us all, either directly or indirectly. We all often work, learn, play, (re) produce, perform, perfect, within systems that are based in logics of ableism. In the next subsection, we explore this idea of intersectional ableism, a bit further.

Intersectionality of Ableism with Other "Isms"

Ableism is deeply intersectional and has consequences for all. Ableism presumes incompetence of marginalized bodyminds, in terms of physical, mental, cognitive, emotional capacity and functioning, resulting in justification of dehumanization and marginalization. Historically, and in present times, such ableist presumption of incompetence combined with savior complex of dominant groups continues to be used to perpetuate other forms of oppression, marginalization, and inequalities (Brown 2017a).

(**Content Warning: Emotionally Heavy Discussion**) For example, consider how often ableist words "crazy" or "mad" is used in everyday language to dehumanize and marginalize, disabled people, women, BIPOC, and LGBTQIA+ people who disrupt standards of imagined "abled" or "normal" bodyminds. Our dominant cultural norms around use of ableism to dehumanize bodyminds of disabled and other marginalized peoples have historical lineages in systems of oppression.

For example, in the 19th century, doctors and scientists like Dr. Samuel Cartwright fabricated psychiatric conditions such as "drapetomania" and "dysacsthesia aethiopica" to "diagnose" and frame enslaved peoples' resistance to oppression and seeking of freedom through escape and/or through work stoppages as "diseases of mind" and psychiatric illness (refer to Brown 2017b, 2017b; Cartwright 1851; Schalk 2022). Even today, in the United States, ableism's intersectionality with racism and white supremacy is evident from the fact that "50 percent of people killed by law enforcement are disabled, and more than half of disabled African Americans have been arrested by the time they turn 28—double the risk in comparison to their white disabled counterparts" (Thompson 2021, 1).

Ableism is used to perpetuate gender- and sexuality-based oppression. At the turn of the 20th century, movement backlash against women's suffrage was often based on claims that women were intellectually disabled, and that the mental exertion of voting could damage their reproductive health (Baynton 2001). Ableism, historically and continues to interlock with racialization, gender- and sexuality-based oppression to marginalize and harm BIPOC, LGBTQIA+ people through control, invalidation, and pathologizing being queer, trans, dark-skinned, feminine, and Indigenous (e.g., refer to Brown 2017a, 2017b; Kean 2021).

Ableism intersects and is used to perpetuate classism. For example, in the United States, despite the existence of laws protecting civil and human rights, numerous organizations can compensate individuals with disabilities below the minimum wage due to Section 14(c) of the Fair Labor Standards Act (FLSA). Section 14(c) empowers the government to issue "special wage certificates" to employers, enabling them to sidestep state or federal minimum wage requirements. Consequently, a significant portion of individuals with disabilities receive wages as low as one to two dollars per day (Friedman 2019; U.S. Department of Labor n.d.).

From the perspective of economic insecurity, existing research reveals the intersectional patterns of disadvantage due to overlapping systems of oppression, encompassing disability, gender, class, race. For example, in their analysis of 2015 American Community Survey (ACS), Maroto, Pettinicchio and Patterson (2019) found that BIPOC women with disabilities and lower level of education experience the highest rates of poverty and the lowest levels of total income.

Maroto et al. (2019) also found that individuals from disadvantaged groups, particularly those with disabilities, do not predominantly rely on the labor market for their income. This finding underscores the significance of public assistance as a crucial supplement for individuals with disabilities and other marginalized groups facing limited employment income. The absence of this support would result in significantly higher poverty rates among these groups and related cycles of harm and oppression. However, reductions in welfare programs and a policy focus on workfare compound the stigma faced by people with disabilities – first, for being perceived as "unable" to work and, second, for receiving benefits aimed at preventing them from falling into poverty (Whittle et al., 2017).

These are just a few illustrative examples to demonstrate deeply intersectional nature of ableism and to highlight how ableism is used to perpetuate and justify other forms of oppression. In the next section, we dive deeper to demonstrate intersectional manifestations of ableism using selected three key policy and administrative areas namely – workplace, education, and healthcare.

Invitation to Pause

We invite you to pause here. If it feels accessible, take one or more deep breaths, hydrate, stand, stretch, move your body, care for your bodymind in ways that feel kind and compassionate. We invite you to return to the next section when you feel ready and resourced enough in your body mind to engage with the content.

Unveiling Institutionalized Ableism in Key Public Policy and Administrative Areas

Intersectional ableism is omnipresent in our everyday lives and in our contemporary organizational/institutional norms. Ableism can manifest in various forms, both overt and subtle, conscious, and unconscious, at macro (societal and cultural), meso (institutional and organizational), and micro (individual and interpersonal) levels. It can impact different aspects of life, including the workplace, education, and healthcare.

Ableism is deeply embedded in our systems. When examined critically, we can observe manifestations of ableism in our policies (e.g., overt, and covert discrimination against older and disabled people during COVID-19 policy responses) and dominant cultural norms, logics, values, and beliefs (e.g., overemphasis on capitalist norms of productivity, norms based on urgency, lack of values for rest and restoration for bodyminds). Ableism manifests through administrative procedures (e.g., administratively burdensome procedures to receive accommodation and/or access to welfare benefits) as well as structures in tangible (e.g., in lack of prioritization of ramps, curb cuts, and elevators) and intangible ways (e.g., in job description and advertisements, and pay structures).

Ableism in the Workplace

Before we dive into reflections and discussions around workplace discrimination based on ableism, we must acknowledge that one of the major ways in which ableism functions in our society is by attaching peoples' worth to "productivity," especially one that is measured in terms of capitalist profit-focused norms. Furthermore, ableism shows up in our society, our policies, and culture by attaching access to resources to meet basic human needs, including shelter, food, and healthcare to participation in "labor" market economy, that is, whether or not we are "working". Disrupting ableism involves countering dominant, exploitative and extractive norms around productivity, creating spaces and investing in non-capitalist forms of labor that enhance and enrich human lives and society in diverse and meaningful ways. It is a recognition that all bodyminds and all peoples are intrinsically valuable (Sins Invalid 2019). We invite grounding into this acknowledgment and what it means for our workspaces as we dive deeper into intersectional manifestations of ableism in workplace contexts.

Intersectional ableism shows up in workplace settings in myriad ways. The consequences of workplace ableism can be felt at recruitment and hiring stages, to everyday on-job experiences, and while navigating career progression and promotion opportunities. When people with disabilities seek job opportunities, they must navigate workplace ableism in recruitment and hiring procedures that are steeped in stereotypes, prejudice, and stigma against disability. These structural, cultural, and procedural biases exclude and prevent people with disabilities from entering the workforce, sometimes literally due to ableist infrastructure that prevents access (Lindsay et al. 2023; Pilling 2013).

To explore ableism in recruitment and hiring from an intersectional perspective, consider the experiences of youth and young adults with disabilities. Some of the common barriers that young people with disabilities encounter when looking for a job include – limited pre-vocational and career preparatory experiences, overly protective parenting, restricted access to transportation, limited availability of accessible employment opportunities, attitudinal barriers, stigma, and discrimination. A frequently cited barrier to the social inclusion of people with disabilities in the workplace is negative attitudes and discrimination. Ableism contributes to the persistence of chronic unemployment and under-employment of people with disabilities (Lindsay et al. 2023).

Once in the workforce, people with disabilities are targeted by ableism through inaccessible work environments, lack of reasonable accommodations, harassment, microaggressions, and gaslighting experiences. For example, people with non-apparent disabilities, find that their bodyminds are being policed and their needs and experiences are gaslighted, including by strangers, family members, medical providers, peers, human resource professionals, and supervisors who challenge their needs and use of accommodations or assume they are "faking" their disabilities (Kattari, Olzman, and Hanna 2018).

For people with apparent disabilities, manifestations of ableism in workplace, in public spaces, and in larger societal contexts, includes the non-disabled gaze that seeks to invalidate impaired bodies. The non-disabled gaze ranges from "pity" to "intrusive curiosity" driven by non-disabled peoples' ableist behaviors. These include a sense of entitlement to "intrude, inquire, and appropriate impairment as a public spectacle." Non-disabled gaze also includes forms of benevolent ableism revealed through habits of making "heroic" attributions. Non-disabled people often turn disabled people's lives into what Stella Young referred to as "inspiration porn" (Loja et al. 2013, pp. 193–194; Young 2014).

Workplace ableism manifests in day-to-day interactions when people with disabilities may be denied opportunities to build social capital, network, and experience social isolation. They may experience exclusion from workplace events, and formal and informal gatherings – this may be direct exclusion when they are not invited to a gathering or indirect exclusion, when gathering is held in a space that is inaccessible for employee/s with disabilities. A culture of disability inclusion is critical to improve employee retention. For example, using the context of the U.S. federal employee experiences, Chordiya (2022) found that even when policies and structures are created to foster disability diversity, in absence of disability inclusive cultures and practices, employees with disabilities exhibit higher turnover intentions (compared to their non-disabled peers).

Ableism shows up in our everyday workplace culture through norms about showing up at all costs – even when we may be in grief, feeling sick and/or in pain, or must care for someone who may be sick and/or in pain. Ableism shows up when we are rewarded for working through pain, hiding our pain, and hiding our disability. Intersectional ableism shows up when asking for and receiving flexibility and support is viewed as a sign of weakness instead of signs of strength, reciprocity, mutuality, and trust building. Ableism shows up in our cultural norms where we run or participate in long meetings without bio-breaks, and where there is a lack of culture for movement and stretching (so our bodies can feel supported and comfortable). When there are no resources, no structure, no culture, no community for practice of self-care and collective care (Chordiya and Protonentis 2024; Protonentis 2021).

Intersectional ableism persists at various stages of career progression and promotion and directly impacts people with disabilities as they may be overlooked and denied opportunities for career progression and professional development. For example, Brown and Moloney (2019) found that women with disabilities, on average, encounter more depressive symptoms because of various employment-related factors. These include overrepresentation in low paying, less prestigious jobs, elevated workplace stress, less autonomous and less creatively engaging job positions.

Intersectional ableism shows up when employees with disabilities are scrutinized more strictly, receive biased performance evaluations, and unfair treatment. For example, Pilling (2013) found that BIPOC, LGTBQIA+ people with mental health conditions face powerful barriers to disability disclosure as they may be viewed as "incompetent" in the workplace and face double standards and stricter scrutiny in their evaluations. Trans BIPOC people with mental health needs may experience multiple stigmas due to the intersectionality of their racialized, gendered, and disability identities. Experience of ableism is compounded by trans oppression in workplace as trans identities may be pathologized as sexually perverse and experience prejudiced behaviors in workplace (Pilling 2013).

Mohamed and Shefer (2015) attribute the challenges experienced by people with disabilities and with multiple intersectional identities to our societal tendency to define disability as a binary and the discourse surrounding "normalcy" that we have come to accept. The authors argue that:

> The normal/abnormal binary is profoundly interwoven into existing power and privilege. The construction of normalcy rationalises and bolsters the marginalisation and "othering" of bodies, minds, affects, and sexualities that do not fit into a particular culture's imaginary of the ordinary, everyday, or acceptable. The suppression of diversity the negation of potential futures (and presents and pasts) and notions about the im/perfectibility of the human are infused with fears about disability.
>
> (Mohamed and Shefer 2015, p. 2)

Ableism in Education

Ableism in education manifests in various ways, often creating barriers and reinforcing discriminatory practices against individuals with disabilities. Some of the common barriers posed by ableism in educational settings include inaccessible physical and psychological environment (e.g., steep stairs inside and outside lecture halls, lack of ramps, elevators, accessible restrooms, and sensory rooms) and lack of assistive technologies (e.g., screen readers, text-to-speech software, braille materials).

Ableism in educational settings also persists and manifests through absence of inclusive educational practices and lack of systemic prioritization of universal design for learning (UDL) approaches that account for learning needs of disability diverse student body. UDL does not offer a complete or perfect solution to all access needs in a learning environment. However, if it used with adaptability, flexibility, care, and intentionality, and understood to serve more "as a floor than a ceiling" to meet diverse access needs, UDL approaches in classroom contexts can serve a diverse range of bodyminds (rather than assuming an imagined ideal learner). UDL approaches include using multiple means of student engagement (why students learn), diverse methods of content delivery (what students learn), and multiple avenues for students to express themselves and act (how students learn). UDL approaches can help to interrupt biases in students' performance assessment and challenge unexamined notions of academic rigor (Dolmage 2017).

Other barriers that contribute to disability oppression in educational settings include stereotyping and low expectations for students with disabilities and inadequate learning, and development opportunities for educators to foster disability affirming classrooms. Ableism manifests through unsafety in academic environments, where people with disabilities (including students, teachers, and staff) may experience microaggressions, gaslighting, bullying, and harassment. For students with disabilities, testing and assessment biases, biased notions of academic rigor, inflexible policies and procedures, limited representation in curriculum, lack of support for mental health and access needs, social isolation, lack of opportunities for peer support, mutual aid, and collective care can contribute to marginalization and hinder their academic progress and success (Brown 2011; Dolmage 2017; Mireles 2022; Piepzna-Samarasinha 2022).

The intersection of ableism with other oppressive systems, such as racism, sexism, and classism, amplifies the complexity and severity of the experiences of individuals subjected to multiple forms of oppression simultaneously (Annamma, Connor, and Ferri 2013; Mireles 2022; Piepzna-Samarasinha 2022). The persistent overrepresentation of BIPOC students in special education in elementary and high school settings and underrepresentation at the postsecondary level, reveal how the historical legacies of racism, classism, sexism, and ableism persistently impact educational practices (Reid and Knight 2006).

(**Content Warning: Emotionally Heavy Discussion**) Intersection of ableism and racism significantly compounds negative educational experiences of BIPOC students with disabilities (Oregon Department of Education n.d.). For example, a teacher might misinterpret a symptom of a student's disability, such as difficulty focusing due to ADHD, as a behavioral problem. When ableism intersects with racialized stereotypes such as Black students as more "disruptive," this intersectionality results in Black students being unfairly disciplined, more frequently and more harshly compared to their peers. Black students experience disproportionately higher rates of school removal and arrests for emotional and behavioral issues compared to their white counterparts. This not only unjustly penalizes the student based on their race and disability but also disrupts their educational progress.

The frequent occurrence of suspensions or expulsions deprives the student of valuable learning time, potentially causing academic setbacks (Meiners 2007; Oregon Department of Education n.d.). These intersectional ableist experiences in educational settings reveal how students with disabilities and multiply marginalized students must cope with and survive persistent prejudice and discrimination that contribute to spiritual wounding and spiritual trauma (refer to Chapter 3 for discussion on spiritual trauma; Love 2016; Revilla 2021).

Ableism in Healthcare

Ableism in healthcare manifests in many ways and varies in intensities. It can lead to unsafety, inequitable treatment, discrimination, marginalization, and barriers to meeting care-related needs, and at times survival needs for multiply marginalized people with disabilities.

People with disabilities need to rely on medical care, including costly pharmacological and technological interventions, legal protections, and public accommodations. However, intersectionality of ableism with other "isms" creates barriers in terms of access to resources, access to disability affirming care providers, communication barriers, physical barriers, institutional barriers, financial barriers, as well as cultural barriers posed by stigma, stereotypes, and prejudice against disability (and other minoritized social identities). Ableism in health means denial of disability affirming care to multiply marginalized people with disabilities that honors their agency, informed consent, choice, and self-determination (Brown 2017a; Kean 2021; Mingus 2015, 2022; Piepzna-Samarasinha 2018, 2022).

Women with disabilities often have later cancer diagnoses, less thorough treatments, and higher cancer mortality rates than those without disabilities (Iezzoni et al. 2008). The challenges faced by individuals with disabilities likely contribute to mental health differences. In 2018, an estimated 17.4 million (32.9%) adults with disabilities experienced frequent mental distress, a number 4.6 times higher than those without disabilities (Cree 2020). Disability has a substantial impact on LGBTQIA+ individuals, and the convergence of disability with race, gender, and other marginalized identities presents numerous challenges. LGBTQIA+ individuals with disabilities are severely vulnerable to mistreatment in health care settings, affecting their access to medical care and mental well-being (Rodríguez-Roldán 2020).

COVID-19 pandemic had disproportionately detrimental effects on BIPOC individuals with disabilities. For example, a study on care providers attending COVID-19 patients from BIPOC communities with disabilities found that health care quality declined during the pandemic due to reduced, delayed, and limited care options. This was influenced by biases, organizational policies, inadequate resources, a stressed medical environment, and provider burnout. Additionally, a lack of cultural competency around disability in the medical community, coupled with ableist messages in COVID-19 guidelines and policies, contributed to the dismissal of people with disabilities in care. This ableism, intersecting with ageism and racism, worsens care inequities, especially for patients who are both older, BIPOC, and have a disability (Lee et al. 2023; Ramirez et al. 2022).

Ableism and Medical Industrial Complex

As discussed previously in this chapter, disability rights and DJ activists have long resisted medical model of disability as a harmful ideology that pathologizes non-conforming, disabled bodyminds, views disability as a deficit in an individual and something to be "fixed" or "cured" (Kean 2021). Mia Mingus (2015) notes, countering ableism in healthcare includes both fight for the right to receive care, and the right to refuse care.

The medical industrial complex (MIC) is an extensive system that extends far beyond the realms of doctors, nurses, clinics, and hospitals. MIC includes medical schools, research labs, pharmaceutical companies, insurance companies, alternatives and natural medicines industry, mental health industry, and more (for a detailed description of MIC, please refer to Mingus 2015). Primarily driven by profit rather than a focus on "health," well-being, and care, its influence pervades various aspects of society. Its historical roots are intertwined with eugenics, capitalism, colonization, slavery, immigration, war, prisons, and reproductive oppression. It doesn't merely contribute significantly to the history of ableism but is intricately connected to all systems of oppression (Mingus 2015).

Mia Mingus (2015) powerfully describes the contradictions of oppressed communities needing to rely on healthcare and MIC while also navigating its painful, traumatic, and unjust history of systemic ableism.

This includes legacies of eugenics that target oppressed communities under the guise of care, health, and safety. Mingus (2015, p. 1) notes:

> (**Content Warning: Emotionally Heavy Discussion**) Oppressed communities have had long and complicated histories with the MIC. From the continued targeting of disabled bodies as something to fix, to the experimentation on black bodies, to the pathologized treatment of and violent attempts to cure queer and trans communities. From the humiliating, lacking or flat-out denial of services to poor communities, to forced sterilization and dangerous contraceptives trafficked to young women of color. From the forced medicalization used in prisons today, to the days when the mental institutions used to be the jails, and the ways that "criminal" and "mentally disabled" are still used interchangeably. From the lack of culturally competent services, to the demonization and erasing of indigenous healing and practices. From the never-ending battle to control populations through controlling birth, birthing and those who give birth in this country, to the countless doctors and practitioners who have raped and sexually assaulted their patients and the survivors who never told a soul. From all the violence that was and is considered standard practice, to the gross abuses of power. In flushing out what the MIC is, we are naming a system. We are calling attention to the systematic targeting of oppressed communities under the guise of care, health, and safety.

Invitation to Pause

> If you are able and willing, we invite you to pause here, to breathe into this quote and reflect. Allow these words to land in your bodymind.

Disability rights and DJ movement builders recognize that while MIC offers living-giving and life-saving care, medicines, medical procedures, and treatments, while many in the system are working dedicatedly to change the system and serve marginalized people, and yet there is a profound need to interrupt oppression and transform the medical industry complex and health care systems (Mingus 2015; Piepzna-Samarasinha 2022). In the next section, we reflect on action and change to counter ableism and foster DJ.

Action and Change for Disability Justice in Public Service: a Liberatory Public Service Perspective

In this section, we reflect on how LPS framework is anchored in and deeply aligned with foundational principles of DJ and seek to advance DJ in public service contexts. DJ is a core building block and foundational to LPS (for detailed discussions refer to Chapter 5). In the following paragraphs, we hope to build on discussions offered in Chapter 5 and offer additional reflections on the theory and practice of DJ followed by reflections on LPS to advance DJ.

Disability Justice

DJ is a liberatory framework that was co-created and is being developed by BIPOC, LGBTQIA+, sick and disabled activists, thinkers, visionaries, and leaders. Together they are innovating and co-creating the cultural foundations for emergence of DJ visions and principles of collective care, collective access, and collective liberation. DJ is anchored in ten foundational principles. These are: intersectionality, leadership of those most impacted, anti-capitalist politic, commitment to cross-movement organizing, recognizing wholeness, sustainability, commitment to cross-disability solidarity, interdependence, collective access, and collective liberation (for interpretative discussion of DJ principles, refer to Chapter 5; Sins Invalid 2019). It seeks to counter intersectional ableism by envisioning and building foundations for systems where multiply marginalized disabled people (and non-disabled people) can arrive as whole people, be their authentic selves, belong, create, innovate, and be free.

DJ is a framework that can guide us in the vulnerable practice of cultivating communities of care through relationality, reciprocity, integrity, and hard work of showing up for each other and supporting each other's needs. DJ elevates the need to build coalitions as necessary elements of liberatory present and futures. DJ invites us to consistently be in the practice of imagination, creation, innovation to counter ableist systems in all work, one small step at a time, one task at a time, one project at a time, moving a pace that is authentic, sustainable, and meaningful. DJ invites us to envision a future anchored in values of collective access, collective care, and collective liberation.

In dreaming about DJ and envisioning disabled futures, Leah Lakshmi Piepzna-Samarasinha (2022, p. 72) writes:

> There is no one disabled future. But in mine, there is guaranteed income, housing, access, food, water, and education for all– or money has been abolished. I get paid to write from my bed. The births of disabled, Autistic, Mad, Neurodivergent, Deaf, and sick kids are celebrated, and there are memorials and healing and reparation sites on every psych ward, institution, nursing home, youth lockup, and "autistic treatment center" where our people have been locked up and abused. Anyone who needs care gets it, with respect and autonomy, not abuse. Caregivers are paid well for the work we do and are often disabled ourselves. Disabled folks are the ones teaching medical

> school students about our bodies. Schools have been taken apart and remade so that there's not one idea of "smart" and "stupid" but many ways of learning. There is a disability justice section in every bookstore and a million examples of sick and disabled and Deaf and autistic and Mad folks thriving. I have a really sick lipstick-red spiral ramp curving around my house.
>
> Because it's beautiful. Because I want it. Because I get to live free.
>
> (p. 72)

LPS Principles and Core Values[3]

The framework of LPS is rooted in the core values of love, courage, repair, healing, joy, efficacy, solidarity, and transformation. The five emergent principles of LPS seek to approach public service and DEILJ work from a trauma-informed, repair and healing-oriented lens that compassionately centers the margins within all our organizational functions structures, designs, policies, procedures, leadership, and cultures. These principles are:

- *Principle 1: LPS integrates inner transformation and collective transformation.*
- *Principle 2: LPS is trauma informed.*
- *Principle 3: LPS is repair and healing oriented.*
- *Principle 4: LPS compassionately centers the margins.*
- *Principle 5: LPS seeks to transform the conditions of harm to end cycles of oppression.*

Reflections on Application and Integration of LPS Perspective

In advancing the work of DJ in public service contexts, LPS invites public service community to engage in the process of learning and unlearning to counter ableism. LPS seeks to cultivate disability affirming public service organizations (also refer to Chordiya and Protonentis Forthcoming). LPS invites us to radically imagine and reimagine our policies, administrative procedures, protocols, and cultural norms to center the needs, lives, and freedom of multiply marginalized people with disabilities. In practicing inner transformation and collective transformation, LPS follows the leadership of DJ thinkers, scholars, visionaries, and movement builders.

LPS invites us to create structures and cultures for collective access and recognizes that access is a floor not the ceiling. As powerfully noted by beloved ancestor Stacey Park Milbern (2017), a founding DJ movement builder and visionary, "*Collective access is revolutionary because disabled people of color (and disabled people in general) choosing each other is revolutionary. And, in many ways access should not be a revolutionary concept.*" Working to build collective access and supporting each other's access needs is a profound practice of care and reciprocity that are the deepest qualities of being human. As humans we inherently know what care and reciprocity look like and feel like. We know how to be in care-centered and reciprocal relationships. However, acting on these core values is not often supported by our dominant cultural norms of urgency and scarcity- and in that sense, collective access both is and should not be a revolutionary idea.

Milbern (2017) further writes, "*It is only the first step in movement building. People talk about access as the outcome, not the process, as if having spaces be accessible is enough to get us all free.*" Working intentionally to meet each other's access needs serves as a foundation to build solidarity. Building structures and cultures for meeting access needs with care and dignity must be at the core, and as Milbern (2017) notes, a routine, everyday part of our liberatory praxis. She writes, "*Disabled people are so much more than our access needs; we can't have a movement without safety and access, and yet there is so much more still waiting for us collectively once we build this skillset of negotiating access needs with each other.*"[4]

LPS invites us to build collectives and communities of practice for DJ. The practice of LPS rooted in DJ means building liberatory consciousness and to imagine and dream visions of DJ for our lives, our collectives, and our future generations. LPS means finding time for nurture and nourishment – including nurture and nourishment for our relationships. LPS is also about building intentional time and space to gather as whole people, to discern, meet, and support each other's access needs, to give ourselves and each other permission and compassionate support to rest, restore, and heal along the way as we seek to transform ourselves and our disability-diverse organizations and collectives.

LPS means being vigilant of internalized ableism and cultivating awareness and skills to interrupt and counter ableist norms of perfection, urgency, and scarcity mindsets. LPS invites us to find a pace that is sustainable and meaningful that allows headspace and embodied space for creation, innovation, and liberation to emerge. LPS invites us to develop norms and practice of efficiency and effectiveness that is generative (not extractive, coercive, or dominating) and is aligned with core public service values of care, equity, and inclusion. LPS understands that we need to build and sustain momentum for transformative work while simultaneously recognizing that sustainability, patience, and slowness are necessary elements for democratic, inclusive, and participatory transformation to emerge.

LPS invites us to engage in the work of solidarity for DJ and always remain accountable to the base movement spaces and movement philosophies that guide our practice. In communities of practice for advancing DJ, LPS invites us to pause consistently to reflect on the ten principles of DJ.

LPS asks us to consistently return to and reflect on the questions – in our public service practice, what it means to follow the leadership of multiply marginalized BIPOC, LGBTQIA+ people with disabilities; and, what it means to leave no bodymind behind?

Summary and Key Teachings

Disability is a core human experience. In this chapter, our goal is to advance meaningful conversations within the public service community, recognizing the significance of disability in both our present and future. We seek to eliminate the stigma surrounding disability, confront and disrupt ableism, and promote LPS that is firmly rooted in the principles of DJ.

We understand ableism as a system of oppression that is based in anti-disability shaming, stigma, and prejudice of bodyminds, one that seeks to prevent disabled people from being whole people, from surviving, from thriving, and being free. We highlight that ableism and other systems of oppression are socially constructed by humans. So, as humans, we have the power to change them. We have the power to create something new that is not oppressive and in fact is liberatory. We have the power to interrupt and counter ableism, to individually and collectively plant the seeds of LPS that is deeply anchored in DJ. We have the power to collectively imagine, co-create, innovate to bring DJ to life.

Deep Dive Resources [Full Citations in References]

Inclusive Language Guidelines

1 Brown, Lydia X.Z. 2022. "Ableism/Language." *Ableism/Language* (blog).

Disability Justice

2 Chordiya, Rashmi, and Adana Protonentis. 2024. "Healing from White Supremacy Culture and Ableism: Disability Justice as an Antidote."
3 Chordiya, Rashmi, and Adana Protonentis. Forthcoming. "Disability-Affirming Diversity, Equity, and Inclusion."
4 Nielsen, Kim E. 2013. *A Disability History of the United States*. Beacon Press.
5 Mingus, Mia. n.d. "About." *Leaving Evidence* (blog). n.d. https://leavingevidence.wordpress.com/about-2/.
6 Piepzna-Samarasinha, Leah Lakshmi. 2018. *Care Work: Dreaming Disability Justice*.
7 Piepzna-Samarasinha, Leah Lakshmi. 2020. "Disability Justice: An Audit Tool."

8 Piepzna-Samarasinha, Leah Lakshmi. 2022. *The Future Is Disabled: Prophecies, Love Notes and Mourning Songs.*
9 Sins Invalid. 2019. "Skin, Tooth, and Bone: The Basis of Movement Is Our People, A Disability Justice Primer."
10 Wong, Alice, ed. 2020. *Disability Visibility: First-Person Stories from the Twenty-First Century.* New York: Knopf Doubleday Publishing Group.

Websites and Podcasts

11 Swenor, Bonnielin, and Nick Reed. n.d. "Included: The Disability Equity Podcast:"
12 Wong, Alice. n.d. "Disability Visibility Project." Disability Visibility Project. n.d. https://disabilityvisibilityproject.com/.

Notes

1 Language note: Language is a powerful tool in promoting respect, dignity, and empathy in conversations about disability. It is important to listen to and respect the preferences of individuals with disabilities while using terminology that is respectful, accurate, and inclusive. We recognize the evolving preference within the disability community to adopt identity-first language as opposed to person-first language. This shift reflects the perspective of many disabled individuals who consider disability an intrinsic part of their identity, akin to race and gender. Nevertheless, it is essential to acknowledge that some community members still favor person-first language. Considering this diversity, in our writing about disability, we use both approaches. We refrain from using euphemisms like "special needs" or "differently abled," except in instances where they are utilized as proper nouns (as exemplified in Brown, 2013).

2 We want to acknowledge our colleague and reviewer Adana Protonentis, a wise disability justice scholar and practitioner, for offering us this profound insight on differentiation between experience of becoming disabled and life as a disabled person. We invite you to refer to her Facebook post on this (Protonentis 2023)– it is dated December 1, 2023, and included in our references.

3 We invite you to read these reflections alongside LPS-focused ideas and visions described in Chapter 5 (thc key tenets of LPS framework), towards the end of Chapter 8 (section on LPS perspectives for racial justice) and Chapter 9 (section on LPS perspectives for gender and LGBTQIA+ justice). These reflections build on each other and their practice is intrinsically aligned and mutually dependent. We think many of the ideas, practices, and strategies for action and change offered in all four chapters (5, 8, 9, and 10) can be applied across various contexts of DEILJ work that are discussed in this book and beyond. We invite you to make these ideas and practices your own and adapt them to your individual and collective/organizational priorities, contexts, and needs with deep care, accountability, and intentionality.

4 For full quote, please refer to Stacey Park Milbern's Facebook post, dated December 22, 2017.

References

arielle, zipporah. 2019. "The Sometimes Hard-To-See Line Between Visible and Invisible Disabilities: "This Is What Disabled...." *M'edium* (blog). July 29, 2019. https://medium.com/@coffeespoonie/the-sometimes-hard-to-see-line-between-visible-and-invisible-disabilities-this-is-what-disabled-eb6dec41bdf6.

Annamma, Subini Ancy, David Connor, and Beth Ferri. 2013. "Dis/Ability Critical Race Studies (DisCrit): Theorizing at the Intersections of Race and Dis/Ability." *Race Ethnicity and Education* 16 (1): 1–31. https://doi.org/10.1080/13613324.2012.730511.

Baynton, Douglas. 2001. "Disability and the Justification of Inequality in American History." In *The New Disability History: American Perspectives*, edited by Longmore Paul K. and Umansky Lauri, 33–57. New York, NY: New York University Press.

Brown, Lydia X.Z. 2011. "Autistic Hoya — A Blog by Lydia X. Z. Brown." *Letter to My AP English Teacher* (blog). December 21, 2011. https://www.autistichoya.com/search/label/invisible%20disability.

———. 2013. "How 'Differently Abled' Marginalizes Disabled People." August 29, 2013. https://www.autistichoya.com/2013/08/differently-abled.html.

———. 2017a. "Ableist Shame and Disruptive Bodies: Survivorship at the Intersection of Queer, Trans, and Disabled Existence." In *Religion, Disability, and Interpersonal Violence*, edited by Johnson, Andy J., J. Ruth Nelson, and Emily M. Lund, 163–178. Springer Cham: Springer International Publishing. https://doi.org/10.1007/978-3-319-56901-7_10.

———. 2017b. "Lydia Brown - Disability Justice Intersection with Racial Justice, and Queer/Trans Liberation." Disability Intersectionality Summit, March 10. https://www.youtube.com/watch?v=4qoc1S_pEXo.

———. 2022. "Ableism/Language." *Ableism/Language* (blog). September 2022. https://www.autistichoya.com/p/ableist-words-and-terms-to-avoid.html.

Brown, Robyn Lewis, and Mairead Eastin Moloney. 2019. "Intersectionality, Work, and Well-Being: The Effects of Gender and Disability." *Gender & Society* 33 (1): 94–122. https://doi.org/10.1177/0891243218800636.

Cartwright, Samuel A. 1851. "Africans in America/Part 4/ "Diseases and Peculiarities"." *De Bow's Review Southern and Western States*, 1851. https://www.pbs.org/wgbh/aia/part4/4h3106t.html.

Center for Disease Control and Prevention. 2023. "Disability Impacts All of Us Infographic | CDC." May 15, 2023. https://www.cdc.gov/ncbddd/disabilityandhealth/infographic-disability-impacts-all.html.

Chordiya, Rashmi. 2022. "Organizational Inclusion and Turnover Intentions of Federal Employees with Disabilities." *Review of Public Personnel Administration* 42 (1): 60–87. https://doi.org/10.1177/0734371X20942305.

Chordiya, Rashmi, Stephanie Dolamore, Jeannine M. Love, Erin L. Borry, Adana Protonentis, Brendan Stern, and Geoffrey Whitebread. 2023. "Staking the Tent at the Margins: Using Disability Justice to Expand the Theory and Praxis of Social Equity in Public Administration." *Administrative Theory & Praxis* 0 (0): 1–26. https://doi.org/10.1080/10841806.2023.2216616.

Chordiya, Rashmi, and Adana Protonentis. Forthcoming. "Disability-Affirming Diversity, Equity, and Inclusion." In *Elgar Handbook on Diversity, Equity, and*

Inclusion, edited by Meghna Sabharwal, Shilpa Viswanath, and Sean McCandless. London, UK: Edward Elgar Publishing Ltd.

Chordiya, Rashmi, and Adana Protonentis. 2024. "Healing from Intersectional White Supremacy Culture and Ableism: Disability Justice as an Antidote." *Journal of Social Equity and Public Administration* 2 (1): 127–52. https://doi.org/10.24926/jsepa.v2i1.4856.

Collier, Danielle. 2016. "Inclusion of People with Disabilities in the Workplace: Best Practices for HR Professionals," October. https://ecommons.cornell.edu/handle/1813/74446.

Cree, Robyn A. 2020. "Frequent Mental Distress Among Adults, by Disability Status, Disability Type, and Selected Characteristics — United States, 2018." *MMWR. Morbidity and Mortality Weekly Report* 69 (36): 1238–1243. https://doi.org/10.15585/mmwr.mm6936a2.

Dolmage, Jay T. 2017. *Academic Ableism: Disability and Higher Education*. Illustrated ed. Ann Arbor, MI: University of Michigan Press.

Forber-Pratt, Anjali J. 2021. Included: The Disability Equity Podcast: 7: Disability Identity Interview by Bonnielin Swenor and Nicholas Reed. https://included.libsyn.com/7-disability-identity.

Friedman, Carli. 2019. "Ableism, Racism, and Subminimum Wage in the United States." *Disability Studies Quarterly* 39 (4). https://doi.org/10.18061/dsq.v39i4.6604.

Iezzoni, Lisa I., Long H. Ngo, Donglin Li, Richard G. Roetzheim, Reed E. Drews, and Ellen P. McCarthy. 2008. "Early Stage Breast Cancer Treatments for Younger Medicare Beneficiaries With Different Disabilities." *Health Services Research* 43 (5p1): 1752–1767. https://doi.org/10.1111/j.1475-6773.2008.00853.x.

Institute on Disabilities, Temple University. 2021. "Disability Rights Timeline." College of Education and Human Development, Institute on Disabilities. June 28, 2021. https://disabilities.temple.edu/resources/disability-rights-timeline.

Kattari, Shanna K., Miranda Olzman, and Michele D. Hanna. 2018. "'You Look Fine!': Ableist Experiences by People With Invisible Disabilities." *Affilia* 33 (4): 477–492. https://doi.org/10.1177/0886109918778073.

Kean, Eli. 2021. "Advancing a Critical Trans Framework for Education." *Curriculum Inquiry* 51 (2): 261–286. https://doi.org/10.1080/03626784.2020.1819147.

Kindred Leaders. 2021. "Who Should Our Organization Be Most Accountable To?" *Instagram*. https://www.instagram.com/p/CLE8ve2DbFX/.

Lee, Danbi, Paula M. Kett, Selina A. Mohammed, Bianca K. Frogner, and Janice Sabin. 2023. "Inequitable Care Delivery Toward COVID-19 Positive People of Color and People With Disabilities." *PLOS Global Public Health* 3 (4): e0001499. https://doi.org/10.1371/journal.pgph.0001499.

Lewis, Talila A. 2022. "Working Definition of Ableism - January 2022 Update." TL's Blog. TALILA A. LEWIS. January 1, 2022. https://www.talilalewis.com/blog.html.

Lindsay, Sally, Kristina Fuentes, Vanessa Tomas, and Shaelynn Hsu. 2023. "Ableism and Workplace Discrimination Among Youth and Young Adults With Disabilities: A Systematic Review." *Journal of Occupational Rehabilitation* 33 (1): 20–36. https://doi.org/10.1007/s10926-022-10049-4.

Loja, Ema, Maria Emília Costa, Bill Hughes, and Isabel Menezes. 2013. "Disability, Embodiment and Ableism: Stories of Resistance." *Disability & Society* 28 (2): 190–203. https://doi.org/10.1080/09687599.2012.705057.

Love, Bettina L. 2016. "Anti-Black State Violence, Classroom Edition: The Spirit Murdering of Black Children." *Journal of Curriculum and Pedagogy* 13 (1): 22–25. https://doi.org/10.1080/15505170.2016.1138258.

Meiners, Erica R. 2007. *Right to Be Hostile: Schools, Prisons, and the Making of Public Enemies*. 1st ed. New York, NY: Routledge.

Mingus, Mia. 2011. "Moving Toward the Ugly: A Politic Beyond Desirability." *Leaving Evidence* (blog). August 22, 2011. https://leavingevidence.wordpress.com/2011/08/22/moving-toward-the-ugly-a-politic-beyond-desirability/.

———. 2015. "Medical Industrial Complex Visual." *Leaving Evidence* (blog). February 6, 2015. https://leavingevidence.wordpress.com/2015/02/06/medical-industrial-complex-visual/.

———. 2022. "You Are Not Entitled to Our Deaths: COVID, Abled Supremacy & Interdependence." *Leaving Evidence* (blog). January 16, 2022. https://leavingevidence.wordpress.com/2022/01/16/you-are-not-entitled-to-our-deaths-covid-abled-supremacy-interdependence/.

Mireles, Danielle. 2022. "Theorizing Racist Ableism in Higher Education." *Teachers College Record* 124 (7): 17–50. https://doi.org/10.1177/01614681221111428.

Milbern, Stacey Park. 2017. Facebook.com. December 22, 2017. https://www.facebook.com/smilbern/posts/780151464677.

Mohamed, Kharnita, and Tamara Shefer. 2015. "Gendering Disability and Disabling Gender: Critical Reflections on Intersections of Gender and Disability." *Agenda* 29 (2): 2–13. https://doi.org/10.1080/10130950.2015.1055878.

Maroto, Michelle, David Pettinicchio, and Andrew C. Patterson. 2019. "Hierarchies of Categorical Disadvantage: Economic Insecurity at the Intersection of Disability, Gender, and Race." *Gender & Society 33 (1):* 64–93. *https://doi.org/10.1177/0891243218794648.*

Nielsen, Kim E. 2013. *A Disability History of the United States*. Beacon Press.

Oregon Department of Education. n.d. "Understanding and Addressing Ableism in Schools." https://www.oregon.gov/ode/students-and-family/SpecialEducation/publications/Documents/informalremovals/understandingableisminschools.pdf

Ostiguy, Benjamin J., Madeline L. Peters, and Davey Shlasko. 2016. "Ableism." In *Teaching for Diversity and Social Justice*, edited by Maurianne Adams, Lee Anne Bell, Diane J. Goodman, and Khyati Y. Joshi, 3rd ed. 299–337. New York, NY: Routledge.

Piepzna-Samarasinha, Leah Lakshmi. 2018. *Care Work: Dreaming Disability Justice*. Vancouver, CA: Arsenal Pulp Press.

———. 2020. "Disability Justice: An Audit Tool." Northwest Health Foundation. https://www.northwesthealth.org/djaudittool.

———. 2022. *The Future Is Disabled: Prophecies, Love Notes and Mourning Songs*. Vancouver, CA: Arsenal Pulp Press.

Pilling, Merrick Daniel. 2013. "Invisible Identity in the Workplace: Intersectional Madness and Processes of Disclosure at Work." *Disability Studies Quarterly* 33 (1). https://doi.org/10.18061/dsq.v33i1.3424.

Protonentis, Adana. 2021. "Keynote by Adana Protonentis - Engaged Employer Symposium 2021." Presented at the SU Career Engagement, Seattle University, August 19. https://www.youtube.com/watch?v=QV4HSBaS2Us.

———. 2023. Facebook.com. December 1, 2023. https://www.facebook.com/adanap/posts/10159163185266268?ref=embed_post.

Protonentis, Adana, Rashmi Chordiya, and ChrisTiana ObeySumner. 2021. "Centering the Margins: Restorative and Transformative Justice as Our Path to Social Equity." *Administrative Theory & Praxis* 43 (3): 333—354. https://doi.org/10.1080/10841806.2020.1868159.

Ramirez, Luisa, Caitlin Monahan, Ximena Palacios-Espinosa, and Sheri R. Levy. 2022. "Intersections of Ageism Toward Older Adults and Other Isms During the COVID-19 Pandemic." *Journal of Social Issues* 78 (4): 965—990. https://doi.org/10.1111/josi.12574.

Reid, D. Kim, and Michelle G. Knight. 2006. "Disability Justifies Exclusion of Minority Students: A Critical History Grounded in Disability Studies." *Educational Researcher* 35, no. 6: 18–23. https://doi.org/10.3102/0013189X035006018.

Revilla, Anita Tijerina. 2021. "Attempted Spirit Murder Who Are Your Spirit Protectors and Your Spirit Restorers?" *The Journal of Educational Foundations* 34 (1): 31–46.

Rodríguez-Roldán, Victoria. 2020. "The Intersection Between Disability and LGBT Discrimination and Marginalization." *American University Journal of Gender, Social Policy & the Law* 28 (3). https://digitalcommons.wcl.american.edu/jgspl/vol28/iss3/2.

Schalk, Sami. 2022. *Black Disability Politics*. Durham: Duke University Press Books.

Schweik, Susan M. 2010. *The Ugly Laws: Disability in Public*. New York Press edition. New York and London: New York University Press.

Shakespeare, Tom. 2006. *Disability Rights and Wrongs*. 1st ed. New York, NY: Routledge.

Sins Invalid. 2019. "Skin, Tooth, and Bone: The Basis of Movement Is Our People, A Disability Justice Primer." https://www.sinsinvalid.org/skin-tooth-and-bone.

Stramondo, Joe. 2021. Included: The Disability Equity Podcast: Disability Moral Asymmetry on Apple Podcasts Interview by Swenor Bonnielin and Nick Reed. https://podcasts.apple.com/us/podcast/disability-moral-asymmetry/id1535129231?i=1000545218061.

Swenor, Bonnielin, and Nick Reed. n.d. "Included: The Disability Equity Podcast:" Accessed November 28, 2023. https://podcasts.apple.com/us/podcast/disability-moral-asymmetry/id1535129231?i=1000545218061.

The World Bank. 2022. "Disability Inclusion Overview." Text/HTML. World Bank. April 14, 2022. https://www.worldbank.org/en/topic/disability.

Thompson, Vilissa. 2021. "Understanding the Policing of Black, Disabled Bodies." *Center for American Progress* (blog). February 10, 2021. https://www.americanprogress.org/article/understanding-policing-black-disabled-bodies/.

U.S. Department of Labor. n.d. "Subminimum Wage." http://www.dol.gov/agencies/whd/special-employment.

Young, Stella. 2014. "Stella Young: I'm Not Your Inspiration, Thank You Very Much | TED Talk." April 2014. https://www.ted.com/talks/stella_young_i_m_not_your_inspiration_thank_you_very_much.

Washington State Governors Office of the Education Ombuds. 2020. "Disability History in the USA Timeline Strips and Answer Key." chrome-extension://

efaidnbmnnnibpcajpcglclefindmkaj/https://www.oeo.wa.gov/sites/default/files/public/Lesson-3-Disability-History-in-USA-Timeline-Strips-and-Answer-Key_.pdf.

Whittle, Erin Louise, Karen R. Fisher, Simone Reppermund, Rhoshel Lenroot, and Julian Trollor. 2017. "Barriers and Enablers to Accessing Mental Health Services for People With Intellectual Disability: A Scoping Review." *Journal of Mental Health Research in Intellectual Disabilities* 11 (1): 69–102. https://doi.org/10.1080/19315864.2017.1408724.

Wolfe, Brendan. 2023. "Buck v. Bell (1927)." Virginia Humanities. Encyclopedia Virginia. July 17, 2023. https://encyclopediavirginia.org/entries/buck-v-bell-1927/.

World Health Organization and World Bank Group. 2011. "World Report on Disability." Malta: World Health Organization. https://www.who.int/disabilities/world_report/2011/report.pdf.

11 Concluding Reflections

Aspiring for Liberatory Public Service

Abstract

In this chapter, we share our concluding reflections on the hard question – can public service organizations be liberatory? If so, what are the core values and principles we must commit to, if we are to dedicate our praxis to dreaming and co-creating a liberatory public service (LPS)?

We emphasize that to align with the core philosophies and principles of its building blocks, such as restorative justice, transformative justice, healing justice, and disability justice, and other critical frameworks such as intersectionality, critical race theory, LPS necessitates working toward the practice and the goal of decolonizing public service, including in connection to the people, and the planet. LPS necessitates collective efforts and shared leadership approaches that are community and survivor-led and seeks to replace inequitable systems with, structures, cultures, policies, procedures, and practices that prioritize the needs of those who are multiply marginalized by inequities. LPS means our public safety, peace keeping, immigration, welfare, education, healthcare, housing, environmental, public utilities, public transit, and all other public service systems, are reimagined, our colonial lineages are acknowledged, and our goals, visions, and values are transformed to serve "all means all" public.

Holding Contradictions: Can Public Service Organizations Be Liberatory?

As we conclude this book, we want to continue reflecting on the hard question – can public service organizations be liberatory? If so, what are the core values and principles we must commit to, if we are to dedicate our praxis to dreaming and co-creating a liberatory public service (LPS)?

Public servants must often wrestle with many historical and present-day contradictions and tensions that entangle our organizations, our institutions, and our day-to-day work. Without building institutional and individual capacity to hold these contradictions and tensions, they can limit our creativity, imagination, and courage for solving wicked problems

DOI: 10.4324/9781032670669-14

facing public service. Especially in contexts where our organizations may have intentionally or unintentionally contributed to perpetuation of systemic harm and inequities against marginalized populations, it is very important for us to develop a collective clarity around the question: Can public service organizations be liberatory and what do we mean by it? Can public service organizations that have complex histories intertwined with settler colonial projects, including their involvement in formulating, and implementing racist and white supremacist policies and administrative processes, transform themselves to be liberating entities?

How can we as a public service community reconcile or hold these huge and overwhelming contradictions? What kind of change needs to occur for systems that have often been weaponized under the guise of public service to cause harm and oppression of people, to undergo transformation? Is such a transformation even possible?

Can all public service organizations be liberatory? Can some public service organizations be liberatory while others remain oppressive? Can some public service organizations lead the way for other organizations to join in the practice of liberatory justice? If we are to collectively imagine the journey from oppressive systems to liberatory systems, what would that look like, feel like? What would be the beginning steps? What would be the next steps for developing and maturing the praxis of liberatory justice in public service contexts? What are the core values and principles we must commit to, if we are to dedicate our praxis to dreaming and co-creating an LPS?

Throughout this book, starting with Chapter 1, we share our discernments around these questions and identify core values and emergent principles that can serve as roots or foundations for LPS theory and praxis. In this final chapter, we wish to return to these hard questions and offer some concluding reflections. We do not consider these reflections to be complete, rather we offer these with a hope to drive more conversations around these hard questions within the public service community – in our classrooms, our organizations, and our community spaces.

We acknowledge that these reflections reveal our emerging understanding and discernments of various contradictions and ideas of liberation involved in public service work that is anchored in values of democracy and social justice. We care deeply and remain humble, open, and invitational in our offerings. We hope to continue these conversations through collective scholarship, practice, education, dialogue, and action.

Concluding Reflections on Liberatory Justice and Liberatory Public Service

In this book, we ground our understanding of liberatory justice as work that is focused on identifying and transforming the conditions of harm that allow social inequities and injustices to persist. It is an ongoing work that seeks to remove all forms of barriers (i.e., inequities) that can have an adverse, marginalizing, and disempowering impact on any group, while centering the needs of groups that are most impacted by inequities. Liberatory justice necessitates collective efforts and shared leadership approaches that are community and survivor-led and seeks to replace inequitable systems with, structures, cultures, policies, procedures, and practices that prioritize the needs of those who are multiply marginalized by inequities (Kaba 2021a; Page and Woodland 2023; Sins Invalid 2019).

To align with the core philosophies and principles of its building blocks, such as restorative justice, transformative justice, healing justice, and disability justice,[1] and other critical frameworks such as critical race theory and intersectionality, LPS necessitates working toward the practice and the goal of decolonizing public service, including in connection to the people, and the planet. LPS would mean divesting from colonial and settler colonial investments and projects. For example, many public service organizations are exploring ways to practice solidarity with racial and social justice, anti-colonial, and climate justice movements led by Black, Indigenous, and People of Color, through actions rooted in values of "interdependence," "relationality," "reparations," and "landback" (Krawec 2022, ; Nonprofit Quarterly n.d.; Page and Woodland 2023).

LPS means envisioning and nurturing new ways of being in ethical relationship with the Indigenous peoples whose ancestral lands we are on and creating intentional ways of repair, healing, relationality, and transformation to emerge. It means honoring and doing the work of repair and healing relationships with Black people whose inter-generational and ancestral labor has been exploited and extracted to build our public service institutions, and infrastructure. LPS means our public safety, peace keeping, immigration, welfare, education, healthcare, housing, environmental, public utilities, public transit, and all other public service systems, are critically examined, our (settler) colonial lineages are acknowledged, and our goals, visions, and values are reimagined and transformed to serve "all means all" public.

LPS: A Practice of Solidarity

Given the responsibility and missions of serving "all means all" public, as public service organizations, and public servants, we are uniquely positioned and empowered to transform existing systems and move toward a liberatory praxis with the help of collective and communal imagination and creativity. We are well positioned to practice solidarity with grassroots, inter-generational social justice, and climate justice movements across the world, by allowing transformation of our organizations, our teams, our policies, procedures, structures, and cultures. Given the wide network of public service organizations – practitioners, community builders, and scholars can collaborate to create micro-models of transformation and share lessons of successes and failures. Through micro-level changes, there is potential for ripple effects and hopefully larger-scale explorations to envision and co-create liberatory systems.

With discipline and a strong anchoring in relationships, in community, and in solidarity rooted in accountability, there is deep potential for the public service community to practice liberatory values at a meaningful scale and in ways that can be impactful for the communities we seek to serve. Scholars and practitioners can help to build empirically tested and sound theories and liberatory tools that can help the praxis of liberatory justice at local, state, national, and global levels, across public service organizations and across policy and administrative domains. This work is already happening, and we need to cultivate it and expand our knowledge.

Depending on our contexts, resources, constraints, hurdles, and challenges, every public service organization, each public servant, and every scholar, may need to be deeply intentional and take the time to discover their specific goals, objectives, and pace that feels sustainable, meaningful, and humane. LPS means we begin the work of inner and collective transformation and sustain it through pushback, backlash, and other challenges one step at a time, one structure at a time, one cultural norm at a time, one policy at a time, and one practice at a time. Sometimes, we might find opportunities for dramatic, radical changes, especially when external and internal forces for collective liberation and solidarity align and are strong enough, and other times we work incrementally, across generations, like many of social justice and liberation workers did, to transform our systems.

As we have explored in this book, transformative social justice work is inter-generational, and we must build on successes and learn from the failures of inter-generational work. We must remember our histories and "not forget" lessons from our ancestors. We must remember to "not forget" that even if we cannot enjoy the fruits of our work, our work matters, public service matters, and it is worth dreaming and envisioning a liberatory future for public service for generations to come after us.

In this book, we describe LPS as a vision, a process, and a practice of creating the conditions for liberation to emerge through alignments across policy work, administrative work, structure and culture change work, and an embodied social justice leadership that serves – "*all means all*" public. It involves the systematic removal of oppressive policies, administrative, and cultural barriers, one step at a time, and work to collectively eliminate the sources of all forms of oppressive policies, administrative, and cultural barriers.

We emphasize, LPS is not about simply dismantling structures or removing burdens to create a void. LPS is about replacing burdensome systems and procedures that are exclusionary, marginalizing, causing hurt and harm, with nourishing systems, inclusive cultures, procedures, and infrastructures that are rooted in collective work, accountability, transparency, demonstrate care. LPS is about integrating inner and systemic transformation to foster public service that is, are trauma-informed, repair and healing- oriented, and compassionately centering the margins.

While checklists are important, transformative work cannot be driven only by checklists. Without falling into narrow mindsets of the checklist approach or ten-step finite processes, we invite you to read, learn, reflect, discern, and imagine, what does trauma-informed, repair and healing-oriented, and compassionate practice of centering the margins look like and feel like in your work, in your team, in your organization? Who must be at the table and whose help do you need to support your transformative change work? For example, we are thinking about diversity, equity, inclusion, and liberatory justice (DEILJ)-focused consultants, practitioners, scholars, coaches, mentors, peers, community members, especially those who identify with multiply marginalized identities and bring experienced expertise, creativity, and knowledge to this work? How can you as a manager, a leader, an organization working in public service contexts, share power with those who act as your support systems and ensure they feel safe-enough to be their authentic selves as they seek to help you and guide you to lean into the unsettling work of transformative change for DEILJ? What foundational skills and capacities must you build at individual and organizational levels to allow transformation of instinctive defensiveness (which is natural) and into opening portals for engaging with curiosity, openness, flexibility, and compassion for self and others?

Remembering "Hope Is a Discipline"

Mariame Kaba (2021b) a transformative justice leader, visionary, teacher, and movement builder, who is dedicated to abolishing systems of harm and oppression and building liberatory futures, reminds us that "Hope is a Discipline." Some may argue that the ideas we present are too radical and politically untenable in a hyper capitalist, extractive, scarcity, and fear-driven ecosystems of our culture and society. Our current dominant systems that are often based on binary win/lose, "power over," (rather than "power with")mindsets, may make it seem like liberatory justice or LPS is a distant or remote possibility. It does not have to be so. We must remember every major transformation begins with an initiative and desire to transform. That's how we have grown and matured to become democratic societies. LPS is not the first liberatory idea, nor is it isolated.

There are many developing examples of collective genius, creativity and innovations that seek to cultivate a liberatory practice in public and nonprofit organizations, that are anchored in decolonizing and trauma-informed, repair and healing-centered approaches, and compassionately center the margins. For example, the contemporary landback vision builds on the inter-generational Indigenous movement and visions for transformative futures that seeks to dismantle the systems that made land theft possible in the first place. The Landback movement has led to many Native communities winning back their ancestral lands and working toward repair, healing, and restoration of relationships between Native communities and our sacred ancestor, the land (Krawec 2022; Tilsen and Strong 2022).

From the return of 523 acres of the Tc'ih-Léh-Dûñ redwood forest in present day Mendocino County, California to the Sinkyone Council, a consortium of 10 federally recognized Northern California tribal nations; to management of 1.9 million acres of land in Utah by the Bears Ears Inter-Tribal Coalition; land reclamation efforts are underway, and settler colonial legacies of land theft are being interrupted and transformed. Tilsen and Strong (2022), powerfully note, "The resources to scale this work exist. The question is: are people in power willing to cede them?" (p. 3) (for many more examples, refer to Krawec 2022; Nonprofit quarterly n.d.; Piepzna-Samarasinha 2022).

We want to lean into the idea that liberation is a possibility for public service; that we can have a future that invests in life-giving, life-enriching, and life-saving public service that at its core, centers the lives of those who are multiply marginalized. LPS is rooted in values of love, courage, repair, healing, joy, efficacy, transformation, and solidarity. The practice of these core values requires us to shift away from "power over" approaches and lean into the philosophies of "power with" the people we serve. The practice of LPS means we understand power to be expansive and infinite, and something that grows as we share it (Kanter 1979). LPS understands power as a tool that can be used to oppress or to liberate. And LPS recognizes that when power is rooted in love and accountability, it can be used in service of liberation (King, Jr. 1967).

As we conclude this book, we believe it's not an end but a beginning of expansive possibilities that lie ahead. We hope our book, has served as a meaningful resource for you and leads you to many other books, especially those authored by disabled, queer, trans, non-binary, Two-Spirit, Black, Indigenous, and People of Color authors, teachers, visionaries, and movement builders (many of which we highlight throughout this book and in our deep dive resources sections). We extend an invitation to you, our reader, to embark on or continue your own explorations and we hope you discover your guiding stars and constellation that serves your liberatory praxis. Please know you are not alone on this journey. There is power that comes through community and solidarity. We hope you find your community of practice, even if it is one other person. We cannot emphasize enough how important that is.

For scholar, thinker, researcher colleagues, if LPS resonates with you as a theoretical framework, we invite you to explore its applications and integrations in your scholarship. As scholars and researchers, we imagine, some of the next steps in developing the LPS framework will be to develop testable hypotheses, measures, identify case studies of practice that align with core values and principles of LPS, as well as identify areas of challenges and growth opportunities to apply and integrate LPS in everyday public service work. As scholars and researchers of public service, we believe one of our key tasks is to help develop and elevate existing tools and promising practices that are anchored in LPS. This work will need collaborations and partnership between scholars, researchers, practitioners, and communities with serve. We invite you to reflect on how LPS principles and core values can guide scholarly practice, research methods, designs, and writings.

We are excited about the potential uses and progress that can come from expanding dialogues on LPS and liberatory justice frameworks in public service contexts. Even though the world presents tough challenges, we hold onto hope. We believe in the power of vision, imagination, ideas, teamwork, and collective efforts. Our hope is grounded in the belief that even when situations seem dire, there's room for transformation and growth. LPS acknowledges and necessitates space for grief, repair, and healing. And it invites us to remain anchored in the mindset and a disciplined practice of hope (Kaba 2021b). Hope that guided our ancestors and that will guide us through uncertain times and offer us the strength and courage we need to find a path forward toward collective liberation.

Note

1 These building blocks are described in detail in Chapter 5.

References

Kaba, Mariame. 2021a. *We Do This 'Til We Free Us: Abolitionist Organizing and Transforming Justice*, edited by Tamara K. Nopper. Chicago, IL: Haymarket Books.

Kaba, Mariame. 2021b. Hope Is a Discipline: Mariame Kaba on Dismantling the Carceral State Interview by Jeremy Scahill. https://theintercept.com/2021/03/17/intercepted-mariame-kaba-abolitionist-organizing/

Kanter, Rosabeth Moss. 1979. "Power Failure in Management Circuits." *Harvard Business Review*. https://hbr.org/1979/07/power-failure-in-management-circuits

King, Martin Luther Jr.. 1967. "Where Do We Go from Here?" Speech Delivered at the 11th Convention of the Southern Christian Leadership Conference, Atlanta, GA. https://kinginstitute.stanford.edu/where-do-we-go-here

Krawec, Patty. 2022. *Becoming Kin: An Indigenous Call to Unforgetting the Past and Reimagining Our Future*. Minneapolis: Broadleaf Books.

Nonprofit Quarterly. n.d. "Homepage." Non Profit News, https://nonprofitquarterly.org/

Page, Cara, and Erica Woodland. 2023. *Healing Justice Lineages: Dreaming at the Crossroads of Liberation, Collective Care, and Safety*. Berkeley, CA: North Atlantic Books.

Piepzna-Samarasinha, Leah Lakshmi. 2022. *The Future is Disabled: Prophecies, Love Notes and Mourning Songs*. Vancouver, CA: Arsenal Pulp Press.

Sins Invalid. 2019. "Skin, Tooth, and Bone: The Basis of Movement is Our People, A Disability Justice Primer." https://www.sinsinvalid.org/skin-tooth-and-bone

Tilsen, Nick, and Gaby Strong. 2022. "Dismantling the Land Theft System: A Land Back Vision for Philanthropy." *Non Profit News | Nonprofit Quarterly* (blog). November 21, 2022. https://nonprofitquarterly.org/dismantling-the-land-theft-system-a-land-back-vision-for-philanthropy/.

Index

Note: Page references in *italics* denote figures, in **bold** tables and with "n" endnotes.

9781032670645